Putting Children First

How Low-Wage Working Mothers Manage Child Care

Ajay Chaudry

Russell Sage Foundation ~ New York

The Russell Sage Foundation

The Russell Sage Foundation, one of the oldest of America's general purpose foundations, was established in 1907 by Mrs. Margaret Olivia Sage for "the improvement of social and living conditions in the United States." The Foundation seeks to fulfill this mandate by fostering the development and dissemination of knowledge about the country's political, social, and economic problems. While the Foundation endeavors to assure the accuracy and objectivity of each book it publishes, the conclusions and interpretations in Russell Sage Foundation publications are those of the authors and not of the Foundation, its Trustees, or its staff. Publication by Russell Sage, therefore, does not imply Foundation endorsement.

Library of Congress Cataloging-in-Publication Data

Chaudry, Ajay.
    Putting children first : how low-wage working mothers manage child care /
by Ajay Chaudry.
        p. cm.
    Includes bibliographical references and index.
    ISBN 0-87154-171-8
    1. Child care—New York (State)—New York.   2. Poor children—Care—New York
(State)—New York.   3. Poor women—Employment—New York (State)—New York.
4. Welfare recipients—Employment—New York (State)—New York.   I. Title.

    HQ778.67.N7C43 2004
    362.71'20'9747—dc22

                                                                        2004040968

The paper used in this publication meets the minimum requirements of American National Standard for Information Sciences—Permanence of Paper for Printed Library Materials. ANSI Z39.48-1992.

Text design by Genna Patacsil.

RUSSELL SAGE FOUNDATION
112 East 64th Street, New York, New York 10021
10   9   8   7   6   5   4   3   2   1

Putting Children First

To my sister, Nina,
and the forty-two mothers who shared their family stories,
without whom this book would not be possible.

~ Contents ~

~ About the Author ~

AJAY CHAUDRY is a writer on social policy issues and faculty and senior research fellow in urban policy and management at New School University.

~ Acknowledgments ~

This research study and book took the better part of four years of my life, and along the way I had a great deal of support. The research was funded in part through grants from the Child Care Bureau at the U.S. Department of Health and Human Services and from the Russell Sage Foundation. I want to thank the bureau for its financial support and its dedicated staff for the opportunity to learn from and share this research with the child care policy research community. I want to thank Eric Wanner and Suzanne Nichols at Russell Sage for showing confidence in me, and in the importance of this work. The five anonymous reviews that Russell Sage commissioned for the manuscript helped improve the final product immeasurably, and I thank the reviewers for their comments and votes of confidence as well.

While working on this project, I have been affiliated with the John F. Kennedy School of Government at Harvard, where I was a student, and the New School for Social Research, where I am a teacher. I have long considered the Kennedy School my intellectual home: my mind has been nurtured there, and my thoughts on public service and social responsibilities have taken root in the extraordinarily rich ground of scholarship at this institution. The New School's Graduate School of Management and Urban Policy has provided a consistent institutional home for my work for over a decade.

My warmest thanks go to Mary Jo Bane, who, as the principal adviser on this project, was supportive from its conception to its completion. In the initial stages of the research, she helped me rein in my vagaries and broad ambitions and channel them into a more manageable and relevant undertaking. Through each step of the field research and writing, she gracefully guided me with simple, profound direction. Her insights were brilliant, and I cannot fully list all the places within this work that reflect her indelible influence. I am grateful for her guidance, patience, and presence. I would truly have to share authorship to give her due credit.

David Ellwood and Mary Jo Bane have been mentors from the beginning of my study of social policy. It was as much through their generosity of thought and kindness as their tutelage that they made the Kennedy School a home to me. David Ellwood has been consistently generous to me with his time and exceptional insight and helped me to develop and articulate my own thinking on American social policy. Sandy Jencks and William Julius Wilson, two of the most eminent scholars in American sociology, helped me graciously in developing this research and inspire me with the examples of their rigorous scholarship. I also wish to thank Olivia Golden, Julie Wilson, and Ken Winston, who taught me much in my days at the Kennedy School: to always think about how people are affected by policy decisions and service delivery systems; to do so sympathetically, with an eye toward better possibilities; and to know that dedicated teachers make a difference in the lives of others and to the common good.

I have benefited from an abundance of great minds who have shared their collective wisdom and guidance in the shaping of this work. Larry Aber advised me wisely throughout and read each chapter, making creative suggestions that otherwise I would not have considered. Carol Stack, whose own work inspired and shaped this inquiry, met and corresponded with me regularly and made inimitable suggestions that could arise only from her grounded approach and lyrical sensibilities. Marty Zaslow, a leading expert on child policies, carefully read and critiqued my review of the literature and offered her guidance and several important suggestions to make the work more complete. Frank Furstenberg, Laura Lein, Ann Lin, Jim Quane, and Hiro Yoshikawa, among many others, shaped my ideas and the research approach to the study.

I am very fortunate to have received an unbelievable amount of research and personal assistance in conducting this project, much of it in-kind and all of it integrated into the body of this work. Shana Brodnax, Nina Chaudry, Zach Church, Elizabeth Fisher, Kimberley Gester, Bronley Luhrs, Sharla Phernetton, Elizabeth Rigby, Elisa Rosman, Suzanne Siegel, Mark Sullivan, Amy Taylor, Wendy Trull, and John Christopher Young have all given generously of their time and their prodigious abilities, and each contributed greatly and uniquely. Their collaboration in this project made it more worthwhile than the final product could ever indicate. My sister Nina contributed directly to the fieldwork with thorough and meticulous interviews that extended the reach and depth of the study, and she provided her acute editing skills when needed. Mark Sullivan designed the database that made most of the analysis possible. Zach Church and Suzanne Siegel read, edited, and reedited every chapter through several versions and helped make words flow where my own drifted. I owe more than just thanks to Amy Taylor, who more than anyone knows the toll that conducting field research and then completing a dissertation took in terms of time and energy; she helped make much of that work possible and shared the dear costs. Her buoyancy kept me afloat through some of the earlier stages when I was sure I would sink. Friends and colleagues, including Sheila Cavanaugh, Jim Kunz, Taeku Lee, and Hiro Yoshikawa, helped me to think through the work at critical stages and provided generous advice. Two friends contributed more to the completion of this project than just about anyone. Jim St. George and Mark Sullivan hosted me for the better part of four years in Cambridge in their warm and beautiful home and made it too easy to grow accustomed to their immense generosity. Susan Juda and Susan Morgan—the two Susans in my life—listened to me while I tried to put my work on this book into some perspective, but more often, when I could not, they showed me patience and humored me, while still directing me toward some better balance.

Many people went out of their way to help me in the course of the two years of field research. I particularly want to thank the community program staff in the four communities where I did this research. In the early stages, Ronni Fisher, Nina Piros, Grace Perez, and Charmaine Wong helped me consider how to approach community programs and residents about this work and truly ground my research.

I thank my family for the support they have given me for much longer than the life of this project. My parents almost to a fault put hopes for their children's happiness and success far ahead of their own. My father emphasized the importance of education and work. My mother taught me the meaning of compassion, consistency, and character. My sister Nina has shown me what family bonds and caring over time mean and in that way informed this work in a way that academic and field research never could.

Finally, my greatest debt of gratitude is owed to the families in this study, the forty-two mothers and their children whose stories are told here but who the requirements of confidentiality do not allow me to thank by name. This study was about the work and the care that women provide in the name of love and family survival. For doing that and for their confidences, let me now praise them, to whom I am ever thankful for sharing with me their lives. I am sure that I have gotten some things wrong in the retelling of their stories and that my best attempt could not do them the full measure of justice. The experience of learning from these families has been a deeply abiding pleasure.

~ Foreword ~

The last decade has witnessed a dramatic change in the experience of low-income single mothers in America. The Personal Responsibility and Work Opportunity Reconciliation Act (PRWORA) of 1996, the most noted policy change, shifted the focus of the social safety net for poor mothers and their children from cash assistance to required work. At the same time, federal support for working families increased about threefold, primarily through the Earned Income Tax Credit (EITC), which supplements the earnings of low-income working families, and through Medicaid expansions and children's health programs. These policy changes reflected underlying behavioral, attitudinal, and economic changes in the society. Welfare rolls declined by more than 50 percent between 1994 and 2000, while labor force participation rates of single mothers increased by about ten percentage points over the same period. Expected to support themselves and their children through their work, single mothers have done just that.

Millions of single mothers are now struggling with the issues that are explored so thoroughly and sensitively in this fine book by Ajay Chaudry. They are in the labor force, holding down jobs that are often low-paying and insecure, and sometimes with odd hours and irregular shifts. They struggle to make ends meet, to pay the rent on costly apartments, and to find health care. And they worry about how their children will be cared for while they work. They look for convenient, compassionate, and affordable in-home care for their young children, and they cope with the frequent disruptions that occur when their own circumstances or those of the caretakers change. They seek educationally and developmentally appropriate group settings for toddlers and preschoolers, only to find that good programs are often expensive, oversubscribed, and out of sync with their work hours.

This book documents in rich detail the child care choices and concerns of forty-two low-income single mothers in New York City. It is not a large or nationally representative sample; New York City is not America in many ways, and it has considerably more child care resources than most cities. This latter fact makes the stories told here even more compelling: if women are having such difficulties arranging care in a resource-rich environment, what must they be experiencing in more ordinary places?

The strength of the analysis in this book lies in the complex detail emerging from the extensive interviews with this relatively small but very diverse group of women. The book documents, through a combination of individual case studies and numerical tabulations for the whole group, the complexity of the lives of low-income single mothers and their difficulties in managing their own work lives and the care of their children. It shows that mothers change jobs and families move with alarming frequency. It shows that mothers devote huge amounts of time, energy, and concern to arranging child care, but that even so, many children experience frequent turnover in their care arrangements, especially in the very early years. It shows that mothers search out care arrangements appropriate for their children's ages, especially educationally oriented group arrangements as their children approach school age, although they often find these to be unaffordable and logistically unmanageable. It shows that mothers confront a bewildering array of eligibility and application rules for the subsidies and slots that become available.

After reading their stories and pondering the analysis, one is filled with admiration for the resourcefulness and persistence of these mothers. But they also leave one convinced that there must be a better way for the polity to respond to the situations of low-income mothers and their children. The final chapter contains a thoughtful and careful review of existing child care policy and a sensible and practical set of suggestions for improvement.

As Chaudry points out, policymaking ought to reflect what is known about the developmental needs of young children. His analysis reflects the fact that both parents and experts on child development perceive that children do best in stable settings with caretakers who understand and love them and that children of different ages flourish in different settings.

The ability of parents to establish stable care settings for their children is compromised by the bewildering array of public programs and subsidies with which low-income parents must contend. Chaudry's research shows poignantly how divided responsibility among public agencies and complex eligibility rules for different programs can force mothers to move from one care setting to another, whether or not the change is appropriate for the child. He makes sensible suggestions for making the system work more easily and coherently, with better coordination and smoother transitions among all its segments. These recommendations require few additional resources beyond a commitment to rationalize the system.

More ambitious are the suggestions for responding more appropriately to the developmental needs of children of different ages. Substantial research suggests that high-quality preschool education programs can help children, especially those from disadvantaged families, get a better start on their schooling. A societal near-consensus on the desirability of preschool for three- and four-year-olds is suggested by the widespread use of nursery schools by middle-class families, the bipartisan political support for the federal Head Start program, and the commitment of many states and school districts to provide, or start to provide, universal prekindergarten programs. All of this has resulted in an increase in the percentage of three- and four-year-olds in preschool programs, from about 20 percent in 1970 to more than 50 percent in 2001. Thinking about preschool for three- and four-year-olds as well as kindergarten for five-year-olds as a normal part of the public education system seems like a logical next step. Moving in the direction of universal preschool, provided with predominantly public funding but through a mixed system of public and private approaches, including Head Start, ought to be a high priority for the country.

The next step is to supplement what are often half-day preschool programs with extended day or wraparound care. Children do not need—and many cannot tolerate—a full day of structured, educationally oriented activities. Other settings can fill the rest of the day with supervised but not necessarily educational programs, as long as there are easy and safe ways for children to make the transitions. Parents could have an even wider range of choices for these programs than for preschool; they could be funded through a range of public and private money, including parental charges.

For toddlers there is more diversity in what optimal child care settings look like. Some parents use or would like center-based group settings; others prefer less formal home or neighborhood settings. Certain standards of safety and supervision should be met in all settings, but there is no reason not to provide and encourage a wide range of options. Americans tend to think about spending on child care as a legitimate work expense, which is logically deducted from income for tax purposes. Through an extension of this thinking, we can imagine providing more substantial tax deductions or credits and making the credits refundable for low-income workers.

Many Americans, as well as many child development experts, believe that infants are best taken care of by their parents, and many, though not all, parents would like to do just that. Honoring that preference in national policy requires a commitment to paid parental leave, not something the country seems poised to mandate at this point. Nevertheless, paid parental leave is an important policy option to keep on the table.

Suggesting universal preschool, expanded public funding for child care, and mandated parental leave seems, I admit, hopelessly utopian in the current political and budget climate. Similar proposals have been discussed for years, with little success, even in better times. But perhaps the dramatic increases in kindergarten and preschool enrollment over the last few decades, much of which has come in public settings, suggest a quiet commitment to at least this part of the agenda. And the political support may well exist for increased spending in support of working parents, particularly if done through the tax system, as with the Earned Income Tax Credit. Chaudry's documentation of the resilience and struggles of low-income single mothers as they try to do what is best for their families ought to both inspire us and increase our commitment to working for policy change. We owe him, and the mothers he introduces us to, great gratitude.

Mary Jo Bane
Kennedy School of Government
Harvard University
February 2004

~ Child Care Terms and Definitions ~

Bridge care: Often short-term care arrangements used between primary care arrangements.

Care exit: The ending of a care spell. In this analysis a care exit is assigned a primary reason or causal "event" that occurred at the time of the ending and is considered the main reason for exiting.

Care spell: The number of consecutive months in which a child is in the same child care arrangement.

Center-based care: Care provided in a range of child care center programs, including day care and nursery programs, Head Start centers, and preschool or prekindergarten (pre-K) programs. Center-based programs are located in a range of settings, such as community-based organizations, schools, or churches, and they are operated under different auspices—by nonprofit organizations, by public agencies, or as private businesses.

Contracted care: A form of child care subsidy. Under contract care, a public agency contracts with a provider, usually a community-based organization, for slots in a child care program.

Family child care (FCC), also called family day care (FDC): Care by a licensed provider who operates a child care business in her home taking care of a small, mostly unrelated, group of (three to six) children. Care may be regulated by the state, and there are wide variations in the states' licensing or registration requirements. A family child care group is an expanded version of family child care where a provider serves a larger group of (eight to twelve) children in her home, usually within a large dedicated care space and with a second adult assistant. A family child care network is a large group of providers (twenty to two hundred) organized by a community-based agency or city-wide social service provider that helps parents find care and matches them with providers.

Father care: Care by the child's father, often in the child's home. In the case of noncohabiting mothers and fathers, care may be in the father's own home or in the home of the father's family.

Group day care centers: Local centers that contract with the city for child care slots in classroom settings; these centers usually offer full-day care (8:00 A.M. to 6:00 P.M.) during the five weekdays.

Head Start: A federally subsidized preschool program in local communities that offers part-day (three to six hours) or full-day care (up to ten hours) at no cost to very low-income (below the federal poverty level) families. The program has an explicit developmental focus, includes family social services, and features parent involvement. Early Head Start (EHS) is a smaller federal program that builds on the Head Start model and with local programs offers a range of service models for the care and development of children from birth to age three.

Home-based care: Child care provided within a home setting (as opposed to a child care center), including, for example, care by a relative, neighbor, or nanny.

Informal care: Care by a nonrelative provider in the caregiver's home. Provider may be a neighbor, friend, or acquaintance, with care arranged on an individual basis for the specific child, but is generally not a child care provider.

Kin care or care by relatives: Care by a relative of the child, most often the child's maternal grandmother, but also other relatives of the mother or father. Care can be in relative's home or the child's home.

Licensed family child care: The state may require family child care providers to be licensed and to meet standards (including, for example, health, safety, group size, and physical space requirements). It often requires an inspection prior to licensing and possibly periodic inspections.

Mother's care while working: Care by mothers who bring their children to work, including mothers who work at home for income.

Multiple care arrangements: The use of more than one regular child care arrangement at a time (for example, within a single week) to cover the mother's work schedule.

Nanny care: Care by a nonrelative care provider in the child's home.

Preschool or prekindergarten (pre-K) programs: Educational programs to prepare children for kindergarten entry.

Primary child care arrangement: When families use multiple care arrangements, the primary child care arrangement is the one in which the children spend the most hours.

Registered family child care: As an alternative to licensing, states may require providers to identify themselves and certify that they comply with state standards. No initial inspection is made.

Secondary care arrangement: Regular, ongoing care arrangement beyond the primary care arrangement. A family may use more than one secondary arrangement.

Sibling care: Child care provided by siblings, generally in the child's home.

Special needs care or specialized care: Child care for children with special health or developmental needs. This care can be offered in specialized institutional settings such as hospitals, therapeutic nurseries, or special needs child care centers, or it can be a therapy offered within a child care center.

Subsidized care: Child care funded by a source other than parents, such as the federal, state, or local government, an employer, or a private funding source.

Unlicensed care: Care in the home of a provider who either is not required by the state to have a license or is not adhering to state licensing requirements. Most informal care is unlicensed.

Voucher care: A form of child care subsidy. In a voucher system parents select care and are given vouchers that pay a certain amount for it. The provider is either reimbursed by the government agency or paid directly by the parent.

Wraparound care: Care arrangements that "wrap around" a primary arrangement so as to accommodate parents' work schedules; for example, most after-school child care can be considered wraparound care.

Mothers and Children
in the Study Sample

MOTHER	∼	CHILD
Angela		Mark
Annette		Aaron
Bernadette		Paul
Brittany		Bethany
Cassandra		Cedric
Clarabel		Robert
Dana		Victor
Diane		Adrienne
Dona		David
Edwina		Emily
Felicidad		Karyn
Francine		Fortune
Gloria		Baldwin
Griselda		Giselle
Harriet		Horace
Hortensia		Ivan
Inez		Jasmine
Iris		Quirina
Josephine		Faith
Julia		Jacqueline
Kari		Jaya
Kiesha		Korey
Lisa		Millie
Lola		Lucas
Magdelena		Marisa
Matilda		Leo
Nadia		Lana

MOTHER   ∼   CHILD

Nora	Nick
Oona	Kiley
Pamela	Venus
Querida	Nyles
Ramona	Flores
Rhonda	Steven
Rita	Rea
Sandra	Shaniqua
Sara	Cristina
Traci	Tanya
Uma	Sade
Vanya	Xavier
Winnie	Willis
Yolanda	Yeats
Zina	Zoe

~ Chapter 1 ~

Introduction: Children's Care in the Age of Personal Responsibility

In August 1996, President Bill Clinton signed welfare reform into law.[1] The Personal Responsibility and Work Opportunity Reconciliation Act (PRWORA) of 1996 instituted rigorous work requirements that compelled welfare recipients to work. This shift to a work-based social policy in the United States had an immediate and dramatic impact on the lives and expectations of mothers and children living in poor neighborhoods. All at once, more single mothers had to both find work and make hurried child care decisions.

In the span of the next five years more than one million additional single mothers went to work, while other mothers who already had jobs worked additional hours, and even additional jobs, to make ends meet. The timing of the welfare reform work mandates coincided with greater work availability during a period of unprecedented economic growth in the United States in the middle and late 1990s. Between 1996 and 2000 low-income single mothers' employment increased by more than 25 percent (U.S. Department of Health and Human Services 2002a). Mothers thus emphatically responded to the work challenges and opportunities by creating a new wave of working mothers: the proportion of low-income, single mothers with children under six who were working grew from 44 to 59 percent between 1996 and 2000.

But what about the children? At the same time government policy was requiring that more low-income mothers go out and find jobs, mothers had to find child care as well. With limited personal resources and minimal assistance from the polity, these mothers had to figure out where to send their children. Even if a strong labor market could absorb the mothers, could the child care markets, which were fractured and incomplete from the start, provide places for their children to go? These families' earnings were meager, so most options even in the limited private child care market were out of their reach. The public child care systems were inadequate; many mothers were already on long waiting lists for subsidized child care or had lost eligibility for subsidized care as their income increased. Thus, the recent shifts in public policy and the wave of new working mothers have resulted in one unresolved question for mothers and American society: What do low-income single mothers do for child care now that they are working more?

This book is about the dilemmas that mothers face in finding care for their children. I followed forty-two low-income families in New York City over three years as the mothers found jobs and lost jobs and the children moved from one care situation to the next. I regularly and repeatedly interviewed mothers to determine what they did for their children's care and what they thought about the care. Each mother has her own story of striving to find work and child care. This volume traces and analyzes the changes they made in care over time and identifies the child care strategies they developed based on what they learned over a succession of care arrangements.

In the course of becoming workers, these low-income mothers have found that the most complicated challenge they face is not finding or keeping a job, but finding and keeping reliable child care they can trust and afford. These mothers are working and taking personal responsibility for their families, and through struggle and ingenuity they manage to find child care. When they do find child care, however, it is often little more than custodial care, and their children are not being stimulated to develop their potential during the most critical time for their brains' and bodies' development. As these mothers go to work and send their children into quite varying care arrangements, they have replaced welfare with worries about their children's well-being.

What is our public responsibility toward children and what social policy can allow these mothers to work and to have child care that fosters their children's development? I believe that the stories of these mothers can help direct policy discussions. To illustrate, I start with one family's story.

Annette and Aaron's Story

In August 1996, Annette was twenty-six years old when she learned she was pregnant with what would be her second child. She said to the nurse, "You made a mistake. That's impossible." When the nurse reminds her now of that moment, they laugh about it. At that point, however, there was no laughter.

After Annette left the hospital, she went to see the father, Franco. He was from the neighborhood, and someone she had known since they were both young. She had been involved with him for only two months and had no intention of having a child with him. "It just happened," she says. She knew he was very unstable and irresponsible, and in fact she had already decided that she did not want to continue a relationship with him. She told him that she was pregnant, that she did not want to see him anymore, and that she did not want his involvement. She made it clear that whatever she did was her own business and none of his.

Annette did not know what to do. She anguished over—as she put it—

"taking the baby out." She felt she was in no position to have another child. She and her only child, Raquela, shared a small apartment in the projects. She did not have the physical room, the emotional stability, the social supports, or the income to provide for a larger family. She remembers being very depressed at the time, not leaving her house or washing for days.

She awoke daily to her fears about how she would raise and provide for her young daughter in a world where her prospects seemed dim. The prospect of another life for which she would be responsible moved her from anxiety to depression, from tears to paralysis. In her struggles she could see no place for a second child. She feared that her difficult, tenuous path to a decent job and self-sufficiency would reach another stumbling block and that her burdens as a lone mother and provider would multiply. All the while, she says, "a voice inside quietly" told her she could not and should not stop this, and that she would have this child, ready or not.

When Aaron was born on April 15, 1997, and in the years later, she says she thanked God for helping her keep him.

When I first met Annette in the spring of 2000, she was living in public housing with her two children. Raquela was then eight and Aaron was just about to turn three. Annette was thirty. They lived close to the river in the poorest part of Pier Points,[2] a notoriously rough neighborhood with a high concentration of housing projects and an active drug trade. Annette had lived in this part of the Points for most of her life. She was raising her children in a housing project within one hundred yards of the project where she grew up, and the two were indistinguishable—as both were from the other thirty beige-brick-exterior, white-cinder-block-interior, high-rise buildings that surrounded them.

Annette has a frank manner, and she does not gloss details in talking about her life. She left school when she was fifteen years old, ostensibly to work at a shoe store in her neighborhood. Dropping out had as much to do with not liking and not learning much at school as it did with the adolescent pressures of the street life in her community. Over the next few years she realized that she wanted to leave the street culture as she saw its dangers. She was nineteen when her brother and brother-in-law were killed outside her building in the Points, and she says most of the people she knew from that time "are not around" anymore.

Annette's first real love was Raul, who was from the neighborhood. She and Raul very much wanted to have a child. During her pregnancy she left her job at the neighborhood shoe store, where she had worked for five years. Annette was twenty-one when their daughter Raquela was born. Several months later they moved to Puerto Rico because she wanted to get them out of the Points and Raul away from the influence of his peers. She and Raul married in Puerto Rico and then moved to Virginia, where he was stationed after joining the military and later worked as a corrections officer. Over a short time she watched her husband return to drug use, neglect their family life, and prove himself unfaithful to her. Escaping her turbulent relationship with Raul, she returned to her native New York with Raquela and later divorced Raul. Soon after she left Raul was caught dealing and possessing drugs, while working as a state corrections officer, and he was sentenced to a Virginia correctional facility, where he remains today.

Leaving behind Raul's bouts of infidelity and drug abuse, Annette thought she might have opportunities for a better life back home. She was able to get housing by moving into her family's old apartment in the projects after her mother migrated back to her native Puerto Rico. Annette also had a job opportunity as a corrections officer in New York. Both she and Raul had applied to the New York City Department of Corrections four years earlier before moving to Puerto Rico. When Annette was thinking of leaving Virginia, she was finally called for a job at Corrections. Even though the work environment would be rough and dangerous, she considered this an ideal job because it offered higher starting pay, security, and greater earning possibilities over time than any other work that she believed might be available to her.

As it turned out, Annette's hopes were dashed: she lost the chance to work for Corrections when she could not find child care for Raquela. Her mother had told her she would move back to New York from Puerto Rico to provide child care, but she backed out the week of Annette's final evaluation for the job. After that Annette mostly worked in the retail trade. She learned that these jobs led nowhere and that the menial work could end abruptly when the business faltered or any family emergency arose, large or small. There was little flexibility on the part of employers, who regarded each low-wage employee as easily replaced. After losing a couple of short-term jobs, she returned to "public assistance" or "PA"—what she and other poor mothers in New York City call cash welfare. She had received welfare from the time she was pregnant with Raquela until she moved to Puerto Rico, and she now cycled back on as she sought some other path to work. She supported her family by juggling minimum-wage jobs and welfare payments, sometimes combining the two. At the same time she also tried training programs and community service jobs in her desire to get ahead. When she became pregnant with Aaron, and after he was born, she had to depend on welfare exclusively.

> I was doing job training and an internship when I became pregnant [with Aaron]. When Aaron was born, I took time off. I really wanted to be a full-time mom, but I struggled a lot for money. I just received PA and food stamps, which, you know, is almost nothing, and all my housing was paid. We ate a lot of peanut butter and bread. That was it. We had no support from family, friends, their fathers, nothing.
>
> I did not work for a year. . . . I was struggling, but Aaron has asthma and he was hospitalized twice for about a week each time before they re-

alized it was asthma. . . . He was sick a lot when he was younger . . . and so I could not get a job.

When Aaron was sixteen months old, Annette was offered an Americorps position for one year working for a social services program in the Points called HELP. When that opportunity came up, Annette again asked her mother to provide care.

> I wanted to stay with him and was scared to leave him, but when I was offered the [Americorps] job . . . I wanted to do it. . . . I told my mother, who lived in Puerto Rico, that I was going to be starting a job, and she said she would move here to take care of him so I could work. A week before I was supposed to start she called me and said she was not coming. That was normal for her; she always does that to me. I did not know what to do. I could not find anyone to take care of Aaron, and I was very upset. I did not know if I could do the internship.

Aaron was already in an Early Head Start (EHS) program, which he attended for four hours each week, in the same umbrella agency that included the HELP program. The staff at the agency knew about Annette's child care problems and suggested an arrangement. A woman who was doing an internship with EHS was going to be starting a family child care program in her home. The program director suggested that Annette ask the provider, Terry, whether she would be able to care for Aaron. Terry agreed, and Annette paid her with an Americorps stipend for child care plus an additional sum because the stipend was not enough.

Aaron was in this arrangement for about seven months, and he seemed to enjoy going to Terry's very much. The care ended, however, because of a conflict between Annette and the provider.

> She was a wonderful provider. She really loved children and had done all this preparation to be a child care provider, making her house really nice for the children and trying to do what they do in the centers. She read to them in reading circles, made up interesting play activities, and took them out to the park. Aaron liked going there. . . .
>
> There was some complaints and problems. . . . It was a mess! . . . First there was a problem between Aaron and another child in her care [they would fight], and that upset her. And she complained about Aaron to everyone. Everyone got involved, including the program directors at my job and at the child care network and the girl's mother. I told her that I thought [fighting] is something kids do. She did not agree and blamed Aaron. . . . She told me that she would not take him anymore. It was really bad. She was a good provider, and I did not know what to do. I had to stop working and was desperate.

Annette did not formally leave the job. Her director was understanding and told Annette to keep searching for child care options. She started working regularly again weeks later when Aaron's grandmother (his father's mother) agreed to watch him on at least a short-term basis. Annette made this arrangement even though she did not want Aaron's father involved in her life or Aaron's and in spite of her serious reservations about Aaron's grandmother.

> There was no one. I tried everything, but I could not find anyone else. The grandmother was willing to do it. I did not want to leave him with her because I thought she was a little strange, but I had nothing else I could do. So I started leaving Aaron in her home. He had trouble transitioning. He told me every day he did not want to go there. I heard from a couple of people in the neighborhood that they kept seeing Aaron out in the street with her, that she was out with him all the time. Then, one day when I was outside her door, I heard her screaming at him, and then a whack, and he was screaming. She hit him, and I told her off. Well, that was it. We had this arrangement: she called in the mornings to tell me she was ready for me to come over with him. That next day she did not call. After waiting, I called her. She said she had trouble dealing with his asthma . . . and she was too sick [to take care of him].

Annette's second care arrangement lasted less than a month. When she again told her director she could not work, the director again told Annette to work something out, at least until the end of the internship. For her third primary care arrangement, Annette turned to a friend's mother for informal care until she could find something better.

> I had to do something. I spoke to a friend who I grew up with who asked her mother if she would watch him. Claudia was my mother's age, and she had been a neighbor I knew since I was a girl. She was poor, and so she was willing to do it for the money until I could finish the internship. It was informal, you know unlicensed care. . . . It was nothing great, but it was better than the other provider, and I could not find anyone else who would do it for the money [provided by the Americorps stipend].

When she finished her internship in August 1999, Annette interviewed for a job at the HELP program as an administrative assistant. They had funding for no more than a part-time position, however, and around this time the Early Head Start program also had a part-time position to fill. Annette did not take either job right away. First, she had to find someone to care for Aaron, and she had to arrange for a child care subsidy through the Agency for Child Development (ACD). She had already applied to ACD a year earlier in the hopes of getting a placement in a child care center or a licensed provider, but she was still on the waiting list. After searching for almost a month, she was about to give up. Then her director called to tell her that there was a space with a family child care provider.

> There was an opening with a woman named Lizette, and I made a visit to the house right away and agreed to put Aaron in the home. I was desperate, so at first I felt lucky, but it turned out it was just terrible. The place was like a shoebox, and Aaron just watched TV there, and he was tortured in the home by the woman's grandkids, who were the other children she was providing care for and were not even part of the program. And she complained that he was difficult and sick. Then he started really misbehaving—jumping on tables and using language he did not use before. I became very worried. He would cry and beg me not to take him to the provider's home.

Aaron was there just two weeks when the problems started, and Annette again thought about leaving her job. She asked the family child care program's director to let her know if a space opened up with another provider. She wanted to move Aaron but decided she would leave him with Lizette and try to keep working as long as possible. After a few months a spot opened with Nelly, another family child care provider.

Nelly's care, in many ways, turned out to be an ideal arrangement for Annette and Aaron. She ran a licensed family child care operation from her two-bedroom apartment in a low-rise housing complex that was very close to Annette's office and Aaron's EHS class. Nelly, who spoke only Spanish, was an older Latina woman who provided very loving, nurturing care. When she started providing child care for her own grandchildren, she also began taking in other neighborhood children, became licensed, and joined a family child care network. She and her husband had raised three children of their own in the Points, and these children were often around the house, making the child care feel like a large family environment. Aaron liked going to Nelly's:

> He calls Nelly "Grandma," and he seems to feel good about being there when I drop him off and pick him up. With Nelly it is really like being with a grandma. It is warm, loving, and safe; he eats well and takes a nap, but he is not learning so much there.

Annette felt confident about the care, but she wished she knew more about Aaron's experiences there and could be more involved.

> I do not know too much about what he does [at Nelly's], which is hard for me because I am an involved parent, and because he spends more time there than he does with me. He does not say too much, which usually means it is okay. I never have a chance to talk with her because I have to rush to work when I drop him off there in the mornings, and when I

go to pick him up we have to rush to get Raquela from her after-school program because they won't watch her after six o'clock.

Annette stuck through the child care changes and "pieced together" the two jobs for almost eight months before the director of the HELP program found the money to hire her full-time. When Annette told her boss at Early Head Start she was going full-time at the other job, the director, not wanting to lose Annette, sought and found a grant to hire her full-time. Annette decided to take the job at Early Head Start.

Three months before she turned thirty Annette started what she called her "first full-time job with a real salary." The new job offered her some stability and better pay, increasing her annual income from $16,000 to $22,000. She was earning more income, but she says her struggles were much the same as other forms of assistance she had received were reduced and her expenses went up.

> So, for a while I had to put these two pieces [two part-time jobs] together when I would have rather just had a full-time job. . . . Now I work one job and I make almost $100 more each week than I made working the two jobs. That was a good raise, but it's still hard because the expenses just go up. Now I have to pay a bigger part of the child care costs—I was just recertified after the new job and pay increase and now have to pay $47 every week. I was paying $24 until last week. . . . I still need my food stamps [$74 per month], but the stamps will go down [to zero] when they recertify me with the new salary. And then, since I live in public housing, my rent is higher the more I make. I now have to pay $297 and before I was paying $167.[3]

Nelly was Aaron's fifth primary child care arrangement before his third birthday, and it turned out to be the smoothest and most durable arrangement yet. Even so, Aaron's care was still complicated because Annette needed to make multiple arrangements to match her work needs with his care needs. In addition to the family child care and his four hours a week in Early Head Start, Aaron regularly had to spend a couple of hours with his mother at her job, and he also stayed with a variety of family and friends for a few hours every Saturday when Annette needed to work. Time was Annette's most pressing concern about her children's care arrangements: how little of it she got with her children, how little she knew about how Aaron spent his days. She worried about whether her working and his child care were adversely affecting his development.

> Time is the biggest issue—there is no time. I get no time to talk to the provider, to be alone with her, to be with my son. . . . I think he is okay over there. I hope he is, but I worry. He's my son, my responsibility, but

I am not with him so much of the time. He has been in the care of so many others, strangers.

The Context for Children's Care in Low-Income Neighborhoods

Annette and Aaron's family life is typical in many respects of life in poor urban neighborhoods for many similarly situated families, including the more than forty whose stories are recounted in this volume. These mothers struggle to fulfill the roles of sole earner and sole parent. Many women must put work first in order to adequately provide for their families, yet they find it very difficult to secure adequate child care. Mothers like Annette do work and do find child care among the limited choices available to them. However, the poor quality of much of the care they use, the succession of child care arrangements that fall apart, and their concerns about the impact of child care on their children combine to *challenge their identities as mothers*.

Annette's need to make simultaneous decisions about work and child care is similar to the work-family trade-offs faced by so many families today as women's labor force participation has increased dramatically in recent decades. Mothers from all walks of life—prosperous and poor, married as well as single—bear much of the responsibility for supplying their family's material and developmental needs. These twin goals of family life require that they ensure that their children have adequate shelter, food, clothing, and medical attention and that other basic needs are met; that their children feel secure, attached, and loved; *and* that they are supervised, shown the limits of acceptable behavior, and stimulated to learn. For any parent, these goals often conflict. Reaching a balance between how much work is needed for the family's income and how much time can be preserved for parenting has become one of the defining calculations that American women now face. And with it comes the decision about who will care for their children when they go to work.

The terms of this conflict can be most severe for working single mothers, especially those who earn low wages. Annette's story illustrates some of the acute problems that low-income single mothers face in their attempts to find and maintain work to support their families while arranging child care for their young. Her desires and quests are universal: to find love and companionship; to have a family; to raise her children to be healthy and successful in life; to work and help meet her family's needs; to find safe and appropriate child care for her children. However, Annette struggles to negotiate these challenges within a context of opportunities and constraints that are very different from those faced by most middle-class or married mothers. She is constrained by her limited resources and the social conditions of her environment. She faces the conflict as a lone parent. She lacks many personal supports. She has limited employment opportunities. She lives in an area of the city with few good care opportunities. She is economically segregated in public housing that is cut off from most mainstream avenues to opportunity. She also must still rely on governmental assistance for child care or housing that she cannot otherwise afford even with a full-time job, and she must consider all of her work and child care decisions within the complicated context of the rules of the social services systems she relies on to hold her family life together.

The Context of Poverty

When I met Aaron, he was more than two years old and his family was not poor by the standard income measure. For a family of three like Annette's, the poverty threshold was $13,874 in 2000 (U.S. Department of Commerce 2000a).[4] Annette's earnings provided 1.75 times that level, and while she could clear the poverty threshold with money to spare, she knew that she barely had an adequate income to provide for her family. As other evidence also confirms, the official poverty threshold levels are very low compared to a family's basic needs (Edin and Lein 1997; Ruggles 1990; Schwarz and Volgy 1992).[5]

In policy terms, "poverty" is assumed to relate to the official income poverty threshold.[6] Even if the threshold is set unrealistically low, it provides a measure of social conditions.[7] By official poverty measures, children under six are demographically the poorest age group: more than one in six (17.2 percent) American children were considered poor in 2000 (See table 1.1). Poverty rates for children under age six in large central cities and for Latino and African American children were even higher, and the rate for single-parent families was the highest among the major demographic classifications. This study's sample was selected from among these groupings—black and Hispanic single-mother families with very young children living in urban areas.

Though Aaron was not poor when we met, his family's income in his young life was such that he had experienced income poverty for two out of his first three years. Given his mother's tenacity and some luck, his family may never be income-poor again. Aaron is now among the nearly half of American children in single-mother families who live on the positive side of the low poverty threshold.[8]

In concentrated urban poverty neighborhoods like the Points where Aaron lives, the poverty rate for young children is about 40 percent, and most of the children Aaron will associate with in his early developmental years come from families living around the poverty line. Poverty in these neighborhoods has many dimensions. The social disadvantages and the non-income dimensions of poverty—the bleak surroundings, the proscribed set of choices for schooling and health care, the exposure to peers who are also disadvantaged—are ever-present for Aaron. He has asthma, as do legions of his peers in New

Table 1.1   *U.S. Poverty Rates for Young Children Under Age Six,*
Compared to Other Age Groups and by Demographic
Subgrouping, 2000

	Rate
Official U.S. poverty rate	11.3%
Young children (under six)	17.2
Children (under eighteen)	16.2
Young adults (eighteen to thirty-five)	12.2
Working-age adults (thirty-five to sixty-four)	8.1
Elderly (over sixty-five)	10.2
Poverty rates for young children (under six)	
Central cities	24.4
Suburbs	13.9
Rural	22.2
Black	33.1
Latino (Hispanic origin)	29.6
White	13.7
In single-mother families (all)	47.1
African Americans in single-mother families	53.9
Latino Americans in single-mother families	52.3
Black, central-city, and single-mother family	55.7
Latino, central-city, and single-mother family	61.0

Source: Tabulations from the March 2000 Current Population Survey, tables 1 and 4.

York's low-income neighborhoods. He lives in public housing that marks one as indigent almost regardless of the income, self-esteem, and behavior modeling his mother may try to bring home. He is largely isolated with his mother in the poorest projects in the Points, where most of the adults he meets come into and out of his life without staying too long. Annette says that he misses having a consistent male presence. She thinks having a man in his life could help with his emotional outbursts and provide a role model as he tries to figure out his place in a world in which all the adults around him—his mother, sister, aunt, cousin, their friends, and his caregivers at family child care homes and day care centers—are women.

The story of Annette's long but successful road from welfare to work and self-sufficiency is remarkable. Without access to a good formal education, Annette learned from her environment, managing to draw from its resources and making steady progress in her own work pathway. However, she also knows that every choice she made had consequences for her children, particularly the child care Aaron experienced in his earliest years. Annette says that the most challenging aspect of her family's story has been finding child care. It is in this area that she feels she has the least amount of control, has some of the worst choices, and has inadequate resources to meet Aaron's needs.

This book is about forty-two low-income single mothers and children like Annette and Aaron. It examines how these mothers made child care arrangements, interprets what they learned through a succession of child care changes, and describes how they used that knowledge to adapt their care choices over time. Using in-depth interviews and participant observation, I documented day by day and month by month the child care that these families used and their transitions during three years of field research. The need for such an analysis is obvious when one considers the neglect of these concerns in American social policy discourse. The difficulties of finding child care, children's experiences in care, and the continuing needs of children living in poor neighborhoods have not been adequately addressed in the policy discussions that have surrounded welfare reform and the movement of more mothers into the labor force.

This book explores how mothers' strategies for coping in low-income, isolated communities change in the context of less welfare and more work and how they incorporate greater child care responsibilities into those strategies. I learned some important lessons from the stories of Annette and the other families:

- Accepting work as necessary to their family's survival, mothers expect and want to work, and low-income mothers are working at greatly increasing rates—both mothers who have lost welfare entitlements and those who never used them.

- Working mothers require child care and want care that can meet their expectations of quality and stability.

- Low-income mothers cannot afford to pay the market costs of child care, and there are not enough subsidies to help very many of them gain access to quality care. In addition, the complicated child care systems created by state and city governments to administer and ration child care make it difficult for even the savvy and diligent to use them, and the immediacy of most job choices available to low-income women do not afford them the patience or flexibility needed to negotiate those systems.

- Low-income children end up in whatever child care their mothers can piece together. These mothers often must use multiple care arrangements concurrently and change settings frequently because the care they find is inadequate and inherently unstable.

- Unstable and low-quality child care has an enormous impact on children's well-being. While mothers are well aware of this, they also know that within the existing child care markets and subsidy system, quality is a luxury that they cannot afford or even properly consider given time constraints. Quality is a huge concern for them, but one that trails their practical concerns about first finding child care on which they can rely and that is safe.

This book attempts to inspire and inform a debate about public responsibilities to support both working motherhood and children's development following the rapid movement to a work-oriented social policy. We live in a society where most mothers work, and this is the explicit expectation of responsible adulthood. Many low-income mothers also come to prefer working because it enhances their sense of control and helps structure their families' lives. There is no reason to expect that fewer mothers will be working anytime soon, especially those whose earnings are their family's primary lifeline. Along with the personal responsibility taken by working mothers, there needs to be far greater public responsibility for children's developmental well-being so that quality child care can be consistent with a mother's attempt to secure her family's economic well-being.

Mother's Work, Children's Care, and Welfare Reform

The changes stemming from the Personal Responsibility and Work Opportunity Reconciliation Act of 1996, which included very strong work requirements for families seeking social services assistance, profoundly changed the context for mothers' work and children's care for families in low-income neighborhoods. Among the policy changes that helped push single mothers to work more were strict work-first policies across the states, strict time limits on how long families may receive assistance, and an end to the federal entitlement that provided poor families with cash assistance based on need. Federal assistance now came in the form of a block grant to the states, a change that more fully shifted to the states the responsibility for the design of programs and services to the poor with minimal federal oversight. In addition, the federal law established mandatory target percentages of those in a state's welfare caseload who must be working and made immigrants ineligible for many services.

Welfare reform, by instituting rigorous work requirements, effectively moved the United States to a work-based social policy. The change marked a fundamental shift in public policy, asserting that parents must take "personal responsibility" for their family's well-being and that all public support follows from a "work-first" policy framework. The rhetoric of personal responsibility further shifted the focus of American social policy away from the protection of children and their interests and toward their mothers' work behavior. From the perspective of mothers, the shift amplified the conflict between their responsibility to work for their family's material well-being and their responsibility for their children's developmental well-being. Mothers now had to put their work first, often before their children's care needs.

Underlying much of the long-fought debate about welfare reform was a tension between two competing interpretations of welfare—the one that promoted social policies designed to improve children's welfare and the one that denigrated policies that provided assistance to able adults, including nonworking parents, who have often been considered the "undeserving poor" (Katz 1986). The volatile politics of welfare reform was rooted in some of the long-standing and conflicting American values that underlie many social welfare policies.[9] The paramount value that Americans place on economic self-sufficiency and the virtues of work (Heclo 1993, 1997, 2001) was pitted against the primacy of the family and communitarian ideals, particularly the ideal of helping vulnerable children and offering them equal opportunities. In the battle of American values that took shape over welfare reform, the bootstrap individualist creed ruled the day in August 1996. Much was deservedly made of personal responsibility, the need for individuals to direct their own lives and marshal their own energies, and the centrality of work in American life. However, at the same time as we were asking the least fortunate to strive and work harder, we were deeply discounting our public responsibility for the children born into poor families and disadvantaged communities. We could have replaced welfare with more supports and opportunities for children in addition to strong work requirements, but the legislation emphasized work, provided few new supports to families, and cut other supports to some families. In society's estimation, and in mothers' minds, the imperatives of earning for a family's self-sufficiency and caring for children have become separated, and mothers with few options are forced to send children into care that is cheap and often of dubious quality.

Central to the 1996 national policy changes was the end of previous federal guarantees of assistance that had been directed toward individual children's minimal needs. The Aid to Families with Dependent Children (AFDC) program was the particular entitlement program that was most often known as welfare. The AFDC entitlement program ended as part of the welfare reform legislation and was replaced with a new block grant program, Temporary Assistance to Needy Families (TANF), which took the same amount of federal money that had been spent on entitlements to families and gave it as a lump-sum block grant to the states. When AFDC was instituted as part of the New Deal in 1935, its intention, as its name implies, was largely to protect the interests of children, and by extension their mothers for them, by offering a buffer against absolute poverty. The welfare reform law abdicated this responsibility and passed along concern for the poor to the states with no guarantees for individual families in need. In the policy push to make mothers take direct responsibility for their families' self-sufficiency, the law made clear the requirement of work but offered little in the way of public responsibility for children and their developmental needs.

Some of the logic for the policy shift was clear. With most mothers working in American society, making work the basis for public assistance was consistent with the expectations of most families. However, the needs of some of the most disadvantaged children were neglected, and the supports that single mothers need to carry out their dual role as worker and parent went unaddressed.

The welfare reform law coincided with other changes—expansions in work-related benefits like the Earned Income Tax Credit (EITC), a modest increase in the minimum wage, and increased federal and state spending on child care subsidies—that also contributed to increased work participation by low-income families, especially single mothers. The EITC was expanded in 1993 to provide greater supplements to the pay of low-wage earners with refundable tax credits that effectively increased their family income. The minimum wage was increased in 1996 from $4.25 to $5.15 an hour. A strong labor market in the initial years after the welfare reform law helped to bring many single mothers into the labor force relatively quickly. Welfare reform pushed single mothers to work, policies to "make work pay" encouraged them to do so, and available jobs pulled many of them into the labor force.

The recent surge of low-income women into the workforce followed already substantial increases in women's labor force participation over the past half-century. In 1950 only one out of eight women with children younger than six worked outside the home. This increased to nearly one in four by 1960. By the year 2000, 65 percent, or almost two-thirds, of mothers worked outside the home—five times the rate of a half-century earlier (see figure 1.1; see also table A.1 in appendix A).

Notable in this figure are the changes in labor force participation between married mothers and lone mothers (never-married, widowed, and divorced mothers). For most of this time lone mothers have had greater levels of labor force participation, largely out of greater necessity. From 1970 to 1990 there was a rapid rise in married mothers' work participation levels following the greater economic independence achieved by women and the increasing expectation and acceptance of work by women and of two-income families. Over these two decades the rate of increase in work participation for married mothers was three times that of single mothers. By 1990 married and lone mothers were both working at about the same rate, 58 percent.

During the 1990s the trend turned markedly in the other direction: single mothers' rate of increase in work participation was three times that of married mothers. Most of this increase occurred between 1995 and 2000, when single mothers' rate of labor force participation increased from 60 percent to 73 percent. This unprecedented increase in a very short time is all the more remarkable because it built on an already high base of work participation by mothers: three of five were already working. Nearly three-quarters of lone

Figure 1.1   *Labor Force Participation Rates of Mothers of Children Under Age Six, 1960 to 2000*

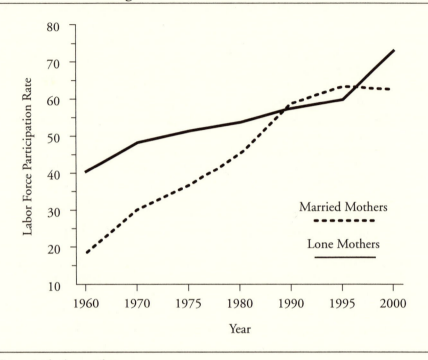

Source: Author's compilation.

mothers were in the labor force by 2000. Married mothers' labor participation also continued to grow in the 1990s, but at a more gradual rate; it had reached 63 percent by the end of the decade.

What About the Children?

As some observers of the welfare reform process have noted, the federal welfare reform legislation passed without much discussion of its potential effects on children (Bane 1997; Edelman 1997, 2001). The welfare reform debates focused most intensely on the behavior of poor single mothers, but the law is likely to have as much consequence on the lives of their children. One of the most direct and far-reaching effects of increased parental work is the corresponding need for child care. Questions about where this care will be found, what care will be used, and what children will experience in this care are all essential matters for public policy.

As welfare was being reformed, there was very limited child care assistance in place even then to meet the need, much less the increased need that would follow with more mothers entering the labor force and unable to pay for many care options.[10] At the time the welfare reform law was signed the total number of children receiving subsidized child care was 1.3 million, while 6.5 million children under the age of thirteen lived in families receiving welfare assistance (Hofferth 1999).[11] When we include the large number of children in low-income working families who were not receiving welfare but also needed and qualified for child care assistance, the proportion of eligible children who could be served, even with marginal increases in funding, drops much further.

As part of the 1996 Personal Responsibility and Work Opportunity Reconciliation Act, the federal government did make some changes in child care policy. Several preexisting federal programs offering low-income child care subsidies were consolidated into a single Child Care Development Fund (CCDF), to be allocated to the states as block grants.[12] Overall child care spending was increased to help states meet some of the increased demand for child care assistance, and states were allowed to use funds from the new TANF welfare block grant for child care needs as well.

The primary source of public funding for child care is the federal government, while the development and administration of child care programs is primarily the individual state's responsibility.[13] Federal block grant funding to the states through the CCDF increased from $3 billion in fiscal year 1997 to $4.8 billion in FY 2002 (U.S. Department of Health and Human Services 2000b, 2003; Gish 2002; see also table A.9).[14] The proportionately large increases in child care assistance, however, have come on top of a very low initial base of support. Even with recent increases, the percentage of eligible children served by the CCDF block grant has been estimated to range from only 12 percent to 25 percent across the states (Burstein, Layzer, and Cahill 2000; U.S. Department of Health and Human Services 2000b).[15] These estimates generally do not include children served in Head Start, state pre-K programs, and other smaller programs offering child care subsidies. Given that these other programs combined serve fewer children than the states serve through CCDF grants, it is fair to conclude that probably well over half of children eligible for child care subsidies do not receive them.

States combine their federal CCDF block grant money with their own funds, and in a few states, like New York, policy responsibility is further devolved to counties and cities, which also contribute child care funding and run the subsidy programs. As federal funding for child care increased in the years following welfare reform, the allocation to New York State increased to $316 million in 2002 (U.S. Department of Health and Human Services 2003).[16] The state contributes funds toward child care subsidies based on federal matching requirements, and in recent years, as its TANF caseload declined, New York, like most of the states, has also used the flexibility to spend federal TANF funds for child care (Schumacher, Greenberg, and Duffy 2001). Child care funding in New York City totaled approximately $470 million in 2002, a 40 percent increase from the level of spending prior to the 1996 welfare reform changes (Child Care, Inc. 2002).[17]

States can administer their child care programs with broad discretion, and in the case of New York, the responsibility for child care programs is transferred to local governments. Because available funding is not enough to serve all children who may be income-eligible, states and localities develop means to ration their limited child care subsidies. States ration subsidies by setting low income eligibility ceilings. New York State, like most states, sets its maximum income cutoff for eligibility lower than the federal maximum. Federal guidelines allow states to set the maximum level for income eligibility at 85 percent of its state median income (SMI), which in New York translates to approximately $41,000 for a family of three in 2001. New York during the period of this study set a maximum income cutoff for child care assistance at near 60 percent of the state's median income ($29,000 for a family of three), which is about the average level across the states. New York, also like most states, sets priority criteria to serve more families at the lower end of the eligible income range and has created complicated rules for who can apply, how one must apply, and what families must do to keep subsidies.[18] With these factors differing across the states and often changing with little notice, the child care systems that families must navigate are very complicated and fluid across the country (Adams, Snyder, and Sandfort 2002) (for further details, see the literature review in appendix A).

During the same period when public child care assistance was growing, there was an unprecedented increase in the number of working single and low-income mothers (figure 1.1). Labor force participation by low-income single mothers (those earning less than 200 percent of the federal income poverty threshold) increased by 25 percent between 1996 and 2000, which followed upon a 25 percent increase in work for this same demographic group from 1992 to 1996 (U.S. Department of Health and Human Services 2000a). Therefore, despite the increase in child care subsidies, the total number of families needing assistance remains high.

As long as the increased pressure to work outstrips the available child care dollars, *many women lack the resources to both mother and work effectively.* One of the biggest concerns of low-income mothers is the relatively high cost of many child care options compared to their earnings. Some of the care they might want to use is not only beyond their means but unavailable in their communities. Even as they are priced out of market-rate child care, many low-income families spend a substantially larger portion of their budgets on child care compared to those who earn more. Linda Giannerelli and James Barsimantov (2000) have found that families that earn less than 200 percent of the federal poverty level who pay for child care spend an average of $217 per month, or 16 percent of their earnings, for child care expenses, while those that earn more than this pay $317 per month, or 6 percent of earnings. Giannerelli and Barsimantov also report that among low-income families, employed single mothers spend 19 percent of their earnings on child care while two-parent families spend 11 percent of their earnings. Because more than one-third of all families with children have incomes below 200 percent of the federal poverty level, and 23 percent of all children are in single-parent families, these high cost barriers affect many families.[19]

The care that low-income mothers do find and use is often of poor quality, leaving them worried about the consequences for their children's development. We know from several assessments by developmental psychologists and child care professionals that the overall quality of care in the United States is relatively low within a fairly wide range and that it does not reach its potential to enhance children's development (Helburn 1995; Kontos et al. 1995; National Institute of Child Health and Development 1996). The research has shown that children in lower-income families on average receive lower quality care and that the potential impact of child care on children's development, both positive and negative, may be greater for disadvantaged children (National Institute of Child Health and Development 1999; Phillips et al. 1994; Scarr and Eisenberg 1993).

With the changes following welfare reform leading to more single mothers working and with a continuing shortage of child care funds, what are low-income mothers doing about child care? This longitudinal ethnographic study of the child care and work patterns of single-mother families in poor urban neighborhoods considers the implications of policies that are meant to serve their families. This study does not explicitly focus on questions about care arrangements before and after welfare reform but rather seeks to describe the care that has emerged in the context that has followed, accepting the work-based focus of social policy as a given.

Research Design and Setting

This qualitative research study investigates how mothers choose the arrangements they make for their children's care and then considers the implications for children's development and the social policy implications. The research design builds on the traditional ethnographic and interviewing methods that have been used to look at mothers' survival strategies to make decisions and provide for their families in poor communities. Carol Stack (1974) and Kathryn Edin and Laura Lein (1997) investigated survival strategies in contexts where the receipt of welfare payments played a primary role in these strategies, and welfare itself is central to their analyses. Similarly, I have explored how mothers develop strategies for their children's care in the context of high levels of work participation.[20]

Another method this study utilizes comes from the dynamics analysis that has been employed in poverty research. Mary Jo Bane and David Ellwood (1983) were the first to study poverty and welfare dynamics, focusing on the lengths of time people spend collecting welfare and what causes people to leave welfare.[21] Bane and Ellwood's findings on the heterogeneity of the poor and the changing conditions of their lives serve as context for this analysis. More important, I adapted their method of looking at the spells of time during which families receive services to study child care.[22] Bane and Ellwood's analysis demonstrates the importance of studying changes and transitions for low-income families.[23] I compiled detailed information about all of the care arrangements made for the children in my sample from birth through completion of the last arrangement made prior to their fourth birthdays, and I looked at not only the durations of these spells but also the reasons why they ended.

The qualitative data for this study were gained primarily from a series of in-depth interviews with forty-two low-income mothers living in four New York City neighborhoods. New York City provided a good setting for studying work and child care dynamics. The city implemented a strong work requirement as part of its welfare policies during the 1990s, and it witnessed a very large increase in the rate of single mothers working—even greater than the employment boom nationwide.[24] As shown in table 1.2, there was a 52 percent decrease in the number of people receiving public assistance (AFDC and home relief)[25] in New York City from 1994 to 2001. At the same time there were equally sharp increases in two other forms of assistance, Supplemental Security Income (SSI) and Medicaid, which many former welfare recipients turned to in place of welfare or sought to retain despite the loss of welfare.[26] In 2000, of the 8.0 million people living in the five boroughs, approximately 1.6 million, or almost 20 percent of the population, were receiving at least one of these forms of assistance. This is almost unchanged compared with recent years. More important, there was also little change in the city's high levels of child poverty. The poverty rate for children under the age of five declined marginally from 29.7 percent in 1990 to 28.8 percent in 2000.

Like other states, New York has a complicated bureaucracy for child care, but unlike most states, New York's system is further complicated because it passes on responsibility for program operations to local government agencies. New York City's administration of child care services is quite complex, and its subsidy system very difficult for families to navigate. Two separate agencies administer child care assistance in New York City, and each administers its program differently and steers families to different forms of care. Families moving from welfare to work go through the city's Human Resources Administration (HRA), which provides vouchers for child care. Another city agency, the Agency for Child Development (ACD), provides subsidized child care to low-income working parents and others, mostly through contracted care and a smaller share of vouchers.[27] Each agency has complicated eligibility systems that can appear opaque to families applying for assistance and require that parents provide extensive documentation and often make multiple in-person visits. This can be challenging for low-income single mothers working in jobs that may offer little employee flexibility. Since instituting its welfare

Table 1.2 *Child Poverty Rates and Level of Social Services Supports in New York City in 1990, 1994, 2000, 2001*

	1990	2000	Percentage Change
Total population	7,322,564	8,008,278	
Children under five years old	502,108	532,676	
Living below the poverty line	29.7%	28.8%	
Living in single-mother household	22.5	21.0	
	1994	2001	
Income support			
Public assistance (AFDC and home relief)	974,818	465,693	−52.2%
Supplemental Security Income	298,063	367,928	23.4
Medicaid only	324,265	756,430	133.3
Total persons assisted	1,597,146	1,590,051	−0.4

Sources: U.S. Department of Commerce (1990, 2000b); New York City Human Resources Administration (1994, 2001).

reforms, New York City has adopted child care policies that promote the use of less expensive, more informal care arrangements. It provided almost all of its child care expansion in the form of vouchers, doing little to create new child care capacity, and it made a stringent work push for welfare recipients that meant these families had to arrange child care quickly. Child care funding in New York City helped to subsidize the care of almost 92,000 children from birth to age twelve (Child Care, Inc. 2002). Much of this 37 percent increase from the 67,000 served in 1995 represented families moving from welfare to work. Fifty-six thousand of the 92,000 were infants, toddlers, and preschoolers, representing about one-fifth of those earning less than 200 percent of the federal poverty level and eligible to receive subsidized child care.

The respondents in this study lived in neighborhoods with very high levels of child poverty (See table 1.3). Two of these neighborhoods were primarily African American, and two had high concentrations of immigrant and Latino families. In all four neighborhoods the number of people receiving cash public assistance declined significantly, between 50 and 67 percent, from 1994 to 2001. The number of families receiving any type of social service assistance declined by much less, by between 5 and 15 percent, as more fami-

Table 1.3   *Racial and Ethnic Composition, Child Poverty Rates, and Level of Social Services Supports in Selected New York City Neighborhoods in 1990, 1994, 2000, 2001*

	The Valley		The Ville	
	1990	2000	1990	2000
Racial and ethnic composition				
Non-Hispanic white	1%	2%	1%	1%
Non-Hispanic black	88	77	84	77
Hispanic	10	17	15	18
Asian and Pacific Islander	<1	<1	<1	<1
American Indian	<1	<1	<1	<1
Other	<1	<1	<1	<1
Non-Hispanic of two or more races	—	3	—	2
Native-born	90	83	87	81
Foreign-born	10	17	13	19
Children under five years old	8,089	7,594	12,041	11,505
Living below the poverty line	49.9%	44.4%	49.3%	45.6%
Living in single-mother households	41.2	40.4	39.1	40.8
Median household income	$13,861	$20,313	$17,159	$23,877

	1994	2001	Percentage Change	1994	2001	Percentage Change
Income support						
Public assistance (AFDC and home relief)	29,348	13,074	−55%	38,871	19,059	−51%
Supplemental security income	7,243	8,191	+13	8,425	9,631	+14
Medicaid only	5,158	14,094	+173	6,382	16,882	+164
Total persons assisted	41,749	35,359	−15	53,678	45,572	−15

Sources: U.S. Department of Commerce (1990, 2000b); New York City Human Resources Administration (1994, 2001).

The Points			The Harbor		
1990	2000		1990	2000	
29%	28%		46%	47%	
9	8		7	5	
32	27		44	38	
30	35		3	3	
<1	<1		<1	<1	
<1	<1		<1	2	
—	2		—	3	
64	60		73	67	
36	40		27	33	
8,112	6,709		13,773	13,427	
39.5%	35.5%		53.6%	50.7%	
22.1	16.6		20.8	11.9	
$20,325	$30,278		$19,891	$27,133	

1994	2001	Percentage Change	1994	2001	Percentage Change
18,807	6,254	−67%	29,080	10,701	−63%
11,093	10,351	−7	7,506	8,681	+16
9,362	16,425	+75	19,304	33,694	+75
39,262	33,030	−16	55,890	53,076	−5

lies received Medicaid and SSI for families that included a member with a disability.

I developed a small sample of families with mother-child pairs living in these neighborhoods. The mothers were single and had a child between the ages of two and three at the time of initial contact. The analysis concentrated on the care of this "focal child" from birth to four, even though many families, like Annette's, had additional children. I selected the sample to have some parameters in common and to differ across others. In addition to residing in one of the neighborhoods, being single, and having a toddler-age child, all of the mothers selected for the study were working at the time of initial contact and had less than fourteen years of formal education (up to two years of college or less). About one-third of the sample had less than a high school education, a little more than one-third had completed high school or received a general equivalency diploma (GED), and slightly fewer than one-third had up to two years of postsecondary education (see table B.1). I stratified the sample by two additional criteria: race and nativity. I did this not so much because I planned to analyze racial, ethnic, and immigrant differences, but because I wanted adequate representation of African American and Latina respondents living in and coming from different contexts. See appendix B for a more detailed discussion of the methodology for the field research, including recruitment, sampling, data collection, and analysis procedures, as well as the interview guide employed.

Overall, the sample of forty-two women included twenty-one African American mothers and twenty-one Latina mothers distributed across the four New York City neighborhoods (see table 1.4). Of the Latina women, seven were of Puerto Rican heritage, eight were Dominican, one was Cuban, and five had family origins in Central and South American countries, one each from Colombia, El Salvador, Honduras, and two from Ecuador. Thirteen of the respondents were foreign-born immigrants, and twenty-nine were born in the United States.

All the mothers were New Yorkers, and they all worked hard and shared a great maternal concern for their children's well-being and (importantly for my work) a willingness to be forthcoming about their families' lives and their own views and actions. These mothers and families also varied in many ways. The mothers ranged widely in age, amount of work experience, and use of public benefit programs. There also were differences across the families in how much the fathers of the children or other partners were involved in their lives and in their housing situations, tenure in their neighborhood, use of family and personal supports, and awareness of community resources.

I diversified my sample of families for the study by using several recruitment methods. I found the first families for the study through initial referrals from community-based organizations and by reaching out directly to families I had met through volunteer work in the neighborhoods. Over time I added to the sample by asking initial respondents for referrals and by writing and

Table 1.4 *Distribution of Sample Across Neighborhoods by Race-Ethnicity and Nativity-Immigration Status*

		Race		Nativity	
Neighborhoods	Total	African American	Latina	Native	Immigrant
Highwall Valley ("The Valley")	13	11	2	11	2
Pier Points ("The Points")	14	2	12	8	6
Centerville ("The Ville")	8	7	1	7	1
Mary's Harbor ("The Harbor")	7	1	6	3	4
Total	42	21	21	29	13

Source: Author's compilation.

calling families whose names I had found on waiting lists for child care services. Most of the women I contacted were willing to participate. Of the fifty-two women I initially contacted, forty-nine agreed to a meeting. Although all forty-nine agreed to be part of the study, seven of the mothers were not eligible by at least one of the selection criteria: residence, child's age, employment, educational level, or single-parenthood. The remaining forty-two formed the sample, and I followed all of them through their child's fourth birthday with zero attrition.

Gathering and tracking information from forty-two families across four different parts of the city over nearly three years of data collection was an enormous undertaking. I used extensive recent-life history interviews at the initial interview followed by semistructured longitudinal interviews every three to six months, regular phone conversations, and informal observational visits with the mothers over the three years to assess changes over time. The mothers gave of their time very generously, but scheduling (and often rescheduling) relatively long interviews with busy and stressed working mothers of small children was arduous. I tracked each family closely throughout the years of data collection. A longitudinal approach was essential because changes and transitions were important to what I was trying to discover about the dynamics of child care. The repeated interviews also greatly improved rapport and helped me verify the accuracy of data. In addition, I observed the children in care settings and homes and had informal interviews and conversations with other family members, child care providers, and staff at community agencies.

Research Questions and Organization of the Book

Four central research questions drove the research design and fieldwork and the logic and organization of this book:

1. What types of care arrangements do single working mothers make for their children? What do they think about the care they use, and how much time do their children spend in care?

2. How stable are child care arrangements over time?

3. How do working single mothers view the care paths of children? How would they prefer to see their children spend their time, and how does that differ from their circumstances?

4. What strategies do mothers employ and develop over time to arrange child care and on which sources of assistance do mothers rely?

The major findings in this book (corresponding to these questions) are provided in chapters 2 through 5. In addition, given that a primary objective of this qualitative study of child care in the context of urban family life is to tell the stories of these mothers and their children, each of these chapters begins with the story of one of the forty-two mother-child pairs.

The goal for the first question was to describe the types of child care arrangements used by working single mothers and to illustrate each with qualitative detail about the aspects of care that mattered to mothers. Chapter 2 provides detailed information on the types of child care used by the low-income mothers in this study, documenting how and why these families arrived at their child care choices and how these choices were shaped by their experiences and preferences. The chapter also provides descriptive data on how many hours children spent in care, how many care arrangements were made for them at one time, and the costs of care arrangements. Exploration of these issues adds important descriptive detail to our understanding of the types of care from a mother's viewpoint. Chapter 2 further considers how child care choices at any point in time are tied to a range of work and family issues, including available child care options and access to child care subsidies.

I approached my next question, about the dynamics of child care arrangements, by examining how long different arrangements lasted and what accounted for changes—both exits and entries—in care arrangements over time. There has been little research on child care dynamics to date. A few studies have examined the durations of arrangements and child care subsidies, but none has tried to explain why care spells end. Chapter 3 describes the families' child care arrangements during the first four years of their children's lives. Here I present findings from a quantitative perspective on how the types of child care used varied by the children's ages, how long these care arrangements lasted, and the reasons why they ended. From a qualitative perspective, this chapter adds narrative detail about how and why child care arrangements change.

Chapter 4 addresses the next question by providing an overall picture of how mothers viewed the quality of care, its availability, and its resemblance to the care that they wanted and their children needed, all within the complexities of their family lives, work and neighborhood contexts. This chapter shows how mothers viewed their children's care together with their work choices and the limitations they faced in balancing work and child care given the surrounding pressures of urban family life in low-income communities.

In looking at the fourth question—about the strategies mothers used to arrange child care over time—I wanted to understand the resources they used, including their personal networks and community institutions. The goal in chapter 5 is to explore in detail, and from mothers' perspectives, the child care strategies revealed in the previous chapters. Framing the range of child care strategies that mothers developed as "survival strategies," the chapter discusses how they pieced together care for their children with limited resources. The complex dilemma of arranging quality child care while finding and maintaining work is also explored in this chapter.

A series of policy implications are discussed in chapter 6, which addresses some of the issues that emerge from this analysis. Among the policy areas discussed are reforming child care systems to make services to children easier to obtain and maintain; moving toward a more public and universal system of early childhood education; and helping families balance their work and care responsibilities in ways that support both self-sufficiency and developmental goals for children. This chapter asks, what can social policy offer American children in the context of increased work by their mothers?

I review the pertinent research literature on low-income families' use of child care and its effects on children's development in appendix A. This appendix focuses on what is known about child care for low-income families, how families choose child care, the quality of care that low-income families receive, and the developmental effects of this care. The appendix also presents a short overview of the policy context for the child care issues of low-income families. Readers may want to use the appendix as a reference or read it at any point for the relevant background to the chapters' findings. Appendix B offers a brief summary and discussion of the field research methods employed in this study, and appendix C is an outline of the interview guide for the study.

~ Chapter 2 ~

Child Care Choices:
"Ain't Nowhere for My Baby to Go"

When Bethany was born on August 28, 1996, in the Highwall Valley Hospital in New York City, Brittany had been dreaming of her future daughter for months. She felt more than ready for the life that was beginning and for the struggles that might come her and her baby's way.

> When I was like six months pregnant, for almost two weeks I dreamt about her, actually dreamt of her every night, but I could not see her face. She had her back to me. . . . I was dreaming the same thing every night, and one night she turned and looked at me. She looked like she was six [years old], like she's starting to look now [at close to age four]. She said to me, "Mommy, it is going to be all right." When she was born and I saw her, I already knew her. . . . And y'know, when I am feelin' it [worried], I remember that dream, and "Mommy, it's going to be all right." . . . I know it will. . . . My faith tells me it will.

Less than a week before Bethany was born, at a quite different occasion in Washington, D.C., President Bill Clinton signed into American law some elemental changes to how mothers like Brittany would view their choices regarding welfare, work, and child care. The law would end governmental assurances of minimal financial assistance during periods of poverty for Brittany and Bethany and would push Brittany to move work up among the competing elements of family life that she would need to balance. On the other hand, the new law would also offer the possibility of more federal assistance for child care to low-income mothers like Brittany—if the states could decide how to expand their systems and the assistance could make the journey from Washington, D.C., to the loosely structured child care markets in New York City's Highwall Valley.

By the time Bethany was born, her mother had been relying on welfare supports for several months. Brittany began receiving emergency public assistance for single adults, which provided cash, food stamps, and, most important, a housing allowance for her rent. She began receiving this assistance after losing a low-paying job in a suburban retail outlet following an illness. After Bethany's birth, she began receiving family public assistance—about $360 per month—along with WIC, food stamps, and the rental subsidy. Her sister and friends handed down some baby clothes and a high chair, and her aunt and father also gave her as much money as they could spare to supplement the small amount of cash and coupons. Bethany's father, Sanford, was incarcerated shortly before Bethany's birth, but after being released from prison he was present and involved in their lives. However, his work was sporadic, so he was often unable to contribute financially.

With this assistance, Brittany took care of Bethany mostly alone for her first seven months. In April 1997 she attended a training program for women moving from welfare to work to become family child care providers. The four-month training period was unpaid, but if successful, she could get a job as a family child care provider in one of the new neighborhood networks this program was starting. Also, the program was recognized as a welfare-to-work activity by the city's welfare program and came with a child care voucher. When she began her training, she left Bethany in the care of Sanford's brother. He watched Bethany because, as Brittany puts it, "he wasn't working so it helped him out."

Brittany's choice was not based on wanting to use Bethany's uncle as a child care provider as much as it was on how the subsidy worked and his immediate availability. The subsidy money was enough to help out a family member who was also poor and needing employment, but not enough to find someone who provided child care services for a living. Bethany's uncle was available at the time, and Brittany had limited information about other options. The subsidy became available when she began the training program, so Brittany had little time to find a child care provider who would take the subsidy, since many providers did not accept the subsidies because of problems in getting payments. As Brittany describes it:

> I decided to leave Bethany with Sanford's brother just for a while. . . . I paid him with money from PA [public assistance] that you had to give to the person that was providing child care. He was getting $95 a week because she was an infant. The amount was not bad for him because he did not know anything about how much people get paid for child care, he was not doing anything else, and he was not doing much with her. He took care of her at my house. That lasted only a short while. He started fine in April, but after a while he started slacking—coming late, not watching her properly.

He cared for Bethany for two months. When she realized he was not reliable, Brittany still had two more months of training. She had to find a new child care arrangement immediately.

> Then I started leaving her at my sister's house because she wasn't working at the time. That was hard too, because she lived in the Bronx, and during the summer they had computer classes for us way downtown. I would take Bethany to my sister's house, and I'd have to leave her there for a few days. I would have to take her early on Monday . . . and pick her up on Thursday or Friday. It was hard, I would cry for her some; I missed her, but I trust my sister, and she had her kids to play with there. Sometimes I would ask my sister if she would stay at my house because I thought she needed to get out of the house too. . . . I had to do that at least until I finished the training program in August. I did not have any other choice; I had no time [to find child care], and I would have had to quit the training program and I really wanted to do this job. I had to go with the only option I had because most regular providers will not take the welfare child care [vouchers] because they don't pay enough and they don't pay on time and they [the providers] find that the paperwork is too much. They also are not sure how long that the child will be there so they don't want to bother. They don't want no sometime child.

After Brittany finished the training program, Highwall Family Child Care Network decided to hire her as a program assistant rather than a family child care provider because they determined that her studio apartment was too small for a family child care program. All the same, she was ecstatic about the opportunity to work. However, she had nowhere to send Bethany.

> I will never forget that 'cause it was August 27, [1997,] right before her birthday, the day I got on payroll. I was so pleased because when I was pregnant I said to myself I would be working again before she was two and never have to get on welfare again, and I was doing it a year before that. . . . But I almost cried, 'cause . . . I had to find some regular child care closer to work because I had to start working at 8:00 A.M. on Monday, and . . . there still ain't nowhere for my baby to go.

Brittany tried to find a care arrangement that would last, not just a patch to cover the weeks of a training program. She could not find a single available provider through the family child care network where she would be working. She called Sandra, a woman she met during the training, who worked at another child care program and knew providers. "I called her upset, and she told me to call this provider and they would help me work something out. And that same night I went to meet her, and Bethany did not want to leave. I said, 'Oh, okay, that's a good sign,' and I thought she was a nice lady."

Bethany would stay there for two years, and for most of that time Brittany had to pay the full cost of the care. Initially Brittany continued to receive child care vouchers through the Human Resources Administration (HRA) for two months until they closed her welfare case, and then she applied for child care subsidies with the Agency for Child Development (ACD), a different city agency that handles child care subsidies for working parents. She was put on the waiting list for ACD child care and tried also to get transitional child care benefits from HRA, to which women moving from welfare to work are entitled. After fighting for these for more than two years, she would receive a back payment for six months of transitional child care almost three years later. Bethany stayed with the family child care provider until she was almost three years old. At that point a dispute between Brittany and the provider over payments for time Bethany was not there grew into a conflict, and the arrangement ended.

> Bethany loved it there. She was an independent provider . . . and I paid her $90 a week out of my pocket. I was giving her $360 a month, that's more than I had paid for anything—more than my rent! I thought she was real nice until I saw her true colors. . . . The provider wanted me to pay her for care when we were on vacation. She started acting funny. She told me to pay her for two weeks when Bethany was with me in the summer, and I could not see how or why I should pay when she was not there. . . . So I told her I work in family child care, and that's how you do it. I brought one of our contracts to her, and oh, that made her mad. That was it—I will never forget what she called me to this day. I heard the message on the machine, and oohhh, she was real nasty to me. I could not believe it. She said we couldn't no longer do business anymore. I said, okay, no problem.
>
> Then I had to tell Bethany, and I told her that she would not be going to her house anymore. She said, "Why, Mommy?" I told her that we just had to find somewhere else to go because I did not want to say anything bad to Bethany about her 'cause she was a nice lady up until that point, and Bethany loved her. That's why it hurt me so bad the way she did me.

The abrupt care ending left Brittany scrambling for the next year to find another stable care arrangement. That September Bethany began staying with her father, Sanford, who had started living with them at that time. He had just lost a security job, and they felt it was better to "save some money while we found something else." She stayed with him for a total of two months, while Brittany continued working on arranging an ACD subsidy and looked for providers. She knew there was going to be a place with a family child care provider who was returning from maternity leave. The provider, Mattie, also lived two blocks from her home, so Brittany decided to keep Bethany with Sanford until January, when Mattie was going back to work. This arrangement lasted only four months and also ended because of a conflict between the provider and Brittany, which in this case was not about money but about trust.

> I thought I knew Mattie, but things did not work out with her either. She started acting funny. I called her one day and nobody answered the phone, so I became worried and went over. I rang the bell and no one answered, so I thought maybe she was outside, so I walked through all the parks looking for my child. Then I went upstairs and now she was home, so I asked her why she did not answer. She said to me, "I don't think you called. Are you sure, because I was here." So I did not like that because I don't have any reason to lie, and I should not have to walk from park to park looking for my child. I mean, my child was supposed to be here. She knows that I call her every day before I leave to let her know that I am on my way. I don't know why she did not answer her phone, but for whatever reason she started acting funny, and I did not feel comfortable anymore, and when I don't feel comfortable and I start to feel bad vibes, I eliminate myself from that situation.

After this experience Brittany says she did not trust anyone else. Bethany was three and a half years old, and Brittany had wanted her in a child care center for a long time by then. For a long time she had been waiting to be approved for ACD subsidies, and when she finally became eligible, she had to find an ACD center with an opening. She had called or visited all eleven centers in Highwall Valley that had ACD contracts, but she could not find an opening. She decided she would wait to find a place in a center, and she brought Bethany with her to work until she could arrange that.

> I started bringing Bethany here with me [to work] during the summer. . . . I did not want to try to find her another home. No, I said, I would keep my baby with me until she starts the ACD program [at a child care center]. She came with me for two to three months until I found her a space in the center across the street. They knew me, seeing me in the neighborhood, and I would just go in with her whenever I could and ask when they would have a space. Then in the summer when some children were leaving they took her in.

Arranging Child Care: The Contextual Settings for Children's Development

Children spend much of their early childhood in care settings away from home while their mothers work. With more low-income mothers working, some working more hours than ever, children are spending more and more time outside their homes in the care of providers. These child care arrangements play a large and growing role in young children's development. The settings, the providers, the content, and the quality of the care vary tremendously.

Looking at the child care arrangements of the forty-two families in this small but diverse sample, it is possible to describe with qualitative detail the types of care working single mothers used, and what they thought about their

Figure 2.1   *Dynamics Timeline for Brittany and Bethany's Story*

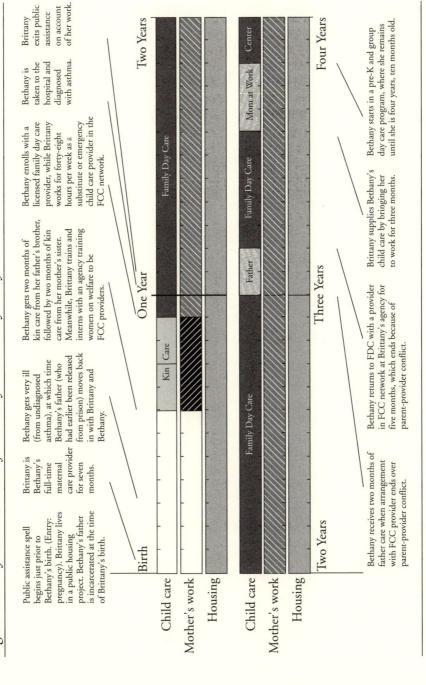

Source: Author's compilation.

care choices. In this chapter, I document how mothers balanced multiple dimensions of child care in their choices, and I analyze how their choices were tied to other factors such as their work or family situations and the complexities of child care subsidies. I also analyze the amount of time that children spent in care, and the cost of care arrangements to families.

Types of Child Care Arrangements Used by Working Single Mothers

The arrangements that mothers in this sample made during the course of this study reflect the broad array of child care types that exist for young children ages zero to four. The major types of care available to urban families, not just to single-mother and lower-income families, vary across several dimensions, including the setting, the provider, and the number and age of the children. These arrangements are summarized here; for a more complete listing, see table A.7.

Home-based, individualized child care

    Father care

    Kin care by an adult relative or close family friend

    Informal care by a nonrelated adult, neighbor, or acquaintance

    Care by paid nanny or sitter in child's home

    Care by older siblings

Family child care in caregiver's home

    Family day care (licensed)

    Family day care network (licensed)

    Family day care group

Center care (child care professionals in community settings)

    Group day care and nursery programs

    Head Start and Early Head Start centers

    Pre-K and preschool programs

Other settings and types

    Mother's care while working

    Specialized care or special needs care

    Day care in shelters, hospitals, or other specialized or service institutions

The patterns of child care use among families in the sample reflect the availability and affordability of care in poor neighborhoods. Mothers make care choices based on their contextual situation, the particular kinds of care available to them, and the interaction of these options with their work needs.

Most of the major types of child care can be seen in the arrangements that Brittany made for Bethany (see the time line summary in figure 2.1). As a first-time mother who knew little about child care and needed to arrange care for her child quickly, Brittany started, like many mothers, by making two relatively brief care arrangements with family members. These arrangements were not ideal, however, in terms of these relatives' commitment to being care providers, the location, or their long-term availability. After these two short spells in kin care, Bethany was switched to what would prove to be her most durable arrangement, one with a family day care provider; this was the one whose ending mother and daughter most regretted. The conflict between Brittany and the provider illustrates the unclear guidelines that parents and providers often face when they negotiate care arrangements, which are made doubly hard when the parent and the provider are both low-income and the conflict is over money. In some care arrangements there may be disagreements and misunderstandings over how much to pay for the care, when to pay, and whether to pay for days or periods children miss.

After that, Brittany scrambled for a year with a variety of short-term, unsatisfactory arrangements, trying to bide time—important time in her daughter's development—until she could get Bethany safely into care at a center she had had her eyes on for three years.

Annette's story (see chapter 1) is similar to Brittany's. She first sought care for her son Aaron when she was struggling to leave welfare. Given a history split between work and joblessness, she was uncertain of her work prospects or their potential durations. Unlike Bethany, though, Aaron had two advantages: he was a second child, and his mother was a long-term resident of their community. She was both experienced in care choices and well connected to community-based organizational resources. The types of care Annette utilized ran the gamut: family day care, care by friends, informal care, and group day care. Like Brittany, she had a couple of care arrangements that she liked very much but that ended in conflict. Most of her arrangements proved short and unsatisfactory, forcing her to use providers who were not really engaged in the care enterprise or who offered poor quality care.

Annette and Brittany struggled with their limited resources and pieced together care over their children's first few years using a wide range of care arrangements. They experienced many of the ways in which families find and lose care arrangements. Their experiences, like those of many other mothers in the study, illustrate some attributes of child care for low-income single-mother families:

- Care pathways are likely to begin with informal types of care by family, friends, or neighbors.

- The choice of care type is dictated by cost and the availability and rules around subsidies.

- Care arrangements are often second-best choices.

- Parents and providers are often in conflict when trying to negotiate the terms of their relationships.

- Care often starts and ends abruptly.

Some of these findings are consistent with the results of the earlier studies of child care among low-income families, which showed that age, availability, and cost constrain choices and that care is often low-quality (discussed in the literature review in appendix A).

Annette's and Brittany's child care arrangements were typical of the care I found across the sample of families, though each story was unique. Table 2.1 aggregates all 215 primary care spells for the 42 children in the sample between birth and age four from a longitudinal analysis of the early childhood care arrangements.[1] Since many families used multiple care arrangements during the workweek, *primary care arrangements* refer to those that provided the most hours of care. These correspond closely to the patterns of child care use by African American and Latina low-income, single-mother families found in national survey samples. (For comparison with data on the distribution of child care use nationally, including by age, income, family structure, race and ethnicity, and trends over time, see tables A.2 through A.6.)

Mothers used a wide variety of care arrangements to meet their care needs, although some types were more prevalent than others.

Together, *kin and informal care* accounted for 84 of 215 primary care arrangements, or 39 percent of all primary care arrangements made by mothers in the sample. With kin and informal care, individuals usually provide care in their homes to one or two children. The care tends to be child-specific, and the hours that such care is available may be more flexible. Kin care is usually care by a relative or someone who has a familylike relationship with the child that may motivate the care. Informal care is usually provided by a non-relative, possibly a neighbor, acquaintance, or other person offering care on an individualized basis and not someone who generally provides child care in their home on an ongoing basis. Of the fifty-two kin care spells, grandmothers accounted for thirty-one instances, mothers' sisters (children's aunts) for ten, mothers' cousins for five, mothers' aunts for three, and a male kin member for the three remaining cases. Parents often pay for kin and informal care, but the amounts are individually negotiated with providers and can vary greatly.

Family child care, also called family day care, is care offered in the home of

Table 2.1　*Distribution of All Primary Care Spells (Birth to Age Four) for Families in Sample, by Type*

Type of Primary Child Care Arrangement	Frequency	Distribution
Kin and informal care		
Kin care	52	24.2%
Informal care	32	14.8
Nanny care in child's home	1	0.5
Subtotal home-based care	85	39.5
Family day care		
Family day care (licensed)	26	12.1
Family day care (unlicensed)	13	6.1
Family day care network (licensed)	9	4.2
Family day care group (licensed)	3	1.4
Subtotal family day care	51	23.7
Center-based care		
Group day care (DC) programs	38	17.8
Head Start (HS) programs	6	2.8
Combined HS and DC programs	2	0.9
Pre-K programs	5	2.3
Subtotal center-based care	51	23.7
Parental care arrangements		
Father care	11	5.1
Mother's care while working	6	2.8
Subtotal parental care arrangements	17	7.9
Other care arrangements		
Special needs care	8	3.7
Shelter care	3	1.4
Subtotal all other care arrangements	11	5.1
Total primary care arrangements	215	100

Source: Author's compilation.

a provider set up to provide care to a small group of children on an ongoing basis. Fifty-one of the primary care spells in the sample were family child care. This kind of care includes independent licensed family day care providers as well as unlicensed providers operating a business outside of government regulations. Some providers expand their operations to what are generally referred to as family day care groups that serve more children, generally up to ten, in their homes, and with a second adult assistant. Some providers may also be a part of a family child care network, which coordinates recruitment, placement and payments, and provides supervision and training.

Of the fifty-one *center-based care* spells in the sample, the most frequent type was *group day care* at local centers, many of which contracted with the city for child care slots. This is usually full-day care available to low-income families with parents making sliding-scale copayments. Other center-based care includes Head Start programs, which often provide part-day (three or six hours) but sometimes full-day (ten hours) care at no cost to very low-income families below the poverty level. Usually better funded on a per-child basis than group day care, Head Start has a developmental focus and is directed to involve parents and provide families with more than just child care services. Local Head Start programs, which receive full federal funding, must meet federal program standards. Two children in the sample were in integrated Head Start and group day care programs that offered extended day care hours with Head Start's richer package of services. Five children were enrolled in prekindergarten or other preschool programs, funded though state education funds, that are mostly used when children are age four or almost four.

Eleven of the 215 primary care arrangements were *other institutional care arrangements*, such as specialized care for children with special needs or care while in a homeless shelter.

I also looked at the *secondary care arrangements* that mothers in the sample used simultaneously with their primary care. Table 2.2 presents the children's primary and secondary care arrangements *at the time of the initial interview*, when they were between ages two and four. When arrangements are aggregated, as in this table, kin care and family child care are again equally prevalent, each accounting for nineteen regular ongoing care arrangements out of a total of ninety-eight among the forty-two families. A significant difference between primary and secondary arrangements, however, is that kin mostly served as secondary care when children were older, between ages two and four. All but three of the nineteen kin arrangements were secondary. On the other hand, family child care was the most common choice for primary care, used in sixteen of the nineteen cases.

Like kin arrangements, care by fathers was an important category for secondary care, with fourteen of the forty-two children receiving this type. Fathers accounted for one-quarter of the secondary care but none of the primary care at the time of the interviews. Kin, informal, father, sibling, and mother care for children while they were working together account for about five out of every six secondary care arrangements, but only one out of every six primary care arrangements.

Of the forty-two mothers in the sample, eighteen had children whose primary care was at a center, and twenty-four had their children in homes—sixteen of these had their children in family child care. At the time of the initial interview, when children were between ages two and four, center care and

Table 2.2   *Distribution of Concurrent Primary and Secondary Care Arrangements at Time of First Interview (Children Age Two to Four), by Type*

Type of Child Care Arrangement	Primary	Secondary	All
Kin and informal care			
Kin care	3	16	19
Informal care	4	9	13
Subtotal home-based care	7	25	32
Family day care			
Family day care (licensed)	13	2	15
Family day care (nonlicensed)	3	1	4
Subtotal family day care	16	3	19
Center-based care			
Group day care (DC) programs	8	1	9
Head Start (HS) programs	5	4	9
Combined HS and DC programs	2	—	2
Pre-K programs	3	—	3
Subtotal center-based care	18	5	23
Other care arrangements			
Father care	—	14	14
Mother's care while working	—	6	6
Sibling care	—	2	2
Special needs care	1	1	2
Subtotal other care arrangements	1	23	24
Total care arrangements	42	56	98

Source: Author's compilation.

family day care accounted for a majority of the primary care arrangements but were used relatively rarely as secondary care arrangements. Kin and informal care were comparatively less frequently used as the ongoing primary arrangement between ages two and four than they were prior to age two. As we shall see when we look closely at the arrangements longitudinally in the next chapter, kin and informal care are most often used for early care, short-term care, or secondary care.

Looking in table 2.2 at the number of primary and secondary care arrangements the mothers made for each child, it becomes clear that for most families one child care arrangement did not meet their full care needs. As table 2.3 indicates, only three of the families used a single care arrange-

Table 2.3   *Number of Concurrent Care Arrangements Used by Families at the Time of Initial Interview (Children Between Ages Two and Four)*

Number of Arrangements (Combined Primary and Secondary Care Arrangements Used at One Time)	Frequency
1	3
2	24
3	13
4	2
Total number of families	42
Average number of arrangements	2.33

Source: Author's compilation.

ment; of the thirty-nine families that had made additional arrangements for their children besides the primary care arrangement, twenty-four had two, thirteen had three, and two had four care arrangements at that point in time. The forty-two families in the sample averaged 2.33 arrangements at one time.

As this table shows, low-income mothers need to mix and match care arrangements because of the nature of their jobs and the nature of the child care resources available to them. Most low-wage jobs offer workers little flexibility, and many mothers have complex and shifting work schedules that may not match the hours that some care arrangements are available. Many mothers also work multiple jobs and often change the mix of jobs, requiring a shifting mix of care. Most of the child care they use offers limited or set hours that do not neatly match their work schedules. Most formal center care and licensed family child care arrangements are available only during traditional weekday working hours; however, many low-wage workers work nontraditional evening and weekend hours. Many informal and kin caregivers also cannot offer enough hours to accommodate the many hours that some mothers work, so those relying mostly on informal care arrangements often have to use several of them. Very often, if families use the center-based care they prefer for developmental and consistency reasons, they must add informal care around the hours offered by the center. Many centers, such as most Head Start and pre-K programs, offer only limited hours—for example, three hours in the mornings—so using these programs requires that working families make complex logistical efforts to set up second and third care arrangements.

Mothers' Views of the Varieties of Care

Types of child care vary in the settings, the providers, the number and ages of children in care, the number of adults, and the activities and environments that frame the day. Many of these characteristics were prominent in mothers' decisions about the care they used and preferred. (For a review of the factors influencing child care choices, see appendix A.) For example, settings range from the child's home to the provider's home, a center or school, a mother's workplace, or a specialized institutional setting, such as a hospital offering special needs care or a homeless shelter with day care for resident families. Providers can be parents, kin, friends, neighbors, strangers, family child care providers, teachers, or other child care professionals. A parent or relative may provide care for just one child or for a few related children. In a family day care home, the group size is usually three to five children, but in some cases it may be as many as six to ten if the provider has a group license and an assistant. Center-based groups can range from eight to twenty children. From a mother's perspective, care ranges from "babysitting" to "nurturing" to "developmental" to "educational" to "special needs," with some differentiation in the meanings that mothers attach to these terms.

The study relied on in-depth interviews with mothers to uncover how they perceive the aspects of child care that shape their decisionmaking and how they arrive at their care choices. Through a grounded analysis of the data gathered from the interviews,[2] I developed an analytic framework (see figure 2.2) from which to understand these mothers' child care choices and to consider the factors that were most relevant to them in making these choices. The primary explanatory variables that helped determine their choices include their children's needs, their own work requirements, their views of appropriate child care, family dynamics, the costs of care, and the availability of care and subsidies.

This model is useful for showing how mothers choose particular care arrangements and which factors contribute most to the instability of child care for low-income families. The model also serves as a framework for understanding the existing problems in the child care market identified by other research, problems that this study bears out in detail. For example, we know that the cost of child care places strong constraints on low-income mothers' choices (Heymann 2000, 2002). The ways in which mothers view the care available to them are thus often determined by supply factors. Mothers who do not earn enough to pay the market rates must either find lower-cost care, such as informal care that may not be reliable over the long term, or base their care choices on the availability of subsidies. Problems on the demand side can limit choices as well. Because low-income women are more likely to have jobs with variable or unusual work hours, it is often more difficult for them to find child care that meets their work needs (Presser 2000). They are also more likely to experience frequent job changes requiring change in their child care arrangements (Pavetti and Acs 2001).

Figure 2.2   *A Grounded Model of Child Care Choices*

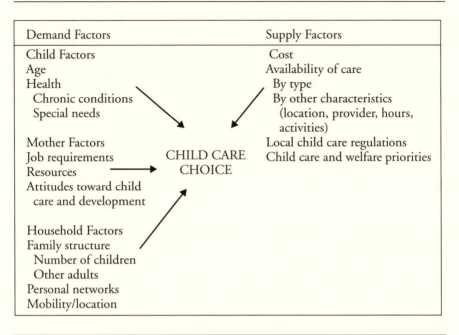

Demand Factors	Supply Factors
Child Factors	Cost
Age	Availability of care
Health	By type
Chronic conditions	By other characteristics
Special needs	(location, provider, hours,
	activities)
Mother Factors	Local child care regulations
Job requirements CHILD CARE	Child care and welfare priorities
Resources CHOICE	
Attitudes toward child	
care and development	
Household Factors	
Family structure	
Number of children	
Other adults	
Personal networks	
Mobility/location	

Source: Author's compilation.
Note: Providing this framework for structuring the presentation of child care choices was first suggested by one of the anonymous peer reviewers commissioned by the Russell Sage Foundation, to whom I owe a debt and due credit.

Beyond Types of Care

Most mothers do not choose their child care by "type" or array their choices this way. There are some major archetypes—kin care, center-based care, and family child care—and it is important to understand these as most mothers do.

Rather than view child care types as discrete categories, it is useful to view them as defined places within a broad continuum of arrangements. Actual care arrangements may blend elements of different types or change over time from one type to another. For example, the distinctions between an informal care provider and a family day care provider are sometimes hard to make. Telling distinctions may be that the provider considers herself a family child care provider, that she is serving several unrelated children at a time and for a longer expected duration, and that she may have reconfigured her home to provide child care on an ongoing basis. The informal care provider, often a neighbor trying to earn some extra money, is usually engaged because of a particular care need for one child for a particular mother. Some informal care providers may take in more children over time and then at some later point decide to become a nonlicensed or a licensed family child care provider. Sometimes the distinction between kin and informal care is blurred, especially when the arrangement involves a friend, neighbor, or distant relative and the provider is someone whose motives are primarily financial, such as when Brittany employed Sanford's brother to take care of Bethany.

Even with the caveat that care is better thought of as a continuum than as set categories, there are some important variations that can be used to organize a discussion of the types of child care used by low-income families. The following analysis helps to identify the range and frequency of child care arrangements used by low-income families and the features of particular types of care that account for their choices. Looking at child care choices in context helps to model the decisionmaking that mothers engage in when selecting care and highlights the factors that are most relevant to their use of particular arrangements. This descriptive analysis is helpful in both developing an analytic framework for child care choices and incorporating into this framework the factors that mothers consider in their choices. In addition, the qualitative data add contextual understanding about the relationship between mothers' child care choices and their decisions about work, housing, family relationships, and their children's health and developmental needs.

Kin Care

One mother in the study, Harriet, prefers kin care for her son Horace. She expects her family to provide care, almost as if it were an obligation. Harriet had a strong family network in which the older generation of female kin often served as primary caregivers. She also thinks that kin care is important because it helps establish an ongoing relationship across generations and preserved a family's identity.

> Little babies need a loving family member, their grandma or aunt. They need to be in a home and have that regular eye on them, and just them, so they will have their diapers changed, they won't be neglected. . . . I trust my aunt with him because I have seen her with children all my life. She helped raise me up, so I know what she is like. . . . She has the blood connection, so she will watch him right.

This concern about trust was the strongest sentiment expressed by the handful of mothers who relied on kin care for infants and young toddlers. Harriet thinks that when children are very young they should not be in centers, and she is distrustful of family child care providers.

Kin were a common starting place for mothers trying to figure out care. Many younger and first-time mothers who still lived with or near family were most likely to seek their family's help. For many mothers, kin care was often "the easiest way to go" the first time. It was familiar, and it was often low-cost or free to them. It was also often the most certain in its immediate availability. Of the thirty-five mothers who worked in their child's first year, sixteen used kin care as their first arrangement.

Matilda, a young mother who still lived with her parents, primarily used kin care for her son Leo because it was readily available. For her, other care options were not feasible, either because she did not trust them or because their cost was prohibitive.

> My mother and sometimes my father took care of Leo when I was work-
> ing at the doughnut shop. It is good I even had family members to take
> care of him because I looked for child care and it was so expensive; I
> would not have worked.

A few months later Matilda was in a new job and still relied on kin care. However, it was getting harder for her to maintain and coordinate, and she was considering group care, which she thought would be more consistent, give him exposure to other children, and yet be safe.

> Right now I am working different shifts at the Burger Joint, so [Leo's
> care] is between me, my parents, and, sometimes, the father's mother. I'd
> rather not have to hustle him so much, and I'd like to put him in a school
> that's got parents involved, coming in and out . . . and with people who
> work in a nursery and want to be there. That would be better for him,
> and for my trusting them.

Griselda had two daughters, Alicia and Giselle. She used primarily kin care followed by care in centers. Though her initial use of kin care was based on her work and living situations, she continued to rely on her mother as a steady primary and secondary care provider as these aspects of her life changed over time:

> My children have gotten a mix of things—a little bit of care at centers,
> some with my mom. . . . When I have lived at my mother's, like now, she
> will watch them more. . . . One time I changed jobs just so my hours
> would be different from my mother's, so I would work late and she
> picked them up and made them dinner, and I worked Saturdays because
> she watched them then too.

Griselda also says that the amount of time she wants each of her children to be with their grandmother depends on their age and developmental stages:

> I am glad my mom is always there for me, but I really wanted them in a
> center. My mom works, and I did not want to leave all of that on her. . . .

For Alicia I knew she was not ready; she is a very quiet, shy child, and she needed more attention, so I stayed home with her for a longer time, and then when I worked she stayed with my mother. . . . With Giselle, she was ready for a learning environment . . . so I tried to register her [in a center] at one [year old].

Lisa first used her mother as her daughter Millie's care provider while she was trying to move off welfare through training programs and work. Her mother provided care for about one year before Millie went to family day care:

I stopped [child care] with my mom and started family day care because my mom was not a young person anymore. Millie had become more active . . . she was now starting to move more and need more attention. She was running around, and my mother could not keep up with her. She would ask to go outside, and my mom would tell me, "It's nice and warm outside, but we can't go outside because if she runs away I cannot chase her." . . . So we talked about it, and she said, "Yes, it's time for her to be around children her own age," and my mother wanted to go live in Jamaica, where she had family. So now she will come here to stay with us during the summer and care for Millie for short stretches.

Kin care was often short in duration because kin had their own life paths—just some of which involved caring for their youngest kinfolk. Kin included grandmothers, like Millie's, who were moving to distant places they considered home, were aging, or had health issues that restricted their ability to provide ongoing care. Kin included not only grandmothers and aunts who faced their own work obligations or family crises but other relatives who found out they were not cut out for child care. Some mothers recognized from the start that kin care was uncertain in its duration, and others realized from experience that it would prove to be short-term. Mothers also quickly realized that they could trust kin care to be loving and safe but that it could also be custodial, isolating, and not as developmentally stimulating as they wanted when their children got older. Griselda says:

With my mom they are just with my mom, you know, confined to the house, stuck in the projects, or going to the little park between the buildings, or sometimes seeing my mom's old friends in the building. At home they act the way they want. But in school they are learning, they are reading, they are learning to interact with other kids, with other adults, learning behavior. They have to learn how to behave in particular places and certain situations.

As children got older, kin care remained a significant form of care, but it was mostly used for shorter *bridge* care between arrangements or secondary *wraparound* care arrangements. Francine's mother provided both primary and secondary child care at critical periods. She watched the children on and off when they were infants and toddlers because Francine sometimes held irregular jobs that ended after a few months. When Francine started working longer hours, and often two jobs, she arranged preschool care for her youngest son, Fortune, and her mother provided secondary care on weekends and at other times. Francine also turned to her mother when her other care arrangements fell apart. As the need for care became more regular, Francine's mother, who was getting older, could not provide as much care as she once had, and eventually Francine's sister picked up some of the secondary child care needs.

Francine appreciated this care and recognized that without it she "could not have made it" down the choppy road from regular welfare to welfare mixed with irregular work, and then to regular work. But Francine also recognized the limits of the kin care she used:

> With kin you can work, but it cannot be the regular care. . . . I like that the care is more like home—but [kin] don't pay no mind to what they are doing. If he is with my mother or sister, he'll just do the PlayStation all the day. . . . I like for him to go there when I am working on the weekends because it is most like being home with me, but I don't want him there for the regular child care. I liked him to be in school as soon as I could do it.

Informal Care

Like kin care, informal care is usually arranged between individuals outside of the market and public systems for child care. It is generally lower-cost and often either lasts for a short term or is of uncertain duration; it is more likely to be used as an initial or early care arrangement when a mother has fewer options or limited information available to her. Along with kin care, informal care is one of the most common forms of secondary care used to wrap around longer, more durable primary care arrangements throughout early childhood. Informal care and family child care share many of the drawbacks of care in a stranger's home, including the potential for a lack of trust and misunderstandings about the parameters of the care arrangement between provider and parent. Yet some lasting informal care arrangements can be like good family day care arrangements and lead to attachments on the part of the children and a complementary, familylike relationship between the mother and the provider.

Sandra describes a typical start to an informal child care arrangement:

> When my mom moved down south, home to Alabama, I asked her, who am I supposed to get to keep Shaniqua? She thought of this woman first.

. . . I did not feel right about throwing her into a day care [center] right away when she was one year old. I didn't want anything formal, I just did not know who I would get. I really don't know people in this building, but my mother said, there's a woman upstairs in her building, Miss Candice, that she didn't have a job and sometimes keeps kids. So I called her. . . .

I had met her before. I had known her 'cause I used to go to the same church until I stopped going when I had my baby. So I had seen her for twelve years, but I had never talked with her. Since she was familiar, I was comfortable with it, because I thought I had to quit my job when my mother said she couldn't keep her no more. So when my mother mentioned her, I was happy, 'cause otherwise I didn't know what to do because to me my baby comes first.

Like many informal care arrangements, this was care by a neighbor whom the mother was acquainted with but did not know very well. There was a community and personal connection in this case through Sandra's mother and the church. The need for care followed an unexpected transition. There was uncertainty about what the care would be like and about the price. Shaniqua was in Miss Candice's care for eight months, and initially Sandra did not know what to expect. It was the first time she had put her child in the care of anyone besides her mother or herself.

The transition was hard for Shaniqua to go from my mom's care to a babysitter, because she only had my mom and was used to being around me or my mom or her dad. At first she used to cry when I took her. It was so scary for me to go to work and leave her with this lady, that was pretty much just a stranger, with my baby crying. I told my supervisor that if it lasted the whole week straight, I don't know if I am going to keep her at this lady's house, or what I am going to do. I don't know what the lady is doing even though I know her some, or if she can handle her. But after two or three days . . . I guess it was just her getting used to me leaving her, bringing her out of the house, leaving her, and she realized I would come back. That would have happened with any kind of child care.

Diane, who used many child care arrangements for her three children, faced similar concerns about how much to pay and what to expect when she used informal child care the first time.

When I needed child care for Adrienne's oldest brother, I started calling centers and they were all filled up. . . . We ended up getting a young lady in the building. I didn't really like that. It wasn't bad care, but it wasn't structured. I got the impression he watched a lot of TV, and it was hard for me because I had to bring all his food. I was paying her $50, and after he was with her three or four months she wanted to go up to $75, so then I decided I needed to find someone else. . . .

Then I sent him to an older lady in the building, who fed him, but I found out she drank a lot. I wouldn't call her an alcoholic, but she drank. A lady whose son was there also claimed they smelled alcohol on the baby or in his bottle or something, so she said we should take our sons to the hospital to get them checked out. So we took them to the hospital, but the doctor didn't find anything. I never thought she would do that. I don't think she did, but we could not take a chance with a child, so we found someone else.

One of the frequently mentioned concerns about informal care was the lack of structure. Parents had the same problems with other types of home care, especially kin and family child care, but the concern was more prevalent in informal care, perhaps because these providers did not have established routines for multiple children in their care, unlike many family child care situations. Mothers complained about a lack of structure in informal care more than they did about kin care, even though it actually might not be more prevalent. With kin care, mothers may be glad that their child is with a family member at least for a short time, and they may not have the same expectations because they do not consider it a care arrangement.

The cost of informal care arrangements was generally lower than it was for family child care and higher than it was for paid kin care, but with a wider range and more instability in the amount. There was often less sense of a basis on which to determine the price and greater anxiety about whether the price was right. In addition to less structure and more variation in price, it was sometimes difficult for mothers to know what to expect from informal care. Diane mentioned one situation that is more common in informal care—the need to bring one's own food and diapers. Many informal care providers did not regularly provide care or did not have young children themselves, so they were less willing to take on this responsibility or expense. When informal care was not ongoing or regular, the food, the diapers, and almost every other detail of the care needed to be individually negotiated.

As often happens, both Sandra and Diane were able to find a woman in the neighborhood with whom to make an informal care arrangement by word of mouth. Also like many others, the arrangement ended after just a few months, out of either a preference for something else or some dissatisfaction with the care.

In addition to being short-term primary care arrangements, informal care and kin care often served as important secondary care to fill gaps in care left by primary care arrangements, especially for mothers with irregular work hours. Traci's arrangement was typical. Two to three days a week a woman in her building picked up her children from day care and school and watched them for an hour until Traci came home from work, and she charged Traci $8 a day, or an average of $20 per week.

Traci's informal secondary arrangement worked out well. In other cases, secondary arrangements did not work out because they were less reliable or more expensive. Iris, who often worked two jobs, had to use informal secondary care to match her work hours. The informal care proved unreliable at times, including once when an informal caregiver who lived in her building and picked up Quirina in the evenings failed to do so one night.

> She was in the day care, and then I also had the babysitter who lived in the building, and I paid her to watch Quirina because I was working the evenings. She picked her up every day, and then she did not that day. The police called me [at my job]. I almost killed her. The police had to take my daughter to the station because if you don't pick up by six o'clock the day care calls the police to take her. And if it happens more than once you can lose your child. Thank God it happened just that time. After that I learned. I gave up the other job.

Often the cost of a few hours of informal care changes the financial calculus of work versus care and mothers leave their jobs and their care situations. Ramona, who worked in a department store, was using a woman from the neighborhood to pick up her daughter from day care. "She was charging me $7 per hour to pick up my daughter and for the hours that she was staying with her, and that was coming out of my expenses . . . and I was paying her grandmother too. . . . That is why I had to quit."

In mothers' child care choices some of the factors most pertinent to their selection of kin and informal care arrangements included:

- *Children's ages, mothers' attitudes about child care, cost, and availability*: The most important factors to these mothers were the ages of their children, their attitudes about child care, the cost of kin care, and the availability of personal networks.

- *Trust*: Kin care was often used very early and by mothers who trusted only family, many of whom equated trustworthy care for infants with kin care.

- *Limited resources and access to subsidies*: This was a time when their resources were limited, and so those with personal networks turned to them. The cost of kin care was often much less than the alternatives, and sometimes it was free. For many mothers, their difficulties in getting subsidized child care led to their choice of kin care, especially when they were first starting to work.

- *Flexible hours*: Mothers whose work situation required that they find child care quickly or who were working a job with variable or unusual work hours were the most likely to use kin or informal care because these were often the only options that offered flexibility in the hours that care was available.

- *Difficult subsidy forms and rules and limited options for other forms of care*: The form and rules of child care subsidies contributed to the use of kin and informal care. Child care subsidies for women moving from welfare to work were not widely accepted at this time because of payment problems. Also, the child care vouchers allowed them to transfer the subsidies to family members or informal care providers they knew, which encouraged them to use those forms of care. The limited availability of other forms of care, particularly for younger children, was another important supply factor contributing to the use of kin and informal care.

Family Day Care

The mothers who preferred that their children spend most of their time when they were very young in the home of someone they knew, often kin, usually ruled out other home-based day care because they feared leaving their children in the care of strangers. In such situations, they expected the quality of the care to be low or hard to discern. Matilda, who was not sure what family child care was, says: "I don't like where you put the child in another person's home with a lot of other people's children—that's called family day care, right? I don't like that, so he won't be going there."

However, many other mothers who also wanted their children to be in a home environment when they were very young did use family child care. Some of these mothers did so in spite of initial fears. When Edwina, for example, was struggling to arrange care for her first child, she was unaware that family day care is a licensed and subsidized form of child care. She eventually did use family day care as the main type of child care for her second child, Emily, for almost three years.

> When I was living in the Bronx with [my older daughter] Nelly, I had the hardest time. . . . I didn't really know about ACD family day care. I thought family day care was something different—it wasn't that I preferred care in the house or the center. I just wanted the care to be reliable, you know, licensed, and I had no money, so I wanted help paying for the care until I could start paying, and I thought you could only do that with the center or [you had] to get the cheap care with the private ladies. With Emily I learned about the family child care through ACD, and I wanted that because it was easier and [the provider] was good.

Edwina and Emily's experience with family child care was positive: the arrangement was long-lasting and consistent, and Emily loved the provider. The same was true for Brittany's daughter Bethany, who loved her first family day care provider. Brittany too appreciated that Bethany had consistent care for more than two years, especially after the two short arrangements during Bethany's first year. Compared with the other arrangements she had used,

Brittany liked family child care for offering hours that corresponded with her full-time work schedule. Family child care was often the most readily available care option for mothers seeking many hours of care.

Annette found that the three family child care arrangements she used for Aaron varied in quality and duration but were generally more available to her than the alternatives. She thought some family day care providers, which she also referred to as "mother providers," were more stable and dedicated to child care, and her assessment of the provider was the most important aspect when it came to choosing child care:

> The important thing to me is the provider's attitude—if they seem like they are doing this work because they like the children and if they seem patient with the child. And I think actually that is true more for the mother providers in the community, who are licensed, than what I have seen even with the private kinds of care when you leave a child with a family member. Those situations do not work out like people like to believe. . . . I like the care arrangement to be more structured, more educational than babysitting, for there to be reading, play, artwork. Family day care providers who are doing this for a living do this more than the informal babysitters.

Like Annette, Yolanda had multiple experiences with family child care providers for her son Yeats, and she found the quality to be mixed. She quickly left her first care arrangement:

> I thought Ms. Bostock was good; however, he started coming down with a diaper rash. And that concerned me, 'cause he never had a rash before. She was telling me that she provided Pampers and all. . . . I was like, I can bring these. "Oh, no. We have plenty." So I had the impression that she wasn't changing him regularly like she should have been. . . . So I let the agency know and they found me someone else.

Yolanda's next family day care provider, Ms. Nancy, was more the "grandmother type," Yolanda says. Ms. Nancy did not teach Yeats very much, while Jane, his third family day care provider, did. Yolanda had planned to move Yeats to a center care sooner, but she chose to leave him in Jane's care because she provided a learning environment coupled with the warmth of a home setting.

Annette and Yolanda each used as many as three family child care providers, and both found wide variations among these arrangements, some of which they liked and some of which they rejected. Annette and Yolanda both liked care that was professional and a provider who showed warmth and a strong desire to care for children. They also preferred providers who structured their time with their charges and who focused on learning activities. In general, they found that if care was high-quality and educational, family child care offered them stability, safety, and many hours of care so they could work.

What Annette and Yolanda did not like was family child care that was largely custodial and offered no learning opportunities. And in some cases they harbored questions about what occurred when the provider was alone with their children.

Family Child Care at Times Is the Best of Care . . .   The range of mothers' experiences with family child care was quite wide. Those who spoke highly of particular family child care situations often described their providers as "second mothers" or "grandmothers" for their children. They described these providers as patient with children, because of their greater experience with children, and the mothers appreciated how much their children were engaged in creative and learning activities that they did not always get at home.

Felicidad used Melanie as the family child care provider for her two children, Cara and Karyn. Both were with Melanie for nearly three years, from shortly after birth until they started in preschool programs. Cara started in child care with Melanie when she was four months old, and three years later Karyn started at Melanie's when she was just five weeks old and replaced Cara, who then moved to center-based care. "I had planned it with Melanie from before the baby was born. She is my best friend's mother and we [she and her best friend] both had children at the same time and asked her to take care of them."

Edwina also prepared in advance for her child care needs. She identified Soraya as her child care provider for her daughter Emily before she even started to work. Edwina had recently moved to a public housing project in a new neighborhood after leaving a homeless shelter. Socially isolated and still not on her road back to work, she ran into Soraya with a group of children and learned that she was a family child care provider who lived downstairs in the same building and was also from the Dominican Republic.

> So that was the first time I had seen her, and like that [*snaps her fingers*] we just started talking. . . . When I saw her apartment, I loved the way she had it set up. Her living room has a small table and lots of toys. I told her, one day when I get a job, I want [Emily] to come here. So when I got a job, I tried right away to get Soraya. . . . I wanted family child care only because I wanted Emily to be with her.

Edwina and Felicidad both chose the provider well in advance of needing the care, and they both remained with the same provider for the bulk of their children's primary care because of the attachment and ease of the arrangement. Bernadette became attached to her infant son Paul's family day care provider, establishing a lasting care arrangement and a close family friendship:

> I love her [the provider]. I went to see three providers . . . and I knew this was the person I wanted right away—I felt I could trust her. I liked the

way Luiza spoke to the children. The house was very child-ready. She
was licensed. There was a fire extinguisher, and all the outlets were covered up. . . . She had special furniture and materials just for the children
and had everything well arranged and clean.

The other places I visited were not the same; they were not child-
proof. They were new providers and still getting licensed. One mother
had seven children including her own, so there would be lots of traffic
and a busy environment.

Bernadette had not expected to feel that comfortable with a child care
provider for her infant son. She had been wary of leaving her child in the care
of anyone besides her own mother. But she liked Luiza because she was mature, spoke Spanish, and had a stable home environment, including a husband who helped with care and played with the children.

Yolanda started with a strong preference for center care for Yeats but found
it was unavailable when he was very young. She was surprised that over time
she came to prefer many of the aspects of family day care, especially when she
found a family day care group that had a strong developmental focus:

If I could choose any one type of child care now, I would use family day
care. I like that they get attention and are safe and they are around other
children. That is really important for him to learn how to get along with
all different children, sharing, knowing that it's not my world only.

Diane was able to keep track of what was going on at the family day care
provider's home with her daughter, Adrienne, and her infant son, because she
called the provider daily from work. The provider, Miss Monique, also became quite involved in the lives of the families whose children she cared for.
"Miss Monique calls on the weekend to see how they are doing, and recently
she has taken them for the weekend to her home in Staten Island so she could
expose them to that environment and to give me a break."

Like the other women, Diane was glad that her children became attached
to their family child care provider; as a result, both a long-term care arrangement and close family friendships were established. For mothers who do not
have family nearby, including many immigrant mothers, family child care
providers can become a close substitute for a kin relationship. Care can be in
a familiar home and language, and it can allow mothers to work more consistently and for longer hours. This was true for Edwina, as well as for Clarabel
and Hortensia, two Spanish-speaking immigrant parents.

After leaving the shelter system, Clarabel started in a literacy program at a
local social service agency. When required to work again because of welfare reform, she returned to the job she had for three years before going into the
shelter and onto welfare. The agency had a family day care network that offered care. It promoted family day care for children younger than three because its centers had limited space and spaces for children age three to five

were given priority. After helping Clarabel establish her eligibility for a child care subsidy, the program told her about two providers, whom she visited:

> When I went to see the first place, I was scared to leave him there. She had a dog and a cat. It was dirty. She did not pay attention to the children. She did not care for nothing. Then I took him to Dolores, and she gave him a banana and hugged him. He liked her right away. He loved that babysitter and calls her "Mamita."

Clarabel was happy to have the family child care because she knew she would be working regularly again. She did not really know what family child care was until she placed Robert with a provider, but she was very happy to learn that Dolores, like her, was an immigrant mother from the Dominican Republic. Since she had no family she could turn to here, Dolores was the closest thing to a family environment for Robert and herself. When Robert was four years old, Clarabel had twins, whom she started to leave with Dolores when they were only two weeks old.

Hortensia was pleased to find a family day care provider from her homeland, Honduras. She had used four different home-based, unlicensed providers before she found Fanny, a stable and subsidized child care provider who reminded Hortensia of her mother. She liked Fanny's manner with her son Ivan, who was nineteen months old at the time, and the warmth and familylike environment in her home. Fanny cared for four children—her own granddaughter, the son of a family friend, Ivan, and another child—and she treated the children with great tenderness. For Clarabel and Hortensia, finding someone who shared many of their views on children and customs was ideal. They felt as if they instinctively knew what their child's time with the provider was like, and they were able to communicate with their provider in a shared tongue.

. . . And at Times Family Child Care Is the Worst of Care   Some mothers had a negative experience with family child care arrangements, especially when they could not communicate effectively with the providers or they did not have a clear sense of what happened in the home. Often this occurred because of language barriers. If the provider spoke only Spanish and the parent did not, the language difference made mothers wonder about how involved and verbally engaged the provider was with their children. Often they suspected that while the provider's home was a warm, safe care environment, the children were mostly watching television. Given that many mothers considered family day care to be the least visible form of care, mothers would sometimes respond to cultural difference by paying particular attention to signs such as the cleanliness of the home or the behavior of the provider's own children.

Cassandra knew about Lydia, an unlicensed child care provider, for some time before she actually hired her to care for her son, Cedric. Although this arrangement ultimately worked out, Cassandra was initially concerned about language differences and about the home environment.

> I had known about Lydia already. She lives around the corner, but I just thought that he was too young because Lydia speaks no English at all. I didn't feel so comfortable with not having any communication with someone taking care of my baby. But then he was older, and I had become so desperate after all the other child care problems. I knew she was maternal and at least had a safe home. He had been through a horrible care situation, when I had to take a leave from my job, so getting him into someplace safe soon became the most important thing.
>
> She's a grandmother type. It's a big Spanish house, and there are like twenty rooms in the apartment, all full with people going in and out of there all the time. She's got about five to ten kids there already. I might be exaggerating a little, but she's got her hands full, plus her children and her children's children. All that traffic made me worry . . . but he seemed to like all the attention they give him.

Traci's concerns about the family child care setting were not anticipatory fears but reactions. She tried two family child care arrangements, both of which she ended abruptly. In the first instance, she found that the provider's house was very dirty, and her daughter Tanya got a virus in her first two weeks there. When Traci saw a liquor bottle on a table when she picked Tanya up one day, she decided not to bring her back there again. Primed to look for something more orderly, she tried another family child care provider. That arrangement ended when her daughter was hurt while in the provider's care and Traci had not been informed. With two abrupt endings to family child care arrangements, Traci said she had "had it" with home-based care and decided to immediately move Tanya into a child care center.

Strong reactions and abrupt exits caused by provider-parent conflicts were not unusual with family day care, owing to fragility of trust, unclear expectations, and lack of boundaries between the provider's home life and workspace. In family child care arrangements, the mother's response to problems was typically to end the care. Given that the range in family day care is so wide, some exits can signify a choice for a better arrangement. However, many family child care endings reflect intrinsic problems in the nature of the exchange of services and in the communication between parent and provider. Parents have incomplete information about the quality of this service and they cannot observe it directly. Although licensed family child care must meet certain requirements, mothers often have lingering concerns about quality and safety. This concern, along with the lack of any venue or process for parents to voice their concerns short of exiting and a shortage of qualified providers for an excess of children, often leads providers to develop "a take it or leave it" attitude toward the exchange.

Several important factors determined the use of family child care by the mothers in the study:

• *Mothers' work requirements*: Family child care was often linked to mothers' work requirements. Those who worked more regular hours were more likely to use family child care because the care generally offered the most hours and was relatively consistent.

• *Lack of personal networks*: Family child care was used more often by mothers who did not have personal networks they could turn to for child care.

• *Experience with other forms of care*: Mothers often needed lead time to arrange subsidies to help pay for family child care and to learn about available options, so many mothers who used family child care had relied first on other types of care.

• *Children's ages*: Family child care was used most consistently across the years of early childhood compared to other forms of care; kin care tended to be for very young children, and center care was often mostly used for preschool-age children.

Center Care

At some point when their children are young, most mothers struggle with questions about when to move them from a home arrangement to a center. Facing these choices is a common decision point for families, and the decision is often shaped by the parents' preferences and by the available options.

Bernadette used both family child care and center care for her two young sons, and she was pleased with each arrangement. Bernadette said she liked the center for her older child and preferred home care for her younger son. Her choices were based in part on the age of each child, the particular child's needs, and the arrangements available at the time:

> Andre was older when I started working, and he needed to be in a large group and learning environment right when he started. I think I would have wanted to care for little Paul like I had for Andre, but I had to work, so I wanted him to be in a nice home environment, and Luiza was so good and paid close attention to him because he needed more attention.

Mothers clearly preferred different types of care arrangements for children at different ages. Many mothers of infants and toddlers wanted individualized care like that given by parents or relatives or in a small family child care home. As their children grew older, mothers stressed the importance of socializing and learning skills. As Annette explains:

> I like the [center] care because it gives him [Aaron] classroom structure, socialization, teaches him the routines of the day and what to expect— he goes out twice a day unless it rains and then he goes to the gym. He learns his environment and the space. . . . [But] sometimes in the group situation you worry that he might not get enough attention, that is why I worried about him leaving Nelly's care . . . [but] he does not need to be babied as much now, he needs to grow with his peers.

Mothers differed as to when they preferred to start their child in a center. A few wanted to wait until a child was three or older. Some wanted to do it much sooner. Most preferred to transition to center care at some point between ages two and three. Felicidad says that young children are better off in a smaller home environment, like that of her family child care provider, where they can get individual attention. She says three years of age is about the time to start in center care. Francine says that "family day care is really for the kids birth to two . . . and when they are two they need to start with the centers and get the educational [care] . . . and more activity." Traci thinks even sooner is better:

> There comes a time when they have to learn to socialize with their peers. They need to be in a different environment with kids their own age. They need that . . . [to] learn how to deal with other people. . . . At a year old they are ready for that. Before that they need to be nurtured by their parent, but then it's better to go to the center and not get spoiled by their mother.

Many mothers prefer center-based care for their children by the age of two or three to get them ready for school, but many mothers in low-income neighborhoods are unable to find center care when they first want it. Vanya wanted to put her son Xavier in a center, but the five in her immediate area were full and all of them had waiting lists.

> He's been on so many waiting lists. I put his name everywhere I could. One new place they were picking names out of a lottery, and he was on the waiting list for three other schools. He got into one, and he did not get into the others. But when we went to that center the first day, they were not organized at all. . . . They had more kids than they could handle . . . and they didn't even have a class for him. We walked right out, and I was able to arrange care for him at the other center [later].

Diane, a veteran of child care searches after making multiple primary and secondary arrangements for her three young children, related her disappointment when she thought she had found a pre-K program for Adrienne but the arrangement fell through.

> We had planned to enroll her in school in September, but it looks like Adrienne won't be able to go. I wanted her in pre-K because she is so bright and could get ready for school, and the pre-K program is free . . . but today was enrollment day and they said that I am not in "the zone." . . . I had already called five times before that to ask about enrolling her, and no one said anything about a zone, and besides, I am only two blocks from there. What can the zone be?

This was the only school in the area with pre-K for three-year-olds, but they gave Diane contradictory information about whether Adrienne was eligible. She speculated that they had no space and so put her off as a way to ration their limited services.

> They have such few places that they want to serve those who live closest to the school, and they know there would be no places available. They told me to try another school, but I knew [the other school's] pre-K program was for four-year-olds. I went back two days later, and they said they had filled up on enrollment day, and there is now a waiting list with more than five hundred names and I could put my name down. There was nothing to do at that point.

Low-income mothers generally prefer the free or subsidized center care available through Head Start, the universal pre-K program, and day care centers contracting with the city's Agency for Child Development. Many mothers planned to put their children into these care situations at the earliest possibility but often found that this was later than they would have liked.

There are many other obstacles to arranging center care besides its limited availability. Issues of affordability and variable quality may also deter mothers from accessing centers. Clarabel, who wanted to send Robert to a center early, mentions a basic and common obstacle: "He needed to be potty-trained and could not go in Pampers to any of the day cares here." After Robert was potty-trained at the age of three by Dolores, his family child care provider, he finally went to center care.

It can be quite hard for mothers looking for a center to find one available, so mothers were especially creative in developing and maintaining these care options. Like other mothers, Francine had to piece together multiple arrangements and juggle them for as long as she could in order to keep a center care arrangement:

> When Fortune was in Head Start, I liked that, but that is only part-day, 8:30 to 11:30, and I tried taking him, and then run over during my lunch to pick him up and take him to the family day care provider. I did that for three or four months, but I could not do that like every day, especially when things got rough at work and it was getting cold, so I had

to take him out of Head Start and put him in just the family day care for a while.

Cassandra had already used four home-based options for Cedric by the time he was fourteen months old, including one arrangement in which he was abused, which caused her to take a leave of absence from her job. After that she found a center that was opening in a church basement. When the woman who started the program lost her lease, Cassandra was so desperate to keep the arrangement that she allowed the woman to run the program with a small group of children from her home. However, that did not work out for long either:

> The provider had an hour commute . . . and she was making me late [for work]. I was watching the other children, who showed up before she did. Then, during a snowstorm, she could not get here at all. . . . That was it. I could not take that responsibility and risk my job.

Mothers will go to great lengths for center care. Uma has put up with some problems at Sade's center, where she has been for the last year and a half:

> A problem at her Head Start program is that there are too many special needs kids, children with behavioral issues, and you just cannot put them into the classroom and let them loose like they do . . . but they won't do anything. They know you have no choice, I mean, when the program is free, what can you do? The program is not that good, but what can you do? It's like when you begging or they think you beggin', you can't be choosy, 'cause all they think is that you complainin' too much . . . and you should just be happy with what you got.

Finding the Center by Pluck or by Luck   Many mothers find it hard to get a place in a center. Factors leading to placement in a center include the neighborhood, the mother's knowledge of the service providers in the community, timing, persistence, and luck. Lola tried to enroll her son Lucas in a multiservice agency with a child care center in her neighborhood, but she never moved up on the waiting list. Later, when she admitted herself to the emergency room because she was "stressed," a psychiatrist referred her for counseling to the same multiservice agency where she had sought child care. When she started counseling, they immediately registered Lucas in both their Head Start and day care programs, even though before she sought treatment for stress they had had no places.

Edwina had so much trouble finding child care for her first daughter, Nelly, in her own neighborhood that she used her mother's address to place Nelly in a center in that neighborhood. Then she had to travel an hour each way to take her child to the center.

When I first started working, I looked for a day care center, but every-where I went the story was the same—the waiting list was for like five hundred children, "Oh, I'm sorry, I don't have a spot for her, come back next month." So first I ended up putting her in a private lady's house. . . . Then I went there to ACD and I lied, telling them Nelly lived at my mother's address, and they found a space for her down there—they had space there, but not uptown. . . . So now I had to commute one place for child care and another for work, and my mother would pick her up at five because I worked until 7:00 P.M. Then I would start to stay overnight at my mom's apartment almost every week, and the little one and me would sleep on a mattress on the floor. . . . It was hard, but I had no choice.

The Pros and Cons of Center Care   Mothers had a wide range of experiences with center care. Cassandra states a preference, based on her experiences with both center and family child care, for center-based care. She says that family day care did not offer enough structure: "It is basic babysitting . . . just a bunch of kids and they do what they want. At Hearts and Minds [day care center] they had a lot of activities for him. There were structured reading times, or play times, or activity areas like sandboxes."

Nevertheless, Cassandra found it prohibitively difficult to arrange center care, and she came to rely heavily on home-based arrangements. A home provider could accommodate her rotating shifts as a nurse-practitioner. Yet she thinks this arrangement may have compromised Cedric's development. Many mothers share Cassandra's preference for the structure and varied activities in centers.

Nora had developed a durable, positive relationship with Nick's family child care provider. When she moved to a new neighborhood, she first placed Nick in a provider's home because it was available, but after three months she found a place in a center. She had been pleased with the provider's care but thought the center would be better for Nick's development.

> You learn the basics in a provider's home day care, but I think there is more to do and more to learn in a center. . . . The woman he was with was wonderful, and I miss her and we still keep in touch, but I really wanted him to start at the center, and I really think he is doing well there, and now I cannot wait for him to go to school, and see him do well there. . . . That boy is my best hope and best effort, and I want to see him go places.

Iris, an immigrant from Santo Domingo, used mostly center-based ar-rangements for her daughter, Quirina. She started Quirina in center care when she was three months old because Quirina's father, Rafael, was a student at the time in one of the city's public colleges that had a full-day child care program. Iris did not have a predisposition for center care, but she developed a preference for it from her experience, and she kept Quirina enrolled there after she and Rafael broke up and she moved into a homeless shelter in another borough. "I liked the center at Rafael's school a lot," she says. "There's many kids in there. It's going to be hard to abuse one child with the others not talking. Everybody can see what's going on."

Sara, like Iris, was also living in shelters during the time her daughter, Cristina, was in a Head Start program. They moved across the city when they were homeless, but Sara kept Cristina enrolled the entire time. Like Iris, Sara pointed to the consistency of her daughter's continuous attendance at the center as an important source of stability when they were homeless.

> I think because she was at the center all the time it was better for her. She would see her teachers every day and the same people—it made things normal for her. . . . It is important the child has the consistency and is learning to belong in a group like that, especially like that time, and because otherwise she has only me, and she was scared. . . . She is timid, so the teachers at the school, they have the right style with her. . . . I don't think I could do it otherwise.

A few mothers mentioned specific developmental improvements they noticed when their children were in center care arrangements. Dona was grateful for the additional developmental assistance and special needs services that came with her son David's center care:

> David is getting speech therapy and is doing well. . . . He was diagnosed with speech delay there, and he's benefited a lot, speaking-wise. . . . He is now well mannered and doesn't have tantrums or rebel. I notice it. The teachers here noticed it. Now he talks and says "thank you" and asks for things.

Annette noted differences in Aaron's verbal engagement following opportunities to develop his speech in center care that he had missed in his interrupted home care arrangements:

> I am very concerned about him not speaking. I notice that he speaks less than other children, and he mumbles a lot. . . . Now that he started full-time at the center I want him to be evaluated because he could get speech therapy there. . . . At the provider's home, if he does not talk so much, she won't see it. She has two infants, and she does not really know if he is not talking right.

Among the mothers who preferred center-based care for their young children, most point out that they felt that it was more standardized—they knew what to expect. Other benefits of center care that mothers mention most often were that centers had spaces designed specifically for children, more structured time with a wide range of activities, more exposure to children of the same age, a more professional staff, and opportunities for children's special needs to be identified and addressed.

On the other hand, mothers also say centers could vary widely in terms of how they operated and how much they offered. They say that some centers tried to serve too many children with inadequate resources. Annette says that she wanted higher-quality care and more individual attention for Aaron, which she says was unavailable at centers serving low-income mothers.

> I want a smaller classroom size, and more attention, and I want him to have teachers who adjust more to each child's needs, and for him to get specialized care too—like anger management. . . . I know they have this around here, but it is private care, and expensive.

Zina found that there were significant differences in care across centers and that the better-quality care cost more than she could afford. She compares two centers that Zoe attended: Hampton, which was available to her through a subsidy program that subsequently expired, and Crosby, the center she went to next:

> I loved the child care center Zoe was in last year. I mean, I loved Hampton. It was like you knew your child was going to learn. I'm sorry I took Zoe out. I wish I could have found a way to pay. But $675 a month—I would've had to struggle hard. . . . That's more than my rent or anything, so I could not do it. . . . Once she got to Crosby, she only learned some Spanish words because everything they were doing she had already learned [at Hampton], so Zoe gets bored half the time.

A common complaint by those who have placed children in centers—and by those who have not—was that center schedules could be rigid. When center schedules did not correspond to work schedules, parents often had to make multiple and complex arrangements, finding one or more additional providers to wrap around the care day or to transport their child. Rhonda was pleased with the pre-K program in which Steven had started, but she had struggled to combine other care with the center care hours to comply with her work schedule as a school safety officer. She started work at 7:30 A.M. and could not be late. She had to rely on her mother, her sister-in-law, and Steven's father to provide early morning care until the center opened at 8:00, but none of them proved reliable.

Most universal pre-K programs consist of three-hour-a-day sessions or at best follow the traditional school schedule, and many mothers faced the wrap-around pressures at the end of the schoolday that Rhonda faced in the mornings. Sometimes there were after-school programs that children could go to from pre-K, but when these were located elsewhere, mothers had to arrange for their child to get from one place to another. Many Head Start programs also have short days, from 8:30 to 11:30. The part-day schedule traces back to the program's original design: it was conceived as a poor child's social enrichment program in which mothers would not be working but participating themselves in related activities in the center. However, Head Start and mothers' work schedules can be incompatible, as we saw in the lengths to which Francine went to keep Fortune in Head Start. When Sterling, her older son, was in Head Start just a year and a half earlier, Francine moved to the Bronx for a short while but maintained her mother's address in Highwall Valley to keep him in the program. Later she struggled with her own schedule at her job in the Valley and with the transportation for all those involved.

> I would have to drop off Fortune so early at the family child care provider's [in the Bronx] and then go to Highwall to leave Sterling at Head Start. Well, I can tell you, you really rely on the kindness of strangers for your child care needs because I cannot even find the words for how grateful I am. This woman who worked in the program there in the kitchen—she made sure he got to class in the morning when I had to leave him to get to work before the center opened, and then she watched him until I got over there at my lunch.

Even when center-based care is full-day, as in many group day care programs, the hours are firmly set, and there is little flexibility for a variant work schedule, a delayed parent, or a missed wrap-around arrangement. The policy at most centers is to call the police at 6:00 P.M. if someone has not picked up a child—to protect the child and avoid liability for the center.

Important factors in mothers' use of center care included:

- *Availability and complexity of subsidy systems*: Center-based child care was the most expensive option and therefore not affordable to most low-income mothers. The availability of subsidies to help pay for day care in centers or the ability to find free forms of center care such as Head Start or pre-K programs seemed to be the most important factors explaining center usage. The complexity of the child care subsidy systems contributed greatly to whether families could gain access to center care and maintain these arrangements.

- *Availability*: The limited availability of care slots, even when families could arrange subsidies, further restricted the use of center care.

- *Children's ages*: The age of children was also important because as children got older and mothers worked more, more stable ongoing child care arrangements became necessary. One factor in the timing of mothers' use of center care was their desire to focus on their children's learning and social needs as they got older.

- *Developmental opportunities*: Many mothers preferred the developmental focus of center-based care, including its specialized spaces and activities, socialization opportunities, and educational activities.

- *Special needs*: Mothers of children with special needs were particularly likely to pursue more formal center care. The early intervention system gave children with special needs greater access to center care.

Other Care Arrangements

Center-based, kin, informal, and family child care are the major categories of care and accounted for nearly seven of every eight primary care arrangements for children in this sample. Other types of care arrangements accounted for 29 of the 215 primary care spells, and more than one-quarter of the secondary arrangements fell into the "other" category. Within this category are three less commonly used care types: father care, mother's care while working, and special needs care.

Father Care   Fathers, while providing relatively little of the overall care, often served as an important bridge during specific periods of their children's lives. Father care as primary care shared many characteristics with kin care, but it was not as prevalent. When used as primary care, father care was typically short-term and concentrated early in the child's life. Because father care was more prevalent when parents were living together, it was particularly vulnerable when family situations changed. When they were living together, Griselda and her daughter's father arranged that he would work nights and then watch the children in the morning when Griselda went to work, before taking them to Griselda's mother later in the day. This arrangement lasted about a year and ended when Griselda moved out because of problems in their relationship. The duration of father care was often dependent on the relationship between the mother and father, and such care commonly came to an end when the relationship ended.

Many times father care was used as primary care for a short time to bridge arrangements or when other care ended unexpectedly. In the chapter's initial story, Bethany's father, Sanford, provided primary care for her after a conflict with the family child care provider prompted Brittany to change care arrangements. The father care arrangement worked out because Sanford was living with them at that time and he was having trouble finding work. Brittany thought that his care was adequate, and it allowed her to keep working to support the three of them. She used this care until she could arrange another family child care provider for Bethany two months later.

At times father care was short because it was not the care that mothers preferred. Kiley's father provided care for a couple of months as well, until Oona decided the care was not good enough:

[I stopped working] because he was just not good. He did not have the patience—that was the main reason. He's not the kind of person who can handle taking care of him. It's not his thing. I can have him come over and watch him for an hour in the morning when I got to get to work, and let him bring him to school, but, you know, he can't be the regular caregiver.

Fathers, however, most often provide secondary care that can be instrumental in allowing the mother to meet her work needs while also helping foster a father-child relationship. As many as one-third of the children in the study received secondary care from their fathers. When used as a secondary arrangement, care by fathers was seen as an opportunity for the child and father to develop their relationship, especially when the father lived elsewhere. Cedric's father had been the secondary care provider during the evenings and on weekends when Cassandra was working as a nurse. She said that despite her own problems in her relationship with Cedric's father, "he's very responsible as far as Cedric's concerned." Yolanda had a similar relationship with Yeats's father:

He's good, very supportive, spends time with him, and calls him all the time. Our relationship faltered, but he's always been there for Yeats. I'm glad about that. That's good for both of them. It helps me because otherwise I might get stuck sometimes for child care. His father and I have an agreement that I'm supposed to call him first if I need help with care, and he's to call me first if he has to go somewhere before we leave him with someone else.

Mother's Care While Working   Like Brittany, some mothers resort to bringing their children to work as a short-term emergency strategy when another care arrangement breaks down. Six of the forty-two mothers in this sample, or one out of seven, provided care while working as a primary arrangement at some point during the study. Nadia brought Lana to the property management office where she worked as a bookkeeper after her mother abruptly moved and stopped providing care for Lana. She related how hard it could be:

Most of the time I would end up bringing Lana to work with me . . . but work was very difficult with her here. . . . And she was sick often and I missed work or I had to bring my sick child to work. . . . One afternoon I remember just looking over at her and crying at work, "This can't be happening." Then I got sick myself and missed another week of work.

Like father care, mothers' care while working was more often a secondary care arrangement that was used only occasionally as needed. It was used to bridge those times when work and care hours did not mesh or as emergency care for days when other care was not available because of holidays, illness, or a provider's day off. For example, Annette brought Aaron to work with her on Mondays and Wednesdays from 9:00 to 10:00 A.M. before his Early Head Start program started. Nadia's and Brittany's need to use it as their primary care for as long as a few months was rare, but it did occur when fragile care situations dissolved and options were limited.

Two of the mothers, however, sought to arrange work that would allow them to care for their children. Rita wanted to be her daughter Rea's full-time caregiver while she continued her own business importing and selling textiles, which involved irregular work hours and travel:

> Her first main arrangement was she was on my back. Wherever I went, she went. I carried her. That's how I liked it, and what I wanted for her. I would bring her with me to the flea market when I was selling if the weather was nice, or she would be home with me when I worked here. From when she was born until I lost that business, I cared for her the most, and families and friends filled in sometimes. . . . I never wanted to put her into a nonfamily, nonpersonal care situation, and I wanted to be her provider as much as I could, for as long as I could.

Similarly, Magdelena quit her job at a department store when Marisa was almost one, in part to spend more time with her. She started selling diet and health products in order to give her more time to care for Marisa:

> The reason I work independently, and not for someone else, somewhere else, is so I can be with her more. I don't want it to be like with the other children where they do not listen to their mother like they do to their babysitter. They love just the babysitter. I prefer that she develop a relationship with me than someone else who is doing the child care.

Special Needs Care   Many children had particular health and developmental needs. Two of the children in the sample suffered from seizures, one had Erb's palsy, and four were born with low birthweight. Other more frequent health and developmental needs included asthma and speech delay, both of which turned out to be prevalent among the sample of children.

Some of the children with special needs received specialized services. Some children received special needs care coordinated with their regular care. A few children received ongoing specialized care for their conditions in institutional settings, with the spaces and activities designed to meet their developmental needs and individualized therapies mixed in with congregate care. Oona described Kiley's care in a specialized setting:

> Kiley started early intervention services when he was two. They placed him in the special school, where he goes from 8:30 to 2:00, and they work with him one on one on his speech and his motor skills, which are

also delayed. For the first six months I watched him after 2:00 before I could find a day care center for him to go to after school. Now he is bused there from 8:30 to 2:00 and then the bus drops him off at the day care center, and he is there until I pick him up from work.

Lana eventually received specialized care in a hospital setting for multiple special needs, and her mother, Nadia, had many problems finding a child care provider willing and able to care for Lana around her specialized care. It was harder still to arrange appropriate treatment as part of Lana's care. First, it took a long time for Nadia to have Lana formally diagnosed with developmental delays, though the delays were fairly pronounced—she started walking very late, and she also did not speak much until the age of two. Once her diagnosis entitled her to specialized therapies, it was hard to find a qualified specialist to take the case and coordinate her therapy with her other child care. A few weeks after the first interview, Nadia managed to arrange specialized care for Lana in a hospital setting. She related her difficulties:

> She has just started going to multiple therapies in a hospital setting five days per week. . . . It has been a hard road, though. I went to the doctor right from the beginning. I told him she had started walking late, and I knew she was speech-delayed. I knew because my first daughter had developed much sooner than her. Finally, a doctor in the Bronx where I used to live sent her to be evaluated. I missed so much work the whole last year taking her to appointments to be evaluated. Finally the therapy plans have come together.

More than eighteen months after Lana's first seizure, and after her mother had tried to explain to doctors that she was almost a year late in walking and talking, Lana began specialized care in a hospital setting five days a week for three hours a day. At the hospital she received occupational therapy, physical therapy, and speech therapy, and at home she received vision therapy twice a week. In all, it took nine months for Lana to be diagnosed, and seven more months to arrange the prescribed care. Other families experienced similar long delays.

Speech delays and asthma were the two most common health and developmental problems for the children in the sample. Seventeen of the forty-two children had at some point been identified or evaluated for speech delays, and some of them had received speech therapy.

Even after their mothers were able to find their way to the city's early intervention program,[3] a federally funded program that serves the special developmental needs of children between birth and age three, it was often several months after the need was identified that services were arranged.

Special needs care was usually available for a limited number of hours, and this made it difficult to coordinate with other child care. For example, it took Oona six months to find a secondary care arrangement to cover the hours from 2:00 to 6:00 P.M. after her son Kiley's specialized school-based care ended. She eventually used three different arrangements paired with the special needs care.

After taking a long time to arrange the appropriate care for her daughter, Nadia faced the problem of arranging for the continuity of the care when Lana turned three. The city's early intervention program served only children aged zero to three; when they turned three, children were supposed to enter the separately administered preschool special education system, a transition that could disrupt not only their special needs treatment but their child care.

Fourteen of the forty-two children in the sample had asthma, and some with serious cases of it. Many mothers mentioned that asthma was commonplace in their neighborhoods, but they had little direct knowledge of asthma before they learned of their children's condition. They became the primary watch guards for any sign of an attack or a change in their children's breathing.

Aaron had his first asthma attack as an infant and was hospitalized twice before it was diagnosed. Over time, Annette learned how to care for his condition, but she still had problems coordinating care for asthma within his care arrangements.

> Aaron misses a lot of time at the center because of the asthma. When it is really bad, he can't come in and I have to stay home with him. When he has to take medication or his nebulizer, I have to go to the center and give it to him. I just had an incident with them [the center] where the nebulizer broke down, and the center refused to get another machine even though maybe thirty children in the building have asthma, some worse than Aaron. They said, "They were not mandated to do it." . . . Finally a parent had an extra machine she lent me for Aaron, but what about all the other children?

Annette, with care and resourcefulness, learned how to handle Aaron's chronic asthma. He had to return to the hospital many times during the worst flare-ups, but they did not have to keep him overnight after the emergency visits.

Brittany, like Annette, found work near her daughter's child care center. Although, like many mothers, she found that the asthma improved as her child aged, Brittany was always prepared to go to the care provider if needed.

> Now I carry the pump with me just in case I have to run over and give it to her. I never leave it behind. It is in my pocketbook wherever I go. I have not had to go to the care providers in a while. Thank God. . . . And each year her asthma seems to be getting a little bit better. Thank God.

Perceived Pros and Cons of Different Types of Care

Mothers of varying ethnicity, employment status, family structure, and neighborhood delivered fairly consistent messages regarding the relative advantages and disadvantages of different forms of care. No one type emerged as the best type of care, but taken as a whole, these perceptions indicate that many mothers are forced to make important trade-offs regarding ease in arranging care, the type of care, the developmental aspects of the care, and the flexibility of care arrangements.

- The care that was initially the easiest to arrange (kin care or informal care) was the least stable over time. Center care and family day care provided greater stability but was much harder for families to arrange.

- Similarly, mothers believed that center care was safer and offered more developmental activities. Yet this was the care that was in the shortest supply, most difficult to access, and least affordable.

- When choosing between centers and family day care, mothers were sometime choosing between what they perceived to be the better arrangement for their child's development (center care) and the setting that allowed the greatest number of hours of care that matched the hours they worked (family day care).

Some of the mothers' experiences amplify what other researchers have concluded, including the finding that parents prefer homelike arrangements for younger children and more structured learning opportunities for older children (Fuller, Holloway, and Liang 1996; Liang, Fuller, and Singer 2000; National Institute of Child Health and Development 2000a). Quality is difficult to assess (Duncan and Gibson 2000), and the subjective characteristics of the provider and the daily program are elements of quality (Emlen, Koren, and Schultze 2000; Henly and Lyons 2000) that are often more important to parents than the structural features of care emphasized by child care researchers; this is an important distinction for understanding how considerations of quality are linked to choices. Mothers' views of child care offer potentially new insights and depth to the existing understanding of child care, such as how the factors that mothers consider are often shaped by the available options. Their experiences also offer a greater understanding of the complexity of multiple care arrangements at a given point in time. It also becomes clear in this study that mothers' choices are tied to a range of other issues they are managing, including family relationships, public assistance, and child care subsidies, in addition to work.

What comes through most clearly in their discussions of child care choices is that these mothers were keenly aware of the advantages and disadvantages

Table 2.4   *Care Characteristics as Perceived by Mothers for the Major Types of Care*

	Pros	Cons
Kin care	A starting place for care for infants or when mother is unaware of care options or has limited choices Care is available, often flexible, and convenient Higher level of trust compared to other care options; familiar with care, provider, and setting Longer-term relationship with caregiver; caregiver and parent are "like-minded" about care; preserves familial and cultural traditions Provider loving due to "blood connection" and "natural" attachment; personal attention; often fewer children Affordable—low-cost or in some cases free Often available for emergencies and secondary care	Shorter-term care; often unstable Less developmental exposure and fewer activities Regarded as babysitting and less stimulating May lack socialization opportunities; fewer children; less peer interaction Child becomes spoiled, sees self as "center of the world" Can complicate family relationships and dynamics Payment ambiguities
Informal care	More individualized care Personal attention from providers; often fewer children leads to greater child-caregiver attachment A starting point for care—often an initial arrangement Flexible, can be used as a wraparound secondary form of care	Often less trust of provider and greater anxiety about the care Informal nature of arrangement can make it difficult to agree on care elements, leaving much to be negotiated (such as, cost, food, diapers, hours) and leading to conflicts

Table 2.4   *Continued*

	Pros	Cons
		Shorter-term care, uncertain durations
		Least structured
		Often considered "babysitting"
Family day care	Long hours of care and flexibility of schedule	Mistrust of type of care and providers by some
	Consistency of care and provider—long care durations	Lack of knowledge or limited information about content of care; care not visible
	Fewer children, so more individual attention than center care, yet with some socialization opportunities with small set of peers	Less structure to the care and care setting
	Children likely to "attach" to providers	Fewer developmental activities and stimulation than in many centers
	Providers are mature, experienced caregivers	Smaller group size and fewer peer interactions compared to center care
	Home-based care in a secure, warm setting; home-cooked meals and home sleeping accommodations	Can be difficult to agree on parameters of care and payments
	Care can be complementary to what children receive from mothers at home	Can take time for parents to find a provider
	Direct communication between provider and parent	Can become "too personal" and unstable
	Providers can be like family, nurturing and caring; often cultural and language compatibility	Language differences can cause difficulties in communication between provider, parents, and children
		Frequent and abrupt exits from care and a "take it or leave it" quality to the care

(*Table continues on p. 72.*)

Table 2.4   *Continued*

	Pros	Cons
Center care	Care regarded as safe because it is public and visible	Problems with availability
	Learning activities, educational, more reading	Less individual attention and direct adult-child interactions, creating potential risks
	School-like setting, classroom structure, consistent schedule	Care requirements (such as, potty-trained prior to entry, food provision)
	Socialization, peer interactions	Head Start and pre-K programs often have restricted eligibility and limited spaces
	Greater environmental exposure, more outdoors time	Limited or rigid care hours
	Long care hours often available	
	Standardized and stable, less variation in quality	
	Accountability to parents, options for redressing grievances	
	Head Start focus on child development and family support services	

Source: Author's compilation.

of the different care settings in which they considered placing their children. These are summarized by the types of child care in table 2.4, which offers a qualitative view gained from the mothers' perspectives and complements table A.7, which summarizes the analysis of the literature on care types. In addition, mothers understood the shortcomings of the care that was available to them compared to the potentially more stimulating and stable care that was not available to them. They also realized that they were forced to place economic self-sufficiency over concerns about child development.

Spending Time Among Providers

Children spend a lot of time in child care away from their mothers. Because of the age group and selection methods in this study, the children I observed spent much of their day, more than ten hours on average, in their care arrangement. As table 2.3 indicated, mothers were piecing together child care, with ninety-eight primary and secondary care arrangements counted at the time of the first interviews. The average was 2.33 care arrangements per child. Thirty-nine of the forty-two children in the sample had multiple care arrangements. In some cases, the mix offered complementary care, but in most cases care was patched together by necessity. Other survey data have also shown that many children are in multiple care arrangements to cover their parents' work schedules. According to the fall 1995 Survey of Income and Program Participation (SIPP), which was the first survey to collect this type of data, 68 percent of preschool-age children of employed mothers were in multiple arrangements, with an overall average of 2.2 care arrangements per child (Smith 2000).

The amount of time that children in this sample spent in nonmaternal care ranged from thirty-nine to seventy-eight hours per week, with fifty-four hours the average. Eleven of these children spent sixty hours or more per week in care arrangements away from their working mothers. The proportion of their care hours spent in their primary arrangements varied from a little less than half of the total care hours to all of them. Overall, a little more than three-quarters of the children's care hours were in a primary care arrangement, and the children spent about one-quarter of their care hours in their secondary care settings.

These results show longer hours in care than the findings from other recent studies that have looked at how much time children spend in care arrangements. Kristin Smith (2000) has found that in the 1995 SIPP children with working parents who were younger than five years old spent an average of thirty-five hours per week in care arrangements, compared with an average of fifty-four hours in this sample.[4] Other studies using large sample sets indicate that children spend between thirty and thirty-five hours per week in child care, with longer hours for African American children, children whose mothers work full-time, and children with single parents (Ehrle, Adams, and Tout 2001; National Institute of Child Health and Development 1997b, 2000a). None of the studies reported data for the hours in care combining some or all of these characteristics.[5]

Table 2.5 aggregates hours of care in a week for each type of care, providing another way to look at the distribution. The first three columns repeat the breakdown of child care arrangements in table 2.2. The rest of the table provides information about how the forty-two children in the sample divided their time. The fourth column gives the hours when the forty-two children were in care in one week. More than 60 percent of their early childhood care hours were spent in homes—the children's own or those of kin, family day care, or informal care providers. Most care in homes was with paid family day care providers, who provided 32 percent of the total care hours. More than one-third of all time in care was spent in group day care, Head Start, and pre-K programs in centers and schools, with day care centers offering the most care hours.

The last column of the table gives the average number of weekly hours per arrangement. Kin and father care averaged fewer hours than the other types. Care in Head Start and informal arrangements averaged moderate lengths of

Table 2.5   *Number of Care Arrangements and Aggregated Hours in Care (Per Week), by Type and Overall Distribution of Time Spent in Care*

Type of Child Care	Number of Arrangements			Aggregate Number of Hours	Care Hours Distribution	Average Hours per Arrangement
	Primary	Secondary	All			
Father care	0	14	14			
Kin care	3	16	19	238	10.5%	12.5
Informal care	4	9	13	324	14.3	24.9
Family day care	16	3	19	731	32.2	38.5
Center-based care	18	5	23	784	34.6	34.1
Other	1	9	10	92	4.1	9.2
Total	42	56	98	2,268	100.0	
Average			2.33	54		23.1

Source: Author's compilation.

time. Family day care homes and day care centers, which together accounted for 54 percent of all care hours, averaged about forty hours weekly per arrangement.

Overall, children spent about 4 percent of their time each week being cared for by their fathers. Much of the time that children spent in the care of their secondary providers—especially their fathers and kin—occurred on weekends, in the summer, or on weekdays wrapped around a primary care arrangement to meet the mothers' work hours. In addition to bridging time, some secondary arrangements were also important for gluing together arrangements; the second provider might transport a child between arrangements, or between home and an arrangement, and then watch the child for a short time until their mother arrived.

The larger survey datasets have also found that the number of hours spent in care vary by type. Smith (2000) has found that children in day care centers and family child care averaged thirty-three hours per week in these primary arrangements, while those in the care of grandmothers or other relatives averaged about half that, seventeen hours—similar proportions to what was found here.

Children spend their time with a wide range of providers and often transition between them while mothers try to manage the combinations and changes. Aaron, who was three years old at the time of the first interview with Annette, spent forty-nine hours a week in four child care arrangements. He was in a family day care home for thirty-eight hours and at an Early Head Start program four hours a week. He was also in two other regular arrangements. Annette's sister or a friend cared for him while she attended a training program for her job, and he stayed with his mother at work to bridge the time from the start of her workday until his Early Head Start program began. One of these patches on her primary care was watching Aaron herself two days a week while working, which often interfered with her work. Yet this was time Annette also valued:

> On those days he comes [to work] with me . . . he sits in my office with me and we share a bagel and talk. We actually sit and eat together and have real quality time together before his [Early Head Start] group starts at ten o'clock. The hour together is the only real time we get together to talk.

Although Annette had to piece together more than one care arrangement to meet her work schedule, some of these arrangements were made by choice rather than necessity, and the timing of the care availability was generally convergent with her regular workweek. Yet she expressed regret about, as she put it, the "all or nothing" expectations of work and child care. "Spending so much time among providers—so much time away from home—cannot be good for him," she says. Other mothers, with lengthier and even more complicated care schedules, express similar feelings about the limited time they spent with their children at the beginning of their lives.

Mothers who worked nontraditional hours struggled especially hard to arrange child care to cover those hours. Cassandra, the nurse-practitioner, was on a rotating schedule that required her to work some shifts in the evening or the middle of the night. For evening shifts she often left Cedric with a family day care provider in the early afternoon. His father picked him up when he got out of his job as a construction worker and kept him at his home before dropping him off at Cassandra's house at about 10:00 P.M. for the night.

Often mothers with high-volume care needs pieced together many care arrangements. Iris worked forty-nine hours a week at a local pharmacy. She had group day care for her daughter Quirina during the week, but she had to pay someone to either take Quirina to school in the morning or pick her up by 6:00 P.M. almost every day. Since she also worked every weekend and most holidays, she relied most often on a kin care provider, Quirina's paternal grandmother.

Some mothers who worked multiple jobs or hours that diverged from most available care hours had to place their children in care for inordinate amounts of time. Kari, who worked from noon until 9:00 P.M. at a digital art printing shop, placed her daughter Jaya in an unlicensed family day care home, even though it was more than an hour from where she lived, because of the amount of care that the provider, Tella, gave Jaya. "Jaya spends far more time with Abuela—that's what Jaya calls her [the provider Tella]—in her home with her family than she does with me, in her own home."

Kari kept Jaya with the provider, who lived in the Bronx near where they used to live, for almost two years after returning to Highwall Valley. She did not think she could find anybody else who could fit her child care needs given her work schedule.

Ramona worked irregular hours as a sales associate at a department store until she had to leave the job because of the complications and costs of the multiple care arrangements needed to accommodate her work schedule. She worked at the store full-time for three months, but her hours included weekends and evenings, and the schedule changed weekly. She tried to talk her supervisor into a set schedule with earlier daytime hours, but she was told that she "had to work according to the store's rules." She was forced then to constantly adjust her daughter's three care providers with little notice.

> I had her grandmother—the father's mother—watch Flores on Saturdays and Sundays. I would pay her $50 for two days. Then I had this lady charging me $7 per hour to pick up my daughter and for the hours that she was staying with her. Sometimes when I was working late, like to ten o'clock, I would sit there and calculate how much I was paying. She picks her up like at 5:45, and I don't get there like until ten o'clock—that was another $50 or $60, 'cause those hours add up.

Paying for Care and Finding Subsidies

Child care is expensive relative to the earnings of low-wage working mothers. As noted earlier, employed, low-income single mothers spent 19 percent of their earnings on child care (Giannerelli and Barsimantov 2000). One result is that mothers choose lower-cost child care alternatives when they begin working, such as kin care, informal care, and father care (see table 2.6). These arrangements may be low-cost or even free. Slightly more than half of the mothers using kin care paid the provider. The average payment was $55 a week. Mothers paid an average of $64 a week for informal care, almost all of which were paid arrangements. Both of these forms of child care were rarely subsidized.

The majority of mothers using family day care and center care received subsidies for part or all of their care expenses. Three-quarters of those using family day care and nearly 80 percent of those using center-based care arrangements were subsidized. Many parents receiving assistance from city government agencies also made copayments, which averaged $21 a week for family day care and $32 a week for center care. For those who were not subsidized and paid fully for family child care, the average cost was $87 a week for family child care and $118 a week for center care. Both Head Start and pre-K programs are fully subsidized at no cost to the mother.

Table 2.6   *Child Care Characteristics: Costs of Care for Families in the Sample*

Types of Care	Cost
Kin care	Affordable, low-cost, or no-cost care Twenty-six out of fifty kin care providers were paid for care; twenty-four were not paid; average payment: $55 Infrequently subsidized: six out of fifty care arrangements were subsidized by HRA (welfare-to-work) child care vouchers
Informal care	Often lower-cost care Twenty-eight out of thirty-one providers were paid for care; three providers provided care at no cost; average payment: $64 Infrequently subsidized: five out of thirty-one care arrangements subsidized with HRA vouchers
Family day care (FDC)	Often subsidized: thirty-seven out of forty-nine care arrangements were subsidized; eight of these were subsidized with HRA vouchers and twenty-nine were ACD-contracted FDC slots; for ACD-subsidized care, mothers made copayments averaging $21 a week In twelve nonsubsidized FDC arrangements that were not publicly subsidized, mothers paid $45 to $145 a week; average was $87 a week
Center-based care (including day care, Head Start, and pre-K programs)	Often subsidized: thirty out of thirty-eight children in day care were in subsidized, contracted care or using welfare-to-work vouchers; some mothers made copayments, which averaged $32 a week In eight day care arrangements that were not subsidized, mothers paid $90 to $143 a week; average payment was $118 a week Head Start is fully subsidized and free to eligible families; most families required secondary care around HS, arrangements for which most paid Pre-K programs are fully subsidized and no-cost, though (paid) secondary arrangements are often required
Father care	No cost

Source: Author's compilation.

Table 2.7   *Distribution of Care Spells, by Payment and Subsidy Status and Average Parent Payment Amounts*

Payment and Subsidy Status of Spells	Distribution of Care Spells by Payment Type	Average Parent Payment Monthly (Weekly)
(Fully) paid care spells	29.3%	$334 ($77)
(Fully) subsidized care spells	24.2	
Subsidized care spells with parent co-pay	26.4	$102 ($24)
Nonpaid (free) care spells	20.0	
Total (215 care spells)	100.0	$223 ($52)

Source: Author's compilation.

There was widespread use of subsidies for child care among families in this sample. Table 2.7 provides the distribution of care spells by payment type as well as the average amount parents paid.[6]

As can be seen in the table, in 29 percent (63 of 215) of the care spells mothers paid fully for the child care and did not have care subsidies, though in some cases providers offered care at a lower cost specifically to that family. In 51 percent (109 of 215) of the care spells the care was subsidized in some part, and for nearly half of these (52 of 109 subsidized care spells) the care was fully subsidized. In 20 percent (43 of 215) of the care spells the provider was not paid directly for child care, and in some cases the care was expected or given as an in-kind exchange or gift, most often by a family member. Overall, parents made payments for care in 55 percent (119 of 215) of care spells and averaged $52 a week for all paid care spells ($223 per paid care month).

More than half of all care arrangements were partially or fully subsidized. The most common source of subsidized care for mothers in the sample was the Agency for Child Development, which accounted for 53 percent of the subsidized care arrangements. The Human Resources Administration provided subsidies for mothers trying to move from welfare to work and accounted for 21 percent of the subsidized care spells. The remaining subsidized care sources included Head Start, universal pre-K, early intervention programs, Board of Education–funded special education programs, Department of Homeless Services, Americorps (for two mothers who were employed in the program), City University of New York (one child's parent was enrolled), one mother's employer (which had a child care center), and Florida's Department of Children and Families (where one family moved during the course of the study).

These rates of subsidy usage by low-income families are actually higher than those reported in some other child care studies and national surveys (Hofferth 1995; Schumacher and Greenberg 1999; U.S. Department of Health and Human Services 2000b). Families in this sample, then, were in a better position from a child care subsidy perspective than it would appear is the case overall. Given the struggles of the families in this study to find care and the compromises they made when they could not find good subsidized care, *the overall situation may be worse for the larger population of low-income families needing child care assistance.*

Overall, mothers paid a relatively large proportion of their low incomes for their children's care. They paid for child care in 55 percent of the care spells, and for these spells they averaged $52 a week in payments, or $223 per paid care month. The payment levels were much higher for the paid, nonsubsidized care spells, which averaged $77 a week, or $334 per paid care month. For spells when the care was also subsidized, the mothers paid $24 a week, or $102 per paid care month.

These figures are very close to the child care payments reported in other studies. Giannerelli and Barsimantov's (2000) analysis of data from the National Survey of American Families finds that low-income families who paid for child care averaged payments of $217 per month, or 16 percent of their earnings. One study of the NICHD (2000a) longitudinal sample finds that low-income families averaged $215 per month in care payments, an 18 percent income share for that subsample. In my sample the $223 average monthly payments that mothers were paying for child care amounted to approximately 18 percent of their net monthly income, comparable to the findings reported for the NSAF and NICHD samples.

Given the relatively high cost of child care, many of the better providers are out of the reach of most families without greater access to subsidies. The 18 percent of their earnings that families in this study spent on child care often paid for the lower-quality, less expensive variety. This confirms Jody Heymann's (2000) findings that the proportion of earnings that low-income families spend on care forces them to choose low-quality care and that inadequate public support to assist families in their care responsibilities worsens the work-family dilemmas of families.

Mothers in this sample were working and earning low wages, so they were income- and/or status-eligible for some form of subsidized care. Most of them were earning incomes below the cutoff for ACD eligibility for child care assistance to working families. Those moving from public assistance to work were eligible for HRA vouchers and for transitional child care benefits for twelve months after leaving welfare. Families were also eligible for child care subsidies if they lived in a shelter, had an open child welfare case, had a child with a diagnosed developmental delay, were income- and age-eligible for Head Start, or were age-eligible for the state's universal pre-K program.

Many families did not receive child care subsidies when they were eligible, usually because there was not enough subsidized care for all those who were eligible. They also missed out on subsidies because the process for establishing and maintaining eligibility proved extremely difficult. The ACD system was constantly at capacity, so the families applying were almost invariably placed on long waiting lists. They were assigned priority code categories and a place at the end of the queue for that category. Working parents were assigned the fifth priority code, and among working parents the lowest-wage-earning families were given higher priority. The rules, as such, were complicated. Given an uncertain probability of getting subsidized care, some families were dissuaded from even applying by the bureaucratic hurdles and opacity of the system. The eligibility process for child care subsidies often required clients to apply in person and to supply multiple documentation that required repeated follow-up visits. Mothers who were relatively new to the labor force and working in low-wage jobs with limited flexibility had the least capacity to apply for the child care subsidies that they needed most.

A few mothers, like Sandra, found the public system of child care subsidies too daunting and did not even pursue subsidies, though financially they needed them for their preferred forms of care. Sandra often worried that she had stunted her daughter Shaniqua's development by leaving her with an informal care provider for a long time when she would have preferred sending her to a center.

> She really needs to be in day care . . . and I would try and get ACD 'cause the day care will run me too much. My friend told me what to do and where to go, I just haven't gone down there. . . . I'll take one day off, but I am dreading it. . . . They'll probably say, "Oh, you gotta come back with such and such." That's what I don't like. If I can do it all in one day, then that's great, but if they tell me, "Oh, you forgot such and such. Can you bring back this paper?" No, I can't. I have a job. You're on your job now, let me work and keep mine.

Almost every other mother in this study did apply for a subsidy at the earliest opportunity but found it hard to arrange. Getting subsidized care was often most difficult when children were youngest because of the time and energy required to establish eligibility and the limited availability of most subsidized care options—such as center care and family child care—for infants and young toddlers. Therefore, much of the care they used when their children were very young was not subsidized, though most were eligible for some sort of subsidized care. They often used care they preferred less because it cost less and because the care they wanted required subsidies that took time and luck to arrange.

The time it took to get child care subsidies varied for mothers in the sample. Yolanda was able to get her eligibility established right away, before her son Yeats started in child care, because she knew what to do from previous experience with her daughter Yesenia.

> Before I even went back to work I hooked up with Agency for Child Development. I already had an affiliation with them because my older daughter, Yesenia, has been with ACD since she was 2.9 [two years and nine months]. So for me it was not hard getting ACD [eligibility] with Yeats—just a matter of letting them know that I had another child and I was seeking child care for him. Plus, I work for the city, so I know a couple of people who work for ACD.

Although a few mothers also secured eligibility for subsidized child care quickly, most did not. Of the mothers who formally applied to ACD for care subsidies, most say that they waited many months or more than a year to receive them, if they received them at all. Many of them found it difficult to locate an available care slot once they had received ACD eligibility. Brittany began applying for an ACD slot as soon as she started the welfare-to-work training program that led to her first job, but she did not receive her eligibility for services for almost thirty months—and a year and a half after her HRA vouchers had run out. For most of those eighteen months she had to pay the full cost of Bethany's care. When she finally received her ACD eligibility, she still could not find a center placement for Bethany, which she would have strongly preferred, so instead she used ACD family child care. Some mothers who applied to ACD early in their children's lives say they have never received a care subsidy.

Griselda found the process of establishing eligibility for an ACD subsidy easier then finding an actual place in an ACD center.

> For the ACD appointment I maybe waited a month or so, and then [after getting an appointment] it's always, you forgot this paper, you have to come back, you forgot that paper, you have to come back, but I had been through it before with Alicia, my older daughter, so I did that part okay. . . . My bigger problem was not the eligibility but finding a place. I spent a year before I found any place in an ACD center, and then I found that I had to wait until she was two before they would take her.

Many mothers experienced significant problems with subsidies even after they became eligible and had placed their child in a subsidized care arrangement. The greatest difficulties occurred with the HRA subsidies that mothers trying to move from welfare to work received during their participation in New York City's Work Experience Program (WEP) and other employment activities. Many mothers who relied on HRA subsidies had difficulty finding providers who would accept the HRA vouchers because of payment problems and lower payment amounts than they received with ACD subsidies. Many

HRA-subsidized care arrangements ended after just a few months when providers stopped the care because they were not getting paid.

Brittany either found ways to pay her provider when she had payment problems or negotiated for time. She maintained the arrangement with her first child care provider for more than two years—even though her initial HRA payments were tardy and even after her HRA payments stopped—by taking it upon herself to pay the full $360 per month cost out of pocket. That was more than one-quarter of her monthly income and more than she paid for rent. This arrangement eventually ended, in large part because Brittany could not afford it. When the provider asked her to pay for the child care during two weeks when Brittany had taken her vacation time just so she could save on her child care payments, the arrangement dissolved in acrimony. This would not have occurred if Brittany had gotten the child care subsidy for which she was eligible.

Having two different agencies in New York City providing child care subsidies with different rules created significant problems (which are discussed in chapter 4). There were often large gaps in the time after mothers left welfare before they received the ACD subsidies for which they were eligible. Brittany, like many mothers leaving welfare, was not given the transitional child care benefits from HRA for which she was also eligible. The welfare department did not even tell her about transitional benefits—a common experience for mothers leaving welfare. Brittany knew about transitional benefits, though, so she appealed to receive them while she continued to pay the full cost of her child care. More than two years later she received lump-sum payments for only some of the care costs owed to her, and long after Bethany had moved on.

Many mothers in the study believe that child care should be publicly provided, and several mothers equate child care with education. Early childhood care, as Traci puts it, "needs to be considered like education, and should be the same for everyone."

Many mothers who worked regularly over time but had previously received cash welfare assistance were pleased to be off of welfare and more economically independent. They often found the welfare system demeaning and questioned its legitimacy as a long-term support. But they seldom question the need for ongoing assistance in other areas of family life. They feel that child care is among the most legitimate of needs, along with housing and health care. Some also suggest that these needs are felt beyond their communities and extend to moderate- and higher-income families as well.

Many think that care subsidies are a basic need because they cannot earn enough to pay for adequate care. Some also say that it is a public responsibility, given the societal expectation that parents will work and the importance of child care to children's development. Some think that child care should be free since it is a need shared by almost all parents.

Most mothers who received subsidies that required a copayment say that they did not mind paying a share of the costs when the care was good—even if they needed that money for other expenses. For example, Brittany was pleased when she finally arranged for Bethany to go to a pre-K program, even though her care costs increased from the $24 weekly copayment she had been making for ACD family child care to $45 for the after-school program that followed her daughter's free pre-K program.

Felicidad did not know she might be eligible for child care subsidies when she first negotiated care payments with Melanie, a family child care provider, for her older daughter, Cara. After becoming eligible, she could pay a lower, more affordable amount for child care from her limited income, and Melanie, who was also low-income, could receive a more appropriate higher rate of compensation.

> When I first started child care for Cara, I did not know about ACD. But when I found out that Melanie could become an ACD provider [from a community agency from which she received other services], and that I would pay based on my income, I thought that was great. I don't mind making the copayment. I think it's all right. I think I should pay something, but it's good that it is something I can afford.

Nora too was glad to pay something for child care while gainfully employed for the first time. She feels that working and paying some amount for care was easier then getting by on welfare and looking for work. "When I was on public assistance, I paid nothing, I don't even know how much child care cost. When I got employed in 2000 and they told me it was $31, they calculated it. . . . I said, `No problem!'"

Finally, although some mothers report concerns about the difficulty in getting subsidies, no one who tried to get subsidies says that she gave up pursuing them because of bad experiences with the system. And only one mother, Sandra, was influenced by what she had learned from her friends about the "hassles" of getting subsidies and so never applied for child care assistance at all.

Summary and Conclusions

The goal of this chapter was to examine the range of child care arrangements available to mothers using a combination of basic distributional data on how much families use different forms of care and qualitative narrative that details what mothers believe about the various types of care they have used. I found that there is often a gap between what people do and what they prefer: much of the child care that mothers used at particular points in time depended on what was available more than on what they wanted. Limited options—what was available to them in their communities, what they could afford, and what they knew in the short time frame in which they needed to arrange care—directed their choices. I also learned that many mothers are very thoughtful about child care and deeply concerned about its quality.

Through the interviews with the mothers and my own observations, I also discovered a lot about the range of care types that families use. There was great heterogeneity across families in this study in the care they used and in how they viewed that care. Mothers differed in their preferences for particular settings and providers at different ages for their children, and they encountered a range of constraints in arranging the types of care they wanted for their children. They had many definitions of good child care, and these definitions and their choices for child care interacted strongly with the nature of their work and the complexity of child care subsidies, among other factors. No single type of child care was preferred across the years of early childhood. Many mothers preferred some form of home-based care when their children were very young; contrary to their expectation, they tended to use family child care more than kin care. Family child care was much more prevalent a form of child care than I had expected, and its quality varied widely between truly inspiring caregiving and simply biding time. Another critical finding, discussed more in later chapters, is that relatives play a variable role in the care of children. Even where kin were available, there were limits to how much care they could provide, and it often was not enough to support a mother's full-time or ongoing work.

In a single case, Brittany and Bethany's story, we can see much of the qualitative discussion of care documented in this chapter. Brittany started Bethany in kin care because it was most readily available to her, but after two kin care spells she learned that this type of care was not durable enough for her to use long-term. She then turned to family child care, which turned out to be the type of care she used the most over the next four years. Mothers usually preferred to transition their children to institutional forms of child care in centers and schools at the age of two or three, but they found these types of care hard to get. Brittany was not able to move her daughter to center care as early as she might have preferred because she could not find an available place in a center. Because Brittany was not able to earn enough to pay for market-rate child care, she had to use informal types of care that were unreliable and had unclear parameters, which led to conflicts with the providers.

Working mothers have to find child care for their children, and in this chapter we found that, yes, they do find child care. They struggle to make arrangements, and they often have to find child care very quickly when making a transition to work. They then struggle to maintain these arrangements in the context of their complicated and dynamic lives. They were often concerned about the quality of these arrangements and the sheer amount of time their children spent in a complex set of often unfamiliar arrangements. These findings point to the need to improve families' initial options when they are starting to use child care and to provide their children with opportunities to transition to educational care settings at a common, earlier point in their development.

~ Chapter 3 ~

Child Care Dynamics: "You Have to Move Your Children Around All the Time"

Jacqueline was born on December 20, 1997, weighing a full eight pounds, on the Franklin Delano Roosevelt Drive on Manhattan's East Side. Julia tells of her daughter's start:

> I never made it to the hospital, so she was born on the FDR around Sixty-third Street. The ambulance guy delivered her. I lived in the shelter up in the Bronx, but I didn't want to go to Jefferson, the hospital there, because I heard some bad things about it, and that's not my hospital, Buena Vista was. . . . It was almost 2:00 A.M. when I called the ambulance. I was really starting to feel the labor pains. The pains became sharp quickly, and we did not even have time to first take Hope and Cambia [her one- and four-year-old girls] to my mother's home, so they came in the ambulance. They were taking me to Jefferson Hospital, and I said no, I didn't want to go there. I showed them paperwork for Buena Vista, so they tried to get me there, but I delivered. The medic in the ambulance delivered the baby, and they were still driving. They had to stop to put a blanket on her and cut the umbilical cord. And they put a sheet on her head because she caught a head cold. When we got to Buena Vista, we spent two days there and then went back to the shelter in the Bronx for two days. And then I got the housing—the next day.

Thus, as winter's solstice started, Julia gave birth to her third daughter, and in the same week—on Christmas Eve—she and her family moved into their first permanent residence after fourteen months in the city's shelter system, which took them through four homeless shelters across three boroughs.

> It was me, her [Jacqueline's] father, and my other two daughters together in the shelter. We were in the shelters starting election day in 1996 until

the end of 1997—from a month after Hope [her second daughter] was born until the week Jacqueline was born. . . . We stayed together in all these places for the year until we were assigned an apartment through section 8. It was in the Points, where I grew up, and not too far from where we had lived before we left my mother's. He lived there with us for the first four or five months, and then we broke up and he left.

After more than a year spent living in the city's shelters and before that under her adopted mother, Julia had finally secured a place to live for her family—the first place she could really call her own. When Jacqueline was born, she had been receiving public assistance for about sixteen months, since the late summer of 1996, and now Julia immediately wanted to find a way to leave welfare. Soon after they moved, Julia decided to enroll in a community college nearby and had their father watch Jacqueline and Hope.

> I left her [Jacqueline] with her father after she was born. I was still getting welfare, and I wanted to start college right away because I wanted to start doing something for myself and not just be staying at home. I went to Stuart College and started taking computer classes. It was for an associate's [degree], though I still needed also to get my GED. That was when she was like one month. Her father took care of her. I was scared to leave her when she was so small, but I did it because it was only three days.

Their father watched the two youngest daughters until the end of the semester, when he and Julia broke up because, as she puts it, "he was doin' nothin' with himself, or for his family, and we did not get along anyhow." He moved out in the summer, when Jacqueline was five months old. (Julia adds that a month after he left, "he was put in jail in New Jersey, and I have really nothing to do with him.") Julia was off from the community college for the summer and still relying on public assistance. she stayed home with her children that summer and explains how difficult and critical this point in her life was:

> If I had to say what times made me who I am now and what was hardest for me, one was then, when I really had to be on my own, when I was nineteen. We had been cut off food stamps because when I was in the shelters I did not get a notice about doing finger-imaging, and so then they cut me off. We had to starve for like a month. I had three kids now, and after I had to cook whatever I could find, wash clothes, and do everything myself, it hit me. Reality just hit me. I remember crying in the apartment, thinking about starving. Now, when I had my own housing and I had no money. There is nothing that teaches you how to get money. It starts to open your eyes little by little. You have to really think who you could talk to and who you could work for.

Julia started the fall semester at Stuart College and also began a three-month internship she arranged through a community agency. Izzy, Julia's eighteen-year-old sister, had moved in to help, and she provided child care for a few months. Izzy grew up in foster care and had wanted to move out of her group home and into Julia's place as soon as she turned eighteen. (Julia herself had been adopted at three months because her birth mother was incapable of providing adequate care for her. Her adopted mother, who was the best friend of Julia's biological grandmother, asked to take her. When Julia was older and her birth mother had died of AIDS, she got to know some of her siblings, including this younger sister who had developed an attachment to her.) Once she moved in, Izzy became the primary care provider for almost five months, but eventually she had to stop when her own work prevented her from continuing to provide the care.

> My sister moved in that September, and now I was going to school and I did an internship for [the Big-Time Cable Company] three days per week. She watched them for three months almost full-time. The internship did not really pay—I got a stipend for $50 every two weeks. I stayed for the three months because I thought maybe I would get a job, but it was no good, no real pay, no real experience.
>
> We needed money, so I found a better job. We [she and Izzy] took jobs working at the Burger Joint, and she did not watch them that much after that because we both were working. So we would try to take different shifts at the Burger Joint. When one was working, the other one would watch the kids, or we used to bring them with us because we had a cool nighttime manager, and the children would just hang out or sleep in their carriages while we were working.
>
> I worked at the Burger Joint for only five or six weeks, because I really couldn't stay on it, but she continued. I just did it for emergency money. I couldn't stay on it because of the PA. My grant would get cut if I worked longer, and the money I was making was not worth it, it was about the same as the PA. Working only made sense if I could do both, which I could for a little while before they found out. I was still getting PA, and I never told them about the job because I was only doin' it seasonally—I needed money for the kids. It didn't pay—it was overtime just to come up with $150 to take home for a week. . . . [Izzy] lived with us for a year, but she helped with the child care for just those few months because she kept working, and then she got another job.

Jacqueline was now one year old, and there was a short time period when Julia had no available care options. She applied to the Agency for Child Development for subsidized day care, but she was placed at the end of the already long waiting list. She did not warrant a high priority code at that point because she was neither working nor attending school. She had stopped attending classes in the fall when she started working at the Burger Joint. She stayed home and provided primary care for her children for a month and a half until she was called to start in the Work Experience Program, the city's mandatory welfare-to-work program. Through WEP, she received child care benefits, and Jacqueline began a family day care arrangement that Julia found through the community agency that had been working with her since she moved into the Points after leaving the shelter.

> I had problems with child care. When I was supposed to start a WEP assignment, instead of just going and doing that I went to the Community for Women's Progress, this group in my neighborhood that helps people. They had sent a caseworker to my house after I moved in from the shelter. They find out who is coming to the neighborhood from the shelters and try to help you get settled and offer casework. When I got the assignment . . . I went to them, and they arranged the child care and another internship for three days a week so that I could still go to the college program at the same time. I did not know where to find child care, and you have no time when you get the assignment, so I asked my caseworker at CWP. She told me that CWP had a client, Leida, in the Mayer Houses, who was taking care of kids for money, and so Jacqueline and Hope started going to her.

Jacqueline and her sister remained in that care arrangement for three or four months, but the welfare program's system was late in making payments, leaving Julia owing the caregiver money and soon out of an arrangement.

> When you are doing WEP, they are supposed to help you with child care. They were giving me babysitting money so I could work, but they kept messing it up. They never gave the checks in time and not the right amount. They give me a check every two weeks, but the provider gets paid every week, and so it kept messing up. I kept owing Leida money. They would give the check to me and I gave it to the provider. I tried to fix it. The first couple times it depended on who I was working with there [at WEP], it was one person and then the other, but they all messed it up. First they were late, and I had to explain that to the provider. Then I was getting the wrong amount. I was getting about $300 to give to the provider for taking care of two kids. The money was on the same case and went to the same provider, but they left one child off my budget, and when they did that they messed up the money, and soon I owed the provider a whole month of child care. I could not pay her. She was so upset, and I felt bad because I knew she needed the money like I did, but that was almost all the money I got from the internship and PA. So I tried to fix it again, but the provider could not wait and I had to change to my cousin.

Julia missed a couple of weeks of work while she and her caseworker sorted it out—"they finally figured the money out, but it was months later"—and before she arranged for her cousin to watch the girls. Her cousin, who was not working and had no children, was Julia's only available option. Julia thought her cousin might tolerate the problems with the welfare payment system longer because of their personal relationship.

> They had stayed with the mother provider [family child care provider] until April or May, and she was better than my cousin, but I went to my cousin when the workfare didn't pay the provider. My cousin stepped in only because she was going to get paid. She was on welfare [general assistance]. She does not have any kids. She's lazy and does not do nothing. She does not do much with the kids, but she lives with my mother. My mother is old and sometimes too sick to watch them alone herself, especially when they are so small, but at least she is there to give them love and watch what is going on.
>
> She [my cousin] took care of Hope and Jacqueline from that June until this year around March. Still the payments were late, but they came, so she waited. Then welfare stopped paying her [altogether] because when they [the welfare agency] moved their offices, they lost all my papers. They didn't know who I was, who was my worker, nothing. They closed my case, I had to go to a fair hearing, and they closed it again. We had to go to another fair hearing. They were awful. So she stopped taking care because she wasn't paid. She said she won't do it. She finally got paid, but it was a couple of months later and it was too late.

At this point Julia was doing better in her work pathway, having moved on to her third paid internship. When the children were with her cousin, Julia was working one internship at a financial news company three days a week while simultaneously continuing part-time paid work at the fund-raising company where she had done her last internship. When her care fell apart for the second time over subsidy payment problems, she risked losing both jobs.

> I was going to lose both the jobs because I missed more than a month of time working, and the only reason I didn't lose one was because Becky from the CWP helped me work it out with my supervisor, and she helped me to finally get ACD. I got ACD in May. Hope was three now, so she went to an ACD day care center, and Jacqueline started going to Sonia, a family child care provider in an ACD network. There was a gap for one month until she started with Sonia in May, and I was out of work.

Jacqueline loved Sonia's care. Julia liked all the direct attention and nurturing that Sonia gave her daughter. She also felt that Sonia was really good with children, and she especially liked the way Sonia communicated with the children, the fact that she was teaching Jacqueline to speak Spanish as well as English, that she kept her house spotless, and the healthy food she gave the children. Julia also liked the other children in Sonia's care, with whom Jacqueline was forming relationships, and the fact that they had all been there for a relatively long time. Julia liked the other family members in her house, including Sonia's husband and her two adolescent sons, who played with the children.

After changing her care arrangements three times in one year, Julia kept Jacqueline with Sonia for as long as she could. Julia maintained her relationship with Sonia despite disruptions and complications stemming from changes in her work situation—she passed through a series of training programs, internships, and jobs with different hours and durations—and the complex and shifting child care situations of her other daughters.

After graduating from a basic computer software training program, completing five welfare-to-work internships, working a couple of short-term jobs and a season at the Burger Joint, Julia landed her first full-time, regular, ongoing job about the time Jacqueline turned three. She started working as an administrator and aide for a neighborhood after-school program. The only problem with this job was the hours: she worked afternoons and early evenings and would now have to alter all of her daughters' schedules and arrangements. She had placed her oldest at the after-school program where she was now working. Julia would pick her up when she escorted twenty other children from her school at 3:00 P.M. to the after-school center. Arranging care for her four-year old, Hope, was more complicated. Hope was in a full-day day care center slot, which was hard to come by in the Points, but Julia had no choice but to take her out of the program each day at 12:30 P.M. and bring her to her mother's house. Her cousin had agreed to watch Hope for a relatively modest sum of money, but Hope would prove to be bored and restless when Julia picked her up at 8:30 P.M.

At this point Jacqueline was three. With her experience, some luck, and some effort, Julia might have been able to find a center slot for her daughter. But Julia needed a care arrangement flexible enough to accommodate her evening work schedule, so she asked Sonia if she could keep Jacqueline past the time when the other children left at 6:00 P.M. and her family day care operation generally ceased. She would have to pay Sonia for this extra care in addition to what she was now paying her cousin to watch Hope.

> Sonia did me a favor to extend the hours. Starting in February, we extended the hours, but I pay her extra for six to eight, $120 every two weeks for like two extra hours. It's good. I also try to bring her in later. I bring her in around 10:00 A.M. or even 12:00 P.M. sometimes so she does not have to stay in the one place for that many hours. . . . If she is there from 9:00 A.M. to 8:00 P.M., that's a lot of hours in a household, and I believe the lady needs a break. I appreciate everything she does. She likes my daughter and treats her good. Jacqueline has been going to her for more than a year. She will still spend like about ten hours a day there and sometimes twelve. I also try to bring her late so I can get some time with her. Mostly it is to give Jacqueline a break, because when I see them [my children], they all look so tired to me.

Julia was choosing a non-exit from care with Sonia because the care could be negotiated to fit with her work hours and because of a desire for continuity for her daughter. Julia said she could afford the extra money because she was not yet required to make an ACD copayment for the regular hours of care with Sonia and she was still receiving public assistance. She did not know what she would do when her public assistance case was finally closed, and she knew that her ACD case would be based on her work earnings, requiring her to make copayments. Yet she still wanted both of these things to happen soon.

> I can pay her the extra money because I am still receiving public assistance and do not have a copayment for ACD. Now I want to close it [her PA case], but they say I can't. Also, I tried to have my ACD case based on my pay stubs, and they said, no, your PA is still open so you can't. The child care people say they can't base the case on my work until PA closes my case. When I leave PA, I'm going to have to go in and show ACD my pay stubs. I mean, it's okay, because it works for me now if I don't have to pay anything this way, but I do not know what will happen when my PA closes or when it is going to close. They say soon I will get a letter in the mail, but you know they take their time. That's the funny part— when you really need the help, they cut you off. Now, when I am working and I'll be all right [if they close the case], they don't close it. It's weird. When you tell them that you have a job, they are like, okay, so, whatever, and when you are trying to look for a job, it's like, well, your case is closed. That's the thing that I don't understand. And I want the PA off, but I still want the help with the child care and food stamps, but when they close it they mess all that up.

Julia in her April interview was prescient. The welfare department did in fact close her case three months later, but they "messed up again," as Julia says. In the summer the welfare agency had summarily closed her case, without sending a letter. When she went to find out why there was no food stamp money on her EBT (electronic benefits transfer) card, the agency said she owed them money for the benefits she had received the last few months while she was working. She requested a fair hearing and won, but her case was still closed. She did not mind losing the cash public assistance, but along with it she lost more than $300 in food stamp benefits, which she still needed, and she had to pay close to $400 for her section 8 housing that the welfare agency had once paid. Having lost all this assistance, her increased housing and food expenses left her unable to pay for child care, and she would eventually have to leave her preferred care arrangement with Sonia.

During the summer Julia kept Jacqueline with Sonia because she needed care only in the daytime; her after-school program had turned into a summer school with regular daytime work hours. Then, in August, Julia had to start making an $8 weekly copayment for her ACD case when she was recertified

Figure 3.1 Dynamics Timeline for Julia and Jacqueline's Story

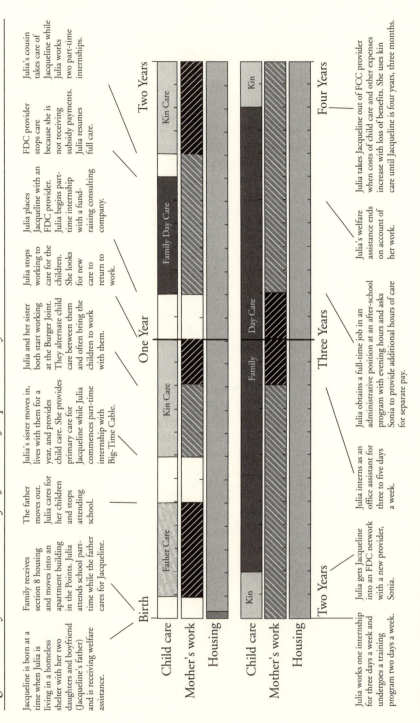

Source: Author's compilation.

as working and earning higher wages. When she returned to her school-year schedule of 2:00 P.M. to 8:00 P.M. in September, she could not afford to pay Sonia for the extra care hours, as she had in the spring. As a result, she started to have Jacqueline spend the mornings at Sonia's, and then, before she went to work around one o'clock, she took Jacqueline to her mother's to pass the rest of the day until she got off work.

Her expenses and debt kept mounting, so with her daughter less than two months away from turning four, she decided she could not afford even the $8 weekly copayment, which she had already missed for almost a month. She left the arrangement with Sonia in favor of using her seventy-three-year-old mother, who was often ill. Julia kept Jacqueline most mornings before taking her to her mother's on her way to work in the early afternoon. She exited Sonia's care after eighteen months because of money—the cost of care rose following her recertification, and her other expenses increased as well. The complications of her work schedule also did not fit well with the available care. She did not tell Jacqueline that the change was permanent. Two weeks later Jacqueline still seemed very unhappy and each day asked her mother, as they walked out the door, if they were going to Sonia's.

Piecing Together Care over Early Childhood

In the last chapter, we examined the continuum of child care arrangements that exist for low-income families, how mothers consider and choose among them, and how many hours children spend in care settings. That analysis focused on the care arrangements at a single point in time. In a given week, mothers were piecing together multiple care arrangements to fit their work schedules, and overall, children spent many hours in care. We began to see that child care choices are complex and that many factors contribute to them. This chapter builds on these findings by showing that for low-income families, in addition to being complex at almost any point, child care changes quickly over time. Among the factors contributing to the instability of children's care are the nature of the care that low-income families use and the relationships between child care dynamics, mothers' work, and other family factors.

Julia and Jacqueline's story illustrates the fast-changing nature of child care and the interactions between Jacqueline's care, Julia's work situations, and changes in their domestic life. The timeline for their story shows that Jacqueline had six different child care spells over four years. Because most of the spells were short, it was difficult for Jacqueline to form a consistent relationship with her caregivers. One arrangement lasted almost two years because all of the previous changes led Julia to value stability and leave Jacqueline with the provider as long as she could. The start of most of the care spells followed directly from Julia's work. As she tried many avenues toward finding steady work, she moved Jacqueline in and out of care. Her child care in turn affected

Julia's work. At points she had to stop working when care broke down. It was when Jacqueline was in her most stable care arrangements that Julia was able to move from progressively better internship experiences into a full-time job and off of welfare.

Jacqueline's child care was also influenced by family factors, including the use of father care and kin care when these sources were available and Julia's need to coordinate Jacqueline's care with her siblings' care. In its short duration, we can see some of the care characteristics of kin care described in the last chapter and analyzed further in this chapter. Spells in kin care are relatively short both because it is less reliable as an ongoing form of care and because mothers tend to use it to bridge time between other care arrangements.

The analysis in this chapter focuses on care arrangements viewed over time, or longitudinally from the time the children were born until they reached age four, instead of taking the snapshots in time used to analyze care in chapter 2. The analysis throughout this chapter focuses on the primary child care spells and excludes the secondary arrangements when families were using multiple care arrangements concurrently.[1] In this chapter I analyze the distribution of care by the children's ages and the total number of primary care spells they experienced during their first four years of life. Next, I analyze the dynamics of care arrangements, including how long care spells lasted and why they ended.

The Timeline of Children's Care

How many child care arrangements do children pass through before they go to preschool? How long are child care arrangements? Do some types of child care last longer than others? How do care arrangements change as children age? What types of child care are most common as initial arrangements? What types are most common for infants, for toddlers, and for preschool-age children? How many total primary care arrangements do children experience in the first four years of their lives? These are all questions that are important to understanding child care dynamics among low-income families.

From the detailed retrospective and longitudinal child care histories of the families in the sample, I developed timelines for each child's primary care arrangements. The timelines in figures 2.1 and 3.1, for instance, capture Brittany's and Julia's child care histories, their work paths, and some of the other dimensions of family life that interact with care dynamics. Figure 3.2 provides a composite timeline for the primary child care arrangements of all forty-two children in the sample from birth through age four. Each row represents one child's progression of primary child care spells over the first forty-eight months of life. The shading and patterns of each box represent the type of primary child care used for that child, and the length of each box indicates the duration of a spell in months.

A quick look at the figure shows the distinctive patterns of care by age, variations in the length of arrangements, and the short durations of many arrangements. The white (blank) boxes indicate the periods during which mothers were not working and so were providing primary child care. These spells were concentrated in the initial years after birth. The number of months prior to a mother beginning work and a child starting child care vary considerably. The four primary types of child care discussed in chapter 2— kin care, informal care, family child care, and center care—are represented by the varying shades of gray. Less frequently used forms of care, such as special needs care and father care, are depicted with patterns and words. The few cases in which two types of care were integrated in relatively equal proportions are represented as striped spells. Table 3.1 aggregates this data and presents an analysis of the overall distribution of primary care arrangements by months for each of the different care types.

Several patterns become apparent when looking at figure 3.2. These are then borne out in the aggregate analysis in table 3.1:

- There was great heterogeneity in the care timelines of individual children, and many children experienced a high degree of flux in their care arrangements. Many children had several care arrangements over four years with many breaks and changes in their providers and the types of care they received, while others had long arrangements without many breaks.

- Mothers were the primary care providers for children in the initial months of early childhood, but there was great variability in how long they were able to remain full-time care providers, and overall mothers' primary care declined significantly after the first year.

- Kin care is a common form of care in the first two years, when family members provided one-sixth of the care for infants and young toddlers. Kin care became less common for primary care after children reached their second birthday.

- Family day care emerged as the most common form of care by the second year, and it was where toddlers were most likely to receive child care.

- Centers emerged more often as care locations for children after they turned two, and for preschoolers it was the dominant form of primary care. Child care in centers amounted to less than 5 percent of care in the first two years and more than 40 percent in the two years after that.

- Informal care, including care by friends, neighbors, or strangers providing mostly individualized care, was consistently used as a form of care. It accounted for about one-tenth of the time in primary care in the first three years.

Figure 3.2   *Composite Timeline of Children's Primary Care Spells from*

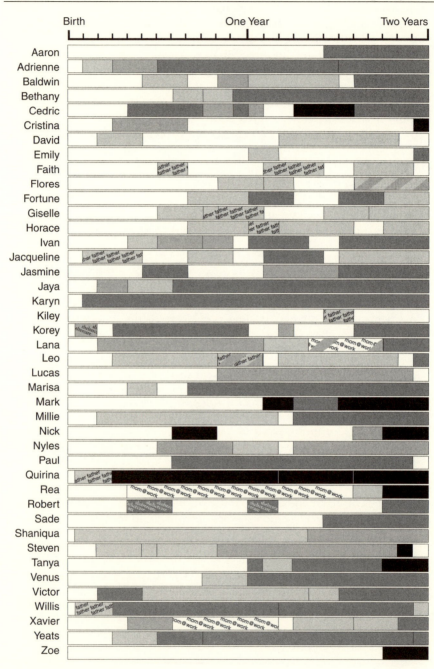

Birth to Age Four

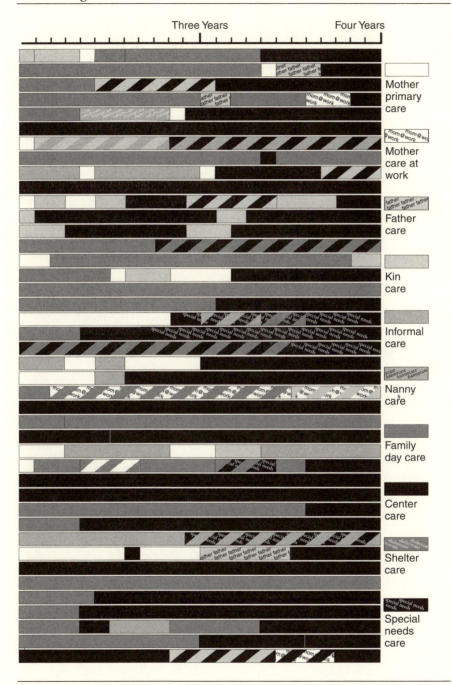

Table 3.1 Longitudinal Patterns in the Types of Child Care Used for Children in the Sample, by Year, and Distribution of Care Arrangements, by Care Months

Caregiver	Year One (Birth to Age One)	Year Two (Ages One to Two)	Year Three (Ages Two to Three)	Year Four (Ages Three to Four)	Total Care Months	Care Months Distribution	Percentage of Non-maternal Care Months
Mother	52.4%	21.4%	10.5%	1.0%	430	21.3%	
Father	2.8	1.6	0.0	1.6	30	1.5	1.9%
Kin	16.9	17.1	4.6	6.0	224	11.1	14.1
Informal	8.3	10.5	9.5	3.0	158	7.8	9.9
Family day care provider	13.7	39.1	39.5	20.0	566	28.1	35.7
Center (all)	2.4	7.5	31.7	59.5	510	25.3	32.2
Other	3.6	2.8	4.2	8.9	98	4.9	6.2
Total	100	100	100	100	2,016	100	100

Source: Author's compilation.

Most of the analysis that follows is a further breakdown of the longitudinal timeline in figure 3.2. First, the total number of primary care spells that mothers made for their children is calculated. A "care spell" is the number of consecutive months a child is in the same primary care arrangement.[2] This is followed by an analysis of the durations of care spells. The chapter then moves to what accounts for the dynamics of child care and mothers' reasons for making child care changes.

Table 3.1 breaks down the distribution of primary care by child age and supplies an aggregate distribution of care by type over the first four years, incorporating the length of the child care spells. This adds another layer to the distributional analyses in chapter 2 (table 2.1) by breaking down primary care spells by the months that children spent in care. When arrangements are weighted by the length of time spent in particular forms of care, family day care emerges as the most prevalent form of care, accounting for 36 percent of all nonmaternal care, followed by center care, which accounts for almost 32 percent of the distribution. Family day care and center care both appear to be more prevalent when care is viewed in terms of care months than they are just looking at the number of arrangements, because their average durations are significantly longer. Kin care and informal care account for a smaller share of the distribution when care is viewed by months, but combined they still amount to about 25 percent of the care, representing quite a significant fraction of care.

In the children's first year they were at home with their mothers as their primary caregiver 52 percent of the time—or, on average, for a little more than six months. When mothers made other arrangements, it was most often for the child to be in a nearby home with a kin, or family day care or informal provider, which together accounted for almost two-fifths of all children's care in the first year. Kin care was the most prevalent among these, and family day care was the next most frequent arrangement. Fathers were the primary source for child care only 2 percent of the time. Only a very small amount of first-year child care occurred in nonhome settings such as day care centers, homeless shelters, and mothers' workplaces.

Primary caregiving by mothers dropped precipitously after the first year. Looking across the first row of data in table 3.1, we see that mothers were primary caregivers for their child 21 percent of the time in the second year, compared to 52 percent in the first year. In the third year this rate was halved again, to 11 percent of the time, and the drop was almost complete after children turned three. In year four only 1 percent of primary care was provided by mothers. Overall, the children in the sample spent 21 percent of the aggregated 2,016 care months in their mother's primary care when she was not working, and most of this was in their first year of life. It is important to note, however, that because the sample was chosen to include mothers who were working at the initial point of contact—when their children were two and three years old—the overall levels of nonmaternal care use, and especially care in the third and fourth years, may be somewhat higher than in the general population.

In the second year family day care emerged as the most dominant care arrangement. Family day care accounted for almost 40 percent of all care in year two, and 50 percent of all nonmaternal care. Kin care and informal care were just as common in the second year as they were in the first year, together accounting for almost one-quarter of the months in care. Father care remained minimal and fell slightly from its low base in the birth year. Primary care in centers increased slightly in the second year, to 7 percent.

Center care emerged much more significantly in the children's third year, accounting for 32 percent of the care at that age and approaching the amount of time children spent in family day care, which was still the dominant care type at 39 percent. Kin care dropped considerably, from 17 percent of the care months in the first two years to just 5 percent by the third year. Informal care remained around 9 percent, as it had been for all of the first three years. Fathers of the children in this sample provided no primary care between their children's second and third birthdays.

As children grew older, they made the transition to more formal care based in institutions. For this sample, the progression was rather dramatic. By the children's fourth year, 60 percent of their primary care was in centers, a doubling from the amount of time they spent in centers in the prior year. In year four, one-fifth of these children's care months were spent in family day care homes, still a significant form of care. Some mothers either felt good enough about family day care to maintain the consistency of this care or continued to use family day care while they waited for a space to open up in a center. Also, children who turned three at some point earlier in the year might not start center care until the September after they have turned three, when more spaces become available at the start of the school year. Kin and informal care accounted for less than 10 percent of the months children were in primary care arrangements after age three, but as we saw in the last chapter, these remained common secondary arrangements as children got older. Special needs care, which is often provided in specialized institutional settings to address a child's identified health and developmental needs and becomes more available as children get older, was used more often in year four.

Family child care homes were the most frequent care setting over the four-year span, accounting for 36 percent of all months in nonmaternal child care. Family child care was also the form of care used most consistently over the four-year time span; it was the most common form of nonmaternal care between the children's first and third birthdays, and the second most common in infancy and in the fourth year of early childhood. Center care was almost as common as family child care, accounting for 32 percent of nonmaternal care months. However, the use of center care was concentrated almost entirely in the last two years of early childhood, when it accounted for more than 45 percent of total care. Kin care and informal care showed the reverse age patterns, accounting for more than 25 percent of children's care months in the first two years and less than 10 percent in the next two years.

Altogether, children in the sample were in family child care homes and child care centers as their primary care locations for more than half of their first four years. Mothers utilized these two dominant types of care for more than two-thirds of nonmaternal care. Kin and informal care together accounted for about 25 percent of all nonmaternal primary care.

The timelines in figure 3.2 and distributions by year in table 3.1 show that these children's care arrangements changed significantly over time as they passed through many care arrangements, in different settings with different providers, in the short period of their early childhood.

The Number of Care Arrangements

Table 3.2 shows the range in the number of primary nonmaternal care spells used from birth to age four by each of the forty-two families in the sample. The number of spells ranged between two and nine, as seen in the first column. Looking at the distribution of the forty-two families across this range (in column 2), twenty-five of the forty-two children in the sample were in five or more care spells.

Table 3.2 shows that the average number of nonmaternal primary care spells was about five per child between birth and age four. For the sample as a whole, there were 215 primary child care spells. In addition to these nonmaternal primary care spells, many children cycled between care with a provider and their mother's care. Following initial entry into care, there were fifty-two instances of spells where children returned to care by their mothers. Not surprisingly, mothers were the default care provider when they stopped working or when other care broke down and no adequate arrangement could be found. Return spells to mothers' care tended to be for short periods. If mothers' care spells are included in the analysis (including the first maternal care spells), the average number of care spells increases to 7.4 per child.[3] Julia made six primary care arrangements for Jacqueline, and she stopped her work activities three times to care for Jacqueline for short spells, including twice when care arrangements broke down. Julia says her situation was particularly unstable since she was trying to leave welfare and her options were limited:

> You are really moving your child around when you get off PA and start to work. You just want to show them that you want to work, but it's hard, especially with the child care. First, you have to get the supplement [the voucher subsidy for child care]. Then you run into too many problems. You try to get the family to help, and then they work hard for little money. You have to use your mother, your cousin, your sister, your brother, and the lady who lives down the block because they don't last. Workfare doesn't give them the money [i.e., payments are late]. And I

Table 3.2   *Number of Primary Care Spells Between Birth and Age Four for Children in the Sample*

Number of Primary Care Spells	Frequency of Families with This Number of Primary (Nonmaternal) Care Spells	Distribution of Primary (Nonmaternal) Care Spells
1	0	0%
2	3	7.1
3	6	14.3
4	8	19.1
5	6	14.3
6	8	19.1
7	8	19.1
8	2	4.8
9	1	2.4
Total families in sample	42	100.0
Total primary care spells	215	
Average number of primary care spells	5.12	

Source: Author's compilation.

> didn't really know that much about the system. I didn't know what's available. So you end up taking any kind of child care just to get the extra income and just to do what workfare tells you. And then you have to move your children around all the time until you find something that works, and I think it's too much for them. But what can you do? . . . At least you've tried.

These changes represent further transitions that children must make, and more care instability. It is important to note such cycling between maternal and nonmaternal care, because it points to an even greater instability that children face over time. The following analysis, however, focuses solely on nonmaternal care spells because it is the duration, dynamics, and use of these arrangements that is central to understanding how child care is arranged and experienced in low-income families. Children's care over time is even more complex when we add in the secondary care that mothers arrange around their primary care. Adding nontransitory secondary care (lasting at least a month) to the number of primary care spells, the average number of care spells per child is twelve.

The Duration of Child Care Spells

For the children in this sample, the durations of care spells were short, as can be inferred from figure 3.2 or from the fact that on average these children were in five primary care arrangements by the time they turned four. Durations of care spells can be further explicated by analyzing the length of each spell to determine how much it varied by type, by the age of the child, and by other factors.[4] This analysis includes all care spells that were started prior to age four. All of the last spells that began prior to age four were followed until completion.

Table 3.3 shows the range in durations of the primary care spells for the children in the sample from birth to age four. The average duration of a child care spell was more than seven months. Thirty-eight percent (82 out of 215) of spells were very short (lasting three months or less), 22 percent were short (four to six months in duration), and 14 percent were of moderate length (seven to nine months). Twenty-six percent (55 out of 215 care spells) lasted more than nine months, and 18 percent lasted longer than a year, constituting relatively long care spells. Twenty-five of the 215 spells were longer than fifteen months.

The exit rates from care spells were significantly higher in the first few months; half of all the spells were over by the fifth month. There are many explanations for the generally short durations of primary care spells. First, the mothers often needed to make arrangements quickly, without much information or many other immediately available options. In addition, the mother and the provider often did not know what to expect from the arrangement, and some arrangements may have been ended quickly by either parent or provider. Finally, care may have ended when a better care option materialized, or the arrangement may have been meant to be short-term from the start.

Table 3.3 *Durations of Primary Care Spells for Families in the Sample*

Duration Length	Completed Care Spells	Distribution
Zero to three months	82	38.2%
Four to six months	48	22.3
Seven to nine months	30	14.0
Ten to twelve months	17	7.9
Thirteen to fifteen months	13	6.0
Fifteen months or longer	25	11.6
Total	215	100.0
Average duration	7.53 months	

Source: Author's compilation.

Table 3.4   *Average Duration of Primary Care Spells for Families in the Sample, by Type*

Care Arrangement	Completed Care Spells	Total Months	Average Duration (Months)
Father care	11	30	2.7
Kin care	52	214	4.1
Informal care	32	158	4.9
Family day care	51	551	10.8
Center care	51	573	11.2
Other	18	92	5.1
Total	215	1,618	7.5

Source: Author's compilation.

The lengths of child care spells in the sample varied considerably by the type of care. Table 3.4 shows that kin care and informal care spells were significantly shorter in duration, lasting on average four to five months. Almost 60 percent of kin care spells were three months or less, as were half of informal care spells. Family day care and center care spells were much longer, averaging about eleven months. Family day care and center care spells accounted for forty-nine of the fifty-five completed care spells of ten months or longer. Nearly two-thirds of family child care and center care arrangements combined lasted for seven months or longer, while this was true of fewer than 20 percent of kin and informal care spells.

Care spells during which children returned to their mother for primary care between other care arrangements were also of relatively short durations (not shown in the table). Mother care spells averaged 3.4 months, and 60 percent of these fifty-two spells were less than two months long.

Spell lengths increase with the age of the child. The median duration of the sixty-one care spells started in the children's first year of life was just three months. The median durations increased to five months for spells begun in the second year, six months for spells begun in year three, and eight months for spells begun in the fourth year. The average duration of spells similarly increased by just over one month for each year as children aged (see table 3.5).

These patterns of increasing care durations by age are consistent with the strong patterns of care use by age seen in table 3.1. Earlier spells were shorter since the types of care used more often in the initial years tended to have shorter durations. Some types became shorter or longer over the early childhood years. Kin care spells, for example, declined in frequency as well as duration over each of the first four years. When kin care was used as primary care, the spells got shorter as the child got older, averaging five months when

Table 3.5 *Duration of Primary Care Spell Months for Children in the Sample, by Age at the State of the Spell*

Age of Child at Start of Care Spell	Completed Care Spells	Average Duration	25th Percentile	Median (50th) Percentile	75th Percentile
Year one	61	6.0	2	3	7
Year two	63	7.4	3	5	10
Year three	46	8.1	3	6	13
Year four	45	8.6	4	8	14
Total	215	7.5	3	5	11

Source: Author's compilation.

begun in a child's first year, four months when started in the second, and less than three months when started after that age.

Center-based care follows the opposite pattern. The frequency of center-based care arrangements increased as children aged, as did the lengths of the care spells of this type initiated at each age of childhood. The durations of family day care spells also declined as children aged. Spells begun during the first year lasted an average of seventeen months, those begun between ages one and three lasted about ten months, and those started after age three lasted less than seven months. Of the very longest care durations (longer than twenty-four months), four were family day care spells begun prior to a child's first birthday and five were center care spells begun in a child's second or third year.

In sum, the durations of children's care spells were short, with the median spell being only five months. Durations were much shorter for kin, informal, and father care: almost 60 percent of the spells of these types lasted three months or less. Family child care and center care arrangements lasted more than twice as long as other types of care arrangements, averaging eleven months per completed spell, and 32 of the 102 spells of these types lasted more than one year.

The duration analysis indicates that there are many discontinuities in these children's care, contributing instability to early childhood experience. This finding is significant in light of the developmental literature that has identified negative consequences of unstable child care. Children with unstable care have been found to be less likely to build trust with providers, more likely to show increased aggression, and more likely to develop less functional relationships with their peers and adults (Barnas and Cummings 1994; Howes and Hamilton 1993; Howes, Matheson, and Hamilton 1994). The stability of caregiving relationships appears to be particularly important for children's early social development because of the strength and quality of attachments that may be formed with stable providers, on the one hand, and the greater emotional insecurity that can result from multiple, unstable caregivers, on the other. Stable care is also important for the reliability it offers parents who must base their work decisions around child care. See appendix A for further discussion of the research on the effects of care instability on children.

The Dynamics of Care Spells

Now that we have an understanding of how long care arrangements last, we can look at how particular care arrangements begin and why they end. These fundamental questions about child care dynamics have rarely been explored, but they can help us to understand the child care arrangements used by low-income families and to formulate policy responses that may help to increase the quality and continuity of children's care.

Care dynamics are complex and multifaceted. Considering the range in types of care, the short average durations of care spells, and the distribution of the durations, it is clear that there was enormous diversity in the care experienced by children in this sample. Many families coped with multiple, inconsistent care arrangements, while others were fortunate enough to find continuous arrangements. Still others made voluntary, conscious transitions to improve their children's care or to pair complementary care arrangements for a period of time, but they also experienced undesired breaks in care or sometimes had to use care that was less than preferred. Any one of a number of factors can make the difference between stable and chaotic care dynamics in the life of a child: the parents' knowledge and resourcefulness, their access to personal and community resources, their work schedules, their preferences, their perceptions of their children's needs, and just plain fortune.

In the story at the start of this chapter, Julia first placed Jacqueline in the care of her father, Felix, soon after she was born, and they all moved into an apartment together in the Points. After securing housing, Julia immediately enrolled in a training program to improve her skills and credentials for getting a job. During the four hours each day when she was in school, she left Jacqueline with Felix, who she thought "was doing nothing" anyway. She started the care spell with Jacqueline's father because she would not be away for many hours and she wanted to find her way off of welfare and into employment, which would eventually enable her to support her family. Felix was an available provider, and he was Julia's only care option. Yet Julia worried that Jacqueline might not be getting the food she left behind or that she might be neglected.

During the four months she was in school and Felix was watching Jacqueline, Julia and Felix fought—more about the relationship than about the child care, but when she told him to leave, she dismissed her child care provider as well. The ending was attributable to a family change, although Julia had expected the care to be short-term from the start.

Julia's next three arrangements all lasted six months or less. Two were with kin—her sister and later her cousin—and one was with a family child care provider. In the first arrangement, her sister ended the care because she was doing it short-term until she found other work. The next arrangement, with the family child care provider, ended because the welfare-to-work agency was not making payments to the provider. Finally, the arrangement with her cousin was a low-quality arrangement that Julia used only until something else became available.

All the while, Julia searched her community for options, worked with a community-based agency, and eventually received a more reliable form of subsidy that led her to a family child care arrangement with Sonia. Julia felt that the arrangement with Sonia offered her and Jacqueline stability and a durable care relationship for the first time. Julia was thankful for Sonia's consistency and flexibility in adapting and continuing to provide care when Julia found stable employment and had to change her work hours. Julia appreciated these aspects of Sonia's care so much that she kept Jacqueline with Sonia past age three and through much of her fourth year, when she could have tried to enroll her in a preschool program. Julia felt that Jacqueline needed the stability that Sonia provided after being bounced around so much.

As we saw in chapter 2, Bethany was in seven child care arrangements between the time her mother, Brittany, began to move from welfare to work, when Bethany was seven months old, and her fourth birthday. One relatively long care spell of twenty-five months was sandwiched between five very short spells, and then one other spell continued past her fourth birthday for a year. When Brittany started a training program to become a child care provider in her effort to leave welfare, she put Bethany in child care for the first time. Like many of the initial situations of mothers in the sample, Brittany had limited choices and information about where to leave her daughter. She started with a kin arrangement with Bethany's uncle, which lasted less than two months and ended because of provider instability and poor-quality care. Then Brittany turned to her sister to care for Bethany because she needed a short-term care arrangement so that she could complete her training program.

When Brittany started working, she found longer-term care with a private family day care provider that lasted for two years. Despite the durability of the care spell over time and the satisfaction of both Brittany and Bethany with the care, the arrangement ended because of a disagreement between Brittany and the provider over payment for child care when the family was on vacation. Provider-parent conflicts were a frequent type of care exit in this study, especially in family day care situations. In the next year Bethany would pass through three other care arrangements. First, she was in her father's care—he was not working at the time and there were no other affordable options. Next, Brittany moved her to a family child care provider when subsidized care became available. Bethany exited this care because of another provider-parent conflict. For three months Brittany cared for Bethany at her job while working. Two months before Bethany turned four, Brittany finally arranged for her entry into a center-based program.

Cassandra, like Brittany, had a relatively stable and flexible work situation as a nurse-practitioner at a hospital, but she had to weather a series of crises that undermined the stability of her son Cedric's care dynamics. Cassandra first put Cedric into a care arrangement at the age of four months, when she returned to work at the hospital. This was earlier than she might have liked from a care perspective, but the financial realities of a mother supporting three boys by herself left no choice. Cedric's first provider was Brenda, whom Cassandra had also used for her second son. Brenda provided family day care for Cedric until he was nine months old. At that point Brenda, who was pregnant, had complications in her pregnancy and was ordered onto bed rest. After this initial provider exit, Cassandra made a short-term arrangement with a friend who was on maternity leave to take care of Cedric until she returned to work two months later. Then Cassandra put him in child care with Mrs. Paul:

> She was a sweet woman. I had met her through church but did not know her too well. I knew she took care of children and lived in a nice (fancy) building on the hill [just on the edge of the Valley]. She suggested I let her care for Cedric. She charged a lot (more than $100 per week), but I had no other alternative. Well, she turned out to have psychiatric troubles, and one day when I went to pick up Cedric I found that Mrs. Paul had apparently not taken her medication that day or something, because she was a completely different person—she was nasty and mean and a little scary. The next day a relation of hers called to say she was being hospitalized and would no longer be providing care.

Next Cassandra put Cedric in an informal care arrangement with a neighbor who lived in his father's building, but this lasted only two weeks. She made a very quick care exit owing to poor-quality care when she found that the neighbor's own children had been hurting Cedric and he was being neglected to the point where he screamed at night. At this point, feeling Cedric had been traumatized by all the changes within his first year, she took a leave of absence from work for almost two months to care for her son and offer him some stability, as well as to seek other child care options.

In these and other mothers' stories, we find almost every type of child care disruption: gaps in care, delays in receiving necessary care, limited options, unforeseen opportunities for care, and a host of other reasons care spells ended and new spells began. Each mother has a unique story to tell about her child care dynamics; some are similar to the stories of Julia, Brittany, and Cassandra, and some involve more compromises of the mother's care, work, and family responsibilities. The detailed retrospective data collection and longitudinal ethnographies allow for a systematic analysis to determine the reasons why child care spells end. An analysis of exits can be most critical for understanding children's care and developing the means for improving it.[5]

Table 3.6 provides information about the reasons for child care endings.[6] The first column gives a broad classification of exits, as interpreted from the interview data.[7] The ending types are grouped according to exits related specifically to aspects of the child care and exits that occurred for noncare reasons, such as work, family, health, or housing. The noncare exit reasons are discussed later in the chapter.

Care-Related Exits

Among the exits from arrangements for care-related reasons were many that were unwanted or involuntary exits. *Provider exits* occurred when caregivers decided for any of myriad reasons to stop providing care. Bethany's uncle decided he did not really want to be a caregiver or to put much energy into it, and Cedric's family day care provider had a health emergency stemming from her own pregnancy complications that required her to stop providing care.

Conflict exits occurred when disagreements between the mothers and their providers escalated acrimoniously into exits, such as the dispute over whether the provider should be paid for the two weeks when Bethany and Brittany were on vacation, or the argument that Brittany had with another provider over the lack of communication about the provider's and child's whereabouts during the day.

Quality exits were those stemming from a mother's decision to remove her child from care she perceived as poor-quality, such as Cassandra's removal of Cedric from the informal care provider in his father's building because he was hurt by the provider's children.

Subsidy exits followed when subsidies ended. Julia experienced an unforeseen exit from care when the Human Resources Administration, the city's welfare-to-work agency, did not make the child care payments to Jacqueline's family child care provider; she underwent a similar exit from the care provided by her cousin when HRA lost her file and discontinued payments. These exits could be traced back to problems in the administration of the subsidy, as in Julia's case, or they occurred when a subsidy ended or was reduced when a family lost its eligibility. Grouped with subsidy exits are *cost exits*; these occurred when mothers could no longer afford the care arrangement or the cost of the arrangement increased, as was the case when Julia exited from the family child care arrangement she had been using for more than eighteen months.

Of the unwanted or involuntary exits, quality concerns and provider decisions to stop providing care were the most common, each accounting for 9 percent of the exits. Altogether the unwanted or involuntary care-related exit

Table 3.6   *Distribution of Reasons for Care Spell Endings for Children in the Sample*

Reason for Care Ending	Frequency	Distribution
Involuntary care-related reasons		
Provider decision—terminates care	19	9%
Conflict—provider-parent disagreement	9	4
Quality—parent perceives care is poor-quality	19	9
Subsidy and cost—increased cost, loss of subsidy, administrative problems, or eligibility ending	21	10
Short-term care—emergency or transitional care expected to be of limited duration	20	9
Voluntary care-related reasons		
Preference or choice—transitions for other preferred care, including developmental, quality, cost preferences	35	17
Age—child ages out or into (other) eligible care	24	11
Non-care-related reasons		
Work—new job, job loss, change in work hours	25	12
Family change	17	8
Housing change	18	9
Health—child's health or mother's health	8	4
Total care spells	215	100

Source: Author's compilation.

categories accounted for 68 of the 215 care-related exits in the sample, or 32 percent of the total.

Somewhat more neutral care-related exits were *short-term exits*. These are relatively clear cases where the care was understood from the start to be a temporary arrangement. These arrangements were often made when no other options were available or to bridge time between care arrangements when a previous arrangement had ended abruptly. Examples include the care provided by Brittany's sister for a couple of months and by Cassandra's friend after each of their first care arrangements ended sooner than they expected. Ten of the twenty care spells in the sample with short-term exits were kin care arrangements. The others were informal care, father care, or mother's care while at work.

There were also occasions when exits from care were desired, or at least expected, and thus could be considered voluntary exits. *Preference exits* usually occurred when another preferred care arrangement became available or the child was newly eligible for it. Most often the change was made to a different type of care and for developmental reasons. For example, Bethany left her father's care to go to the second family child care provider because Brittany wanted her to be with more children and a more experienced caregiver. Transitions also occurred between similar types of care because a new care situation was perceived as an improvement in quality. Preference exits also occurred when a new care arrangement offered a lower cost or a higher subsidy. Specific preferences also came into play. For example, Cassandra changed from an informal care situation she thought was adequate to a woman she hired to come to the house because it reduced the complexity of arranging care for Cedric and his brother. Preference exits accounted for about one-sixth of the exits, and they generally preceded more positive transitions. Of the preference exits, twenty-four of the thirty-five exits, or 12 percent of all exits, were for developmental reasons. Most common among these preference exits were transfers from a home-based care arrangement to a center.

Age exits were a related, though separate, care exit category in which the child aged out of one care situation into another one. These exits were usually based on transitions to programs with eligibility related to age. The age exits included those from a family child care provider who provided only infant and toddler care as well as those from Head Start, pre-K, and other later arrangements with age-specific eligibility rules. Most of these exits occurred later in the four-year span, including twenty for spells begun in the third or fourth year, and many were for the last arrangement in the timeline, with the exit occurring after forty-eight months. Altogether these two generally voluntary forms of care exits, preference exits and age exits, amounted to 28 percent of all spell endings.

Table 3.7 provides data on the exit reasons for child care spells based on children's age, combining some of the care-related exit categories. Many exit categories were evenly distributed over the first four years. The cost and sub-

Table 3.7   *Distribution of Reasons for Care Spells Ending for Children in the Sample, by Children's Age (at Start of Spell)*

Exit Reason	Year One	Year Two	Year Three	Year Four	Total
Quality, conflicts, and provider decisions	23.3%	30.2%	13.0%	17.8%	21.9%
Cost and subsidy	8.3	4.8	17.4	11.1	9.8
Short-term	10.0	9.5	8.7	8.9	9.3
Preference and age transitions	5.0	26.9	45.7	42.2	27.4
Work	13.3	12.7	8.7	11.1	11.6
Family	20.0	4.8	0.0	4.4	7.9
Housing	18.3	6.3	2.2	4.4	8.4
Health	1.7	4.8	4.3	4.4	3.7
Total (215 spell endings)	100	100	100	100	100

Source: Author's compilation.

sidy exits peaked in year three, in part owing to the difficulty of getting subsidized care in years one and two because of the time it took to arrange subsidies and the limited availability of subsidized care for infants and toddlers. Preference and age exits were more frequent in years three and four, accounting for almost half of the care exits in those years.

Non-Care-Related Exits

Sixty-eight of the 215 exits were for non-care-related reasons, including exits related to changes in work, family, housing, and health. Of these, work exits were the most frequent at 12 percent of all exits. Family and housing changes each accounted for nearly one out of twelve exits, and health-related exits accounted for about 4 percent. I will briefly discuss the dynamic interactions between child care and these factors, focusing on them as exit factors, with some discussion of the more general interactions between child care and work, family, and housing in later chapters.

Changes in mothers' work situations accounted for the largest share of the noncare exits—*work exits* occurred twenty-five times. In twenty of these cases the work change that led to a child care exit was involuntary. Work exits included those stemming from job losses (twelve exits), job changes (six), or changes in working hours (four). Yolanda describes a typical care exit related to a job change: she took Yeats out of a family child care arrangement she liked when her job change made commuting to his care too difficult. She tried to time the care change so that it would be easier for Yeats, who she felt had already been through too many changes.

> Jane was a great family child care provider . . . but I had to take him out when I changed jobs. . . . Jane is all the way up where I used to work. . . . I decided to try to keep him at Jane's to have his birthday party with Jane and his friends when he turned three. I left him there for three months, but I had a hard time. . . . I did the going uptown thing to take him and then go to work. . . . It's funny because I always wanted him in a center, but I took him out because of the commuting to my job.

Yolanda's example shows how child care and work dynamics are paired: changes in one often lead to changes in the other. Work came first for Yolanda, as it did for many other mothers in the sample.

> It seems like work and child care change all the time, and one changes the other. For me, work is most important, because you gotta work or you can't do anything else, cannot do a thing for your children. That's most important, you gotta maintain the job. I'll find child care. I can use my mom as backup, 'cause she doesn't work, and that's free child care.

Yolanda, an older mother in the sample with some of the most work experience, was savvy about searching for other care possibilities prior to changes in work. Bernadette, on the other hand, was a younger mother with limited work experience; she started with the expectation that she would work only if she could find appropriate child care. Like Yolanda, Bernadette exited a care arrangement she liked when a job ended and she started a job search. When she took her son, Paul, out of his family child care arrangement with Luiza, she worried about whether she would be able to take him back there if she found work.

> I was doing an internship as a substitute teacher for a few months, but that was just short-term for experience. When that ended in August, I had to take him out of child care because I did not have the regular job. I was not working, so I was not going to pay her, and I was going to be home most days and I wanted to take care of him. But she had been my regular, stable child care from the beginning, and I did not want to lose her, because Luiza was his provider for over a year. I did not know if she would take him back when I got a job, because the agency [a family child care network] could have given her a new child. So I risked losing that child care and beginning all over, and if I found a job but not soon, I then would have had the problem of finding child care. She did take him back, as it turned out, because no other person took his place, when I started the new job.

Just as work changes can lead to care exits, care changes may cause work exits as well. Work for many low-income mothers is unstable, and problems in their children's care can cause them to leave work. For example, Inez left her first job to take care of her daughter Jasmine when she got sick at the provider's house. She then decided to care for Jasmine for a while before putting her back in child care.

> I was working for a cleaning service for like two months and left Jasmine at a family child care home that I found through an agency. One day when I picked her up, she had a bad fever and I got scared. I did not like the idea of putting her in someone else's care when she was six months, and this lady was all right, but she was not going to give her the attention I could. I decided I did not want anyone else to take care of her. I left that job that day.

Inez decided she wanted to take care of Jasmine herself and so did not want to work again for some time. Similarly, Harriet left a job when she could not accommodate her son Horace's care needs.

> Before I had my baby, I had been working two jobs and making good money. One was a full-time position at the Big Bank, and the other was a weekend job at Coffee Time. I wanted to go back to that situation after I had the baby, but I could not because of Horace's condition [Erb's palsy]. I had to take him to the hospital every Wednesday for occupational therapy, and I could not do that while working at the bank. I tried for almost a month, but because of the schedule and the problems I was having with the child care, I could not do it. My aunt was watching him, but she could not watch him every day, and could not take him for his appointments. [So] I kept working at Coffee Time on the weekends, and my aunt watched him for five months until I got the home health aide position, and then had to again work out my work schedule around my child's needs and the new child care problems.

Overall, work is a significant source contributing to frequent changes and adding to the instability of children's care. It was the second most common reason for child care exits among the individual categories. However, work is less prevalent as a source of exits than reasons related to child care, and it may be less prevalent in percentage terms than we might expect: *12 percent of child care exits were directly linked to work changes.* In part, this percentage seems low because other factors were contributing significantly to the instability of the care spells, particularly the inherent instability of the child care itself. It is also low in percentage terms because there were just so many exits. However, work seems to be a more common exit reason when we look at it as forty-two women losing child care twenty-five times for work-related reasons. Or in other words, more than one of every two mothers, on average, experience a work-related care exit during their children's first four years.

The relationship between work and child care is also complex. Work can lead to care exits, as it did twenty-five times for mothers in this sample over four years, and child care instability can cause work to end, which also occurred almost as often in the sample—twenty times. Sometimes one ended the other, but more often changes in one led to continuing adjustments in the other. Work interacts with child care throughout and shapes the choice of care, the timing of care, and the complexity of care, such as whether multiple arrangements are needed.

Family structure also shifted frequently in these low-income families' lives, creating potential problems because mothers often relied on kin for child care. *Family exits* brought on by family change accounted for seventeen care exits in the sample, or 8 percent of the total. For example, Jacqueline's first care arrangement was with her father, Felix, who was living with them at the time. Felix moved out when Jacqueline's mother Julia ended their relationship, ending the care spell as well. Griselda had a similar experience with the use of father care for Giselle and her sister.

> When we were living together, he watched them regularly, like every day. He worked at night, and I worked in the daytime. . . . That ended when I moved out and back to my mother's. For a while then, he did not want to take care of them, even on the weekends, I think because he was hurt and wanted to take it out on me. Now he will watch them, but not as a regular provider like before.

Kin care spells were the most likely to end because of family changes. Many times kin care ended when the provider moved away. These mothers' family members were very mobile, at times residing with the mothers, they also moved back and forth between New York and other places they called home, providing care when they were able to. Sandra, who lived with her mother and used her as Shaniqua's first caregiver, trusted only her mother when she started working after Shaniqua was born. Her mother provided care for more than a year before she moved, at which point Sandra transitioned to an informal care provider.

Changes caused by *housing exits* had a significant influence on family life, and the very important destabilizing role that housing changes played in some families' experience was one of the major findings in this study. Some of the families moved frequently, and when they did, the move usually coincided with or led to changes in other domains of family life, including work, child care, and family structure. In fact, many of the mothers say that their reliance on housing assistance was a greater factor in their family's stability than cash public assistance or other areas of assistance. A surprising number of the mothers in the sample experienced homelessness, including six who had been homeless over the course of their child's first four years, the period of analysis in this study, and three who had been homeless prior to that. Julia's exit from homelessness coincided with the birth of Jacqueline, so Jacqueline's early childhood was not greatly influenced by unstable housing except for the complexity around the time of her birth. However, child care, school, and living situations for both of her older siblings were very much affected by the family's unstable housing.

Housing changes were the reason for eighteen care exits, or 8 percent of the total. Lola, who had a turbulent relationship with her children's father, moved four times in two years. Although the moves led to only one care exit, the instability in her housing was one reason Lola did not work or use child care for long stretches. She finally settled in a housing project when her son Lucas was two.

> When my son was two or three months, I decided not to live with his father anymore, and left. I moved to Queens, and he used to come and visit me in the apartment there. He stayed with me but didn't live there. We didn't stay there long because he fought with the landlord, and the landlord kicked us out. . . . Then I moved to the Harbor, and I was no longer living with his father. He was doing drugs and started living in the street after Queens. I lived there in the Harbor for like two months [until] . . . when he was almost a year old . . . his father stabbed me. They moved me to Coney Island for my protection, which was okay, but it was kind of far. Out there I started working and going to therapy and found a Russian lady who watched him. I lived there not even a year. Then the courts moved me here after he was sent to prison. I started living here, and I was back where I grew up, but it was harder to find child care here where I lived than where I did not know anybody, but it's nice to be settled in the same place now.

Nora, who was homeless when her son Nick was an infant, received housing in a dangerous part of Highwall Valley and then continued to seek a better apartment through the section 8 program. When she finally got the living arrangement she wanted, she also rearranged Nick's care.

> [After the shelters] we moved to a section 8 apartment on Border Street and lived there a year. Then we moved again because . . . I was tired of dealing with my landlord and the conditions of his building. There was always break-ins—I was always nervous. There were break-ins in the store on the first floor; bums kept on sleeping in my hallway; and the man under me, his dog scared the boys, and he would just laugh at us. . . . I thought me and my boyfriend was splitting, and I didn't want to be there by myself, with that man with the dog always threatening me and my kids. . . . A lady in the building that I was friends with, she had an application for here [the building where Nora now lives], but she didn't want to live here. She said she had lived up this way—not to say that it

was bad—but she experienced living up this way and she did not want to move here again. So she got the place and put it in that it's all right for me to take her place, she don't want it or whatever. When we moved here, I was lucky because I got a place in this [child care] center for Nick, while I could not find any down there for him, so that worked out because I prefer the centers for the learning.

One-third of the care endings were for noncare reasons, and housing and family exits together accounted for almost one-sixth of all care exits. Family and housing exits were heavily concentrated in children's first two years, when families' situations were often particularly unstable. Thirty-eight percent of the exits from care arrangements begun in the first year of life were due to family and housing changes. Unstable housing situations and changing family structures are often dominant dynamic factors in low-income families' lives, especially when children are very young. When there are changes in these aspects of family life, they can shape and alter both child care and mothers' work significantly.

Children's health issues, and to a lesser degree mothers' health issues, affected care arrangements, but they did not directly lead to many exits from care. There were eight *health exits*: cases in which care spells ended primarily for health reasons. Hortensia related one health-related exit: when her son Ivan became ill, she was forced to quit her job when her employer would not grant her time to care of her child.

When he was still a baby, I first worked for a cleaning service, and I got paid $20 per apartment I cleaned. Ivan was very sick one day, and I called the man who ran the cleaning service, and I told him my son is sick and I cannot go that day. He yelled at me and said I had to go. I said I could not. He said the man whose apartment I was supposed to clean was having a party that day, and what should he tell the man to do. I said, tell him to clean his own apartment. My son was sick and there was no one else to take care of him. I lost that job that day on the phone . . . and I stayed home with Ivan until I found the next job.

Another type of health exit occurs when a parent needs to make new arrangements because of a child's chronic condition or special developmental needs. For example, Oona ended Kiley's care with his father because she thought he could not fully meet Kiley's special needs; she decided to quit her job until she could find the appropriate care for him. Sandra exited a primary informal care arrangement in favor of a specialized school setting after her daughter Shaniqua was diagnosed with a speech delay. However, she continued to use the informal care in combination with the special needs care since the specialized care did not cover the whole day. In some instances, children began to receive special needs services that did not require an exit from care because services were arranged within the current care context.

Summary and Conclusions

Mothers piece together care arrangements for their children from the time they are born until the children reach age four to make child care fit their work needs over time. The children in this sample passed through many child care arrangements in their first four years. A majority of these children experienced five or more primary nonmaternal care spells. When we count as spells the times when children returned to their mother's care, the average number of changes in primary care is more than seven. These children changed care relationships and locations with great frequency and experienced significant instability during the crucial time of their early development.

The duration of most primary care spells was very brief, with almost 60 percent of care spells lasting fewer than six months and almost 40 percent lasting less than three months. The lengths of child care spells varied considerably by the type of care; kin care and informal care spells were significantly shorter in duration than family day care and center care spells. The lengths of child care spells also increased as children got older.

The analysis of spell durations is paired here with mothers' reasons for why care arrangements end, looking beyond the fact that spell durations are short to try to understand what accounts for this. Most child care arrangements in this sample ended because of factors related to the nature and quality of the child care itself rather than because of other family and work dynamics. Child care was often unstable owing to poor quality, providers who ended care, and conflicts between providers and parents. Although work was not the direct cause of a high proportion of care exits, it affected child care most directly. More than any other factor, work shaped when and why children started care spells and whether mothers needed secondary care arrangements to correspond with their work schedules. In addition, it was often the case that much more than just child care was unstable in families' lives, particularly in the earliest years of children's lives when family and housing crises vied with the frequent changes in mothers' work and children's care. Finally, it was interesting to note that during periods of stable child care the lives of some families, like Julia's, were better anchored and that with greater stability in their children's lives, these mothers were able to work more consistently.

~ Chapter 4 ~

Child Care Concerns: "It's the Worst System Ever"

Traci is a Brooklyn native. She was born in Centerville, the same neighborhood in which she has lived almost all her life and where she now resides with her son, her daughter, and the father of her children. Some would find this quaint. Traci, on the other hand, would like nothing more than to have this be her last year in New York City.

> I want to leave New York City, for one, because my family is in South Carolina and I would have more help with my kids. And it's just a better way of life for my kids. . . . It's a harder struggle here. Unless you are rich or well off, where you have a nanny or somebody who's there for you that you trust and you know. It's just too hard here. The hustle, the bustle. Every morning, rushing to get to the train station. Rushing to get to that job. Rushing to get the kids ready to get to the day care on time so you can catch that 8:15 train. It's just too much.
> . . . I want something else for my kids.

Traci, mother of Tanya and Tariq, has precariously juggled her work and child care since she went back into the job market in 1998. Traci had been on and off public assistance since the birth of her first child, Tariq, in August 1993.

About a year after Tanya's birth in the summer of 1997, she decided to look for full-time work and began researching her child care options—which did not prove encouraging.

> When you go from receiving public assistance and then you get a job, it is so much red tape. You have to find a day care. They have a list of day cares. Then you have to run back and forth down there with all these kind of papers they want. They want pay stubs. They want children's birth certificate. They want all this stuff. . . . And you miss so many days

sometimes from your job 'cause you're trying to supply these people with all these documents to get your child into day care. Meanwhile, I'm going to lose the job because I keep running three or four days for different interviews for damn welfare. And then when you finally get the day care that's approved—'cause not all of them are approved—it's like you have to pay this much money a week or whatever. Meanwhile, they [the city] are supposed to pick up a certain amount. The day care is sending letters home in the kid's bookbag, "We have not yet received payment for such, such, such, and such." So now I have to go back down to welfare. Meanwhile, I've missed maybe two or three days on my new job, with the letter from day care stating that they haven't received any payment. Forget about it. It's the worst system ever. Ever. I'm telling you. . . . When it comes to day care and the children and your job, you almost want to give up and say, What do I do? Do I sit home and take care of the kids? But if I sit home, I can't live off the money that they giving me.

After finally getting approved by the city's Human Resources Administration, Traci put Tanya into a family day care home, which turned out to be awful. When picking a child care arrangement, Traci looked for a clean environment and did not want to see a messy bathroom or a sink full of dishes. She thought that good lighting was important, as well as bright colors and photos. She also noted how the day care provider treated the other children: "I want to see how she's going to care for that student over there when there's snot running out of his nose. I'm going to see if she's going to just wipe it, or is she going to take the time and clean it like she cares, like it's her kid." This home seemed to be devoid of all of Traci's stipulations.

The lady's house was filthy. I couldn't leave my baby there. She had like eight or ten other kids. And the two weeks that Tanya was there, she came down with the worst stomach virus. She probably ate something off her nasty floor or something. I just took her out. I figure these other parents got to know that this lady's house is filthy too. But they're dropping them off, but I'm not going to drop Tanya off. I don't care if I don't ever get a job. I didn't say anything. I just left. The lady was nice, and I didn't want to rain on her parade or whatever. I just left it alone. I'm sure [the city agency] had to know her house is a wreck. Or maybe they clean up when they come.

Traci's mother stepped in to help temporarily. She started picking Tanya up on Monday and keeping her until Friday night. Soon after, Traci found another family day care home with Miss Ernestine, whom Traci had known for a while and who watched other kids from the neighborhood. But that arrangement lasted only a few months before Traci had to find another option.

She was good. She lives right across the street. Her house was really nice and clean, but . . . one day after I picked Tanya up I noticed her lip was busted. And I immediately about-faced and knocked on the door. "What happened to Tanya today?" She said, "Oh, she was running in the playground, and she fell and almost knocked her teeth out." I said, "You wasn't going to tell me? You didn't call me. You didn't say anything." And that kinda like turned me off with her, and then that's when I started to go down the block and see if they could take care of her. I took her out.

Tanya started going to Help Thy Neighbor, the day care center "down the block," in May 1999. This center care spell worked out for a relatively long period of time, although Traci continued to keep a watchful eye on her children's care. Traci liked Help Thy Neighbor when Tanya started there, although she was still hoping to place her in Head Start, which she herself had attended as a child, as had her son, Tariq. She says that she preferred the quality of care at Head Start and that it was no cost. HRA vouchers paid most of the cost at Help Thy Neighbor, but she still had to pay $38 every week.

When Traci tried to enroll Tanya in Head Start, they told her she was not income-eligible. Traci could not gain access to her preferred care for Tanya because she worked and earned more than was permitted for participation. The eligibility standard for Head Start was set at the poverty level, dating back to the time when the program was designed as a part-time early child development program without working mothers in mind.

> It was hard to get her in the place I wanted. I had Head Start in mind, but they didn't have space. So finally when they got space, they gave me a call and told me to come down and make an application. When I told them my income and showed them my pay stubs, they told me I was not eligible. I make $10 an hour, and they say I am not eligible.
>
> I mean, I liked the center Tanya was at, but Centerville Head Start was better-quality, more activities, more professional people, people in the classrooms who are teachers. . . . Also, it was much less expensive. Paying that $38 was hard. I mean, I know it was small compared to the cost, but I only bring home like $300 or $350, and I can't pay my bills.

Tanya and Tariq stayed at Help Thy Neighbor almost two years until two more incidents prompted Traci to move them again. Traci was upset when staff had taken Tanya to the sprinklers without notifying her, especially after Traci had asked them to be extra-vigilant after Tanya experienced an asthma attack earlier that week. Then Tariq broke his arm at the school while he was wrestling. That was the last straw. Traci had known she would soon have to change centers regardless of these events because her eligibility for the HRA vouchers she used to pay for the center care during her transition from welfare to work would soon expire. She would be able to keep them at the center only if she received an ACD voucher, which she had not been able to get even though she had submitted an application two years earlier. Traci soon moved her children to Miracle Ville, a day care center that even Tanya preferred.

At Miracle Ville there are older people there, mature women, mature men. They read to the children, and they do a lot of writing. At Help Thy Neighbor they did read to the children, but they weren't capturing Tanya's interest anymore. Over here, I don't know if the technique is different 'cause I don't really get to sit in and watch, but whatever they doing, she loves them. . . . They just seem like they are there because they care about the kids, they are not just there 'cause that's their job, whereas at Help Thy Neighbor that was their job. It wasn't like they were there because of the best interest of the child. You have to care about kids in order to work with them.

Finding a primary care arrangement for Tanya while she was at work was Traci's first priority. She also had to secure a backup arrangement for nights, weekends, and unexpected events. In the beginning she had her mother; after her mother moved to South Carolina, Traci asked her neighbor down the hall, Miss Janice, if she could help out.

I also have a babysitter who picks them up on the nights that I don't get here on time. She lives down the hall—Miss Janice—I just call her and say, "I'm running late, can you pick them up for me?" She's home 'cause she usually has little kids at her home. She has two other kids at her house. And if she picks them up for a whole week, I have to give her $40. . . . I'm here within the hour. She's like my backup. You need it. You just got to have it.

When things got hectic for Miss Janice, Traci went downstairs and asked Miss Beverly if she was available.

I switched from Miss Janice to Miss Beverly 'cause Miss Janice has three little kids that she watches during the day, so she can't really help me out. And Miss Beverly's kid is like eleven or twelve. She's in fact helped me a lot in the past couple of weeks. Like if Tanya's sick, I'll call her up. I'm like, "Can you please pick up Tanya? I'm on my way." And by the time I get here she usually has her. She's really good. I don't know what I would do without her. . . . I do try to give her something, or if I go out to the store, I'll bring her back some fruits, some stuff, just to let her know that I do appreciate her. . . . She's really good. Thank God, 'cause my mother is not here. . . . I've been [in this building] so long, and they've watched me grow up, like Miss Janice has watched me grow up, Miss Beverly has watched me grow up. Those are like the pioneers of the building. I can depend on them. I can call on them when I need them. And I only call on them when I need them for one of the kids. And they know I'm good decent people, so they help out. Thank God for that.

Up to this point Traci had been doing only unreported work in the informal labor market and was not making enough to make ends meet. In October 1998 she went to an employment agency to try to find regular work. She was placed at National Copy Machines (NCM) to work as a copy operator. At NCM, Traci was assigned to operate machines at different corporate sites where she had to remain for indefinite periods of time. Her first assignment highlighted the problems between juggling work and child care.

> The J train had some trouble, so I was taking four trains to get to work and I was late a lot. And they couldn't understand that. I even had cab receipts where I jumped off the L train and took a cab from downtown Brooklyn to catch the F train to get there on time. And I had this boss that just didn't care. He didn't care that I had to drop my kids off in the morning. He didn't care how many trains I had to take. It was just crazy. And I had proof. The whole city knew that the J train wasn't going over the bridge. Why don't you know? I'm a good worker. I'm a parent. You should be happy that you have me here. It was just the worst. . . . He didn't care about anybody. I was transferred. I couldn't take it anymore. He was driving me crazy. Can you imagine taking four trains to work and four trains back home? That was crazy. I was crazy.

Traci was transferred to a new site a few months later, and she stayed there for a year and a half. She didn't get along with her manager and was fired in April 2001. She remained unemployed for a couple of weeks, living primarily off her Earned Income Tax Credit payment, or "tax refund," as she put it, until she got a new placement through her agency as a customer service representative at a cellular phone company. She preferred this job because she felt that she was learning new skills and dealing with people more than with just machines. All in all, Traci preferred working to receiving public assistance, but she regretted the restrictions that work placed on her ability to care for her children.

> I'm better off working because it gives me a sense of self-satisfaction. When I was home receiving public assistance, I was just there more for my children. If they were sick, I didn't have to worry about calling in or taking the day off, threatening losing the job. An employer doesn't understand that your child may be sick for a day or a week. That's the thing that messes you up when you work and you have children. You can never say, my children aren't going to get sick until I have sick days. Sometimes in the middle of the night the kids have a fever, in the middle of the night they may have an asthma attack. So that's the only thing—when I received the public assistance, I was always there for them. And when I'm working, some days they may not feel that good and I still send them to the day care, because I have to make a living for them. That's what I don't like about work.

Traci also worried that her family responsibilities led to job insecurity.

[I've had trouble with work] ever since I've had my kids 'cause you're out more than the average person. Or you're out more than the girl who doesn't have any kids, especially when you have two children with asthma. So you always have your boss have the screw face for you today because you were out on Monday and you know nobody likes you to be out on Monday. So always there's that pressure. I haven't had a full check in weeks 'cause I'm running to Medicaid or this one is sick.

Traci's life has always been short on stability. The father of her children was incarcerated twice on drug-related charges. The first time was for nine months when Tariq was one year old. The second time was for three years when Tanya was only two months old. He was released from prison in the summer of 2000 and has lived with Traci and his children since.

I almost think that I know he learned his lesson because he was taken away from his family. . . . I see the amount of time he spends with the kids now and how every little thing matters to him now. . . . I'm just glad he's here to be part of the kids' life and stuff like that. 'Cause they really need him, especially my son. Well, Tanya too. My son used to cry for him and cry for him. Not only that he was crying for him, you know what he'd say to me? "Mommy, I need him." That used to just tear me to pieces. You don't even know.

While Traci was obviously glad to have that chapter of her life closed, she also said that the extra income derived from his drug dealing had been necessary for survival.

But, you know, I know drugs are bad and everything, but you know what, thank God he did sell drugs, because the months that they gave me maybe $100 in food stamps and I was pregnant with my daughter, we wouldn't have been able to make it without dirty drug money. It's not good. I wouldn't want him to do it again because at least now I can go to sleep. I don't have to worry about anybody maybe following him. I don't have to worry about my children. But it helped us. We needed the money sometimes to survive. Now I would rather be broke and struggling, but at that time I was pregnant and we did need it.

Traci most wants to put an end to her struggles. The last thing she wants is for her children to relive her life.

I grew up here. I want them to grow up someplace else. . . . Even today, my son wanted to hang out around here, and when he goes outside around here, he's okay for a little while, then they end up having a fight. It's always a fight. I don't like that. . . . What happened to football and baseball? We used to do that around here. We used to play double-Dutch. And then we have so many young girls, and their main thing is

Figure 4.1 *Dynamics Timeline for Traci and Tanya's Story*

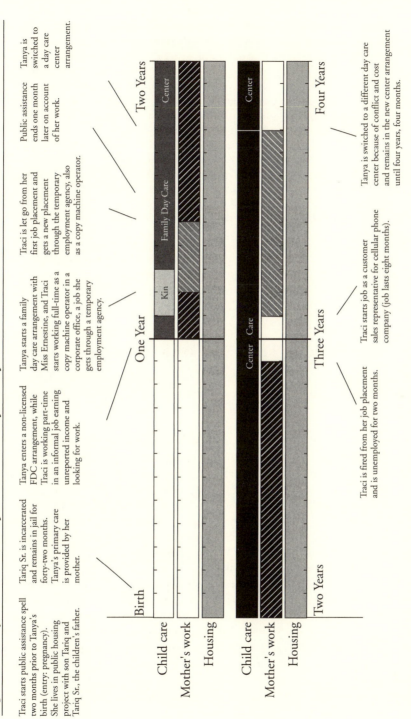

Source: Author's compilation.

to have a baby. I feel responsible for that in a lot of ways. . . . Maybe if we had gotten a husband first and did things differently instead of them imitating our just having a baby out of wedlock, maybe they would have went and got a husband or they would have went away to college. I feel like the examples that have been set by me and other women in my age category wasn't really good. You have young girls that maybe will like the way you look or like the way you carry yourself, so they want to be like that. And when they see me with the baby [Tariq] and just a boyfriend that was a drug dealer, that's what they think life is about. And it's not. In a lot of ways we are responsible for our environment. . . . The guys want to sell drugs. That's like the highlight of their life. The girls want to have a baby, that's what they think life is all about. I don't want my kids to feel like that's all they can get or that's all they can do. Even though you teach them at home, you go to school, you get your education, you go to college, you can be anything you want, but it's the peer pressure. Even right now, my daughter, sometimes she's pushing her baby stroller and has the basketball in her shirt. It's not going to happen like that. You are not going to be walking down Fences Avenue pushing a stroller and pregnant with a baby. What she sees. I don't want that.

Mothers Making Their Way with Child Care Worries

Traci and Tanya's story illustrates how child care is one of many complex elements of family life in low-income communities. For Traci and her family, it is not just that child care involves a lot of the child's time and is complicated, often unsatisfactory, and subject to frequent change. These aspects of Tanya's care were also related to the nature of Traci's work—unstable contingency labor that offered low pay and no benefits (see figure 4.1).

Traci struggled to find child care and to get care that was subsidized and long-lasting. She could not find child care when she decided to begin work and make her way off of welfare. So first she did some informal, unreported work that she had "rather not talk about" to stretch out her welfare check while she tried to locate full-time child care so she could pursue work through a temporary employment agency. At times she had to use care that was unsatisfactory. Traci remained wary, however, and vigilantly watched for problems in care and was quick to pull her children out. She regularly searched for other care possibilities, even though the long hours in care were hard on her and on her children. When she paid for care, it was more than she could afford on her sole income. She did not find much quality child care to choose from and had no sure way to decipher quality except to heed signals like the appearance of the setting and the provider's attitude toward the children in her charge. Tanya experienced five primary care spells in her early childhood and four secondary arrangements. Traci juggled care arrangements when what she most wanted was stability for Tanya and a better life for both of her children.

Traci and Tanya's story also shows how child care choices and dynamics are shaped by the conditions of urban poverty, which have influenced many mothers' own developments. Traci is a forceful presence. You can see her fighting for her children. In this way she is like Annette, Julia, and many of the other mothers who also grew up in the rough-and-tumble struggle of life in the "villes," "valleys," "points," and "harbors" of the city. The lives lie in the shadows of the city's stately heights and glistening towers of wealth and opportunity. Traci had few avenues to the world of work, and little formal work experience prior to parenting. None of the jobs she held during the time of this study were managed with a working parent in mind. She regularly had transportation problems, but working as a temporary employee, she was cut no slack for these problems or to cope with the emergencies that arose with her daughter's care. She could only harbor the guilt of being forced to send her sick asthmatic child to day care while she was at work and expend her rage toward the child care provider at the end of the day when her daughter was more ill than when she dropped her off. In each job Traci continued to work as much as she could despite transportation, child care, and family problems, testing her employers' patience as long as she could. But eventually she would fail those tests and move to find the next job.

Traci has had a man she loves in her life, but while he is devoted to her and his children, he has also been incarcerated twice when she most needed him. He dealt drugs, the only way he has been able to find to provide for his children. At times Traci has had to weigh the risks of such activity, and her fears about it, against the reality of her family's struggles to stave off hunger. She probably still does not know where she stands on this. What she does know is that she does not want her children to know about this world and to face these no-win situations. Her children interact only with other children who are poor. They model themselves after the young adults they see and role-play the limited possibilities offered them. She worries that they might be condemned to follow the common courses for boys and girls in Centerville. She does not yet have a way to get them out of there through her work, and she thinks that little of what they have experienced in their early care environments has helped prepare them to find a way out either.

Traci's constraints in making care arrangements and the quality of the care she has used were among the universal concerns of low-income families in this study. In this chapter, I interpret mothers' concerns about piecing together child care while also coping with the many other pressures of urban life in low-income neighborhoods. When we view care choices within this context, it is possible to begin to distinguish between the impact of living in a poor urban community on children's care and some of the more universal problems that parents have with child care across social contexts.

Child Care as a Component of Contemporary Urban Family Life

William Julius Wilson (1987, 1993, 1996) has offered a comprehensive model of contemporary urban poverty. Wilson focuses on the interaction of several social problems that have led to the deterioration of family life in inner-city neighborhoods, and on two in particular: the decline in urban labor markets and the out-migration of better-employed residents.[1] The combination of these factors isolates the remaining poor inner-city residents in neighborhoods with greater concentrations of absolute poverty and weakened socializing institutions such as schools and churches, and it reduces their access to jobs. These interrelated dynamics have contributed to dramatic changes in urban family life: male joblessness and incarceration have reduced the possibilities of marriage, leading to disproportionate numbers of single-mother families. One adult then has to struggle to survive in the roles of sole parent and sole income earner. At the same time that families' personal resource bases have declined, there have been losses in child-serving institutions within these isolated communities. Together these constrain mothers' choices and diminish their ability to attain the child care they prefer for their children.

In *When Work Disappears: The World of the New Urban Poor* (1996), Wilson and his team of researchers in the Urban Poverty and Family Life Study in Chicago analyze an enormous amount of demographic data and interpret interviews collected from residents of low-income neighborhoods. Wilson and the neighborhood respondents themselves describe in poignant terms the elements of what Wilson terms "the new urban poverty" and the ways in which these disadvantages truly afflict and limit the lives of urban residents, including:

- Joblessness

- Declines in residential real estate and the deterioration and abandonment of homes

- The loss of businesses, basic services, and legitimate enterprise

- The flight of the middle class and any signs of affluence

- Increasing concentrations of poverty, lone-mother families, and dependence on welfare

- Poorly functioning public schools in deteriorating condition with dim expectations of learning

- Crime and high levels of concern for the safety of residents, especially children and the elderly

- Violence

- Increases in drug consumption, abuse, and trafficking and the fear and havoc these cause

- The emptiness of the streets and the decline of meaningful social exchange

- Growing disconnection and isolation from the larger city and society

- The dimming of residents' personal outlook and concern for their neighborhoods

Peter Marcuse (1997) has used the term "outcast ghetto"—a ghetto of the excluded—to refer to neighborhoods that exhibit these characteristics. People living in the outcast ghetto are removed from the dominant society both physically and economically. Although some members of the outcast ghetto may be peripherally tied to the mainstream economy through low-paying jobs, part-time or occasional labor, or illegal activities such as drug dealing, the ghetto economy remains isolated and separate from the mainstream. Loic Wacquant (1993, 368) further characterizes the outcast ghetto as lacking social potency and social organization; it is "an impossible community," he notes, "perpetually divided against itself." Wacquant (1993), Wilson (1987, 1996), and others (Coleman 1990; Sampson 1992) have developed a central research focus on how *neighborhood social organization*—defined broadly by Wilson (1996, 20) as "the extent to which residents of a neighborhood are able to maintain effective social control and realize their common goals"— serves as a critical perspective for understanding how urban residents adapt to their conditions.[2]

Recent empirical research studies have focused on the economic disadvantages in these neighborhoods and the impacts of poverty on child and adolescent development outcomes. Robert Sampson, Jeffrey Morenoff, and Felton Earls (1999) highlight three dimensions of neighborhood social organization that affect the lives of children: the neighborhood context of childrearing, reciprocated exchange or the exchange of information among adults with respect to child-rearing, and the informal social control and mutual support of children. Sampson, Raudenbush, and Earls (1997) argue that extreme resource deprivation in poor, urban communities, combined with racial exclusion, acts as a centrifugal force that hinders such collective efficacy. Even in areas where personal ties are strong, distrust, fear, uncertainty, and economic dependency are likely to reduce effective collective aspects of child-rearing. (See appendix A for more information on the effects of poverty on childhood development.)

Wilson's social isolation model provides an essential context for understanding how the relative isolation of families in low-income neighborhoods places structural and cultural limits on mothers' child care choices. Traci herself discusses the contribution of many of these factors to the instability in her children's lives and to her fears for her children. She also describes the effect on her children of their father's incarceration. Paternal incarceration was common across the sample: more than one-third of the fathers of children in the study served jail time at some point in their children's first four years. In Traci's discussion of her family's reliance on informal and illegal work in the drug economy, it is clear that, while participation in these activities was sometimes perceived as a financial necessity, it created enormous fear, uncertainty, instability, and moral ambiguity in family life. Traci expresses concern about how the neighborhood's culture will influence her children's development, particularly when they approach adolescence. She regrets seeing children internalize what they observe and invent violent games with their peers, and she even fears Tanya's early fertility while her daughter was still just a preschooler. These fears drove Traci to want to leave this environment, even though it was her knowledge of the environment that gave her some of her only advantages in making child care choices to match her work and support her family. These same fears made Traci vigilant about her children's safety; she would react forcefully to the first sign of problems in their care, even though these responses sometimes seemed like overreactions that led to quick care exits and disruption for her children.

Given the significant increase in work by low-income mothers like Traci over the last several years, "child care instability" can be added to the elements of the new urban poverty. The problems of finding and keeping child care have become a part of the urban poverty landscape as child care has grown to join the troubled institutions of schools, residential housing, commerce, and policing that Wilson identified.

When Work Appears: Child Care and Work Interactions

The mothers in this sample worked a lot during their children's earliest years. Most worked at least one job with full-time hours, and one-third of the sample had more than one job at one time during the study.[3] This high work effort made the sample ideal for observing how work and child care interact in the context of high work participation, which is the direction that urban family life and American social policy have taken.

Mothers in the sample were employed in a wide range of jobs with varying degrees of stability, and most of the jobs were relatively low-paying. Traci earned just under $10 per hour in her two jobs as a temporary office worker and a customer service representative for a cellular phone company; that rate put her just above the mean for the sample, $9.27 per hour. Table 4.1 lists all of the mothers in the sample and the primary jobs they held at the time of the initial interview. They were all working, since this was one selection criterion for the sample. Their jobs included clerical and office positions, work in health care, social services, and retail, and mandatory welfare-to-work assignments. The number of primary jobs that mothers held during these four years ranged from one to seven, with an average of more than three.

In addition to her two on-the-books jobs, Traci worked in the informal labor market for a few months before her job with the office machines company. While she made the switch from the informal labor market to more formal work, she ended up in the contingency labor force, and she eventually lost this job. She worked full-time for most of Tanya's early childhood but still found it difficult to afford what she considered decent child care. She paid a relatively small proportion, less than one-sixth of the cost of Tanya's center care, since she received child subsidies for the bulk of the cost, but her share of the costs still amounted to more than 12 percent of her income.

Some mothers who worked more than one job or worked nontraditional hours required more complex, multiple care arrangements. Mothers who worked one job with traditional hours also regularly pieced together primary and secondary arrangements because individual care arrangements did not fully match up with their work schedules. Traci, who worked in a series of office jobs, had a traditional work schedule and full-time care yet still required regular secondary care arrangements at the end of the day because it took her a long time to commute from work and because some days she could not leave work right at five o'clock. She made four secondary care arrangements over a two-year span, mostly relying on neighbors who provided the care as an in-kind favor because Traci could not afford to pay much for this care.

Rhonda also arranged a complicated combination of care to fit her work schedule, which varied only slightly from traditional work hours. Her work started at 7:30 A.M., an hour earlier than the start of Steven's pre-K program. She relied on her sister-in-law for morning child care for Steven and her eight-year-old daughter, but this caused daily anxiety and job insecurity:

> I usually get [Steven] up at 6:30 because when [her sister-in-law] comes at 6:45 like she's supposed to, they are eating breakfast. All she has to do besides get herself ready to be here is to put on their coats and go to school at 8:00. So every morning I am watching that clock and worrying if she is going to get here on time, and like today I could not go to work because she came at 7:15, and by that time it's too late. I have to be at work at 7:30. I am a school safety officer, so that is when my work happens, and if I am late I get written up, and if you are written up too many times, forget about it. I am a new employee, and I can't lose my job. I called the desk sergeant and excused myself today for a family emergency . . . 'cause it's better than being late. I just started a couple months ago, and I have been late and written up three times already.

Rhonda had worked a series of short-term jobs, but this was her first full-time job since Steven was born. She worried about losing the security of a steady job, especially while she was still in a probationary stage. Matching the

Table 4.1 *Mother's Primary Jobs and Number of Jobs from Child's Birth to Age Four*

Mother's Name	Job at Initial Interview	Number of Jobs
Angela	Payroll and timekeeper	3
Annette	Social services assistant	3
Bernadette	Day care center substitute teacher	3
Brittany	Day care provider	1
Cassandra	Nurse-practitioner	3
Clarabel	Mail clerk	1
Dana	Administrator	2
Diane	Advertising assistant	5
Dona	Stadium vendor	6
Edwina	Child care aide	2
Felicidad	Secretary	1
Francine	Health care provider	5
Gloria	Office assistant	4
Griselda	Cafeteria worker	3
Harriet	Receptionist	3
Hortensia	Cleaning service	4
Inez	WEP—office assistant at nonprofit	4
Iris	Retail—pharmacy	5
Josephine	Retail—photo shop	7
Julia	Office assistant	6
Kari	Computer operator	1
Kiesha	WEP—custodial service at nonprofit	2
Lisa	Administrative assistant	3
Lola	School aide	4
Magdelena	Sales—health product (self-employed)	2
Matilda	Retail-sales—drugstore chain	4
Nadia	Bookkeeper	3
Nora	Real estate office assistant	4
Oona	Sales—department store (seasonal)	3
Pamela	Services aide at homeless shelter	1
Querida	Hair braider	4
Ramona	Telemarketing	5
Rhonda	School crossing guard	5
Rita	Photographer's assistant	3

Table 4.1 *Continued*

Mother's Name	Job at Initial Interview	Number of Jobs
Sandra	Scheduler—media advertisements	3
Sara	Spanish tutor	4
Traci	Copier operator (office)	4
Uma	Personal trainer	5
Vanya	Customer service—telephone company	3
Winnie	Assistant—commercial advertising	4
Yolanda	Eligibility worker—city agency	3
Zina	Office assistant—community college	3
Average		3.43

Source: Author's compilation.

timing of work and care was a common problem. Lisa, who was making her way off welfare, participated for more than a year in a community-based job training program that she had arranged to count toward her work requirements. Then, when her daughter Millie was two years old, the city required Lisa to go to a job center in Queens, which was more than an hour away from Centerville in Brooklyn where she lived. This created a child care problem: she had to be at work by 9:00 A.M., but Millie's day care did not start until 8:00 A.M., making drop-off at care and on-time arrival at work impossible for her.

> When Millie was two, [HRA] said I now have to do job search, and they sent me to Queens, and I would have to take two trains and a bus. It was too far to get my daughter to day care, and they are telling me I am not allowed to be late or I will be sanctioned. I said, how can you tell me not to be late when you want me here at 9:00 A.M. but the day care doesn't open until 8:00 A.M.? . . . Then I had the same problem at the other end. I had to get back to pick her up at 6 P.M. . . . . I thought I was going to have to risk being sanctioned, but then that [job] center closed down.

Francine was working two jobs and many hours when her son Fortune was almost four years old. On weekends she worked in a residential nursing facility for disabled adults. After eight previous primary care spells for Fortune, she had finally arranged reliable care for him during the week that combined pre-K and an after-school placement at a public school. She still had to scramble for care to accommodate her weekend work schedule. For this, she relied on kin and informal care from her mother, her sister, and her best friend. None of these were always reliable, and she was constantly juggling them. The secondary care was hard to arrange, and it caused some anguish for Francine because she was not sure if the time spent away from her children was worth the few extra dollars she netted after paying her family to watch them:

> It is almost not worth it for me [to work], since I only make $8 an hour in the second job and pay my mother and sister $50 each for the [two days and one night of] child care. . . . In the end I'm not making nothing, but I am keeping the job, having a little [left over], and giving some to my kin . . . 'cause they don't work, and this way I help them out some, but I cannot afford [it] . . . and besides, it is a lot of hours [to care for her children]—more than they would do if it wasn't for my work.

The mothers in the sample experienced a wide range of work dynamics across their children's early years. Mothers averaged 3.4 changes in their primary employment over the course of four years. In many cases they also experienced shifts in their schedules and other work changes that affected their child care but were not full work exits. Frequent changes in employment combined with an average of five primary care spells added up to significant turbulence in these families' lives. Adding to the difficulty were changes in secondary care arrangements and second jobs and changes in family and housing situations. Other studies have similarly found that children in low-income families experience a high level of turbulence in a great many aspects of their lives, and significantly more than is experienced by children in higher-income families (Moore, Vandivere, and Ehrle 2000). Mothers have no choice but to make decisions for their children's care within the constraints and turmoil they face, but they nevertheless worry about the paths their children's care will take.

Mothers' Views of Their Children's Care Paths

Between birth and age four, children take their first steps, form attachments, and reach many developmental milestones. Mothers negotiate their journey and all their care arrangements within the context of family life and with any available resources. In this study, mothers reveal some of their key concerns about the care terrain they faced:

- Their children started child care away from their homes earlier than they might have liked.

- The first care arrangement was often the hardest to make.

- Their children were in care for too much time and in too many care arrangements at one time.

- Over time, their children passed through many care arrangements, with frequent disruptions.

- Mothers transitioned their children into the care they wanted much later than they would have liked.

- Child care subsidies were hard to come by and hard to keep.

- The care their children received was often not the right care for their health needs.

- It was hard to find care for a sick child or in an emergency.

Care Too Early

One of the first decisions mothers face is how long they will remain their child's sole caregiver before going to work. The length of time after childbirth that mothers in the sample were the primary care provider for their children varied from one week to twenty-one months. The factors that determined when they started work included whether they were returning to a job they had held prior to giving birth; what their work options were if they were not returning to a prior job; the available care; and other related factors, including their family, housing, and income situations. All eighteen mothers who were returning to a previous job did so within six months, and thirteen of them returned to work within the first three months. Thirty-five of the forty-two mothers placed their children in some form of care arrangement in the first year. The vast majority put their children in care so they could work, and two mothers used child care in the first year primarily for reasons related to their health.

The early labor force participation rates for mothers in the sample after their child's birth were comparable to those found in large national datasets. While 60 percent of mothers in the United States were working in their child's first year (U.S. Department of Labor 2001), 79 percent of mothers in the sample did so. National data show that for mothers working in their child's first year, the average time before returning to work was three months (Hofferth 1999). For this sample, it was about five months. Though on average the women in the sample started work a little later, proportionately more women in the sample worked during their child's first year compared to the national average. The sample is mostly single mothers, for whom work participation rates are higher, particularly with the relatively rapid recent increase in lone mothers' work rates. Also, since this sample was selected from among those working when their children were ages two to three, we might expect higher early work participation levels in the sample as well.

Most of the mothers wanted to be home with their children for longer periods than they were able, in the belief that doing so was important for their children's sense of security and the mother-child primary relationship. Cassandra, a single mother of three children who worked as a nurse-practitioner at a hospital near where she lived, expresses this sentiment strongly when she talks about leaving her youngest son, Cedric, in his first care arrangement.

> I took a leave from my job when Cedric was born in 1998. I worked right up to the time I had him because he came early. I went back to work four months later. I felt it was much sooner than he would have liked . . . but you know, me and the father are not married and we do not live together, so I have to work for myself and the children. It bothered me, because I had been able to be home with [my two older boys] for most of the first two or three years. I felt that helped them get started, and I feel I did not do well by Cedric by going back to work so soon.

Cassandra says that she became depressed for the next six months or so. She felt guilty about "just dropping my little baby at the provider's house and returning almost nine hours later to pick him up," but her earnings were the family's main source of income. Cassandra had just gotten a full-time position within the past year after a series of per-diem jobs with nursing agencies, and she was pleased with the newfound security it offered. Although she believed there was a trade-off between working to maintain her family's living standard and making an early care arrangement for Cedric, she said she did not have much of a choice: "I had to work for my family."

Bernadette, a twenty-three-year-old mother with a more limited work history, describes how she felt when she first placed her son Paul with a caregiver. She compares Paul's history, which included child care for most of his early life, with that of his older brother Andre, who stayed at home with her until he was almost three.

> I was on public assistance when I needed to start working, and so Paul started at the provider's house when he was seven months. . . . I was scared to leave him, and I wanted to be the one to care for him when he was little, like I had with Andre. . . . He is attached to her, but when I first started to take him, he would start crying very loudly when I would leave him. He did that for months. The provider said he would stop crying after ten minutes of being coaxed with the cars and toys he'd brought along, but it was very hard to hear him crying from the other side of the door and then get into the elevator and go to my training.

Diane, who had never received welfare and started working within the first few months of her first two children's births, returned to work earlier than she expected or wanted after her daughter Adrienne was born. Diane was fired from a job that would have given her paid maternity leave a month before giving birth. She had to begin work immediately to support her family rather than take the three months she had planned to stay home with Adrienne.

A week after Adrienne was born, I got a job through a temp agency. I did not want to go back to work right after Adrienne was born—she was only a week old. If I hadn't been fired, I would have had maternity leave that was paid. And the maternity leave was six weeks, but because of what happened at Can-Do Copier, I had to go back to work. I had no time to arrange child care, so Adrienne went to my mother's, who lives an hour from here in Brooklyn. Her father drove, and he picked her up and dropped her off every day on his way to and from his job.

Many mothers in the study expected to work relatively soon after having their children. Cassandra was thirty-nine years old and had previously struggled on and off welfare for several years. While she received some financial support from her sons' fathers, she assumed that her family's self-sufficiency was only attainable through her work income. For Cassandra, early child care placement was a necessary trade-off.

The same was true for Bernadette and Diane, even though both had partners who were involved fathers and lived with them and contributed to the family income. However, their partners' incomes were either irregular (in Bernadette's case) or less than their own income (in Diane's case). Both now believed that one parent's income was not sufficient or reliable and that both parents needed to work. Diane had always expected that she would work while she had young children, even though her children's father helped support the family, because her earnings were needed for their economic survival.

Bernadette's initial expectation as a mother was that her children would be primarily in her care. She received public assistance. She lived with Pablo, her sons' father, without the welfare department's knowledge. He contributed his income from restaurant work, but this income was unsteady and not always enough to meet their family needs. She joined the labor force after Pablo lost his job and the welfare department had begun to pressure her to get a job.

Bernadette's expectations of motherhood, work, and child care changed over time after she began working. She was a relatively young mother, still moving through internships at the time of my first interview with her. She believed then that three years was the ideal length of time for the mother to be the primary, if not sole, caregiver to her child. By a later interview she had successfully started her first full-time job, left welfare altogether, and come to see that her family's financial condition had been significantly improved when her higher wages were combined with the children's fathers' irregular earnings from informal work. At this point she was both earning and working more than she had expected and was pleased with the consistency of Paul's care with his family child care provider. She then revised her preference for how long mothers should stay at home with their children to between one and two years, "if you can find a good provider."

Some mothers report that they moved their children into care early because a particular and trusted caregiver was available. This eased some of their anxiety over not meeting their maternal obligations. Sandra worked regularly as an adult. She returned to work within the first month after her daughter Shaniqua was born because at the time she was still living with her mother, who was the only person Sandra could trust with her child. Yet she still regrets missing the opportunity of that early time with Shaniqua and has considered what she might have done if she could have stayed at home with her daughter.

> I think that if people could be at-home moms, that's the greatest thing, for as long as possible, or even up until it's time for them to start school. They can learn so much. They're like sponges. . . . I would do all the things that I did when I was in Head Start. I would have reading time— even when she was a baby, I used to set out an hour every day when I came home from work and like sit her in her little bouncer and read a book. I would have the activity time and the snack time. I would allot these different times: now it's time to read, now it's time to color, now it's time to do the puzzle, let's do the sing-a-long now. That is what I wish I could do, but I had to get back to work to support us. . . . I was living with my mom. So my mom would babysit her and I could go to work.

Kin care, especially by a grandmother who lived with the family or nearby, was often used for early care arrangements. Other mothers used other female kin, including their sisters, aunts, or cousins. When Hortensia, an immigrant from Honduras, first went to work for a home cleaning service, she only considered leaving her son Ivan with a relative, in this case her cousin. Hortensia's worries about not being the primary caregiver were similar to those of many other mothers.

> Working when you are a mother is hard because you are sacrificing your babies; no one takes care of the child like the mother, especially when they are babies—you have that bond with them. As the mother you know when to feed him, how to bathe him. . . . It does not make me feel good leaving him with my cousin when he was so young, but I had nothing, and the [public] assistance was not enough. I trust only my cousin; she is good, but she cannot know him like I do.

Like Bernadette, Hortensia felt some ambivalence about leaving her child in nonmaternal care, in part because of her own traditional upbringing. She had anticipated that she would stay at home and raise her children as her primary occupation in early adulthood, as her own mother had done. She explains that after living in America for a while she began to want a job and the fulfillment of providing for her family. "Working makes me feel better. . . . It helps me to grow more than I expected . . . and to help my whole family grow more."

Starting the first nonmaternal care arrangement is an important step in children's care paths, and mothers have to weigh their basic need to work with their child's developmental needs. Most mothers returned to work sooner than they preferred.[4] The women in the sample needed to work to provide for their family's income, and some were compelled to move off welfare. Their work expectations often conflicted with their expectations of motherhood. Many of the mothers maintained the stay-at-home model of motherhood as an ideal preference. Even though they worked out of economic necessity, they worried that failing to meet their maternal obligations harmed their children's sense of security.

The First Care Was Hard to Get

When first seeking child care, mothers started with limited information about care options but quickly learned that some options were unavailable and others were beyond their means. Many mothers made their initial care arrangements with the only available provider, usually a family member or friend. Initial care spells were most often kin care or some other kind of home-based, informal care arrangement, like father's care or low-cost care with a nonrelative. Table 4.2 shows that of the thirty-five mothers in the sample who made care arrangements in their children's first year, sixteen, or almost half, were in kin care.

These mothers found that care by relatives, friends, or the child's father was usually the most immediately available at a time when options appeared most limited. These types of care also most resembled their children's home environment.

When Angela made her first care arrangement for her son Mark with a woman in her neighborhood, Ms. Watson, it was the only available option she could find.

Table 4.2　*Distribution and Duration of Initial Child Care Spells Started in Year One for Children in the Sample*

Care Arrangement	Number of Initial Spells	Average Duration (Months)
Father care	4	2.8
Kin care	16	4.6
Informal care	6	5.2
Family day care	5	10.3
Center care	1	3.0
Other	3	5.7
Total	35	5.4

Source: Author's compilation.

The first home care provider I used was Ms. Watson, who lives in the building next to me. She was advertising for children. I knew her for twenty years, but I did not like her . . . well . . . because I knew her for twenty years. I just didn't like her personality, and she had too many kids. I knew that before I left the kids with her, but I was in a desperate situation. She was the only care I knew about that was for sure, and I needed child care right away, and the list ACD [Agency for Child Development] provided was not satisfactory enough. They weren't sure who was licensed and who had spaces. They gave me a list of providers who I was supposed to get in contact with. Well, a lot of them didn't call me back. Some, their licenses were still pending, and I should call them back in a month or so. It was just crazy. So I was desperate. So I just went with her, and I knew it was going to be a short period of time if I could find something else.

Provider availability was the most common reason for initial care entries. In twenty-nine of the thirty-five first primary care spells made in children's first years (83 percent), mothers say they chose that care arrangement because the provider was the only option they had.

The cost of many of the initial care spells was often lower, at a time when mothers had less income. For example, kin care that was used for initial care arrangements was less likely to be paid for than kin care arrangements that came later: only one-quarter of the sixteen initial kin care arrangements were paid, compared with more than half of all kin care that was paid. The four father care arrangements were free, and three of the five family child care arrangements were fully subsidized, requiring no parental payment. In total, mothers paid for care in only twelve of the thirty-five initial care spells for children starting nonmaternal care in their first year, while over the four years they paid for care in 55 percent of all the care spells.

After making their initial care arrangements, many mothers found that their first primary care spells did not last long. The average duration of the initial care spells made in the first year was 5.4 months, 25 percent shorter than the average duration of all care spells. The first care spells were shorter in part because they were disproportionately made up of father care and informal care, which are on average significantly shorter than other types. As the mothers in this study would learn, these types of care were often the least stable because the provider was not necessarily committed to working in child care but just trying to help out when the mother needed to get started on her work path.

Too Much Time in Child Care

The amount of time that children spent in care away from home was a common concern of many of the mothers. As we saw in chapter 2 (table 2.5), at the time of the initial interviews, when the children were between ages two and three, they were in nonmaternal care an average of more than fifty hours a week. Bernadette, who was unhappy with how early her son Paul started in child care, was also concerned about how much time he spent away from her.

> Paul is with his provider more than me. I think Luiza is great, and I am glad he has been with her so long, but I only wish he did not spend more time with her than he does with me when he is so small. She [his provider] has seen him do everything first—she saw him walk first, she heard him say his first word.

Like Bernadette, Annette expresses the same wish that many mothers had—wanting more of her time to be involved in her child's care. She wanted to rearrange her schedule to better meet what she saw as her maternal obligations and to spend "more family time" with both of her children:

> I like my work situation. In terms of child care and being with my children, I wish I could work until 3:00 P.M. or so and have more time caring for the children and not have them away from home and me for so long. That would be better, but you cannot have that. I know by his reactions and his acting out that he spends too much time among providers. It is so much time spent away from home; it cannot be good for him.

Magdelena, an immigrant mother who had primarily used family child care in her daughter's first two years of life, says that her daughter Marisa loved Viola, her provider. While she was glad her daughter became attached to Viola, she wanted Marisa to primarily be in her own care, and she changed her work to try to accomplish this.

> I am lucky to have found Viola—she is so good with the children, and she lives right down the hall—but I do think that in this country the children sometimes love the babysitter more because they are with them more. That is why I want to try to work less hours, and work this kind of job [selling diet and health products based from home] so that she can be with me and I can still be working.

Most mothers were not able to claim this level of independence by arranging their own work schedule. Others who were worried about the time their children spent in care had no expectation of being able to arrange things differently. Felicidad expresses this sentiment about her two daughters' care arrangements, at ages four and two.

> Sometimes I wish I did not have to work so much and see them so little during the week. But you have to work so much to make enough to sup-

port your family, so what can you do? You do what you have to do. I am
with them on weekends and after work.

Annette, Magdelena, and Felicidad all worked full-time traditional jobs
with steady work schedules over time, and all were able to find child care that
converged with their work schedule. Mothers who worked nontraditional
hours, changed jobs frequently, or had primary care arrangements with limited care hours had to make more complicated multiple care arrangements.

Some mothers, because they worked multiple jobs or worked hours that
did not match most available care hours, had to place their children in care
for extraordinary amounts of time to accommodate their work. Kari used the
same care arrangement for her daughter Jaya for almost three years mostly because of the extraordinary number of hours that Tella looked after Jaya—an
average of seventy-eight hours per week, the most of any arrangement in the
sample.

> I kept Jaya with the provider who lives in the Bronx where we used to
> live even after we moved back to [Highwall Valley] two years ago. I did
> not think I could find child care like that here given I work 12:00 P.M. to
> 9:00 P.M. . . . Sometimes I leave Jaya there overnight for two or three days
> because it does not make sense to pick her up that late and bring her
> back. . . . Also, when the provider goes away, like to visit her family, I
> have to let Tella take Jaya with her, like to Providence one time for a
> week, and last month to Santo Domingo for a month.

More often, mothers who needed care for so many hours used multiple
care arrangements. Francine, a single mother with three children, worked two
jobs, which together added up to almost seventy-five work hours per week.
She had reliable center care for her son Fortune during weekday work hours
but had to scramble for care on the weekends. She primarily used kin and informal care, which were not always reliable, so she juggled these secondary
arrangements.

> My mother wants them sometimes, and sometimes she don't want to do
> it 'cause she old, and then it's my sister, and she watches them, but she
> won't do things with them. I will leave them at times with my best
> friend, and they like that 'cause they have kids their age, but I feel bad
> about that 'cause it's too much for her—she works all week, and then she
> has four boys runnin' round her house.

One consequence of the long hours that children needed to be in child
care was that mothers often had to use multiple care arrangements at the same
time. As described in chapter 2, thirty-nine of the forty-two mothers made
more than one care arrangement, and secondary arrangements accounted for
one-fifth of children's care hours. Most of the mothers who worked full-time

needed full-day care, but some were unable to make that kind of arrangement. Finding child care that covered their work hours was especially difficult for low-income mothers whose work opportunities did not always fit the formalized child care schedules of most centers and family day care homes.

Over time the mothers learned to pick care that offered longer care hours; increasingly they used family child care and center care as these became available. At the same time they continued to use kin care and informal care arrangements to supplement their primary care and fully cover the hours when they needed child care. The need to find care to cover many hours and to piece together primary with secondary care arrangements added a burden to their families' lives and further complicated their children's development.

Too Many Care Arrangements over Time

Most of the children in this sample passed through many care arrangements in different settings with different providers in the short period of their early lives. As we saw in chapter 4, children in the sample experienced between two and nine primary care spells other than their mother's care, with an average of more than five. There were many breakdowns in care arrangements over time, and as a result, care spells were short in duration, averaging just over seven months.

As some of the stories have shown, early child care can be highly unstable; mothers are constantly making new arrangements of varying quality, and children must adjust to these new arrangements. Annette moved Aaron through six care spells of varying durations—from an informal care arrangement of three weeks to his longest completed care spell of nine months.

> Aaron has been in so many child care situations and has had a hard time. The change is hard for him—he needs adjustment time, he acts aggressive and tough, but he is scared by an uncomfortable situation. He demonstrates now when he is unhappy, when he does not feel comfortable with a new provider and other children. He needs to work on his emotional development and learn to express himself with words instead of demonstrations. That is why speech therapy and emotional counseling is important—so he can express himself. He may be behind some of the other children in other stuff like learning numbers and colors, but his bigger issue is getting along with people . . . and it's because he has been passed along through so many hands.

Nadia, a single mother with two children who worked as a bookkeeper for a neighborhood-based company that managed low-income housing units, struggled to find adequate care for her daughter, Lana, so that she could work and provide for Lana's developmental needs. After caring for Lana for two and a half months on maternity leave, Nadia returned to work and left her daughter with a family friend who lived nearby. Like other mothers in the sample, she initially had few choices and limited information about where to leave her child. This was the only care option she knew about, and at $60 a week it was all she could afford.

Nadia used this home-based child care with the family friend for eleven months until she moved to an apartment in Highwall Valley and her mother moved with her and initially provided care for Lana. This care spell lasted only three months, and when her mother moved out, Nadia had to scramble to find another care arrangement. For almost five months, Nadia could not find any consistent care. She usually brought Lana to work with her, but that made her work much more difficult to do. She applied to community agencies and to the city for child care assistance, and she was placed on many waiting lists. She wanted to arrange appropriate care to address the delays in Lana's development, but out of necessity she applied for any care she could get.

> I applied everywhere for child care, and I hoped she would only be with me at work for a short time, but everywhere it was the same thing—they put me on waiting lists. . . . Lana was sick a lot, and I had to stay home with her for a few weeks, and I was missing a lot of time at work.

Nadia almost quit her job during this period. She was not paid for the time she missed from work, and she was missing so much time at work that her employer told her she might be fired. At one point she had to turn down a family child care arrangement that she was offered by an agency because the care setting scared her and the location was too hard for her to reach. She felt the constraints of needing a care arrangement desperately, but despite having no other options, she rejected this arrangement, hoping the agency would still call her when another spot opened up. A month later the same agency offered her a place in a family day care home one block from her home, and Nadia quickly took it. She liked the setting and placed her daughter in care the next day.

> I needed something right away, and . . . she [the provider] was a block away. . . . And since this provider has worked as a nurse's assistant, or something like that, she said she did not mind taking care of Lana or that I call two or three times a day to see how Lana is doing during the day.

When Nadia finally found an arrangement for Lana, it was considerably better than the makeshift care she had found it necessary to use for the previous five months, but it was still not the developmental care that Lana needed. As Nadia started Lana in family child care—her fourth primary care spell in Lana's first twenty-two months—she continued to try to arrange the specialized care that her child needed, even though it would involve at least one more care spell.

Almost every mother has a unique story about child care disruptions, gaps in care, and delays in receiving necessary care. The child care histories in this sample reveal great heterogeneity across the early childhood years, but irregular care patterns were most common in the earliest years, prior to age two. Mothers report that they were gradually learning over time how to make good care arrangements and that more stable forms of care sometimes grew out of prior arrangements. There was a progression in the stability of their care arrangements, with the durations of spells getting longer as their children got older. Nevertheless, the bottom line was that many children from low-income single-mother families spent a lot of time among a range of providers during their early childhood and mothers were piecing together care with a high level of instability.

Center Care Comes Through Too Late

For many mothers, the transition to center care came later than they preferred. Their reasons for preferring center care varied, as well as the times when they wanted it for their children, but most emphasized the need for an educational focus ("to get ready for school" and to "start their learning") and for greater peer socialization with children their age ("to be in a group"). As a result of their unfavorable experiences with other types of care, many of the mothers wanted to move their children into some formal, institutional care setting sooner than they had expected. As mothers worked more and worked more regularly, they sought the greater stability of center-based care, and they sought to get beyond the need to constantly piece together care.

Mothers offered a range of responses for when they preferred to start their children in center care.[5] Traci was among those who said that sooner is better:

> I would say that the center care is ideal for children from a year. . . . At a year old, they're pretty much ready to go. Before that they need to be nurtured by their parent. When they're ready, centers are the best care setting. . . . It's even better than staying home with the mother. Yes, there comes a time when they have to learn to socialize with their peers. They need to be in a different environment with kids their own age. They just need that . . . [to] learn how to deal with other people.

A few mothers believed that around age three, when there is more availability for center slots, was the right time to move children to a center, but many came to believe that sooner is better for many children. Felicidad generally believes that young children are ready for center care and learning with peers at age three. Felicidad also expresses a sentiment, shared by several mothers, that all children need to make the transition to center care at some point, but some are ready earlier than others. She believes her older daughter Cara could have made the transition to center care sooner than she did at age three, and more easily than Karyn, her younger daughter, for whom she thought age three was the appropriate age because she was more timid and strongly attached to Melanie, her family day care provider.

> I wanted to keep Karyn with Melanie as long as I could. I know she needs to start to get ready for school and be more in a socialization setting, but she is no Cara, and still needs attention, and she is not ready for all-day care at once. I wish she could do both a little care at the center and some with Melanie for a little longer.

Like Felicidad, Griselda says that the time to start center care should depend on the child, but in her case the default primary care setting was the center. Griselda wanted to start her daughter Giselle in center care as soon as she could arrange a child care slot.

> I think whenever they are ready for the center they should go. . . . For Alicia, I knew she wasn't ready. . . . She needed more attention, so I stayed with her at home [more] and left her in my mother's care longer . . . until she was almost three. With Giselle, I knew she was ready for a learning environment right away when she could walk and talk at one. I looked everywhere for a center to take her, and when I found a place where they would take her at two, I arranged it, and at two years old, on her birthday, she started at the Freedom Child Care Center.

Mothers of children at every age found it hard to get a place in a center. It took luck and considerable effort to secure an available slot that was also subsidized so they could afford it.[6] The difficulties and delays experienced in finding a center slot led many mothers to believe their children were getting a "late start" in their learning and their readiness for school.

Child Care Subsidies Are Scarce and Complex

Contributing more than anything to children's delayed entry into center-based forms of care were the high cost, the difficulties of getting child care subsidy benefits, and the unavailability of center care slots even when families became eligible for subsidies. All of these constraints were worse when children were very young. As described in chapter 2, most mothers were eligible for subsidized child care, either through the city's Administration for Children Services (ACS) (which families referred to as ACD, the Agency for Child Development, the organization's prior name), which administered child care assistance to low-income working families, or through the city's Human Resources Administration (HRA), which distributed child care vouchers to mothers moving from welfare to work and then twelve months of transitional child care benefits after they left welfare. Many mothers applied for this assistance but were unable to arrange subsidies because of bureaucratic problems or the time it would take them to qualify. Even when they did receive subsidies, the process of maintaining them and moving between different subsidy programs was extremely complex. Families would gain and lose subsidies in the administrative churning and complexities of the two bureaucracies.

A frequent problem for many mothers in this study occurred when their subsidy either ended because of administrative problems or did not start at the same time as their work began. A few mothers tried to maintain a child care arrangement despite the frequent payment and other administrative problems they encountered, especially with the HRA vouchers. For most of them, however, affording the care was impossible, especially with the wages they earned in their jobs, or when doing internships or Work Experience Program (WEP) assignments while on welfare.

The time needed to arrange child care caused complications for mothers starting work. When Traci decided to leave welfare for work, she found it took her about three months to secure child care subsidies. She said it first took her time to understand that she needed to get her care through HRA rather than ACD because she had been on welfare; then she had to get her HRA vouchers approved and secured to coincide with when she was starting work. In the interim, she was doing informal work and used limited informal and kin care until she had the child care voucher in place. When her care was approved, she discovered that she had no real options for providers. She left Tanya with a neighbor even though she really wanted center care from the start; she could not find it, however, in her neighborhood.

Traci started Tanya's care using HRA vouchers, which were the least reliable form of financial assistance. These vouchers went to the lowest-income mothers whose balancing of work and care was the most tenuous. Traci had been in education and training programs for more than two years before Tanya was born, and when she started to work, it was with a temporary jobs agency. Mothers like Traci were left on their own to find care and may have known little about care options, including who would accept the vouchers. They received little information or help from the public agencies, which just wanted them to work. The cumbersome paperwork, administrative processing problems, low payments the vouchers offered, and difficulties receiving payments made many providers reluctant to take HRA vouchers, leaving many mothers no choice but to use less-desired care providers who would.

In the ACD system subsidies were scarce and waiting lists long. For ACD child care, obtaining a subsidy and finding placement with a contracted ACD provider was a matter of luck as much as determination or experience. Arranging subsidies across two systems was a huge obstacle, since each had its own opaque rules. Traci was one of the few mothers in the sample who was able to arrange for the transitional welfare-to-work benefits when she exited welfare. Most mothers say they were never even told about these transitional benefits. The mothers who did seek these benefits generally did not receive them owing to the complicated administrative processes and the fact that, once they were working, they had less time to manage them.

Maintaining care was very difficult for mothers trying to transition between the two subsidy sources; the disjointed nature of the two systems created discontinuities in care for families and child care problems for many mothers. Bernadette was making a strong effort to move from welfare to work: she had completed a nine-month training and paid internship and had been working part-time for eight months. She lost her HRA child care subsidies as soon as the part-time job ended, but she could not get eligibility with ACD. She was actively searching for a full-time salaried job and had applied for ACD subsidies more than a year earlier. While she was looking for work, she had to take her son Paul out of family child care because she could not afford to pay the provider. She paid the provider on specific days she needed child care for her job search, and within two months she found a full-time job. Yet when she started the job, she still had not received her ACD subsidies, and no one from HRA informed her about transitional benefits for families leaving welfare. As a result, after years of trying to get her first full-time job, she had to use her entire first paycheck (after taxes) to pay the provider the full cost of the child care.

> I went from paying nothing to paying $254 [for two weeks of care]. I am supposed to get transitional benefits, but that takes months. The [neighborhood agency that has helped her get needed services] wants me to try and get the benefits back later, but how? . . . I don't know how, and I don't want the trouble. I'd rather quit. Maybe when I get ACD they can go back and give me back money, but I don't think so. It takes so long— what happens to a parent who does not make enough money and has to pay child care? It is so hard. My first paycheck from the job, I had to pay for the child care because I owed her for four weeks. It was the whole check. I started keeping receipts for every time I paid her, but what can I do?
>
> I wanted to quit, but also I just want to stick to it, because once I go to my ACD appointment next month on the twenty-fifth, I hope it can be okay—now I know the system because the agency here has helped me. . . . Also, I like my job.

For Bernadette, arranging child care subsidies across two systems was a huge obstacle. The more she got used to the time constraints of working, the more of a hassle it became to deal with the child care bureaucracy. But she was forced to keep trying because she could not afford child care on the income she earned. Most of the mothers in this sample could not afford to use anything but the most inexpensive forms of child care unless they received a subsidy.

Bernadette struggled financially but was able to maintain her care despite the problems her subsidy seam caused. She was fortunate that an agency advocated for her to break through the unresponsive bureaucracy or she would have had to stop working. Often mothers had to make new care arrangements when the source of their subsidy changed. Traci's child care arrangements for Tanya and Tariq ended at Help Thy Neighbor in part because of such a subsidy seam. Tanya and Tariq attended the center, which accepted Traci's HRA vouchers during the time she was on welfare and the twelve months afterward when she received transitional child care benefits. As the HRA vouchers were about to expire, the center told her that she needed to arrange for ACD vouchers or pay the full cost of the care, which she could not afford. Traci applied for ACD eligibility even while she had the HRA vouchers, because of the problems she had had with nonpayments and late payments to the center. She sought to push ACD so she could keep her children in care, but no vouchers were to be had. As it turned out, Traci removed her children from Help Thy Neighbor because of quality concerns just as her HRA vouchers were ending, but in the end she would have had to make a change anyway owing to the subsidy seam.

Care for Children with Special Needs Is Hard to Arrange

Families with children with special needs, such as developmental delays or severe health conditions that required special care and treatment, had particular difficulties arranging appropriate care. Mothers often found that they were the only person identifying their children's special needs. They found a long gap between the identification of their children's special needs and receipt of the appropriate care.

Oona described her difficulties in both identifying her son Kiley's special needs and receiving the appropriate therapies and treatments in a timely fashion.

> It was a difficult route to get him into the care because he got evaluated a lot before he got help. Kiley did not start his treatment until he was two, and I had stopped working when he was about one, 'cause I knew there was something wrong with Kiley. . . . I knew there was something wrong because he should've been doing certain things by that age. I just know he should've been talking; he should've been verbal. I did not know what he was saying at all. No one knew what it was, and I went through a different chain of command, and it was hard to figure out who to turn to for help. I went to the pediatrician, then I went to the ENT [ear, nose, and throat specialist], and that's when I learned that a bad ear infection he had when he was very young delayed his speech and comprehension. I went through being referred to different people to try and get him treatment, and then people had to find the right person before we got EI [early intervention] services.

Many of the children in the sample were speech-delayed, but mothers were often not sure about this and had to rely on their own judgment. Yolanda too was the first to suspect that her son Yeats's speech might be delayed, but like other mothers, she often doubted her own suspicions and was not sure who to turn to for assistance.

> I am concerned with his speech. He speaks well sometimes. However, there are times when he says things and you don't understand a word he's saying, and he's looking at you for this response. I did not know if being in family child care, and not in an educational setting, was delaying his speech. And I did not know what to do. So I called an agency, and then I went to WIC, and they told me about a resource agency that offered speech therapy. I called a speech therapist, and actually I'm going to get him evaluated next month. So when I called them, the lady was saying that at age three they should be saying 350 different words. He can stand here and hold a conversation with you, but I'm not sure that he's saying 350 different words. I may just be thinking that because at his age Yesenia [Yeats's sister], she could hold a conversation like you and I are holding. But later I found out that she was gifted. So I'm like comparing apples and oranges, but I don't know, so I want to have him assessed by a speech therapist.

While some mothers suspect developmental delays or other special needs, many are not able to identify delays in their children's development. Often it was when children were in institutional care settings that staff were first able to identify special needs, so that those who gained access to center care earlier had the added benefit of having their children's developmental needs identified earlier. Besides parents and child care staff, it was often children's pediatricians who identified special needs and developmental delays. Sandra acted quickly when a doctor confirmed her suspicion that Shaniqua could be speech-delayed; however, even after the problem was diagnosed, it still took nine months to enroll her in specialized care.

> I wanted to get the early intervention as soon as possible. I first started to think that she had a speech delay when I went to her physician in December. She talks, but he just thought her vocabulary should have been higher or her response to questions should have been clearer. . . . He gave me a number of a social worker at College Hospital. I called her, and she gave me a list of schools outside of this district that help children with speech delays, because I told her I did not want her to go to the district school. She told me if I wanted her to go to a school outside my district, I could apply for that. I was familiar with this one school that was on the list because I did my prenatal care at a hospital in that area. It's a good neighborhood, and I used to pass the school all the time when I was pregnant and think, wow, that's a nice school, I wish I could send my daughter here. That's what I was thinking when I was pregnant. I didn't know that they helped kids with speech delays. So when she mentioned that school, I was like, "Oh God, okay." She said, "Call right away." It

was by now the summer, and they usually have the school filled for the next year. So I called and luckily they got me in. We had to go through a week of evaluations right away. That was the first step, and then after that you write to the district and you go through the district meetings. Then they approved it. And that's it. She was able to get in, and so she started school in September.

Lana continued to need specialized services when she turned three, but since the early intervention program helped to provide special needs care only for children up to age three, Nadia had to scramble to arrange both the special needs care and child care around those hours. Nadia wanted to arrange both within one center, but the only center-based special needs care she could find would take Lana only for special needs services and had no day care slots available. Nadia had to start Lana in a new combination of care that was less than ideal: continuing in the family day care, which was becoming less developmentally appropriate as Lana grew older, and starting a new special needs program that was of far lesser quality than the previous one. This was the best she could do while she waited.

A very common health condition afflicting children in the sample was asthma, which significantly affected their care and their mothers' work. Iris's daughter Quirina had a severe asthmatic condition that led to many visits to hospitals:

> The first time she was in the hospital she was two months old and stayed there three weeks because she developed pneumonia. . . . She has been to the emergency room more than seventy times, and kept overnight fifty times. I keep a book about her asthma. She was hospitalized last Friday night at Buena Vista for one night, and she has been to five other hospitals in New York.

Quirina was hospitalized for days or weeks at a stretch, during which time Iris did not go to work. Iris estimates that she missed thirty days of work each year. More than once she lost a job because she had to respond to her daughter's asthma attacks. In one instance Iris was called by her day care center and told that Quirina had had an attack and was on her way to the hospital in an ambulance—but her employer would not permit her to leave. (She went anyway and lost the job.) Iris describes how Quirina's asthma condition shaped child care and work:

> The centers are not allowed to treat her asthma. They can call me or call the ambulance. . . . Another thing is that when I take her to the hospital and they keep her or release her, I cannot take her to the day care, because the medication is required during the hours she is in day care and they cannot give it. She has a nebulizer with a pump, and she takes the medication with that. It's easy, but they cannot do it at the center. So I

have to keep her home to give her the medication. In the last year this has happened six times. I find a way. I will call her father's mother. I miss work sometimes because she is sick or something and I cannot find no one. They understand at this job, and that's why I stay even though the pay is little and I have to work more hours. Most of the time they do not cut my pay if I have to miss one day.

No Care for the Sick Child or in an Emergency

Almost every mother discusses bringing her children to work when they were sick or using up all of her own sick leave on her children's illnesses. Traci discussed sending her children to day care despite being sick. A few mothers say they lost a job because their employer would not excuse the time away, and others discuss the need to seek a job with more flexibility for children's health needs. As discussed earlier, Iris twice lost a job to tend to Quirina's health. Then she found a job that required her to work forty-nine hours a week and paid lower wages than she had earned in many of her previous jobs. She took the job anyway because her boss and coworkers accommodated her sick-child care needs and the job was located five minutes from her daughter's child care center. Annette says Aaron's asthma affected her work over time; without some employer flexibility to care for his illnesses, she might not have been able to work at all.

> He gets sick a lot in the winter. It seems I am in the emergency room every other week. . . . This winter I'd say he was sick five times. And this winter was not as bad as last winter—when I was out for more than a week twice. He was sick more when he was younger, and I could not get a job. I have learned to deal with asthma now, and I have had great, flexible bosses, which has made [working] possible. When he has gotten really sick, I have wanted to quit, but my bosses have supported me. They helped me to deal with it, and as he gets older it is getting better than it used to be. . . . Still, if he gets sick, I have to stay home. I really can only work where my boss allows me some flexibility for his care needs.

Francine found that arranging child care when her children were sick was just another strategy for coping. In addition to flexibility at work, she needed backup care when her children were sick. Children's health issues highlighted the importance of child care compared to other elements of family life.

> My boys are healthy kids, but I know that time we were living in the Bronx the moving about was getting to them. We lived up there but were still coming down here for my work and the child care, and they were up and they were out, and we're in the weather, you know, we are walking to the train station, we got to get here, get there, come back, it gets to them, and they were sick a lot. They both got ear infections that year.

[Fortune's] child care was in the Bronx, but it was not close to me, so I had to walk so much with them. And the block we lived on was dangerous, so I was always scared to walk with them, and they feel that, you know. It was terrible, so then we moved back here to the neighborhood. It became about survival—how you work, how you put food on the table, how you get from here to there, how you take care of your kids, how you handle when your child is sick and there is no one to provide child care. The child care is critical—I know some mothers who leave their sick child home alone by themself but they got to go to work, and they have nobody to watch them. And then when I call out because they are sick—like three weeks ago—and I will just sit here and look at the bills and know I am not getting paid. When they are sick a little, I can leave them with my mom or sister, but when they have an ear infection like that or a bad fever, you just have to lose the work.

Summary and Conclusions

As a whole, the mothers in this study express several concerns about the timing, quantity, and quality of care their children received. They were frustrated when they could not arrange the care they thought their children needed at the time they wanted it, when they could not get the specialized care their children required to address developmental and health problems, and when their child care was unstable. They regret the limited time they spent as their children's primary care provider at the start of their lives and, as several of them put it, the "all or nothing" expectations of work and child care. Some express guilt over returning to work very early in their children's lives and putting their children into care for long hours. In general, however, most feel that there was not much choice given the need to support their families and make ends meet. In their current contexts, for most, work came first.

These mothers worry about the care paths of their children and the limited care options in their neighborhoods. Many of the concerns that they raise about their children's relationships with their caregivers and the pace of their learning are the same concerns raised by developmental psychologists in the literature on child care and its effect on development. It is the children of low-income families who the literature says could most benefit from consistent early care and education, yet they are the ones for whom it is most missing.

The mothers in this study universally discuss their worries about having started their children in care too early, before they and their children were ready. The literature has reported that early entry into child care poses a developmental concern because it may cut short the time needed to build a strong mother-child attachment (Belsky 1986; Brooks-Gunn, Han, and Waldfogel 2002). Researchers have added that these negative effects are most prevalent for infants in low-quality care, which was the case in many of the first arrangements made by families in this sample. Many mothers report that their earliest arrangements were often the worst and most worrisome. Researchers have found that the effects of low-quality early care are seen in children's early social development and in later cognitive outcomes and school performance (Brooks-Gunn, Han, and Waldfogel 2002; National Institute of Child Health and Development 1997b; Waldfogel, Han, and Brooks-Gunn 2002).

Mothers also worry about their children being in care for too many hours. Many of the low-income mothers in this study worked many hours for still small incomes, in part because an hour's marginal wage could make a difference in meeting their family's needs. An NICHD study (1997a) has found that infants who spent more time in child care experienced less positive mother-infant interaction and that higher quantities of care were associated with more insecure attachments. A more recent study of the NICHD cohort finds that children who spent long hours in child care demonstrated more problem behaviors and more difficulty getting along with peers when they reached kindergarten (National Institute of Child Health and Development 2003). According to this and other research, the quantity effects of care are more significant for children who are in lower-quality care arrangements (Howes 1990; National Institute of Child Health and Development 1997a).

Perhaps the greatest worries experienced by the mothers in the study were about the instability of child care over time and their inability to find the right care for children. Some of the instability resulted from their need to use inherently unstable care options when nothing else was available, especially when they were starting their children in care. Mothers also worry about the effects of delayed access to center care that would have offered their children the early educational opportunities they needed. As discussed earlier, developmental studies have found that frequent changes in children's care arrangements interfere with development, making it more difficult for children to build trust with their providers. Multiple unstable caregivers can result in greater emotional insecurity, particularly when children are in the early stages of development (Howes and Hamilton 1993; Howes, Matheson, and Hamilton 1994). Studies have also found that center care on average is more developmentally appropriate for preschool children's cognitive and language development and for improving their competence with peers (Howes, Phillips, and Whitebook 1992; National Institute of Child Health and Development 2000b; Scarr and Eisenberg 1993). As Heymann (2000) has similarly found, the child care problems of low-income families are exacerbated by the fact that their children have more health and developmental problems than other children but these families lack access to the special needs care their children require. Low-income parents also have the least work-related flexibility and benefits to cope with a sick child and often have to bring a sick child to the care setting rather than stay home with the child and risk losing their job (Heymann 2000).

These issues are ultimately related to both the lack of available funding for child care assistance to low-income families and the bureaucratic hurdles that families face in gaining access to and retaining child care subsidies. Subsidies were limited, establishing eligibility was difficult, and the available care for very young children was hard to come by. As seen in this analysis, low-income families generally have the most trouble getting needed care subsidies when their children are very young because of the bureaucratic hurdles and the lack of child care options for infants and toddlers.

As problematic to families as the limited availability of subsidies was their administration. The child care systems seem irrational to many mothers: the confusion that results from multiple, separated systems with very different rules and approaches to child care complicates the process of obtaining subsidized care. The various social service agencies categorize need and split up child care in ways that do not account for the many changes in mothers' lives.

These mothers were piecing together their child care and working with a great deal of flux, with care and work often running counter to each other. As they balanced work expectations and children's care, they were dealing with many other problems, such as their children's health problems and family instability. Yet these mothers did their best to manage this balancing act, an amazing accomplishment in many cases. Despite their concerns about the care their children received, over time these mothers had little choice but to develop care strategies and arrange care the best they could for their children as they negotiated their passage from birth to preschool—or as Francine put it, "how you get from here to there."

~ Chapter 5 ~

Care Strategies: "They Say If I Cannot Do It Myself, They Help Me"

Sara first came to the United States from Ecuador at the age of sixteen to live with her mother. Sara now lives with her own daughter, Cristina, and has combined study and work, both at a New York City community college, since September 1999.

The first time Sara came to the United States in 1991, her mother's family was living in the Hell's Kitchen, or Clinton section, of Manhattan. Sara's mother had left her and her three siblings behind in Ecuador when she came over to the United States ten years before, and Sara met her stepfather and her three new half-siblings for the first time when she arrived to live in their home. As she put it, Sara and her mother had "a difficult relationship" for much of the time she lived there. When Sara arrived, she started high school, but she did not like the school or the city very much because she found the culture to be "very aggressive." That and the tense relationship with her mother led Sara to move back to Ecuador after one year.

After that first arrival in the United States, Sara went back and forth between her first home, Guayaquil in Ecuador, and her eventual home, New York City. When she returned to the United States in August 1997, she was twenty-two years old and seven months pregnant. The previous Christmas she had traveled to Ecuador to see Javier, a man with whom she had been involved since they met and fell in love in July 1995 during one of her long stays in Ecuador. After she became pregnant, Sara stayed in Ecuador until deciding to leave in her seventh month because she wanted her child to be born in the United States, with access to the opportunities here.

Sara's daughter, Cristina, was born prematurely on the first of October, weighing just three pounds. Cristina stayed in the hospital for two weeks in an incubator because she was so underweight. Then Sara and Cristina moved in with Sara's mother at first, but this became a difficult situation. The home was very crowded, her mother made her feel unwelcome, and there were constant arguments between mother and daughter. Yet Sara did not have any other real housing options, so she stayed with her mother for as long as she could—six months, as it turned out.

For a long time Sara had no real child care options either. She was very worried about where to leave Cristina given that she was so small. Leaving her with her mother was not an option. As Sara put it, "Her life is much harder than mine—you know, she had three children of her own from her second marriage, and everything with her is so complicated." Yet Sara did want to make some other arrangement because she wanted to go back to school. She had started a semester at a community college before her last return to Ecuador, and now she was anxious to resume her studies. She also needed to earn money to support herself and Cristina and maintain some independence from her mother. If she could find someone to watch Cristina, she could get out of the home, and that might help relieve some of the tension in her living situation.

Sara stayed home and took care of Cristina until she was three months old. Because Cristina was so small, and ate so little, Sara could not leave her very long between her brief breast-feedings. After three months, Sara began to work as a hostess at what she called a "fancy Spanish restaurant," receiving the coats at the entrance. She received no salary and worked just for tips, but, she said, "it was good money."

Sara made her first child care arrangement with a neighbor, Dolores, a Puerto Rican woman in her forties or fifties who lived down the hall in her mother's building. Dolores had been quite friendly to Sara, speaking with her a few times when she was with Cristina. Sara approached Dolores about taking care of Cristina, and she agreed. Sara paid her very little for child care and sometimes nothing at all, and Dolores was fine with that. Cristina was in this child care arrangement for almost five months, until she was eight months old.

> It was very convenient for me because this woman was living in the same building, and she would take care of Cristina all day long. I was paying her just $5 for all day, and sometimes when I didn't have the money, I did not even pay her. She said, don't worry about paying if you don't have the money, I like taking care of Cristina. She was okay with that, and Cristina was very attached to her.

At one point Sara and Cristina moved out of her mother's home, "after some more fights," Sara says. They had nowhere to go at first, so they stayed with Dolores, the woman who was caring for Cristina. They were there for about two weeks, until this posed an even greater problem.

> The problem came when this woman proposed to me that I give her my daughter. She said that she loved Cristina very much and that she would

like to keep her. That I did not have even a home or $5 to pay for child care, and it would be easier for me if I did not have a baby, and better for Cristina too. I was shocked. I did not know what to do. After that, I was always scared even to go to school, of leaving Cristina with her, because maybe she would steal her and take her to Puerto Rico or something like that. I became very paranoid, so I left, and I took my child with me to Ecuador. I was very scared.

Sara was stunned by her babysitter's request. Dolores even had papers drawn up for Sara to sign for her to pass over formal custody. Sara still had a week or two to go in her school semester, but she was scared to go each day. She was able to complete some of her coursework before she decided to go to Ecuador in May 1998, pleased at least that her daughter would meet her father for the first time.

Sara then spent a year in Ecuador, living with Cristina's father, Javier, and his family:

> I like to be there, but the economic situation is unbearable, and we [she and Cristina and Javier] had no place we could live of our own. It makes us very anxious to see that the money is never enough. We were ten people living in that house, and at the end we are always fighting because the money situation is so bad. I prefer being in Ecuador, but then I think about my future and the future of Cristina, and it's better for us to be here [in the United States]. I want to continue studying and working, and down there it is impossible. I did not really work in Ecuador, and that was hard for me because I am not the type to stay home.

Since "home" now was with her child's father's family with eight more in the home, it was hard for Sara to feel in control of anything that was hers. She could not work because there were no jobs there and because his family expected her to stay home since she was a mother. Economic conditions were severe in Ecuador, and the bank where Cristina's father worked went bankrupt soon after she arrived in Ecuador. After that, he could find only sporadic informal work and earned little.

Sara and Cristina stayed in Ecuador and lived with Javier and his family until Cristina was eighteen months old. While in Ecuador, Sara received a forwarded letter from Girls and Boys Head Start Center, where she had quite desperately applied and literally begged for a child care spot. The letter stated there was a slot now open for Cristina. The deadline for this application had already passed by the time she got the notice, but it prompted Sara to return with Cristina back to New York quickly with the hope that they could still get the place, allowing Sara to work again and return to school. Sara said, "It was very hard for him [Javier], but he saw this is what I wanted for Cristina." During that summer after they returned, they lived again with her mother, and Sara took care of Cristina until she finally started at Girls and Boys in September 1999, when Cristina was almost two years old.

Sara's persistence led to Cristina's placement in Girls and Boys. She had first seen the center when Cristina was just three months old, after which she says she began going to the center every day to see whether she could arrange to have Cristina cared for there.

> When she was a baby, I looked around all over the city because I did not know too much about the programs and did not know people here. I was walking with her when I saw the center, and when I went the first time I asked them, how is the process for getting into the program, and how they pick the children that are going to be for next year. They said they didn't have a waiting list because they are a program to serve poor children, so if they see the worst case they are going to take that kid. So that was easy because I went every day saying, I don't have place for Cristina, I have nothing, I need to do this to go to school. That was easy. It was the truth. They could not believe when I came there every day.

Sara was pleased with most aspects of her daughter's child care program at Girls and Boys, and she kept her there through preschool.

When Sara returned from Ecuador in the spring of 1999, she moved back into her mother's home. Again, she stayed only about six months. In October 1999, when Cristina was two, and a month after she had started at Girls and Boys, Sara decided to leave her mother's house and became homeless. At first, she did not qualify to live in a shelter because she was not receiving welfare, so she stayed with a friend and applied for welfare so she could enter the homeless shelter system.

> In January 2000, I left with all my things. My mother didn't believe me when I said I was going to live in a shelter, she said that I was not going to stand it because it was horrible. But I have always had an independent spirit, and I prefer to live in my own place, and I thought, it does not matter if it is small, horrible, or whatever. While I was living with my mother, I was emotionally and psychologically in a very bad condition, I was feeling very bad, always crying, and I knew that it was not good for Cristina.
> . . . Now we don't fight anymore because we don't live together. She left me when I was six years old, and we saw each other again when I was sixteen. Her character is very strong, and so we simply don't get along well. She used to say things to me like, "The groceries are getting finished," or, "There's too much people in this house." She said those things every day, so I got tired. I left.

Sara describes her experience living in the shelter as a terrifying time in her life, but she endured in the hope of eventually getting a housing situation of her own, something she had never had before and that she wanted for herself and Cristina, and where one day she hoped Javier might join them if he could find a way to immigrate from Ecuador.

> To get to live in a shelter, you have to go to the Bronx [to the Emergency Assistance Unit (EAU)] to apply. It's really a horrible place, it is a huge place with big seats in which people they lay down. They make you wait forever. I waited all day with Cristina, without being able to let her rest, or even to change her Pampers. They gave me food, but it was horrible food, it makes you sick in your stomach, so I never gave this food to Cristina. . . . They sent us to a temporary shelter to spend one night, and the next day I had to come back to apply again. Again they did not process my application, and that night they sent me to a horrible place, a room without locks, so I put a table against the door, but I couldn't sleep all night long, because I was so afraid of somebody coming into my room. The next day, the same thing, I had to come back to the place of the application and wait all day long for them to find a permanent place for you. Finally I was sent to a shelter in Brooklyn, which I heard from others at the EAU was the worst place of all. . . . But I was so tired, and after the psychological trauma, I just wanted a bed to sleep. We got a little room . . . and we stayed there for ten days, in this terrible place. . . . The last day I received a note telling me that my petition for permanent shelter was denied, and that I had to go back to the EAU and appeal. I did not take my things because I really didn't have a place to stay or leave them. My petition was denied again that night. I appeal that same day, and so again, I had to go back to the Bronx, stayed there for the night, and the next day they found me a place in Jamaica, Queens, for another ten days, while they were examining my application again. When I went back to the Brooklyn shelter (after two or three days), I found out that they threw all my clothes and Cristina's clothes away, and I had good clothes, I lost everything.

This condensed version of her earliest experiences in New York's homeless system leaves out many individual incidents that left Sara fearful and worried about her ability to cope with her instability. Through all her experiences she said she focused on the routine of having to get Cristina ready to go to the day care center each day and to get herself ready for school and her job. Her next shelter was in Queens. There she was interviewed by a social worker who saw that Cristina was very thin and insisted that Sara must not have been feeding her properly, so she ordered a medical investigation. Once again, Sara was frightened at the thought of losing her daughter.

> I began to feel scared, because you know that they have the freedom to take your child away, and I was nobody at that point: I was homeless, and if she wanted, she could take Cristina away from me. Then I talked to the doctor to see if he could explain the situation to the social worker,

because she didn't want to believe that Cristina was all right. Finally the doctor talked to her, so things got better. Nobody really knows it, but in the shelters children are separated from their mothers all the time, every day you could hear about it, but the mothers don't say anything.

Sara stayed in the temporary shelter in Queens, waiting for her shelter application to be accepted, so that she could be moved into the "tier" system by which she might eventually get housing. She says: "I appeal again, and this time I told them, I said that 'my lawyer' has told me that I had the right to stay in the shelter." Sara did not have a lawyer, but she did know what her rights were. The next day she got a letter accepting her, and she moved to a shelter in Manhattan. That was the last shelter, after having been moved across the ends of the city, and Sara and Cristina stayed there eight months until October 2000. Sara had some bad experiences at the last shelter; she was poorly treated by the staff, she says, but overall the place was better than the others. After ten months in the shelter system, they finally moved into a public housing project in the Points. It was the week of Cristina's third birthday and Sara's twenty-fifth. Overall, she says, the shelter experience, while difficult, helped her establish her independence and the ability to survive.

> For me, I preferred being homeless and not being with my mother. It was horrible, but I was happy that I didn't have anyone telling me what to do all the time and that I could make sure Cristina was okay all that time.

Sara came to believe that during her experience of being homeless and moving between shelters, the stability of Cristina's child care became the most important element supporting them at the time.

> I think all the movements and adjustments were hard for Cristina. She was born here, we went to Ecuador, came back and lived with my mother, and then lived in shelters in Queens, Brooklyn, Manhattan, and a few nights in Bronx. Cristina was like crying when we were moving all the time, but it wasn't so hard because she stayed in the same day care. So everything was changing but the day care, and she was there from 8:30 to 5:45. Yes, that was her house. It didn't change. For me, it was so hard. I was going from Queens to day care to my job working at the community college. During the whole time she stayed in the child care, and I stayed at the community college.
> Because she had the stability at the center for child care, that was good for Cristina, because she saw the same people every day. She spent so much time there. I never wanted to take her out. The social workers [in the shelters] were telling me, take her to this one [at the shelter] because it's better for you because you go to school and you just leave Cristina in this place, and she doesn't have to travel. I didn't trust them,

Figure 5.1 Dynamics Timeline for Sara and Cristina's Story

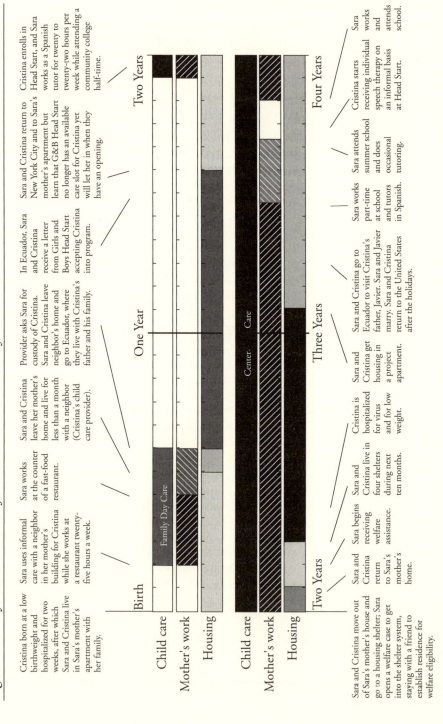

Source: Author's compilation.

because I didn't know how those day cares in the shelters work. Everybody there used them, but that wasn't an option for me.

The stability of her being in the same place every day was very important for her development. The staff at Girls and Boys knew we were homeless, and they were helpful. We were late, and you are not supposed to come late, but they didn't ask me why because they already knew. And they said that if I wanted to use the laundry, I can give them my clothes and the guy who does the laundry, he can wash it for me. I started to give them some of Cristina's clothes to do, but not mine. Also, she would eat something there sometimes, because I never let her eat the shelter cafeteria food, but always eat outside with Cristina.

The people from the day care center told me that anything I need I can ask them. When I moved here, someone gave me this sofa. I didn't have a way to transport it, so the director did it. They say if I cannot do it myself, they help me. They help me a lot.

Getting From Here to There: Developing Care Strategies

Sara's story illustrates how a mother can learn about child care as she goes along, making new care decisions following prior experiences. Sara's care choices were affected by her own background and the social context: she was relatively isolated as a young immigrant woman with few personal and financial resources. Yet she was tenacious in navigating her way through the complex public social services bureaucracies to protect and advance her daughter's cause, getting coveted Head Start care while also living a year in homeless shelters. Throughout her ordeal, Sara maintained her daughter's care and her own work goals, using Cristina's child care arrangement as an anchor around which to base other choices. She made strategic decisions with regard to child care, work, family, housing, and public welfare in ways that helped her and Cristina survive with the most limited resources (see figure 5.1).

Under urban poverty conditions, poor families' options for income, work, housing, child care, and meeting almost all of life's basic needs are tightly constrained. The strategies that single mothers employ are necessarily two-generational (at least) and multidimensional. They integrate decisions about their own work and their child care with choices about housing, income supports, family relationships, marriage, and immigration. The child care strategies described in this chapter were made within this broader context. Sara preferred Head Start for her daughter because it was care she thought was developmentally beneficial and professional. She also figured out that Head Start bases eligibility on income and need and that once she had qualified to enter the program, her daughter's place there would be secure throughout her early childhood. At the same time, she wanted to be able to work and continue her schooling, but based on her earlier child care experience, she decided that she would not do that unless she could get safe, professional, institutional child care. She also had no secure place to live. She and Cristina were not very welcome in her mother's home, and she found living in Ecuador with Cristina's father's family to be very difficult financially, and limiting for her daughter, whom she wanted to have the benefit of an American education and to grow up with a feeling of belonging to a society and having more life opportunities than she had.

It is around her daughter's admittance into Head Start that she based her next steps to return to the United States, resume her work and studies, and become homeless. It was to prove her homelessness that she then applied for welfare assistance. Along the way, she was also making choices to live in the United States separated from Javier and to distance herself from her mother. Her decisions around work, immigration, child development, and housing were all tied up together, and these were intertwined with the complex program rules around eligibility for Head Start, welfare, homeless services, and public housing.

The detailed study of the strategies that women employ to cope with poverty in disadvantaged communities builds on a line of research that looks at how the poor cope with the conditions they face within their life and cultural contexts. Carol Stack (1974) was among the first scholars to directly explore culturally based survival strategies within low-income communities. Stack looked in depth at the broad organization of family life in an urban black community where she lived during the field research to develop and explain the characteristics of sharing networks. The sharing of resources across these networks serves as a primary cultural response to poverty conditions. She identified one broad coping strategy—kin-based support networks—and documented how this strategy is used for sharing food and clothing, child responsibility, and financial resources and how the exchange reinforces a sense of mutual obligations. Stack's examination of coping strategies started a line of research in which others have followed: documenting strategies around family functioning, adolescent motherhood, children's early schooling, household budgeting, and residential mobility in poor communities.[1]

I apply the survival strategies frame to child care to analyze how child care decisions develop over time and how what mothers want for child care is integrated with their decisions about how they were going to pursue work, where the family will live, and the contexts of their relationships with their children's fathers and their families. Viewed in this way, care strategies can be seen as what mothers do when they face the gap between what they prefer with respect to optimal child care situations and what is real and possible given the constraints that characterize their lives. Finally, the focus on care strategies looks at whom mothers turn to and what resources they use to arrange care and what they learn over time.

In prior chapters, I focused on how low-income single mothers chose care arrangements, what their patterns of care looked like over time, what led to changes in their care arrangements, and what their biggest concerns were about the care their children received. Just as chapter 3 offered a dynamic view that built on chapter 2's more static, detailed view of the dimensions of individual care types, this chapter explores from mothers' perspectives how they coped—adapting and learning over time—with their concerns about child care revealed in the previous chapter.

Getting Care Started Quickly

As we saw in the last chapter, mothers in the study generally started with kin or people they knew when they first placed their children in care. Many mothers reported that they had little or no information about other care possibilities while making their first care arrangement and that they relied primarily on friends and family for information. Mothers who sought assistance from community agencies found that care options for children younger than two were the hardest to find and those that existed had the longest waiting lists.

Mothers usually had to arrange child care quickly when starting a new job. Because mothers initially were working less than full-time or were less certain how long they would work, they believed that these informal types of care would be more flexible for their initial needs. Additionally, given that they often earned little, particularly when they first started, mothers sought the most inexpensive form of care they could find if it was not subsidized. If they were subsidized with child care vouchers, there were incentives to keep that subsidy money within their personal network by making a kin or informal care arrangement. First care arrangements were more likely than later arrangements to be no cost or very low cost options, with the provider, most often kin, providing the care in-kind to the mother.

These initial care arrangements did not last very long. Kin care, father care, and informal care were generally unstable. In some cases, the short-term, part-time, or intermittent pattern of mothers' work also contributed to the shortness of these initial care spells.

In addition, many of these first care arrangements turned out to be low in quality, leading to poor care beginnings for the children. Sara's first care arrangement with her mother's neighbor who ultimately wanted custody of her daughter Cristina is a dramatic, if atypical, example. More common experiences with low-quality first care arrangements included one linked to an unstable personal relationship in Julia's case (see chapter 3), an unreliable provider in Brittany's (see chapter 2), and a conflict between the provider and the parent in Annette's (see chapter 1). Other informal care providers, such as the one Traci used for Tanya's first care arrangement (see chapter 4), simply did not provide care with the quality that mothers sought for their children.

Family and Friends Serve as Starting Points in Care Paths . . .   Kin often served an instrumental role in helping some mothers start working when no other care was available to them. Brittany turned to family first when she started a welfare-to-work training program and she knew of no other options for Bethany's care. The care in Bethany's first two short kin spells, with her uncle and then her aunt, were instrumental to her mother's ability to get on a work path, even though the care turned out to be inconsistent and of subpar quality in the first case and inconvenient in the second.

While kin were most often used to allow the mother to return to work, in Lisa's case her mother provided initial care because of Lisa's poor health. Her mother wanted to help her daughter in a time of need and to give her granddaughter early care and continued to do so until Lisa's epilepsy improved; once Lisa started working and found another caregiver, her mother resumed her own plans.

> That first year, my mom lived with us, and she was taking care of Millie. She spent a long time here because my seizures weren't under control, and I was heavily medicated and spent time at the hospital. I once seized and dropped Millie when she was young, so my mother was worried and said she would spend a year here. She couldn't go to Jamaica, where she had just recently moved with her sister, because someone had to take care of the baby. And from there the situation [my health] actually went under control in six months.
>
> She stayed until I was better, and even until I was called in for WEP [Work Experience Program, New York City's mandatory work program]. I went on public assistance after I had a first epileptic seizure when I was six weeks pregnant and could no longer work, and that is when I was receiving public assistance. . . . I was lucky because when I got called for WEP, I found child care in this program that helped single mothers receiving welfare. They will arrange a training [program] and internship that can count for the work requirements, and they provide you with child care. I did that. They provided the child care for the first year, and my mother moved back to Jamaica.

. . . But Not All Our Kin Are Available . . . Despite the frequent use of kin for initial primary care, the overall availability and reliability of relatives for child care varied across the sample. Many mothers did not expect to use kin care as a primary care option very often. In characterizing mothers' reliance on kin care, only eight of the forty-two mothers preferred kin care and thought that it would be consistently available to them. More mothers—nineteen out of forty-two—considered kin to be a limited source of care that was used as primary care in necessary stretches and as a more significant source of secondary care. The remaining fifteen mothers did not see kin as an available option at all, except for very occasional secondary care or short-term care.

For many mothers, kin were not living close enough to provide care, especially among immigrants and interregional migrants. There was high mobility of kin across the sample. Some grandmothers and aunts who provided initial care moved to their home countries or to other parts of the United States. As mentioned earlier, Lisa's mother moved to Jamaica. Diane, Rhonda, Sandra, Winnie, and Zina all had some family roots in the southern United States and had relatives who provided care but then moved to the South.[2] Dana and Traci, who both preferred their mother's care over anyone else's, had kin they would have wanted to provide care who were living in the South. Several immigrant mothers had relatives who migrated between the United States and the Caribbean or Central America and provided care at times but could not do so consistently.[3] Other immigrant mothers in the sample had few relatives living in the United States.

Many mothers did not consider kin a real care option for other reasons. In Sara's case, for example, there was tension with family members. Some of the mothers in the sample were not close to their own mothers, or at least they had no expectation that the grandmother would provide child care. Annette's mother had discussed returning to New York from Puerto Rico to care for Annette's son Aaron when she was beginning work in her Americorps internship, but Annette expected this might not happen: "Me and my mother have the worst relationship ever. I did things when I was younger she did not like, and she is negative—always putting me down—and we just blow up at each other . . . and she shows no love for her grandchildren."

Many mothers said that even if they were close to their own mother or other family members, kin did not always want to provide child care. Iris says:

> My mom, she is now living in the neighborhood, but she goes back and forth between here and Santo Domingo, but she is not an option. My mother says, "I don't take care of grandchildren. I raised my kids, so I am done, you raise your own kids." And you know, it's good in a way, because now I only have the one [child]. If she had babysat, maybe I would have had two or three more.

Angela says she had two sisters in the city but they were not available for child care. That made it hard to arrange her son Mark's first care because she had trouble trusting anyone but family.

> He has his two aunts—my two sisters live near here—but they are not helping out with day care. Nobody helps with that really. It is just myself, his father, and whoever I hire. . . . You have to pay for child care; it's not something you can count on family for, unless it is the onetime thing.

Others had no family at all available to them. Cassandra, Julia, Kiesha, Nora, Sara, and Uma were raised by relatives, adopted, or orphaned. Uma was adopted as a child and raised by an older couple who died before she had her daughter, Sade. Uma recognized that without grandparents, Sade's care options were limited, especially secondary care, which Uma thought was important in being able to make work adjustments and sustain work.

> I don't have family, you see. If you have that mother or that sister that can give that couple of hours [of care], then you could take the extra job, work late, or run an errand—that makes all the difference in the world. You can earn a little more, and you don't always have to pay babysitters, and you know getting that extra fifty or sixty makes a whole lot of difference in the world we live in.

. . . And All Our Kin Is Not Enough . . .   Those who did rely on kin care to get started eventually recognized that while it was instrumental in the beginning, it proved to be of limited reliability and uncertain in its duration. Family members had their own life paths, work obligations, or family crises. Grandmothers were the kin most likely to provide care, but some could not do so for long periods of time because of age or for health reasons. It also became complicated for relatives to sustain these arrangements for the intensive full-time care needs of mothers working long hours. Mothers also learned through their experiences with child care and their exposure to other working mothers that kin care over the long term did not enrich their children's learning and social needs as much as the other forms of care that they came to prefer as their children got older. The more they worked and were exposed to other working mothers' views of appropriate early care, mothers revised their expectations to prefer more formal institutional forms of care that could enhance their child's development.

In sum, because kin often were most available and most helpful during children's infancy or during a particular time of need, their care was a dominant form of care as a starting place for working mothers. Most of the time kin care was used so mothers could start a new job and kin would provide care until something else was arranged. Later, as children got older, and as kin got older or attended to their own work and lives, it became more complicated to sustain these arrangements as primary care for the many hours needed to cover mothers' workdays. As they turned to other primary forms of care, mothers used their personal networks of kin differently—to act more as bridge care between other primary care arrangements or as wraparound care to fill in the hours around primary care, and when they most needed care in a pinch.

Managing Care over Time: Developing Second-Best Care Strategies

Given that mothers' use of care was constrained, they were not free to choose the care they might prefer for their children. Yet, most mothers in this study had clear underlying preferences that came through in the discussions of the care they used (see chapter 2) and concerns about care (see chapter 4). For many, the best care for their children was to place them from the beginning with a safe, consistently available home care provider they knew and trusted, who was low-cost or partially subsidized and flexible in meeting their care needs, until the appropriate time for their child to move to a subsidized center care arrangement. At that point they would find a place in a good center where their children would learn and become ready for school.

Few mothers got close to this preferred care path for their children. Felicidad, who planned her children's care from before the time she decided to have children, came closest to meeting her goals. Her daughter, Karyn, started care with Melanie, a home care provider, at two months; Karyn stayed there until she turned three and then moved directly to center care—all of which was subsidized. Felicidad had some additional preferences for Karyn's primary care: to stay home with her longer after birth before returning to work, to use fewer hours of child care per day, and to provide Karyn with a more gradual transition into center care (possibly combining it with family child care for some time before moving to a full center-based schedule). However, these were secondary concerns because she had what she most wanted for Karyn's care: consistency, safety, trust, a nurturing home environment, direct attention, and a small group of children. Felicidad had similar consistency in her work path and her family and housing dynamics over most of Karyn's first four years.

Millie, Quirina, and Venus were three other children whose child care paths were fairly consistent and roughly followed their mothers' preferences. In these cases, there was greater stability in their care dynamics despite significant upsets in their mothers' work, family, housing, or health situations. Lisa, who was ill for part of Millie's early years and then struggled to leave welfare for work, relied on the consistency of her mother's care and then found an educational family child care group. Millie did very well upon entering school, while her mother eventually left welfare for regular employment. Iris relied on the consistency of Quirina's center care arrangements as she managed her separation from Quirina's father, homelessness, and Quirina's severe asthma attacks. Venus was able to stay with an extraordinary academically oriented family child care provider while living in one of the poorest, most isolated housing projects in Highwall Valley and as her mother battled substance abuse problems that put Venus in her grandmother's custody for much of her early childhood. Later she was found to be "gifted and talented" upon her entry into a competitive private school that would offer her a full scholarship.

In these cases, mothers were able to find child care arrangements that provided stability and a warm and developmentally appropriate environment for their children and a solid base from which they could base other decisions for their families' lives.

Other mothers who did not come as close to their aspirations for child care made arrangements that were second best or third best or went with the least unacceptable option that might in some ways satisfy them and allow them to work. Some mothers combined different strategic elements at different points in their children's care paths.

A fairly common second-best strategy was to patch together care wherever needed to maintain steady employment. Mothers would start with care that they knew, then seek other care and subsidies as they went along, and change arrangements quickly when one care arrangement ended or another was preferred, all the while seeking a more durable care arrangement at each phase. While their children were in care, the mothers would constantly seek backup primary and secondary care possibilities and work to get subsidies for child care. Over time these mothers also used more agency-based care resources. The earlier their informally arranged care arrangements broke down, the sooner mothers would consider center-based care a preferred option.

Yolanda adapted her care preferences to the constraints she confronted in arranging child care for her son Yeats as well as to his changing needs as he got older. After Yeats was born, Yolanda needed to return to her job at a city agency where she had worked for years, and she wanted the best care she could find for Yeats. For Yolanda, work was a given, so she had to make sure she was always planning ahead for her child's care, making regular adjustments and seeking assistance and agency-based services as she went along.

> One thing I know is that my children will always be somewhere until 6:00. . . . So I think if you are working, regardless of what you're making, you really need to seek out what's best for your child. . . . I had to find something for him so I could return to work. . . . I went to this agency, and they told me there was no centers for babies, only family child care. . . . I did not know much about family child care . . . but basically I just had two months to visit whatever places I could to get the feel of who to leave my child with. Many places were full. . . . Finally I left him with this lady . . . but she was not watching him properly so I . . . found me someone else.

Yeats then went to two other family child care providers. Yolanda kept him in family child care arrangements longer than she would have expected because it was hard to find center care slots until Yeats was age-eligible. All this time Yolanda was canvassing for center care options. When Yeats turned three, she decided to send him to the first center where he received a place while she maintained his name on the waiting list for another center just in case:

> You have to do some serious work beforehand to know where you are going to send your child, especially when they are getting to that age when they can go to the center. . . . I debated between ABC and 123 and preferred 123, but they didn't have space for him. I had placed him on ABC's waiting list since I was pregnant . . . and when ABC said they had

a place for him in January, I put him there, since I thought it would be hard to get a spot later if I let this one go.

I thought it [ABC] would be good, but it wasn't. He had two bad accidents there in the first few months. He got hurt, which is going to happen to children, I know, but I was so dissatisfied with his teacher's attitude when they happened. . . . I tried to change his classroom, and they would not do it. I was still waiting for 123, and I started looking at more places. 123 kept telling me it was going to come through next month. I called so many times, and then when I got into 123, I started him in August. And when I took him out, ABC called me to say they had an opening now in another classroom. I said, no, that's okay, I don't want it now.

Yolanda wanted to stay with a consistent, safe provider as long as she could. When she was worried about the quality of the first family child care arrangement, she immediately moved Yeats to another arrangement. Her preference for center care grew stronger at this point, and she canvassed even more for centers while making her second family child care arrangement. She had good experiences with her next two family child care providers, and in the second one the educational environment was similar to a center, so she stayed with it longer than she had expected.

Annette started working later than most mothers so that she could care for Aaron, but once she started work she developed a strategy of maintaining work while arranging care and also adjusting to care changes. Including Annette and Yolanda, about ten mothers developed some variation on this strategy of working more or less continuously while piecing together care as best they could. They arranged new care quickly and took the best care or whatever care they could arrange while searching for something better. Many of these mothers used agency-based care resources more as they went along, learning these were often better for maintaining work stability and longer child care spells.

Another second-best option was to find a long-term reliable care arrangement and stay with it even while making other compromises, like forgoing other possibly preferred care arrangements for the care they had in hand. Kari maintained a single care arrangement for more than three years with a nonlicensed family child care provider in her old neighborhood who lived an hour from her home and her job. Kari relied on this care because she said she could not find anyone else who could watch her daughter Jaya for the evening hours when she worked, and also because Jaya had grown quite comfortable with the provider, who gave Jaya individual attention. Jaya stayed in this family child care arrangement well past the age of four. Kari's mother wanted her to take Jaya out of this care arrangement, because she thought it limited her granddaughter's socialization and peer interactions and contributed to her limited vocabulary because the provider spoke only Spanish. Kari and her mother fought about this from the time Jaya was two, when the grandmother thought that Jaya should go to school. Kari said her mother, while meaning well, did not understand her limitations:

> My mom wants me to get her into a school or a center or something pro-
> gram, but she does not understand I cannot do that with the job I have.
> I can't pick her up at 6 p.m., so it's hard for me to put her in school, and
> she [my mother] is not going to watch her every day.

Julia maintained Jacqueline's care with Sonia, a family child care provider, for a long spell even though her daughter had turned three and center care options had become available. Like Kari, Julia had started working evening hours and had no one to pick up her daughter from a center. However, she was able to rely on the relationship she had with Sonia to get the additional hours of care she needed. Seven mothers similarly used one long care arrangement because of the difficulty of finding other child care or the constraints of matching care with work. Most of these long care spells were family child care because this option often offered longer hours and sometimes had greater flexibility to accommodate mothers' work hours and changes over time.

Another second-best care strategy used by some mothers was to pursue subsidized care from the start, most often a center care arrangement, and then scramble for care until the preferred form of subsidized care materialized. During the period they were scrambling to piece together care, these mothers would sometimes stop working for a while when care broke down or other elements of their family life became more difficult. Often they would return to more consistent work after arranging the more stable care arrangements they preferred. Griselda applied for and received eligibility for ACD-subsidized child care when her daughter Giselle was one, but it took her a longer time to find an available child care opening. In the interim, she juggled Giselle's care between her mother, Giselle's father, and an aunt, and around her changing work, family, and housing situations.

> [I] wanted my girls in a center. My mom has her own life to take care of,
> and the center is best for them. It took me like a year or so just looking
> at places and calling and visiting. I wanted to find the right place. I went
> to ACD and all the community agencies, and they give you a list of the
> child care centers, but none had space, and most did not take them un-
> til they were two or three. I also went to the other places, the private
> places, but they were extremely expensive. One place took infants in di-
> apers, and it was so wonderful, it was educational, and they had a lot of
> different cultural activities. I realized it was way too expensive. My friend
> told me about the Freedom Child Care Center, and she knew someone
> there. I went there, and I got [Giselle] accepted. But then I had to wait
> until she was two for Freedom because they take from two to six.

Sara knew little about child care options when she returned to New York from Ecuador pregnant with Cristina. Sara decided to go door to door look-ing for care, and through persistence she finally found it in a full-day Head

Start center where her daughter stayed for almost three years in fully subsidized care. Including Sara and Griselda, eight mothers found subsidized care as early as they could while working with other less satisfactory arrangements in the interim.

Eight mothers pursued a strategy of using care that was available to them for free or at low cost and then found work around the availability of this arrangement. These mothers often had more sporadic work and care timelines. Dona, a single mother with three sons who had received welfare for long spells over the previous fifteen years, did a series of mostly part-time jobs, internships, and training programs during her son David's early childhood while using no-cost care provided by her mother. She found she was better off with a strategy of combining work with welfare payments and limiting child care costs.

> I only worked part-time from even before David was born because my second son, Denny, was also young when I started, and my mother provided my child care, but I can only get her to watch them for so much time, and I only wanted to work when I could get the child care. I went back to work when David was six months to this job where I helped do political surveys on the phone. I had been at this job part-time for three years before he was born, and they told me I could come back when I wanted to after having the baby. . . . But then I was let go two to three months after I came back because the company moved out of state.
>
> After that I did internships and a fourteen-month job training for a medical [patient] specialist. I did that around my mother's schedule too. . . . Now I'm working at the Big Sports Arena. I do concessions, and the work is irregular. I do one or two days some weeks and three or four days some weeks. Sometimes I don't have any work at all for like one week or two. This way I am just arranging someone to watch the kids here and there, and I can mix it up. If my mother won't do it, then I get my friends. Also, I'm still on PA. If I worked all the time, I would exceed the amount you are supposed to get paid before they will close your case, and then I would also have to pay for child care. I have never done that . . . so I do the seasonal jobs.

In several cases, mothers stopped using child care altogether and stopped working for a while following a bad care experience. Cassandra took a leave from her hospital job after she found Cedric bruised during a very short child care spell with a neighbor in his father's building.

> [After] the horrible care when he was at the woman's house in his father's building for like two weeks, no longer than that, and he was all scratched up, I just left my job for a little while to take care of him, because he did not seem the same to me; it was like he was traumatized. I did not know what to do. I just took a leave of absence and [her employer] understood.

I took two months off; I looked for everything I could find next that would be a safe place.

Sara's experience with the very low-cost informal care provider who wanted to take custody of Cristina was one of the worst care experiences for a mother in arranging care. She abandoned child care arrangements altogether until she could find something she could trust or that was more publicly accountable. More typically, the worst problems are experienced directly by the child, who must endure the low-quality care, as Cedric did.

In sum, mothers learned how to get from their first care arrangement to the next and to manage the care spells that followed by developing second-best care strategies when they could not find the care they most preferred. Many of these second-best care strategies involved an increasing reliance on community-based organizations for care assistance as time went on.

Turning to Agency-Based Care

While mothers often relied on their personal networks at the start of their children's care paths, some of the mothers in this study relied on the support of nonprofit social service agencies in their communities at the beginning of their children's care. And turning to agency-based care was a care strategy that many mothers adopted over time.

Uma, who had no living family, turned to community agencies to help arrange housing and health care for years before she had her daughter Sade when she was in her thirties. When Sade was born, Uma was unemployed and went on welfare. An agency in the Points that served women who were economically struggling helped her move back to work. She eventually started an Americorps placement with another agency that had links to child care programs, through which she made her first two care arrangements. Uma wanted Sade in Head Start so that she would receive the most comprehensive services at no cost. She went to more than a dozen Head Start centers in her community until she found one with an Early Head Start program that accepted Sade when she was twenty-eight months old.

Annette started her path from welfare to work as an Americorps volunteer after having her son Aaron, and she also arranged her first care spells through a community agency. Annette relied on agencies for a wide range of social supports over the years, and she eventually found a job working as a family advocate herself in a community agency. She arranged four of her six care spells through agency contacts, including the only three that she liked. Her agency-developed care spells accounted for twenty-six of Aaron's thirty months in care.

Although Uma and Annette had no kin or extensive personal networks to help them with child care, they did have previous successful experiences with agencies that led them to their primary reliance on agencies as a source for child care. Other mothers who were younger and had little agency experience and few family supports learned to use community agency services over time. These mothers often had multiple service needs that led them to seek agency supports; some of them first came to the agencies' attention because of these other needs.

Several mothers who had experienced homelessness became experts in finding and utilizing agency services. Iris ultimately relied on local agencies to find housing, to arrange her daughter Quirina's child care, to negotiate her welfare benefits, and to help with health care resources for her daughter's asthma condition. Iris returned to work two weeks after Quirina was born, and her first child care arrangement was with her father, Rafael. They were all living with his family at the time, and Rafael was attending one of the city colleges. Iris figured out that they could enroll Quirina in a full-day center at the college for free since he was a student, and they did so when her daughter was three months old. When Quirina was seven months old, Iris and Rafael broke up, and she and Quirina entered the city's homeless shelter system. While homeless, Iris continued to take Quirina to the day care center at Rafael's college in Brooklyn even though she was moving among shelters in the other boroughs. Within a few months she was able to find a charity organization, the Sisters of Galilee, that provided shelter and had a program that could lead to a subsidized apartment that was not in a city housing project. Staff at Galilee helped put Iris in contact with a child care agency in her community that helped her apply for ACD assistance and found Quirina's next two care arrangements. Both were placements in day care centers—the first near the shelter, and the second near the housing development where they moved.

Iris sought help from community agencies at numerous points in her struggles to find housing, work, and child care, and Quirina was in three centers for forty-five of her first forty-eight months, with relatively smooth transitions between them. Iris was able to accomplish this only because she received the agencies' help at many points where care might otherwise have ended because of breaks in her work and housing paths. Iris credited the support service agencies in her community for helping her maintain her spot at the day care center after she lost her job and the center was prepared to terminate her daughter's care because eligibility was based on employment.

> When I lost my job last year after one time she was hospitalized for the asthma, the center wanted to take away my spot because they said I was not working—take it away because they say I am not doing nothing, but they [the community agency] helped me so I can keep her child care. How was I going to look for a job if she was not in child care? I have no babysitting options. None. I found another job in two weeks, but if I lost the child care, I would have to stop working to find another center. Finding a job is easy for me, but child care is hard.

Julia was very young when she became a mother. She started with father and kin care arrangements for her daughter Jacqueline in her first year after leaving a homeless shelter and taking the first steps in her work path. She went back and forth between the care supports she found from service agencies and kin supports, but over time she came to rely more on agencies. Like many of the mothers, her first use of agencies was for help with problems related to her welfare benefits. Through this she found links to other services, including job placements and child care. She also learned "the system," as she puts it, of benefit programs from people at the agency. She says she would recommend the agency path to anyone in the same position.

> I would tell any young girl who is having kids and trying to work the system that it's hard. If they have a child, then it's hard, and the best resource is the community resource. It's more reliable than family. They will help you more than anything, because at least they will teach you about the system and how to work the system. They are more educated than the people that work at workfare—the workers and even the supervisors. The people at the community programs, they know more and they educate you. They tell you the truth, like when the people at welfare or housing are lying to you. Workfare will tell you that you don't have this [things like eligibility for different kinds of child care or for transitional benefits], but you do have all these resources. They just don't want to give it to you and go through the paperwork. The caseworkers here [at the community agency], they know. They are the ones that help you get them. They empower you. They stay on top of you and on top of the worker. They tell you how things are done.

Iris and Julia both gained extensive experience using community-based agencies to help them get the benefits and services they needed. They used agencies for placements in child care centers with ACD-contracted care, to broker other services in the community, to gain information about resources and the workings of bureaucracies, and to troubleshoot at times of need or when services ended. Sara also found community organizations instrumental in helping her to get services, and also for the legitimacy they conferred on her needs, which otherwise might have been overlooked in the labyrinthine public benefits systems that "churn" families on and off welfare and send them through the welfare system's "fair hearings" appeal process.

> The welfare department, they create so many problems for you. I get $40 in cash public assistance [every two weeks] and some food stamps, and they give me so much trouble. I have been to so many fair hearings, and I know all the welfare rules and laws now, so I always fight them when they cut my benefits. But I cannot do it myself. Rosemary at the [community] agency helps me. When something happens, I get a letter, I call Rosemary, and she calls them, because if I call they don't answer the

phone, or pass me to the right person, so she does it. . . . Then, at the hearings—it is in Brooklyn, and it takes two hours and Rosemary comes with me. . . . I tell her what to say, and we have always won, I know the laws so I know if I am right or not. I would not go to a fair hearing if I did not know I was right, but it would be hard without her, because if they see me alone, they make my life impossible, but they see me with her they give us respect.

Julia and Sara both relied to varying degrees on personal networks initially and later moved to agency-based strategies when the care they started with could not reliably meet their needs. About two dozen of the families in the sample followed this path from personal networks to local social service agencies in their care strategies, compared to twelve who used agencies from beginning to end as their primary resource. Julia and Sara combined the use of personal networks and agency supports in their care strategies, and they relied more on agency-based supports over time. They used kin and informal care arranged through personal networks at their children's earliest ages, when agency-based services were least available. They moved to agencies when they needed longer-term care and when their personal resources were exhausted. Julia used informal or kin care for fifteen months and agency-derived care for twenty-four months in the four years of her daughter's early childhood. Sara used the Head Start care she found for Cristina for twenty-five of her thirty care months.

Brittany also used both personal networks and agencies to arrange primary care. Personal networks were the source of nine months of Bethany's care, and agencies for thirty-two months. Brittany, like Sara and Julia, started with care from her personal network, and when this became unstable, she moved to a family child care arrangement derived from an agency source. Like Julia, Brittany returned to her personal network for care assistance when there were breakdowns in the agency care she used. Many mothers combined network and agency supports, returning to personal networks to bridge primary care spells or for secondary care to wrap around the primary care that they found through community agencies.

In addition to moving between the primary arrangements they derived from their personal networks and from agencies, mothers integrated their use of these resources as part of their care strategies in several ways. They often relied on their personal networks for information about available agency care and used care from their personal networks for secondary, short-term, or emergency care even when they sought out or relied on agencies as a primary care source.

Mothers often learned about agencies through their personal networks. Bernadette, a shy, reserved woman, learned about the agency through which she would arrange most of the child care services for her sons when she happened to go into the agency with her cousin, who was receiving other services there.

Griselda wanted to place her daughter Giselle in a center when she was one, but she was unable to find a center that accepted infants and toddlers. She undertook an extensive search for agencies offering care as well as child care resources and referral networks. But she had little luck until her best friend, also a young mother and someone who was well versed in the word-of-mouth information passed around by mothers in the Points, told her she had heard of an opening at the Freedom Child Care Center. Griselda eventually enrolled Giselle there when she was two years old.

> It took me like a year or so looking at places and calling and visiting. . . . I got lists from ACD and this agency for Hispanic families that help you find child care, and I did not find one place I could send her until she was 2.9. I never knew about Freedom, but Dahlia told me about it. It's a small center . . . and she was the only one who knew about it.

As mothers came to depend less on their personal networks for child care, many continued to rely on them for information about community agencies, the child care resources available through those agencies, and which staff members to seek out. Thus, the personal networks of kith and kin served as trusted and reliable information resources, while the local agencies became the source of services. For example, Bernadette learned about child care and other assistance offered by agencies through family members who used these services. Over time she came to rely primarily on agencies for assistance and invested time learning more about the range of child care sources on her own, but she needed her personal network as a starting point.

Some mothers continued to use kin for care while they waited for agency services, which could be hard to arrange. Matilda made five kin and informal child care arrangements during Leo's first three years while she cycled through six low-wage jobs, none lasting longer than seven months. A young mother, she originally turned for child care to each of her parents, Leo's paternal grandmother, and friends. When Leo was two, Matilda realized that her personal networks would not provide steady care arrangements to facilitate ongoing work, but she learned from friends about agencies offering child care. Matilda originally found agency-based resources promising but unavailable, and she waited for a place in a center care arrangement when she was able to work more regularly.

> Right now I'm still juggling his child care between my parents and friends. . . . I think it would be better for him, and for my working . . . [if] Leo went to [the community center]. Next year I hope he's gonna go for care all day at their Head Start program, but he has a whole 'nother year almost, so I have to figure how to get him from here to there so I can work steady.

A significant finding in this study was that over time *most of the mothers in this study came to prefer agency-based strategies in the domain of child care.* The strong reliance on community-based service agencies in this study differs from earlier findings on low-income mothers' strategies when more mothers worked intermittently, part-time, or off the books or relied on welfare (Edin and Lein 1997; Stack 1974).[4] These authors studied low-income women and found a heavy reliance on personal networks of female kin, as I did, but the use of kin networks within my sample varied considerably. Many of the mothers in my sample had little or no access to personal networks, and the pressures and outcomes are different when mothers are working full-time jobs. Nevertheless, the heavy use of agency-based assistance was notable and in some cases grew out of greater work participation and an evolving view of child care that emphasized cognitive goals for children and care stability.

In the context of child care and higher work levels, the use of agencies was the most notable difference in survival strategies among the mothers in my study. Edin and Lein (1997) found that community-based social service agencies were not a major part of mothers' strategies for meeting their families' material needs. Agencies may have become important for child care, in part, because of the range of services they could provide. Families knew they could turn to agencies for help with child care. The mothers in this study were able to rely on agencies to provide the institutional care they wanted as well as access to the child care subsidies they needed. They might have felt less stigma turning to an agency to provide child care than they did applying to an agency for other services, such as food or financial assistance, for which they might principally rely on their personal networks. In the context of this time and place, the agencies providing care support and helping to arrange care were committed to getting mothers to work and promoting financial self-sufficiency. Child care was seen as a crucial factor in achieving these goals. Many of those who relied primarily on agencies for assistance and who had agency help seemed better equipped to balance work and child care.

Adapting Survival Strategies After Welfare Reform

The adaptive strategies of mothers in this study highlights the enormous heterogeneity in the life situations of these women and the actions they took to cope with their problems, as well as in the learning that occurred over time as they changed their care preferences and strategies. The survival strategies themselves were dynamic: mothers altered them according to changing circumstances, adjusting to changes in their work course to make their care correspond and vice versa. Mothers adapted their changing strategies to the changing context of welfare that emphasized work. They charted their care and work paths together to obtain public subsidies to afford higher-quality and consistent care and to secure a place for their child in stable, center-based care.

Charting Work Paths and Care Paths Together

The mothers I spoke with clearly saw work and care as strategically interrelated. Some of them made child care arrangements to support their work schedules, and others sought to structure their work around the availability of child care. In almost all cases, however, mothers knew they had to determine work and child care almost simultaneously, and they were not sure which to put first. Cassandra, who was working as a nurse at a hospital when her son Cedric was two, tried at first to arrange her shifts so that they fit her child care needs, but then later she adjusted her child care to fit her work schedule.

> I try to get my work schedule around my child care. Actually, I think it's the other way around, to tell you the truth. I've been working around my child care. . . . When I had the center care, I would try to get the day [shift] as often as I could, and my supervisor was generally accommodating. Now that I got Miss Leslie watching all the kids, I am asking for the evening shifts [4:00 p.m. to 12:00 a.m.], because that way I can be here when they [her older sons] get home from school, and she will stay with them until the young ones go to sleep, and then I'm okay with them being alone with just my oldest son until I come home. And there have been times when I've had to take some time off when the child care fell apart altogether, where I know in other places I would have lost my job. But also, when I do come to work, I do my job, and do it well. And they pretty much like me there, and sometimes they just look the other way.

These mothers also describe how their priorities changed as their children aged. When their children were younger, they generally worked less or stopped working if they had care problems. As their children got older, they arranged new care more quickly in favor of work. Inez says that she was especially vigilant about the importance of placing care first when her daughter Jasmine was an infant and that she preferred to be Jasmine's caregiver.

> I left one job. . . . I quit after three months because when I picked up Jasmine . . . she was on the floor in front of the TV in her wet diaper while the other kids were running all around, and she [the provider] was not doing anything. I decided I would let them sanction me, but I was not going to leave her with anyone when I could care for her best.

Uma also placed child care before her work decisions when her daughter Sade was very young. She believed that the scarcity of adequate child care slowed down her own development and work opportunities as a physical fitness trainer.

> For me, the child care has to be set before I make work decisions. If she has child care, like now in Head Start, that is 9:00 a.m. to 3:00 p.m., I

have to fit my work around that because my heart would not let me put her in some care I don't know about. I could not imagine her where she is unhappy and where I am not sure about the safety while I am away from her. I just can't. I am trying to get extended hours for Head Start, but it is still hard in my work to do this work when you have a young child. A lot of training and things happen in the evening, and I could probably progress in my work quicker if I had that time available. I have finally found something in my life that I enjoy doing that could possibly be lucrative, and there is something else that is a priority, but that is okay because she is my girl.

Mothers in the sample spent enormous amounts of time and energy developing strategies for work and child care. Ramona, who cycled through several work and training experiences—including some with work hours different from the hours at her daughter Flores's child care center, requiring some multiple care arrangements—developed an expertise in moving between strategies for combining care and work, as evidenced in her advice to other mothers:

A mother can make more if she works full-time, but then she has to find two, three, four places to leave her kids, and some of these are with strangers. I think it's better to work part-time, even two part-time jobs, or find work at home. The full-time jobs we get don't have benefits, and you lose more taxes. If you have one part-time job and one off-the-books job, you can still get food stamps and medical [benefits] for the kids . . . and [*she adds later*] more in the tax refunds [a larger EITC payment].

Most of the mothers in the sample, however, did work full-time jobs and receive all of their income "on the books," and they did so consistently for most of the study's duration, quickly moving from one job to another during work transitions. Many talked about the difficulties of working long, often nontraditional hours and finding child care to correspond with their work schedules. Most of these mothers wanted to work and took satisfaction from it. However, they also wanted to minimize the complex, multiple care arrangements they had to make and the instability that this created in their children's development. As Annette says: "I feel good when I am working. When I am at home doing nothing, I do not feel valuable. Now I wish I had more time at home with the children. I just don't know how you can have it right between work and raising your children."

Getting Subsidized

Even as these mothers felt compelled to work and manage their families' complex lives with little money or resources, they spent a great deal of time and energy concerned about their children's development and care. While their children were young, they constantly worried about how much they should work and what sacrifices they should make in terms of where they put their children. Yet most of them accepted that they would work for most of their children's early developmental years and viewed economic stability as a precondition to their children's healthy development.

Some mothers were committed to work, no matter what, but needed subsidies to make employment a worthwhile proposition and to arrange child care that could at least be adequate and durable, while others worked only if they had subsidized and stable child care. Almost every mother in this study sought out subsidies for child care as a key and early part of their care strategies.

Without subsidized child care, Sara could not have worked or gone to school. She could not have gotten her daughter the developmental care or early education that she needed. Many mothers used very low-cost care that was not subsidized, as Sara did, but these arrangements were often unstable and good for neither the mother's work path nor the child's development.

The most difficult period for mothers was when their children were youngest, because there were so few subsidized care options for infants and young toddlers. Sara found one possibility and pursued it obstinately, waiting more than a year for a place in a Head Start center with an infant and toddler component. After the frightening experience she had with her first informal care arrangement, Sara did not use care again until subsidized institutional care became available.

Mothers' experiences in getting and finding subsidies varied greatly. Most persevered until they got subsidized child care, which often came later in their children's care paths, after they themselves had paid for care arrangements. At a time when what their child most needed was stability and what they most needed was help in making sure their child was in a good arrangement, these unsubsidized arrangements often proved unstable.

Seeing Care as a Stabilizing Force

Sara and Cristina's story also demonstrates the importance that mothers place on finding stable, quality care arrangements as they react to negative experiences, as well as the important role that good, reliable care can play in the lives of low-income families.

After the first poor care arrangement, Sara made concerted efforts to secure and then maintain a place for Cristina in Head Start for the rest of her early childhood; the subsequent consistency of her care over nearly three years proved extremely important to both Cristina and Sara. Cristina thrived in her early cognitive development despite her constant movement back and forth between the United States and Ecuador and across homes and homeless shelters. And Sara was also able to make consistent work and educational plans when Cristina's care was set.

In circumstances of great family and child need, quality preschool programs can serve as both a balm and a developing force for children coping with the severe stresses of their family's poverty. In visits to Cristina's Head Start center, I found other children like her who had lived in a series of homeless shelters, including two toddlers who had become homeless owing to domestic violence they had witnessed between their parents. These children continued to attend the Head Start center and receive additional attention and services, and the mothers were also able to consider the center a home base for their family needs. Other children had been exposed to alcohol or drugs in utero, and one boy had experienced foster care in five settings before he was three years old. Children with such experiences of poverty and family disorder benefit tremendously from a solid, stable developmental base of child care. Several research studies confirm that the benefits of higher-quality child care are greater for children in low-income families and those facing other childhood disadvantages (National Institute of Child Health and Development 1999; Phillips et al. 1994; Scarr and Eisenberg 1993) and that preschool itself can be a stabilizing experience for children living in poor areas (Karoly et al. 1998; McKey et al. 1985; Reynolds et al. 2001).

As has already been discussed, Cristina's stable care allowed Sara to pursue her work and schooling and to base her schedule of classes, work at school, and private work she did as a Spanish tutor around Cristina's Head Start program schedule, and to do so continuously once Cristina started her care arrangement. Stable care helped to stabilize work paths for several other mothers, including Julia, who eventually got her first full-time job and left welfare once she found a stable care arrangement for Jacqueline with a family child care provider whom she liked and to whom Jacqueline became very close.

Another important role that higher-quality early care offered some families was earlier identification of and interventions for special needs. A great many children in this sample had special needs, and sometimes it was the professional staff in a high-quality child care program who identified developmental delays, most commonly speech delays or behavioral problems. Cristina's Head Start program started to work with her immediately on speech and eating problems they identified. Although she continued to be a picky eater and remained shy with many people, over time she ate more while at the center and her speech was fine following her therapy.

Summary and Conclusions

In this chapter, I have explored how mothers developed strategies that allowed them to work and to arrange child care. From their perspectives, there were a range of possible strategies to best approximate the care they wanted for their children from birth to age four. These strategies were generally purposeful, reflecting the practical constraints that characterized their families' lives. They often adopted "second-best" strategies, including: maintaining steady employment and piecing together care around a primary focus on work; staying with long-term care for as long as possible, for the sake of stability; pursuing subsidized care as early and as aggressively as possible and piecing together very-low-cost care until subsidized care came through; and working only when low-cost or no-cost care was available. Mothers who adopted each of these strategies sought to optimize family and child care outcomes in the face of the difficult constraints they faced. For each, their children incurred some costs and received some benefits.

Sometimes facing a paucity of care resources, these mothers regularly worked within their expectations for care to develop strategies that helped them come closer to meeting their aspirations. Mothers also learned along the way and revised their care strategies as their work paths developed and their information and available resources for care changed with time. At the outset, they often took care that was available to them through personal relationships with individual caregivers. Over time they developed stronger preferences for agency-derived institutional care arrangements, which offered greater learning opportunities and stability.

A critical finding from this analysis of survival strategies is that kin play a variable and complex role in the development of mothers' care strategies over time. Kin networks were vital for initial, respite, and wraparound care for the families in this study. Kin, when available, were also instrumental in helping mothers get started along care and work paths, and they were the resource most used to smooth things out in troubled times or when other care fell apart. In addition, kin were often the essential second care arrangement that helped mothers keep their jobs. For some mothers, at some times, kin were able to provide child care, but for others they were not. The analysis further shows the limits of kin care as children mature.

When mothers in this study did use their personal networks for child care, they did not often exchange or swap care in a reciprocal manner, as they did with the many resources they shared in the context of Stack's (1974) study of the Flats.[5] Mothers in this study were working extensively, and most often the personal network assistance went in one direction from the kin who gave care to the mothers in need. This is similar to what Edin and Lein (1997) found when they studied the strategies that mothers used for getting needed financial support; they found that support generally flowed on an as-needed basis in one direction from the better-off to the less-well-off within personal networks. When many family members were working and some were not, as was the case in my own study, those who were able to offer child care were doing so to support the needs of their working kin; without reciprocal care necessarily expected in return.

Many mothers in this study paid for their kin care, while others provided for other family expenses in relation to the caregiver, such as covering their common rent with a rental subsidy when they shared a residence.[6] For example, Dona used the rental supplement that was part of her welfare case to pay about half the rent for her mother's apartment, where she and her three sons all shared a small bedroom. Her mother was often Dona's primary source for child care when Dona worked part-time in the evenings as a concessionaire at a sports arena, and Dona did not pay her mother for this care. These types of exchanges within her extended family had been going on for most of Dona's life. Many members of her family had relied on welfare at several points, and they frequently coresided. These arrangements were fairly common for those mothers who had received welfare and housing assistance and who coresided with their kin at points when their children were very young. It seemed that these types of indirect exchange may be less common now than they were a few years ago, in the context of more work demands and less welfare, and that in many instances these exchanges did not endure or were not reliable.

Thus, even with some examples of child care being exchanged for assistance of a different sort, or for cash, the ongoing interfamily exchange that others have found was neither as common nor as intense an exchange for the care strategies of the women in this study. In the context of welfare reform and participation in the labor force by single mothers, it became harder for mothers to provide assistance to the kin who might be helping them. Most often in this study the provision of child care within personal networks was one-sided support from kin on an as-needed basis. Looked at over a longer time, we might see more levels of exchange across personal networks. At different life stages, the flow of exchanges may reverse direction.[7]

The support from one relative to another was limited overall, because the need for child care assistance was so extensive—kin were needed to provide more hours of care than they could give. Factors in their relatives' own lives, some of whom were older or overstressed by other work and family obligations, did not allow such an intense commitment to full-time, ongoing care. Over time mothers understood that and turned less and less to kin networks for the bulk of their child care assistance.

In the course of developing their care strategies, many mothers turned to agencies in their community for help in arranging care, even though many of them preferred care from members of their personal networks when they first started to arrange care. Mothers increasingly relied on neighborhood agencies as their children got older and they learned that they could not use personal networks as exhaustively as their child care needs required. Over time, most mothers came to prefer agency-based care because care arranged through these sources was more likely to offer stability and access to center care that could offer learning opportunities, which they valued more over time.

The greater reliance on community agencies was partly explained by the difference in the domain of child care: the family need involved a regular, highly intensive need that was hard to exchange when mothers were working much more and needed to rely on regular, long-term forms of support. Relatives' time resources were often stretched thin because they were working as well. As many more women have moved in and out of the labor force, the reserve of female kin who can help with child care has diminished, as has the consistency of this support when it is available. For the mothers in this study, the sources of child care assistance, including kin care and the subsidy systems, were irregular and unreliable. As they made frequent changes to their strategies for cobbling together child care resources, their use of kin and agency-based care often overlapped and their primary reliance on one or the other shifted with changing circumstances.

The detailed narratives of these women's lives and their adaptive care strategies reflect the heterogeneity in the life situations of mothers and the actions they take to cope with the problems presented by child care. The mothers in this study showed enormous resourcefulness navigating employment and children's care arrangements alongside difficult and changing family, housing, and employment situations. Single working mothers struggling for a modicum of self-sufficiency were found to use whatever resources they could employ to manage their children's care and continue to work. Many were still anchored in family networks, and many also relied on community organizations for support. The African American and Latina mothers in this study demonstrated resiliency and varying degrees of independence as responses to the socioeconomic conditions of poverty that persist in the age of welfare reform.

~ Chapter 6 ~

Choosing Our Future: Child Care Policies in the Age of Work and Personal Responsibility

The findings discussed in the preceding chapters provide some reasons to be encouraged, and some cause for concern. The optimism comes, in part, from seeing that many mothers have made great strides in their paths to greater economic self-sufficiency. Most mothers in this study were able to work regularly despite turmoil in many areas of their lives. Many earned enough to lift their families above the defined levels for income poverty, and they report fewer material hardships and less social isolation than they say they experienced in earlier years. Furthermore, they showed remarkable resilience and capacity to develop and implement individual strategies for child care that fit their family's particular circumstances and their expectations for their children's early childhood. It was encouraging to witness them make much out of little as they knit together pieces of care here and there to make their way to work and keep their children largely safe and provided for from birth to pre-school.

Yet these signs of confidence were often accompanied by concerns about the low-paid work, the turbulence of so many changes, and the stress of holding together the different and shifting aspects of the lives of their families. Especially worrisome was the often tattered quilt of care they pieced together for their children's earliest years. The developmental experiences many of their children missed will be hard to compensate for later on. In their own words, these mothers echo the warnings of developmental experts about the deleterious effects of low-quality child care and the lost opportunities that more developmentally appropriate and stable care might have provided for children starting off from disadvantaged positions of poverty and socially isolated neighborhoods.

The evidence in this study clearly suggests that there are major problem areas in child care among low-income families that have been exacerbated in some respects by recent changes in social policy. The analysis in the preceding chapters highlights several significant findings that American public policy must confront:

- Mothers spent an inordinate amount of time and energy locating affordable, accessible child care, and they expended great efforts trying to secure child care subsidies that were insufficiently funded. As a result, mothers spent a high proportion of their income on child care, much of which they found to be low-quality.

A powerful finding in this research study was that low-income mothers make remarkable work efforts, which challenges existing stereotypes of poor single mothers, especially those who had been welfare recipients. In the political debate leading up to welfare reform, many worried that mothers leaving welfare would not find work or make solid gains toward economic independence (Holzer 1996; Holzer and Danziger 1998; Nightingale and Haveman 1995). These mothers did so quite convincingly. They also showed enormous resolve and guile in finding one care arrangement after another and piecing these together, transitioning their children into and out of so many other people's care. They also learned more than any person should have to about negotiating an inchoate child care system in their efforts to finance the quality of care they preferred. These mothers, despite their hard and steady work, did not earn much, and yet they spent an average of 18 percent of their earnings on child care. The further away mothers were from the welfare system, the less likely they were to receive child care assistance. In an era when the virtue of work for the poor is held to be sacrosanct, policy sends the perverse signal that the public purse most supports those who are first going to work but not so much thereafter when they begin to work consistently.

- The children in this study changed care relationships and locations frequently, experiencing instability during their earliest development. The child care that families relied on was inherently unstable, and the frequent shifts in care resulted from and added to the often chaotic changes in work and family life.

There was an astonishingly high level of dynamics in child care during the first four years of childhood. Care arrangements frequently ended because the child care was inherently unstable or because of work, housing, health, or relationship issues. Most child care spells were short, with 60 percent lasting less than six months. Children in the sample passed through an average of more than five primary nonmaternal care spells in their first four years. In addition, families experienced frequent and sometimes extended periods of insufficient care or had to combine multiple care arrangements at a time. In-

cluding the number of changes in secondary care arrangements and the number of times disruptions in child care led children to return to their mother's
primary care, the average number of care changes in these children's first four
years was more than twelve.

• The child care issues that families faced changed as children aged. The stability of child care spells, the availability of subsidies, and the strategies
  that families employed to make their arrangements all varied significantly
  across the years of early childhood.

Most of the families in this study primarily used informal care and kin care
during the first two years of their children's lives, in part because some mothers preferred their children to be in a safe home setting, but also because these
were the only options available to them and they could not obtain child care
subsidies to use other forms of care. Almost all mothers strongly preferred formal institutional care for their children when they were three to four years
old, but some could not make these arrangements then either because of the
complexity of their work or their children's needs. Also, because families were
often better able to access child care subsidies over time, they were more likely
to use more formal care and experience more stable child care spells when
their children got older. Many mothers relied on their personal networks for
arranging care when their children were very young, but as mothers developed care strategies over time and their children got older, more mothers
turned to agencies in their community for help in arranging care.

• Child care difficulties were intensified for mothers of infants, mothers of
  children with special needs, and mothers working nontraditional work
  hours. Infant child care was especially scarce, and institutional child care
  in centers and schools was also less available than many families preferred.

Care choices were especially constrained for mothers when their children
were infants. Many mothers worried about starting their children in care too
early when they had the fewest child care choices, and the earliest arrangements they used often turned out to provide the lowest-quality care. For
mothers working unconventional or rotating schedules, or for children with
special needs, institutional care and alternative options were also in short supply. The supply of formal child care options was limited, though these
arrangements were more stable and ultimately preferred by many families.
Most mothers in this study wanted to place their children in center-based
forms of care earlier than they were able, and they worried that delayed access
to institutional care would affect their children's development and prepara-
tion for school. In many instances there were not enough centers, families
could not access the subsidies required to afford center care, or centers did not
accept certain types of subsidies, such as vouchers.

The Current Policy Context for
Early Care and Education

The challenges faced by these families are not surprising given the incoherent, almost byzantine system of child care and education that exists in the United States. There is no unified system for child care and limited integration of child care and education.

As we saw in the child care arrangements used by low-income working families in this study, children are cared for in a mix of settings that include the homes of relatives or family friends; the homes of neighbors or other informal, nonlicensed child care providers; the homes of licensed, professional family child care providers; their own homes by parents; their parents' jobs; publicly funded day care centers and preschool programs; Head Start centers; center-based programs in homeless shelters; and prekindergarten programs in public schools. Children with disabilities are sometimes served in these programs or others specifically designed for children with greater developmental needs. In addition to these types and settings of care, higher-income families use private child care centers, private nurseries and preschool programs, and nannies.

Many parents agree that finding affordable, available, quality care and education is a significant challenge. In this study, most parents found and arranged child care with difficulty. About half of all the spending for child care tracked in this study was paid for by parents, and the rest was either subsidized by the government or given in-kind by the provider, usually relatives. This finding is consistent with the results of other broader-based survey studies that report that most child care is arranged and paid for by parents who report great difficulties finding care and education programs for their children (Heymann 2000; Mitchell, Stoney, and Dichter 2001; U.S. General Accounting Office 1997).[1] Anne Mitchell and her colleagues (2001) estimate that 60 percent of all child care in the United States is funded by parents.[2] Because of limitations on what the parents in this study could afford, the care that they themselves paid for was often lower-quality, shorter in duration, and unlikely to offer the developmental opportunities they wanted for their children. Large-scale research studies confirm that the care parents are able to arrange is often low in quality (Galinsky et al. 1994; Helburn 1995), short-term in nature (Meyers et al. 2001), very expensive relative to earnings (Giannarelli and Barsimantov 2000; Schulman 2000; Smith 2000, 2002), and lacking in the continuity and stimulation that young children need for optimal development (Helburn 1995).

The United States has an assortment of child care programs and services that have been developed at the federal, state, and local levels (U.S. General Accounting Office 2000; Gomby et al. 1995; Kagan 1993; for a summary of the primary programs, see table A.4). In most states, there are at least four major types of care and education programs for children four years and younger: group day care and nursery programs; Head Start centers; prekindergarten programs; and a range of less formal options. The service models and administrative structure of these programs vary tremendously across states and communities, creating a hodgepodge of programs that parents have great difficulty navigating to make child care arrangements. There are often gaps and overlaps in program funding, the targeting of services and eligibility, schedules of services, fees, and other critical elements of program operations. One comprehensive review argues that this "welter of diverse policy aims, target groups, and service strategies is unacceptably inefficient and wasteful, especially when resources are scarce" (Gomby et al. 1995, 20). This crisis in the coordination of services often means that some families receive fragmented, inappropriate, and inconsistent services, while other equally needy and eligible families receive no services at all. The system can appear opaque, and the resulting distribution of child care services arbitrary and capricious. This fragmented child care system makes the management of child care programs inefficient from the policy level, and despite their real needs for better care opportunities, families often find engagement with this system a frustrating and fruitless experience.

Because of their limited care choices and the tenuous nature of many child care arrangements, the mothers in this study pieced together care arrangements in extremely intricate, but unstable, ways. This resulted in children being sent from one place to the next with great frequency and little continuity. These mothers acquired a rich knowledge of this crazy patchwork system, developing the most rational strategies under the circumstances to make their way through an inherently irrational "system" as they tried to reconcile their work and family responsibilities. For this they certainly deserve our praise, but they also deserve much better. The children do especially.

What We Can Do

America needs to decide what role it wants to play in the lives of young children. The case for a social policy designed to enrich low-income children's early development can be made on many grounds—sociological, economic, developmental, and moral. Overall, the United States of America provides relatively little public support for young children, and there is no unified system of early care and education for children (Heymann 2000; Polakow 1993).[3] This is in contrast to what exists in many other industrialized countries (Gornick and Meyers 2001).[4]

American society has changed remarkably over the last three decades. There have been dramatic increases in women's labor force participation. Following sharp increases in the rates of divorce and childbearing outside of marriage, many more women now raise children as lone parents. These trends have changed American childhood and where and how early childhood time is spent, and they have contributed to making child care a nearly universal part of child development. Mothers are working, contributing their labors to the economy, and have adapted to the changes in American society and social policy, and yet they still need stable, high-quality care for their children so that they can work consistently and productively. Reforming child care was largely unaddressed when welfare policy was reformed in the mid-1990s to incorporate a greater expectation that mothers would work.

Both economic and developmental arguments support efforts to improve child care opportunities as well as maternal employment. Public policies could effectively promote both. When one accepts maternal employment as a given, it becomes important from an early point in children's lives to shift the focus from custodial care to providing opportunities for their educational enrichment. Finally, given the wide disparities in the United States in income and opportunities, as a matter of distributive justice, the accident of birth into conditions of poverty should not limit a child's early possibilities to develop and later compete for better opportunities in life.

The difficulties experienced by mothers in this study offer insights into systematic reforms that might provide better early childhood opportunities and more continuous care for children. Some of the dissatisfaction reported by these mothers resulted from the shortcomings inherent in means-tested categorical programs that were not funded to meet all eligible families' needs, producing the problems in access and maintenance associated with other rationed services. Some of their dissatisfaction resulted from unnecessary and irrational complexities in the child care system itself. The problems I observed—limited access to services and frequent breaks in care continuity—lead me to conclude that we need a much simpler system for administering child care subsidies. This will require building up child care systems and coordinating across diverse programs, while at the same time integrating them with a more consistent educational focus. A reformed child care system must allow mothers to work continuously, make quality care affordable, and provide children with meaningful developmental opportunities from the start of their care paths. The care we offer young children can be improved through a few targeted policy changes.

1. Increase Available Care Options and Supports for Families with Infants

The most critical need for child care subsidies is among low-income working families with infants and toddlers. However, given the limited supplies of child care subsidies and how the system has developed over time, infants and toddlers are often the last and least served. Contrary to current practices, a broadened child care subsidy program should prioritize children younger than three for subsidies, given that families' options for care are most limited at these times, when the subsidies are most needed.

In this study, families had the fewest care options when children were youngest—infants and young toddlers—a time when their incomes were often lowest and their jobs less steady. It was in these most important developmental years that care was least stable: the median length of care arrangements started in the children's first two years was four months compared to a median of seven months for arrangements begun in children's third and fourth years. It was also during the children's earliest care spells that families had the greatest unmet need for subsidies. Most of the very young children were cycled through various low-cost care spells while waiting on lists for subsidized forms of care. The families that did receive subsidies gained them by chance, perseverance, or having better information about the complex subsidy systems.

Most early childhood programs were first built to serve the needs of preschool-age children, then expanded somewhat to serve the after-school needs of school-age children, and then lastly the needs of infants and toddlers. This is partly the result of historical accident. With more infants and toddlers needing care at a time when funding constraints have grown tighter, and with existing child care systems and institutions designed to serve older children, the care of infants and toddlers has been overlooked in an era of increasing working motherhood and earlier working motherhood.

A substantially larger base of services has long existed for preschool-age care in many New York City communities, but there has never been much capacity to serve infants and toddlers in any forms of licensed care—whether in centers or family day care homes. Much of the child care infrastructure was originally built to serve preschool-age children and most expansions have tended to work from this base. Of the licensed capacity of child care slots in the city, fewer than 8 percent are licensed to serve infants. With the recent upsurge in maternal employment, much of the increased demand for child care has been for mothers of very young children. Furthermore, the high demand for more and better subsidized options has been met with almost no public funding for additional child care capacity, since the city has spent most of the recent increases in funding to finance vouchers. Vouchers, while possibly a more efficient way to distribute child care money, do nothing to address the supply constraints for formal care or care for children whose mothers work nonstandard hours, where the primary problem is a lack of supply.

The small nonprofit organizations that operate most child care centers do not have the capital resources to develop new infant care centers or expand to serve younger children. States should help build up the supply of more quality infant care options by creating financing mechanisms, including grants and low-interest loans, to nonprofit organizations interested in expanding institutional care or developing higher-quality family child care networks to serve more infants in more durable care arrangements. As critical as it is to increase access to the subsidy system for families with infants, it is just as important for policy to support the creation of greater child care capacity to serve children age birth to two.

In addition to better meeting their need for initial care arrangements, mothers need help in the first year of their children's lives to determine the

best time to return to work and balance employment and child care responsibilities. Many mothers in this study said their biggest worry was about placing their children in care too early as they were first returning to work. The
first year after birth was also a time when family incomes were often lowest,
when care options were most limited, and when higher-quality care was generally most expensive. Many mothers preferred to be their child's caregiver for
much of the first year because they felt they best understood their child's
needs and they wanted to build a strong bond with their infant before returning to work. The child development research generally concludes that
early maternal employment and high usage of child care for infants is associated with negative effects on children's early development, particularly when
the care is low-quality and combined with other family disadvantages (Belsky
2001; Brooks-Gunn, Han, and Waldfogel 2002; Lamb 1998; National Institute of Child Health and Development 1997a).

Policy supports to mothers in the first year of life can take several forms,
including providing a first-year exemption from work requirements for
women on welfare with newborns, establishing more generous and broad-
based parental leave policies for some part of the first year, and creating child
allowances as a birth-year benefit. Currently, twenty-eight states set their
work requirement exemption periods so that mothers on welfare can care for
their children during the first year of life or longer. Given mothers' worries
about placing children in care too early and the low quality of many infant
care arrangements, states that do not have such exemption periods, including
New York, should defer mandatory work requirements for women receiving
public benefits until their child's first birthday.[5]

Concerns about the timing of mothers' return to work and early child care
are generally shared by families across the income spectrum, and parental leave
or child allowance policies could be broad-based universal policies to support
all families. The differences in parental leave policies and child allowances are
that child allowances could offer broader coverage than parental leave and be
designed to offer greater help to low-income families. Many existing parental
leave measures primarily benefit higher-earning women and disproportionately miss low-income working mothers. Sheila Kamerman (2000) estimates
that currently only about 55 percent of the workforce is covered by the U.S.
Family and Medical Leave Act (FMLA).[6] Low-income mothers are much more
often employed in less secure jobs, work for small employers, or hold informal
and part-time jobs and do not benefit from parental leave laws (Heymann
2000). Single mothers and members of minority groups are much more likely
to be ineligible for the leave (Waldfogel 1999a, 1999b).

Both California and Minnesota have a promising state parental leave program for families with newborns. In 2002 California became the first state to
establish paid family leave. The Family Temporary Disability Insurance
(FTDI) program, which took effect in January 2004, extends disability compensation to individuals who take time off from work to care for a newborn
or seriously ill family member.[7] Minnesota's At-Home Infant Child Care Pro-

gram allows families with a child younger than one that are eligible for basic sliding-fee child care assistance (75 percent of state median income) to provide full-time care for their infant child and receive a subsidy (equal to 90 percent of the sliding-fee rate) in lieu of child care assistance. A family is eligible for this program for a total of one year. Families may choose to segment this time if they plan to have more than one child. The program is funded through Minnesota's basic sliding-fee child care program but does not use Child Care Development Fund (CCDF) funds (Fenichel, Lurie-Hurvitz, and Griffin 1999).

A cash allowance provided to a mother during her child's birth year can provide needed cash when her family's size and expenses rise and its income declines. It can serve as a buffer to allow mothers or fathers to take additional time to parent exclusively or arrange for a preferred care arrangement before returning to work. A child allowance could be made in lieu of the child tax credit and exemptions in the first year, though the existing tax benefits would continue for children age one to eighteen (or older for children in college). It should be universal but progressively scaled so that it provides greater assistance at lower levels of family income, with higher-income families getting the equivalent of what they currently receive in the child tax credit and exemptions. As a primary form of family assistance in the first year of a child's life, this benefit should be neutral with respect to family structure and parental employment. The benefit should be targeted at children regardless of family or parents' work situations, and it should be the same for all families with the same level of earned income.

A child allowance could help promote healthy child development by providing families with the flexibility to use the assistance in the manner most appropriate for their needs, perhaps serving as the financial buffer needed to arrange more stable care with fewer disruptions during the first year of life. A birth-year child allowance could give low-income lone mothers more flexibility in deciding how long to stay home with their children and additional resources to pay for child care at a time when child care subsidies and options are limited. Many mothers would still choose to work, and nothing in the design of the allowance should discourage mothers who still need to work, especially those who are struggling in entry-level work and those for whom long absences from work could be detrimental to their future employment prospects. More analysis would be needed to determine an appropriate level for child allowances, how to structure these levels inversely with income, the net cost when replacing the child tax credit for children's first year, and any negative effects that might result from moving to a child allowance system.

2. Make Educational Investments to Foster Early Childhood Development

In addition to giving children a far better start from birth, public policy must support families by giving them a clearer view of when their child can begin a more focused life of learning and development. Once families in this study started their children on their rocky child care paths, what they increasingly realized they wanted was to get them off that path as quickly as possible and into a formal educational setting that would prepare them better for school. There was no set path for reaching that goal, and there was as much variation in when children started their first center care as there was for when mothers started their children in care after birth. At some much earlier and consistent point in children's lives, the major focus of policy has to move well past just offering vouchers for care of any kind to educational programs that offer developmental opportunities to all children, as early as age three. This is long overdue given the changes in work and mothers' often sole responsibility for their children.

American family life has recently been undergoing dramatic changes comparable to other seminal periods of historical change that have affected conceptions of public responsibilities for education. The industrial revolution had fundamentally changed the conception of childhood by the late nineteenth and early twentieth centuries (Zelizer 1985), moving the country toward universal schooling, first through public elementary education and then to secondary education (Osterman 1980; Ravitch 1988; Tyack 1974; Tyack and Cuban 1995). During the mid- to late-twentieth century the technological revolution again changed our human capital needs and educational expectations, and access to higher education was greatly expanded.

The current changes in American society toward nearly universal working motherhood, coinciding with a greater understanding of early brain development and the importance of early childhood developmental opportunities for later educational achievement, are just as profound. One might call it a "mother and child revolution." Creating a program that offers children optimal access to early educational opportunities requires making educational development a central goal for all types of children's care and providing universal access to preschool programs for three- and four-year-olds.

Many experts in child development and early education have forged a consensus that all children—across the range of family incomes and structures—gain from a stimulating educational environment at ages three and four (Blau 2001; Garces, Thomas, and Currie 2000; Karoly et al. 1998; National Institute of Child Health and Development 2000b, 2002; Peisner-Feinberg and Burchinal 1997; Scrivner and Wolfe 2002; Shonkoff and Phillips 2000) and that a movement to more universal earlier preschool education for children, starting preferably at age three, is the appropriate next step in the development of early childhood care and education. This movement now appears to be under way (Mitchell 2001; Scrivner and Wolfe 2002). The growing body of research finds that there are both short-term and long-term gains when children participate in preschool programs (Reynolds et al. 2002; Shonkoff and Phillips 2000).[8] This is as much a matter of equal educational opportunity for children living in low-income families as an economic benefit to society (Polakow 1993). The present study is a small-scale addition to that research base, and it indicates that mothers echo the concerns of the developmental experts and are part of the increasing demand for universal early education.

By the time their children were three years old, the choices that mothers in this study made for their children were often largely independent of their employment and based solely on their children's developmental needs. Moving children into the educational system at this age supports their school-readiness and helps them move out of the complicated patchwork of child care systems. Currently, the byzantine administrative structures of child care grow more complex when children reach age three and a greater variety of day care, preschool, and nursery programs become available. The care of children from age three—the time by which every mother in this study wanted her child to primarily be in an institutional setting—should become part of the state's system of universal public education. The building blocks for these systems are present in the form of states' pre-K programs and the federal Head Start program. There is now a need to invest more resources, integrate them, and make them universal.

Building on State Pre-K Initiatives   The movement toward more universal early childhood education is clearly under way in most of the states, but states vary enormously in both the types of universal early education programs available and the degree to which they are developing and implementing them. Forty-two states currently fund pre-K programs, and twenty-one states began or expanded pre-K programs in the last decade. Annual spending on state-funded pre-K programs in FY 1999 was $1.98 billion, and the majority of this spending was in ten states that had made major commitments to pre-K programs in the past decade (Mitchell 2001).[9]

The state of Georgia has probably gone the furthest in developing a universal pre-K early education program. It created a free universal education program that serves all four-year olds regardless of family income and funds the program with proceeds from the state lottery. The state funds public schools, Head Start centers, child care centers, and a range of public and private agencies to provide pre-K services and requires that programs be available for a minimum of six and a half hours a day during the school year (Scrivner and Wolfe 2002). In FY 2002 the program was funded at $238 million and served approximately 63,000 four-year-olds.[10]

New York State established a universal prekindergarten (UPK) program for four-year olds in 1998, which was to have been phased in over five years.[11] Some UPK programs are operated within the school system, while others are contracted out to community-based agencies with child care programs. The proportion of UPK services provided in nonschool settings was more than 50 percent statewide and more than 60 percent in New York City in the 1999–2000 and 2000–2001 school years (Scrivner and Wolfe 2002). Much of the initial development of the UPK program in New York State has been for a very short program day of less than three hours, which is inconsistent with the needs of working families. The state design for the program included half-day, school-day, and full-working-day options, with more of the longer day programs developed in community-based programs.[12] Most of the families in this study found it difficult to find a UPK program or to combine the program with other care. A few families were able to find a child care program through community-based agencies that ran both pre-K and day care programs or schools with after-school programs.

State pre-K programs, like child care programs, vary in the degree to which they are universal. Pre-K programs generally serve a broader eligibility pool than a program like Head Start, which is targeted to children in families below the poverty line, or child care subsidy programs that serve low-income families up to relatively higher multiples of the federal poverty level, such as twice the poverty line. A few states use strict income eligibility criteria for pre-K, while others may use low income or some measure of economic or educational disadvantage as a priority criteria. Most states seek to serve four-year-olds in pre-K; only a few include three-year-olds as well. In some states all pre-K programs are school-based, and in others they are located in both schools and other early childhood locations. For example, in New York and at least seven other states, more than 50 percent of pre-K programs operate in programs other than public schools, such as day care and Head Start centers. Most states offer only part-day or school-day-length programs, and only during the school year. Although the development of state pre-K programs advances the goal of educational development, the limited part-day, part-year nature of the care conflicts with the goals of assisting working families seeking economic self-sufficiency and consistency in care arrangements. Only full-year programs for at least the length of the full school day or up to a full working day can provide continuity in care for the children of working parents.

Until recently, many states were assertively building their state pre-K programs and making varied efforts to serve more children, to extend the length of program days, and to find collaboration and funding mechanisms to help them blend pre-K and other program models and funding. These efforts have slowed significantly during the economic downturn of 2001 to 2003, when several states proposed cutting programs as part of larger budget cuts, maintaining only part-day, part-year programs, or limiting availability to the neediest children (Children's Defense Fund 2003).

In some respects, newly expanded pre-K programs could add to the fragmentation and complexity of the early care and education systems in the states if these efforts are not well integrated with other existing programs for preschoolers or if they are limited to part-day services that do not serve full-time working families. Nevertheless, the development of pre-K programs offers promise for building toward universal early education. The policy questions for early education programs should focus on shaping these changes so that they are more universal, serve children's needs more comprehensively, and are coordinated with a reformed child care system so that they meet the needs of working families. With some greater federal contribution, states should continue to develop pre-K programs, first making them universal programs for four-year-olds for the length of the typical school day, then gradually expanding the program to include three-year-olds and longer hours of service. Creating common universal entry points for children into an educational track at age three will provide children with secure, consistent learning environments and an educational path beginning at an early developmentally appropriate point.

Building on Head Start and Transforming It into a Broader Model of Early Care and Education   Head Start is a good program to further incorporate into a broader system of early childhood care and education. Over the years Head Start has matured into the nation's only federally sponsored child development program. From its beginning, Head Start has followed a comprehensive child and family development model that encompasses health and nutrition, social services, and parental involvement in addition to its educational program for children. Several comprehensive reviews of the research on Head Start and other intensive child care for low-income children have found that these programs provide positive outcomes for children (Barnett 1995; Currie 2001; Currie and Thomas 1995; 1999; Karoly et al. 1998; McKey et al. 1985).[13]

In 2002 the federal government spent $6.7 billion on Head Start programs in the fifty states, serving more than 900,000 children at an average annual cost of about $7,000 per child (U.S. Department of Health and Human Services 2003).[14] Head Start has enjoyed popular and political support over the last quarter-century as an educational and antipoverty initiative, with significant annual expansions in funding over the past decade. While the number and percentage of children served have grown steadily over the past decade, the program is not an entitlement, and those served are still only about half of all eligible preschool-age children (Scrivner and Wolfe 2002). Some states supplement their federal Head Start funding to serve a greater proportion of the eligible population. Most notably, Ohio, which has expanded its Head Start program with a significant supplement of state funds, estimates that it serves more than 80 percent of the children eligible for Head Start (Mitchell 2001).

Among Head Start's positive attributes are its comprehensive services, existing infrastructure in very poor communities, higher standards for quality care, federal involvement, and broad support within low-income communities. Head Start already has a presence in neighborhoods, and its funding of the construction of new centers and expansions of existing ones can be very important to building the supply of institutional child care in low-income urban areas, where the shortage of physical space and capital financing can be obstacles to developing an infrastructure for high-quality institutional care and educational opportunities. Yet Head Start is also a categorical program and mostly offered only for a part-day; it could benefit from collaborative models to be more relevant to families' needs in this age of nearly universal working motherhood.

Most of the longer-term residents interviewed in this study knew of Head Start programs in their community and thought highly of them. Some had been in Head Start themselves. Some had used Head Start for their older children and then found they were not income-eligible for their younger children because they were now working; some found the part-day model incompatible with full-time work schedules.

Head Start funding should be expanded to cover more three- and four-year-olds over a broader range of low-income families. The program could be expanded at a rate higher than the recent average annual increases, to more than 10 percent annually. The program primarily serves children from families with incomes below the poverty line. Because the current poverty measure is set quite low, both as an absolute measure of family poverty and increasingly as a relative measure, eligibility for Head Start service should be broadened so that children in families with incomes up to 150 percent of the federal poverty level are eligible. Also, because many low-income families are working and yet poor or near-poor, the higher standard would ensure a greater mix of children from working and nonworking households. An additional way to encourage greater income mixing in Head Start would be to allow a marginal increase in the number of over-income families served. Under current Head Start guidelines, up to 10 percent of children can be over-income. Some localities use this provision to serve children with special needs. This allowance could be changed over time to 15 or 20 percent in order to serve more children with special needs through Head Start and to encourage more diversity in income and experience among the population served.

In many ways Head Start is an ideal program around which to center the integration of children's care services and build in greater child development and early intervention services. The states and the federal government should collaborate to further integrate Head Start with pre-K and other early childhood services in order to meet the need for earlier care and educational services for children, possibly starting with demonstration efforts in a few states. Many states have recently expanded care resources for four-year-olds through their pre-K programs, and Head Start is also focused on this age group. Integrating these program resources and expanding both over time to serve comparable numbers of three- and four-year-olds would foster earlier entry for children into educational programming and increased continuity of services.[15] Further integrating Head Start and pre-K funding would allow Head Start programs to expand eligibility to include children in families with incomes over the poverty level, creating a more heterogeneous learning environment, meeting family needs for longer service days, and extending services toward becoming a year-round program. Head Start, while maintaining a developmental focus on preschool-age children, should also accelerate the development of its Early Head Start programs for children age zero to three.

Some of the advantages of integrated early education are evidenced in this study. Two of the children in this sample were in Head Start/day care collaboration programs that integrated program funding and services. A few of the children in Head Start benefited from community-based early intervention services that were coordinated through their Head Start centers.

In this study, some community-based organizations ran both Head Start and day care programs. Most such organizations ran these programs separately, with different program administrators, staff, budgets, schedules, and program components, but with similar goals and populations served and some overlapping criteria. In the two cases noted earlier, the agencies had formally integrated child care programs, which had streamlined the administrative process and provided families with richer and more seamless services. These examples point the way toward even greater opportunities to develop more universal and seamless systems of care. One can envision integrating more early intervention services into the Head Start apparatus, given the program's existing emphasis on support services for children and families. Both of these initiatives appear to be promising models for further development, evaluation, and possibly replication.

Placing Development First Among the Goals for Child Care Policy and Parental Responsibility Much of the unmet potential for child care to serve as a better developmental context for children can be traced to unresolved, underlying conflicts in child care policy objectives. Within child care policy, there is an abiding tension between two different goals: facilitating the employment of mothers and enhancing the developmental experiences of children. Most child care policy has tended to favor the employment objective, and the recent push toward work-based social policy has only increased the focus of child care as first and foremost a means to increase mothers' employment (Adams and Rohacek 2002).

Early childhood care and education programs that do not explicitly try to relate both goals are likely to promote one goal to the near-exclusion of the other. Most child care subsidy programs, such as those funded through the Child Care Development Fund, are designed and implemented to support parental employment. Employment is most often the eligibility basis for receiving child care subsidies, and work is the direct reason for entry into most subsidized care arrangements. Given that states' subsidy systems do not have funding to support all those who are working and in need of child care, states have designed their systems to support as many working families as they can with limited funding. Much less attention has been given to the types and quality of the care that families might use. Moreover, because subsidy receipt largely depends on employment, a change in a mother's job status is likely to end the child's care abruptly as well, even though from a developmental perspective, there is a strong value in continuity of care independent of employment changes.

On the other hand, programs like Head Start are regarded primarily as child development programs, and these programs have been developed from the opposite perspective, largely neglecting parental employment as a factor in the design of services. Head Start has a very low-income eligibility threshold for those below the federal poverty line and offers mostly part-day and part-year child care schedules. This excludes participation by many families with working parents, even though these parents may be low-income and want the program for its developmental enrichment and stability.

Employment versus development is an enduring tension of child care policy, but these goals need not be irreconcilable. Care-oriented policies that support consistent, developmental early care and education need not be incompatible with requiring adults to work regularly and to be as economically self-sufficient as possible. Fostering both goals, policy changes could help with the initial entry into better-quality care in children's birth year so that their mothers can transition to work. Then child care policy could help children make the transition from care to education at a common, appropriate point in their development, while designing programs with the fact that parents work in mind so that they offer more hours of education and are better integrated with wraparound care options. Finally, the initial access to child care subsidies could be made smoother, and care more continuous, as children make their way from their first care to their first school.

3. Improve Access to Child Care Systems and Promote Continuity in Care

The mothers in this study express frustration about several aspects of the child care system: the poor information they received from government entities about child care; the difficult subsidy application process; the cumbersome procedures for maintaining subsidies; and the disruptions in care that were caused by problems within and divisions between subsidy sources. Overall, the system had a greater demand for subsidies than it could supply, which fostered a culture in which clients were discouraged from participating and encountered a "take it or leave it" attitude in many of their interactions with the system.

To a significant degree, the instability of child care experienced by families in this study was a direct result of complex policies and practices that limited access to and retention of subsidies and of the lack of coherence across systems. The ways in which states design and implement their child care programs can make the difference in whether families get needed assistance. These factors include:

- Eligibility and prioritizing criteria that determine which applicants can get assistance

- The administrative structure of child care agencies, their complexity, and their focus

- Administrative practices that determine how easy it is for families to obtain subsidies and to know whether they are eligible for subsidies

- The procedures for maintaining child care subsidies

Setting Priorities for Child Care Assistance   Most states set the maximum income levels for eligibility lower than the allowable federal maximum level, which is 85 percent of state median income (SMI).[16] The average state maximum is about 60 percent of SMI, with state maximum income-eligibility thresholds ranging from 45 to 85 percent of SMI (Gish 2001).[17] New York State's income cutoff was roughly 60 percent of its SMI, or about $29,000, for a family of three in the year 2000. Even at the maximum levels set by the states, however, states are not able to serve most eligible families, and they usually target their services more specifically to the very lowest-income families who are or have been in their public assistance programs.

States further control child care funds by setting prioritizing categories for subsidies. There are generally at least three categories of recipients: those who are receiving welfare, those who have recently transitioned off welfare, and low-wage working parents who have never or not recently received welfare. Following welfare reform changes, most states initially targeted welfare recipients over nonwelfare low-income working families because of the immediate need to move families from welfare to work. Like other states, New York gives highest priority for child care subsidies to families receiving welfare who are meeting their work requirements and those that are transitioning off welfare.[18] Many states use similar criteria. For example, between FY 1999 and FY 2002, roughly 52 percent of child care spending in California was for families in the state's welfare-to-work programs; 39 percent was spent on families who had transitioned from welfare (who in California are guaranteed child care assistance for twenty-four months after they stop receiving cash assistance); and only 8 percent went to low-income working parents, mostly those who earned the lowest incomes, including some who had been diverted from welfare (Montgomery et al. 2002). California's and New York's prioritization of welfare recipients and separation of child care eligibility and administration by welfare status has also been a common policy direction in other states since the enactment of welfare reform.

All eligible low-income families should be served equally without the added complications and discontinuities in care that come with priority categories and separate systems of care. Providing disproportionate assistance to families receiving welfare sends the wrong signal to those who have left welfare and those who have worked steadily for low wages without receiving welfare, and this message does not comport with the public values of work and greater self-sufficiency. As is also clear from this study, these categories are also illusory because these are often the same families at different points in time. It is when mothers have made progress in their work paths and most need consistent child care that they often lose eligibility or slip between the seams of different child care categories or systems.

A few states have sought to provide equal access to welfare and nonwelfare low-income families. Illinois makes no distinctions in its caseload between families receiving Temporary Assistance to Needy Families (TANF), those transitioning off TANF, and non-TANF families. Beginning in 1997, the state set its income eligibility at 50 percent of SMI, a relatively low level, in order to be able to do this.[19] Illinois, as a result, does not have a waiting list for child care services, and over time it has seen its caseload shift away from TANF recipients as it established the single, simplified income criteria and as its welfare caseload declined. TANF cases represented 65 percent of the child care caseload in July 1998, but by January 2003 they accounted for only 23 percent.[20] Similarly, the state of Washington sets its eligibility at 54 percent of SMI and also does not make distinctions between subgroups of low-income families. Washington has no waiting list for child care, bases eligibility on income and work status, and estimates that 19 percent of its caseload are families receiving TANF, while 81 percent of the caseload are non-TANF families (Gira 2003).

Nebraska's experience in trying to expand its income eligibility range for child care is illustrative of the difficulties that states have in creating these programs with limited funds. In 1998 Nebraska began serving all families whose income was up to 185 percent of the federal poverty level regardless of whether they were currently receiving or transitioning off welfare, using savings from its welfare block grants when its caseloads declined. Following an increase in child care applications, however, Nebraska determined that the state could not serve most of the additional working families, and as of July 2002 it had scaled back its eligibility for guaranteed assistance to 120 percent of the poverty level, instituted much more rigorous resource and asset tests for eligibility, and limited eligibility for child care assistance to twenty-four months (Urzedowski and Scott 2002).

Administering a Single, Simpler, Streamlined System   The existence of two administrative entities in New York City—the Human Resources Administration (HRA), which provides vouchers for welfare-related child care, and the Administration for Children's Services (ACS), which subsidizes nonwelfare-related child care using contracted care and vouchers—makes it more difficult for families to gain access to and retain subsidies. Many families first applying for child care do not know to which agency they should apply. Families moving from welfare to work, for instance, need at some point to move from one agency to the other for child care assistance. A mother who starts working while on welfare is eligible to receive HRA vouchers but needs to reapply to HRA for subsidies when she leaves welfare to receive twelve months of transitional child care. After her transitional benefits expire, she has to apply to ACS for child care benefits for low-income working families. None of the mothers in this study who started receiving child care subsidies through HRA while on welfare and eventually moved to work were able to move across these three categories of subsidy receipt in a continuous manner. Many of the families did not receive transitional child care benefits after leaving welfare, and many of those applying to ACS did not receive subsidies because of the long waiting lists for ACS child care.[21]

New York is not alone in creating a complicated obstacle course for families seeking child care assistance. In California the Department of Social Services offers child care as a support service to the welfare population, and the Department of Education administers child care funding to the population who have transitioned off welfare as well as to the nonwelfare working population as an educational service.

Having two or more child care programs with separate funding and bureaucratic systems can make the process complex and irrational to families seeking benefits. Separate systems can exacerbate many of the problems that characterize the child care system, including its opacity, barriers to entry, discontinuities in care, and the fragmentation and categorical organization of services that do not meet the needs of families and children over time.

Many administrative failures occur when families are caught between New York City's two child care subsidy systems. Some mothers experience long gaps between the time when their HRA vouchers end and the time when they can establish ACS eligibility, if at all. These seams between subsidy systems disrupt children's care and sometimes mothers' ability to work as well. In this study, most mothers leaving welfare were not informed about transitional child care benefits, even though this program was run by HRA, the same agency that administered child care benefits for those receiving welfare. Several mothers who knew about the benefits and asked for applications were told by the HRA Job Center staff that they were out of applications, a form of diversion. Others thought that because they were now working they needed to seek assistance from ACS, which either directed them back to HRA to apply for transitional child care vouchers or simply told them there were no ACS subsidies to be had, only waiting lists. Other studies of child care subsidy utilization by welfare recipients and "welfare leavers" have also found low usage rates and significant "churning" of families in an uncoordinated administrative system for child care benefits (Meyers, Heintze, and Wolf 1999; Meyers et al. 2001; Schumacher and Greenberg 1999).[22]

States and localities must integrate the administration of publicly funded child care into a single, more effective child care system that is less focused on welfare and eligibility determination. This should be part of refocusing the mission of child care agencies to emphasize child development, aligning the expectations of parents, providers, and administrators with the needs of children. Supporting child development would require redirecting program administrators away from a primary concern with compliance and toward the goal of facilitating child care access and choice. An improved child care subsidy system must provide care that helps families support both developmental and employment goals, encourages continuity in children's care and parental work, and recognizes and accepts that families' lives change.

In addition, a single child care system that is less categorical and more collaborative would allow more integrated care arrangements at a point in time, instead of the complicated mix of multiple care arrangements that families must now manage. In such a system, parents would have more flexibility to arrange child care schedules to comport and possibly change with their work schedules. Such a system could be designed to avoid situations where families make a work change or undergo some other status change, only to lose their eligibility for a child care program they preferred. A simpler child care subsidy system could also be combined with other child care and development resources such as Head Start to serve the needs of children more comprehensively.

Improving Access and Simplifying the Application Process   Mothers in this study experienced many administrative problems in getting subsidized child care even though they were usually eligible for some form of subsidy. The administrative problems associated with HRA vouchers were especially troubling for the very low-income mothers trying to transition from welfare to work. These families often had little knowledge of their child care options and no time to choose an arrangement, and the voucher system did not help. They made whatever arrangement they could quickly, but then found their child care spells shortened because of problems with payments to their providers. The linkage between their welfare cases and their child care often exacerbated their problems. Families experienced mistaken case closings, lost benefits, failures to make child care payments, and child care disruptions—all notorious elements of the welfare bureaucracy that had been transferred to and further complicated the administration of child care.

The ACD system, while offering better benefits to mothers than HRA child care, was overrun with long waiting lists for eligibility and programs that were filled to capacity in most neighborhoods. The process of applying for subsidized child care was obscure to many mothers, and it was especially difficult for working mothers, some of whom had not interacted with public bureaucracies very often. The time it took to apply and qualify for subsidies varied, but many of the mothers in this study were nevertheless frustrated by the cumbersome eligibility process. It often took them months to get an interview, and once they did, they were often required to make repeated in-person visits, provide extensive documentation, and take time off from jobs, many of which offered little such flexibility. Then, after all that, most of them received only a priority code and a place on the waiting list. There were long waiting lists for both ACD-contracted care and vouchers. Systemwide, there were more than 47,000 children on the waiting list for ACD child care as of December 2002 (Romaner and Finch 2003).[23] Some of the mothers in this study who applied to ACD waited months or years to receive eligibility, while others applied but either never received eligibility or had difficulty finding an available place in an ACD-contracted center. A review of child care assistance policies in March 2000 by the Children's Defense Fund found that many states had long waiting lists or had frozen intake, with 34,000 waiting in Florida, 31,000 in Texas, and 17,000 in Massachusetts (Blank and Poersch 2000).

Many of the barriers to access to child care can be addressed directly by states. There are some models that states can use to make their child care systems more accessible and to streamline the application process to better serve the needs of working families. Several states and localities have begun to change their application processes to facilitate child care enrollment by mail, e-mail, fax, or telephone and to offer families evening and weekend hours for face-to-face appointments. Minnesota and Texas, for example, accept applications by mail or over the phone, eliminating the need for many face-to-face appointments, and have found that most families use these means, expediting their receipt of subsidies. In Houston 96 percent of families apply by telephone (Adams, Snyder, and Sandfort 2002). Oregon has adopted a eligibility system that combines a phone interview with an application by mail and has found that, over time, more new applicants apply by mail as they learn about this option (Anderson 2003). Washington implemented a pilot call center in one county and has started to use this method statewide. Applications can be made over the phone to a decentralized system of call centers, and thus far 50 to 60 percent of applications are being received by telephone.[24]

Some states have expanded their weekend and evening hours while others allow families to download applications from the Internet. For example, Illinois has a paper process but is developing an online application that will operate similarly to online income tax forms. This effort is progressing slowly owing to the difficulties in verifying income eligibility online as well as the cutbacks in state staffing for the project.[25] After South Dakota began an online application process in January 2002, about 20 percent of the child care applications were received online in the first year of the program, with the percentage increasing significantly over the course of the year.[26] Some states have also experimented with having contract agencies, such as community-based service providers, determine eligibility for child care assistance.

Prioritizing Continuity of Care   The process of recertifying families' eligibility should be greatly simplified as well, in order to provide continuity in care for children. The churning of families from the subsidy system because of income or employment status changes, which may at times be short-lived, adds instability to children's lives and complicates families' efforts to retain the child care they need to achieve self-sufficiency. Once families in this study entered the ACD child care system, they were required to regularly recertify their eligibility for child care assistance and redetermine their copayment amount by returning in person to ACD every twelve months with their wage information. If mothers did not make their scheduled appointments, they could lose their eligibility. Most often, if a mother's income did not exceed the upper eligibility threshold, the main result of the recertification was to adjust her copayment in light of changes in her income. If she lost her job, she would lose her child care subsidy as well, even though she continued to need care while she sought other employment. Also, because many times the specific care placements mothers used were designated for ACD-subsidized care, they sometimes had to disrupt their children's care even if they could have paid for the care themselves while searching for work.

A priority for child care policy should be providing children with continuity of care and families that receive child care assistance with continuity of subsidy supports while adjusting family copayments if their income changes. One option would be to allow children who meet the child care eligibility requirements at the time of the initial application to be considered eligible throughout early childhood until the start of pre-K or kindergarten.[27] The Head Start program, which serves families with incomes below the federal poverty level, uses only income to determine initial eligibility and allows children to remain in the program continuously through their preschool years without regard to income changes.

Another option is to use different income cutoffs for determinations of initial eligibility and continued eligibility. Eight states do this now. Massachusetts has an income cutoff of 50 percent of SMI when families are applying for child care, and 85 percent of SMI to maintain subsidies if their income changes. This restricts access but emphasizes the need for continuity. Alabama, which has one of the lowest income cutoffs for initial eligibility at $18,000, allows families to maintain subsidies as long as their incomes are below $28,000.

States should also extend the time period and simplify the process for recertification of continued eligibility and changes in parent fees. Family incomes may not change frequently enough to make short recertification periods beneficial from a state's fiscal perspective. Thirty-six states require families to recertify for benefits at least every six months, and only thirteen states, including New York, provide twelve months of eligibility before requiring a redetermination of benefits (U.S. Department of Health and Human Services 2002a). Twelve months should be the shortest time period or the norm for recertification. Families should be able to recertify by mail to make the process less onerous. When a family's income has risen above the eligibility threshold and the child is no longer eligible for the current care arrangement, states should provide a short period of continued benefits (roughly sixty days) to allow parents to secure new care rather than cutting off eligibility immediately.[28]

Additionally, it might be more efficient for states to consider establishing a common recertification process at the start of a program year rather than have the recertification period tied to the time of the initial application. For example, child care recertification could be linked to the school calendar. Parents could recertify in the summer for the following year and plan changes in care to coincide with the school year.[29] This could help make transitions and integrations between care and school arrangements more seamless and better coordinate the arrangements for younger and older siblings.

Finally, the easiest way to eliminate a child care seam while also simplifying the system would be to make families automatically eligible for twelve months of transitional benefits following a welfare exit, without an additional application. States could simply provide continual benefits as part of the closing of the cash part of assistance. Minnesota and Oregon are among the few states to do this. In Minnesota families that are no longer eligible to receive child care subsidies from TANF automatically receive one year of child care benefits through a simple administrative recoding of their case.[30] In Oregon a family on TANF that is working and leaves welfare becomes eligible for transitional benefits without filing a new application. The file is shifted to the Employment Related Day Care (ERDC) system by making a phone call. State administrative data estimate that 60 percent of the families that exit TANF end up receiving the child care subsidy as a result. Since ERDC is also the system used by working families seeking child care assistance, it is relatively easy for families to apply for child care benefits for working families when their transitional benefits end. Following this example, states could directly transfer families that exhaust child care benefits from one source (such as welfare-to-work vouchers) to another type of benefit (such as child care benefits for low-income working families) if the family remains income-eligible. This, of course, would be much easier to do if states and localities were successful in creating one simpler, more seamless system that would be far more transparent to families.

4. Provide Child Care Assistance to All Eligible Families

As we saw in the analysis of children's care dynamics and strategies, finding subsidized child care was an important element in mothers' care strategies. Many mothers found that without subsidized child care, work did not pay and they could not work steadily. For most mothers earning low wages, the full-market costs of many child care options consumed such a large part of their income that without low-cost child care options or subsidies, work alone was not good enough as a strategy for their family's survival. The lower-cost care options that some mothers could afford were generally lower-quality as well, limiting their children's opportunities for development. They said that this was a difficult compromise to make for the sake of work. However, given the imperative to work for financial subsistence, many mothers did use low-cost care in order to start working while they also doggedly sought subsidies.

Getting subsidized child care was often most difficult when children were youngest because of long waiting lists. In addition, there were fewer available care options for infants and young toddlers in centers and licensed family child care homes, which are the forms of care most likely to be subsidized. Many times mothers' only alternatives were less-preferred care options.

This study illustrates the need for greater public provision of child care for low-income families. The personal narratives of the mothers in this study who placed their children in care they knew to be of dubious quality document an acute child care crisis. The federal government and the states should increase child care funding and broaden child care assistance to cover more low-income working families over a broader range of income levels. States should reward work by serving low-income working families to the same degree that they serve welfare-to-work families. In addition, states may want to concentrate more of their child care resources on families with the youngest children. The findings of this study and of previous research outline the rationale for greater child care assistance to low-income families, particularly when their children are younger:

- The cost of child care was high relative to family income, especially for low-income families, and the cost of high-quality care was even higher.

- Cost constraints were often a stronger factor than mothers' preferences in determining the care their children received.

- Most mothers considered the institutional forms of care that were subsidized as more appropriate for their child at an early point in their development, but they found that such care was hard to arrange or afford.

- Most mothers wanted higher-quality care options and the financial assistance to find and use the care they preferred, and they believed this was a legitimate area of public support that should be available universally.

- Developmental research on child care suggests that more stable care over time and higher-quality care appropriate to children's developmental stages are associated with improved child outcomes—and that the potential positive and negative effects of child care appear to be much more significant for children from low-income families.

At current levels of state spending on child care, a great many families need and seek child care assistance and cannot find it when they need it (Heymann

2000). Most state child care systems that have been studied have long waiting lists for child care assistance (Schulman, Blank, and Ewen 2001). The long waiting lists strongly suggest that there is a substantial unmet need for subsidized child care services, though they are a relatively crude indicator of the size of the need. For one thing, waiting lists may be poorly maintained, so their size may not be a reliable estimate of the actual current need. Waiting lists also may underestimate need because the very existence of the lists may deter others from applying. Long waiting lists may also lead states to establish priority criteria, and families in lower-priority categories may not bother getting on the queue.

Given the percentage of single mothers in this sample—and nationally—who are paying substantial shares of their income for child care, and the tenuous nature of many of the nonsubsidized care types observed in this study, it seems reasonable to conclude that many families could benefit from additional assistance. The high cost of care limits options and is a burden for more than just the very lowest-income families. A National Institute of Child Health and Development (2000a) study has found that among very low-income families with earnings below the poverty level ($14,400), child care expenses are 25 percent of the average family's total household budget. Child care expenses were approximately 18 percent of the budget of low-income families earning between 100 and 200 percent of the poverty level ($28,800), and 7 percent of the budgets of those who earned more than 200 percent of the poverty level. While all strata of low-income families spend substantial sums on child care, the very lowest-income families are much more likely to receive child care subsidies. Using survey data collected prior to welfare reform, Sandra Hofferth (1995) found that families with incomes below the poverty level reported receiving subsidies at twice the rate of those earning above the poverty level but less than 75 percent of median family income— 26 percent compared to 12 percent. Given that the emphasis on assisting the very lowest-income families has increased in many states since the implementation of welfare reform, child care assistance may have become more concentrated on very low-income families in recent years. Studies have further found that child care centers attended by children from low- to moderate-income families (those with incomes above the poverty level and below the level of median family income) were lower in quality than those attended by children from lower-income families (those with incomes below the poverty level) (Phillips et al. 1994; Whitebook, Howes, and Phillips 1990).

The federal government, together with the states, should significantly increase funding for child care subsidies with a goal of guaranteeing child care assistance for families with children from birth at least up to age three. Funding should be made sufficient to cover all eligible working families with earnings at least up to 60 percent of a state's median income or as much as up to 85 percent of SMI. Parents should also be required to contribute to the cost of the care, with the amount and proportion of their income contributed increasing with their income, up to 10 percent of their total earnings. The broadening of income eligibility and guarantee of child care assistance for low-income families with children younger than three could be implemented gradually by increasing the minimum income eligibility cutoff over time or by raising the income eligibility standard for a birth cohort in a given year. For example, guaranteed child care assistance could be provided for all children born in 2003 to families with incomes up to 60 percent of a state's median income, with a guarantee of continual assistance as long as family income remains below 60 percent of SMI. Starting with a birth cohort would mean that any new babies born would not be subjected to the current fragmented, inconsistent system we have now, and it would clearly put infants and toddlers at an advantage relative to the current system. Also, allowing states to begin with newborns could facilitate a more gradual expansion in funding. With additional funding, the benefit could be expanded by raising the income cutoff in following years to 65 percent of SMI for newborns and to higher levels of family income over time, up to 85 percent.[31]

The total cost of child care for low-income families should be a shared public and private expense, with the level of public subsidy inversely related to income. Most low-income parents, except for the very poorest, should be expected to contribute up to 10 percent of their earnings for child care.

Determining the timing of expansions, the projected take-up rate among eligible working families, and the estimated funding that would be required, as well as defining the federal and state funding shares, would require cost and utilization analyses.[32] The experience of Rhode Island, a state that established a broad child care entitlement early in its welfare reform efforts, could be useful in projecting the potential take-up rates and costs of guaranteed benefits. Beginning in 1997, Rhode Island guaranteed child care assistance to all working families with incomes up to 185 percent of the federal poverty level (FPL). The following year the state further expanded guarantees of eligibility when it passed an early childhood education initiative called Starting RIght, which was originally planned to gradually phase in higher income thresholds, up to 250 percent of FPL, by 2001. However, since July 2000 the eligibility level for guaranteed child care assistance has remained at 225 percent of FPL because of fiscal constraints. Rhode Island covered the greater cost of establishing a full entitlement program with state funds. After passage of the Starting RIght program, there was a rapid increase in caseload matched by increased expenditures, which leveled off after 2000 when the eligibility level reached 225 percent of FPL, with only a slight rise (1 percent annually) since (Murphy 2003).

Many mothers in the study believed that child care should be publicly provided and that access to child care assistance should be consistently available to all eligible families. Many mothers who worked more regularly over time but had previously received cash welfare assistance were pleased to be off welfare and more self-reliant in meeting their family's needs. They often found the cash welfare system demeaning and questioned its legitimacy as a long-term support. But they seldom did so for other areas of family life for which they needed ongoing assistance. They felt that child care was among the most legitimate needs, along with housing and health care, for the families requiring assistance in their communities and beyond.

Many thought subsidies were a basic need because they could not earn enough from work to pay for adequate care for their children. Some said it was a public responsibility given the societal expectation that parents will work and the importance of child care to all children's development. Most mothers who received subsidies that came with a copayment requirement did not mind paying a share of the cost, even if they needed that money for other family needs, if the care was good, and some even thought it was appropriate for them to pay something—an amount they could afford.

Summary and Conclusions

Determining what public policy should offer American children in the context of increased work by their mothers follows from looking deeply into the child care dynamics of low-income families and using this knowledge to help define the personal and public responsibilities for our children's care. In this study of forty-two families in low-income New York City neighborhoods, I followed a group of single mothers who were working, and working a lot. They responded to the challenge of American public policy that has entreated them to work more to support their families and make their way out of income poverty. Most wanted to work and viewed work as a central element in their families' lives and their struggles to move ahead. They showed enormous resourcefulness to arrange child care over time and continue to work relatively consistently over the first four years of their children's lives. They learned how to arrange care in the context of significant constraints, a resourcefulness low-income mothers in isolated communities have repeatedly shown across many aspects of their family life. The strategies they adopted were often the best they could manage, but the outcomes were not always what they wanted for their children. Public policy could help close the gap by helping mothers meet their responsibilities in their dual roles as full-time workers and full-time mothers, while meeting our collective responsibility to provide adequate and appropriate opportunities to support the development of our next generation.

The proposals in this chapter could be a starting point for developing the policy changes needed to address the critical issues that have emerged from this study and other recent research on child care. More analysis would be needed before some of these proposals could become targeted policy responses, and implementing them would require significant public investment. These proposals most directly address the findings in the study about child care complexity, instability in care over time, access and retention problems with subsidies, poor care beginnings, and the need to resort to less desired care types when access to preferred care is constrained. These proposals could lead to improved child care quality by giving families greater access to better care by expanding Head Start, broadening subsidies, and providing families with cash assistance when they are making initial care choices.

In the reshaping of America's social contract, much was deservedly made of personal responsibility as a bedrock American principle, along with the central role that work opportunities must play in American life for the poor and nonpoor alike. Yet, by setting up a policy that compels low-income parents to work mostly for very low wages and punishes those who do not, without examining the other consequences of this policy, we almost literally threw out the baby with the bathwater. We have in effect asked parents to send their children wherever they might find someone to mind those children—for a day or a week or a year—without the care that parents and society as a whole might expect. Expecting parents to work for their family's well-being is an established and appropriate American value. Yet there is no more common personal responsibility in the human experience than parents taking care of their own children—or finding the most appropriate care when they are away. In the movement to an age of work opportunities, what are we defining as our personal responsibilities, and for whom are we defining these? Work by adults is understandably one part of the equation, but is children's early care and development a personal responsibility we rest upon our children's young shoulders as they make their way wherever we may send them? Are children personally responsible for the poverty conditions they find themselves in, and responsible for making a decent life for themselves without good child care or early educational opportunities? Is this the contract we make with our children? Is this the future we choose?

~ Appendix A ~

Our Children's Care: A Review of the Literature

This appendix reviews the relevant research literature appropriate to understanding the child care issues of low-income families. It focuses on how child care is used by these families, including the available choices and constraints, the costs of care, the quality of care that children receive, the developmental effects of this care, and the policies that support the child care needs of low-income families.

The use of nonmaternal child care has grown enormously over the past forty years as more mothers have joined the workforce. During this time child care has become increasingly complicated as changes in American society, particularly in family structure, labor markets, and social policy, have altered the contexts of early childhood. Even the meaning of "child care" has changed with the times. When Dr. Benjamin Spock wrote his best-selling guide *Baby and Child Care* in 1957, his use of "child care" throughout the 597 pages refers solely to maternal care. Only on page 569, in a last section entitled "Special Problems," are working mothers discussed, as well as in-home or out-of-home providers (Spock 1957). In recent years the strategies that mothers use for children's care have come to mean something quite different: not only do families commonly need to arrange substitute care when mothers work, but finding such care is often a problem as well.

The massive movement of women into the paid labor force has significantly changed many industrial societies, as is strongly evidenced in the United States. The remarkable rise in women's participation in the labor force (see table A.1) constitutes both a major demographic and economic shift.[1] In the year 2000, 65 percent, or almost two-thirds, worked outside the home, and almost 60 percent of all new mothers returned to work before their child's first birthday (U.S. Department of Labor 2001).

Lone mothers, who prior to 1960 were more often widowed, divorced, or separated than never married, were already working in significant propor-

Table A.1   *Labor Force Participation Rates of Mothers of Children
Under Age Six, 1960 to 2000*

Year	All Mothers	Married Mothers	Lone Mothers[a]
1960	23.8	18.6	40.5
1970	31.9	30.3	48.1
1975	39.0	36.7	51.3
1980	46.8	45.1	53.7
1990	58.2	58.9	57.5
1995	62.3	63.5	59.9
2000	65.3	62.8	73.2

Source: U.S. Department of Labor, Bureau of Labor Statistics (2001), Current Population Survey, March supplement 2000, published and unpublished tables; Census 2000 Supplementary Survey Summary Tables, table P063.
[a]Lone mothers include never-married, widowed, and divorced mothers.

tions: 40 percent of mothers who were widowed, divorced, or separated worked (outside the home) in 1960, compared to 20 percent of the much higher number of married mothers at the time. From 1960 to 1990, a period that encompassed the women's movement and rapid changes in the American family and U.S. labor markets, both married mothers' and lone mothers' labor force participation increased considerably. Over three decades, the work rates of married mothers rose by 40 percent, escalating steadily—with the fastest rate of increase in the 1970s—and equaling the work rates for lone mothers, whose labor force participation increased by 20 percent in the same period. The gap between married mothers and lone mothers had narrowed by 1990, when 60 percent of each cohort was working. During the last decade of the twentieth century, the labor force participation rates of lone mothers rose rapidly again, ahead of married mothers' participation levels. The work participation rate for lone mothers was 73 percent in 2000, compared to 63 percent for married mothers.

Child Care Usage

The number of children under age five in care arrangements because their mothers worked grew from 3.8 million in 1965 to 10.1 million in 1997 (see table A.2). When we add in both working and nonworking mothers who use some form of regular child care, the number of children in care increases to 12.4 million, or two-thirds of all the children under five in the United States (Smith 2002).[2]

As the use of child care expanded dramatically over the past thirty years, the distribution in the types of care shifted as well. Child care in organized centers was not very common in 1965, comprising only 6 percent of arrange-

Table A.2   *Children Under Age Five with Employed Mothers in Care Arrangements, 1965 to 1997*

	1965	1977	1985	1997
Number of children in child care	3.8 million	4.4 million	8.2 million	10.1 million
Type of arrangement				
Parental care	28%	26%	24%	24%
Father		14.4	15.7	20.2
Mother at work		11.4	8.1	3.4
Relative care	33	30	25	27
Nanny or sitter care	15	7	6	4
Nonrelative provider	16	24	22	19
Center-based care	6	13	23	25

Source: U.S. Department of Commerce, Bureau of the Census, *Current Population Reports*, series P70-9 (1987), series P70-20 (1991), series P70-52 (1995), series P70-53 (1997), series P70-70 (2000), and series P70-86 (2002); Hofferth (1996).

ments. By 1997 center-based arrangements had grown to more than 25 percent of the primary child care arrangements used by employed mothers. Nonrelative care in a provider's home, generally referred to as "family child care" or "informal care" arrangements, accounted for about one-fifth of the care by 1997, up from 16 percent in 1965. The use of a nonrelative provider in the child's own home, sometimes referred to as "nanny care," accounted for about 4 percent of child care in 1997. Nanny care is a small, somewhat diminishing share of care used mostly by higher-income families.

Relatives and parents provided a steady but slowly declining share of care from 1965 to 1995; interestingly, however, both forms of care seemed to increase again rather markedly when measured in the Survey of Income and Program Participation (SIPP) in 1995 and 1997. Care by relatives, or "kin care," declined from 33 percent of care to 21 percent between 1965 and 1995, then increased to 27 percent in 1997 (Smith 2000, 2002). Parental care of preschool children with a working mother held steady at around one-quarter of care arrangements throughout the time period: fathers provided between 14 and 17 percent of care between 1965 and 1995. By 1997 fathers had increased their share of care to 20 percent of primary care arrangements, while mothers caring for children while at work declined from 11 percent of the primary care arrangements in 1977 to about 3 percent of care in 1997.

The usage patterns for different types of child care vary along several dimensions, the most significant of which are age, income, family structure, and race and ethnicity.

Age

There is much less use of centers for infants and young toddlers and much greater use of home-based care arrangements for this age group (see table A.3). Relative and parental care account for more than half of the child care in a child's first two years. Center-based care became the more prevalent form of care starting in the third year, accounting for more than one-third of all care in children's third and fourth years. Relative and nonrelative care in home-based settings continues to be the chosen form of care for significant proportions of children throughout early childhood.[3]

Income

Care by relatives is used more often by low-income families than by higher-income families. Relatives care for 33 percent of preschoolers in families earning up to twice the poverty line. In comparison, only 21 percent of families with incomes higher than that use relative care, and the rates drop further as income increases (see table A.4). In contrast, only 21 percent of children in

Table A.3   *Distributions of Types of Primary Child Care Used for Children Under Age Four with Employed Mothers, by Child's Age (Composite Distributions from 1997, 1999 SIPP data)*

Type of Primary Child Care Arrangement	Year One: Birth to Age One	Year Two: Ages One to Two	Year Three: Ages Two to Three	Year Four: Ages Three to Four
Parental care	29%	24%	20%	19%
Relative care	36	29	25	21
Nanny or sitter care (in child's home)	3	4	5	4
Family child care and informal care	18	19	19	16
Center-based care	15	23	30	39

Sources: Author's analysis and tabulations of published and unpublished data from Survey of Income and Program Participation; U.S. Department of Commerce, Census Bureau, *Current Population Reports*, P70-86 (2002); Boushey (2003).

Table A.4 *Distributions of Types of Primary Care Used for Children Under Four with Employed Mothers, by Income Levels (Composite Distributions from 1997, 1999 SIPP Data)*

Type of Primary Child Care Arrangement	Very Low-Income: 0 to 100 Percent FPL	Low-Income: 100 to 200 Percent FPL	Moderate Income: 200 to 375 Percent FPL	Middle- to Higher-Income: 375+ Percent FPL
Parental care	27%	27%	25%	20%
Relative care	35	31	24	19
Nanny or sitter care (in child's home)	4	3	4	9
Family child care and informal care	11	14	17	17
Center-based care	21	25	28	36

Sources: Author's analysis and tabulations of published and unpublished data from Survey of Income and Program Participation; U.S. Department of Commerce, Census Bureau, *Current Population Reports*, P70-86 (2002); Boushey (2003).
Note: FPL = federal poverty line

poor families are cared for in organized child care facilities, while 36 percent of children in middle-income and higher-income families are in center-based care. Parental care arrangements did not vary as much by income.[4]

Family Structure

The largest variations in the child care used by single-parent families are in the rates of parental care and relative care. Young children under age four in married-couple families are four times more likely to be cared for by their fathers than were young children living in single-mother families. In total, children in single-parent families are cared for by their fathers 6 percent of the time and by their mothers while they are working 3 percent of the time, significantly less than the parental care rates for married-couple families (23 percent and 6 percent, respectively). Single mothers, for whom father care is less available, use relative care much more often (see table A.5). Relatives provide care for children 39 percent of the time in single-parent families, and only 19 percent of the time for children in married-couple families. Usage of other

Table A.5   *Distributions of Types of Primary Child Care Used for Children Under Four with Employed Mothers, by Family Structure (Composite Distributions from 1997, 1999 SIPP Data)*

Type of Primary Child Care Arrangement	Married-Couple Families	Single-Mother Families
Parental care	29%	9%
Relative care	19	39
Nanny or sitter care (in child's home)	5	3
Family child care and informal care	18	17
Center-based care	28	30

Sources: Author's analysis and tabulations of published and unpublished data from Survey of Income and Program Participation; U.S. Department of Commerce, Census Bureau, *Current Population Reports*, P70-86 (2002); Boushey (2003).

care arrangements—center care and all types of nonrelative care—is remarkably similar across family structure.[5]

Race and Ethnicity

Hispanic families are nearly twice as likely, and African American families nearly 50 percent more likely, to use relatives for child care as white families (see table A.6). By contrast, white families have higher rates of parental care than both Hispanic and black families. Hispanic families use center-based care proportionately much less than other families. Qualitative studies suggest that a combination of cultural and institutional factors—including more limited child care options in some areas, language barriers, and cultural differences in child-rearing and expectations of family networks—contribute to these differences, which persist even when controlling for factors covarying with child care use and ethnicity, though these differences are smaller (Liang, Fuller, and Singer 2000; Rosina and Chi 1992).[6] Bruce Fuller, Susan Holloway, and Xiaoyan Liang (1996) have found that African American families are more likely than white or Latino families to use center-based care, and that cultural differences in child-rearing practices contribute to these differences. Table A.6 summarizes the care use data by race and ethnicity.

Table A.6 *Distributions of Primary Care Used for Children Under Four with Employed Mothers, by Race and Ethnicity (Composite Distributions from 1997, 1999 SIPP Data)*

Type of Primary Child Care Arrangement	Non-Hispanic Black	All of Hispanic Origin	Non-Hispanic White
Parental care	19%	24%	27%
Relative care	31	40	21
Nanny or sitter care (in child's home)	3	3	4
Family child care and informal care	16	15	20
Center-based care	30	16	28

Sources: Author's analysis and tabulations of published and unpublished data from Survey of Income and Program Participation; U.S. Department of Commerce, Census Bureau, *Current Population Reports*, P70-86 (2002); Boushey (2003).

Child Care Choices

National survey data inform us that young children are in a wide variety of care arrangements. However, we know relatively little about parents' preferences for child care or how they choose among types of child care. The factors that families are likely to consider include:

- *Child's age and needs*: What care is appropriate for an infant? A toddler? A preschooler? Who can best care for a child with particular health needs?

- *Setting*: Is the care in the child's home? A provider's home? A center?

- *Location*: Where is the care? Are the area and the building safe? Is it convenient for the mother to get to work and to drop off and pick up the child's siblings from school or after-school programs?

- *Provider*: What is her training? What is her background? How comfortable does the mother feel with the provider? How comfortable does the child seem with the provider? Do the provider and family share some characteristics important to the mother?

- *Group size and composition*: How many other children are being cared for in the setting, and what are these children like? Will the child get individual attention? How will the child interact with the other children?

- *Hours of care*: How many hours can this provider offer care? How flexible are the hours?

- *Cost*: How much does the care arrangement cost the mother? Can the mother get a subsidy for the care arrangement?

- *Compatibility with parental care*: How much does the child care comply with the mother's views of appropriate care? Is the care consistent with the care that the child gets at home? Is the child care complementary to the child's home experiences?

- *Educational content and developmental activities*: Is there an emphasis on learning or reading in the care setting? Is the child stimulated and wanting to engage with his environment when in child care?

- *Consistency and stability*: How consistent is the child care? Is the provider not available on certain days? How long might this care arrangement last? How long has the provider been offering care?

- *Oversight*: Is the child care licensed? Does the provider receive training? Is the provider supervised?

- *Quality aspects of the care*: How much is the provider engaged with the child? Is the environment stimulating to the child, providing a range of activities? Are the children fed regularly, and how is the food? Do the children have a comfortable place to sleep? Does the provider take the children outside regularly?

- *Rules governing the care*: Who provides the food for the child? What does a provider do if a child is mildly sick? What happens if a child arrives late to care? What happens if a mother is late picking up the child?

When looking at child care options, mothers do not consider all these factors but assess the perceived advantages and disadvantages of those most relevant to their choice. (Table A.7 summarizes what is known from the literature about each type of care along some of these dimensions.) Mothers often consider a child's age and try to determine appropriate care for meeting the needs of a child that age. They consider whether the setting is appropriate and how comfortable they are with a particular provider. They almost always consider the cost of the care and whether they can get subsidies for the care. They also consider the compatibility of the care hours with their work schedule.

Only a few studies have looked at parents' preferences using many of these criteria, and very few have looked at how they factor into parents' choices (Sonenstein 1991). The 1995 National Household Education Survey (NHES) asked parents using all types of care which of a list of factors were most important to them (Hofferth et al. 1998). The factors parents cited most were: the provider's training in taking care of children; the overall quality of care; the number of children in the class or home setting; the cost; whether the provider spoke English with the child; and the proximity of the provider to the home. Surveys such as this, however, do not tell the whole story. They provide pertinent information about which characteristics are important to families, but they give parents closed-ended choices, many of which reflect the values emphasized by child care professionals and not necessarily the ones that parents consider. They do not reveal how low-income parents consider these factors when choosing care at different moments of children's development or in different circumstances. They also miss other factors that mothers may consider and how parents weigh the trade-offs across the factors they consider in making actual care decisions. Liang, Fuller, and Singer (2000) find that parents' preferences for center care were related to family income, household family structure, family language spoken at home, and mothers' views on child-rearing. When the early preschool years were viewed as an important time to impart school-related skills and corresponding behaviors were present—such as reading to children, frequenting libraries, and speaking English—families used center care at earlier ages.

A few recent qualitative studies have also looked at parents' care choices (Fuller, Holloway, and Liang 1996; Holloway et al. 1997; Henly and Lyons 2000). In onetime interviews looking at the child care arrangements of fifty-seven mothers in low-wage, entry-level jobs in Los Angeles, Julia Henly and Sandra Lyons (2000) found that these low-income mothers emphasized affordability, convenience, and safety as foremost concerns and that job schedule constraints, resource constraints, and the relatively high cost of many child care options compared to their income contributed to these preferences. They found that these factors were often most compatible with informal care arrangements. Fuller and his colleagues (1996) have done more in-depth, repeated probing with a smaller sample in Boston and found that mothers often viewed center-based care as being appropriate as their children approached preschool age to help them begin to prepare for school.

As we can see from table A.2, the proportion of working mothers who use center-based care has increased more than fourfold over thirty years, from 6 percent of all care arrangements for young children in 1965 to more than one-quarter of all care arrangements in 1997. As the use of care has grown tremendously overall, presumably the preference for center care has grown as well. This conclusion is suggested by findings that higher-income families, who would seem to have a greater range of options, use center care the most (Hofferth 1995).[7] Survey data analyzed by Hofferth and her colleagues (1998) also show that families wanting to change their care arrangements most often want to change to center care, and that single mothers are more likely than two-parent families to want to change to center-based care.[8] The

(Text continues on p. 230.)

Table A.7   *Basic Dimensions of Child Care Arrangements, by Type*

Type of Care	Setting	Care Provider(s)	Group Size and Composition
Group day care center (DCC)	Centers at Community Based Organizations (CBOs)	Center staff; two to three adults per group	Generally twelve to twenty children grouped by age (four and under); serves children from two months to school-age, but full-time center care is most often for two-, three-, and four-year-olds; average child-staff ratio is 6.5 to 1 (Hofferth et al. 1998)
Head Start (HS)	Centers at CBOs	Center staff; two to three adults per group in classrooms, with more staff for social services, health, and parental assistance	Mostly serves three- and four-year-olds; ten to eighteen per group; some infants and toddlers served in pilot Early Head Start programs; nationally 7 percent are under three, 36 percent are three-year-olds, 52 percent are four-year-olds, and 5 percent are five or older (U.S. DHHS 2003); 10 percent served are special needs children

Hours (Time of Day)	Cost (Amount and Who Pays)	Care Characteristics
Generally full-day program during traditional work hours, 8:00 A.M. to 6:00 P.M., Monday to Friday	Cost at centers serving primarily low-income families ranges from $100 to $150 per week, with subsidized slots and vouchers for some low-income families; parents make sliding-scale copayments if receiving subsidized care; average cost is $2.39 per hour (Hofferth et al. 1998); 43 percent of families are subsidized (Hofferth et al. 1991)	Most peer interactions Perception of a school-like setting, academic preparation Consistent, set schedule Long care hours Licensed and inspected annually Popular form of primary care arrangement for three- and four-year-olds With HS and pre-K, most likely to have a trained provider (Hofferth et al. 1998)
Generally three-hour part-day (such as, 8:00 to 11:00 A.M.) program, with some longer six-hour sessions and full-day sessions	Services are free to very low income parents (up to 100 percent of FPL) or families on public assistance; 10 percent of children are allowed to be non-low-income	Similar characteristics to DCC: shorter care hours, fewer long days Focused on early childhood development (Fenichel et al. 1999) Package of intensive and comprehensive family support services (Hofferth et al. 1998; Fenichel et al. 1999) With DCC and pre-K, most likely to have a trained provider (Hofferth et al. 1998) Component of parent involvement (Hofferth et al. 1998)

(Table continues on p. 226.)

Table A.7   *Continued*

Type of Care	Setting	Care Provider(s)	Group Size and Composition
Prekindergarten (and other preschool programs)	Schools and centers at CBOs	School or center staff; two to three adults per group	Mostly serves four-year-olds; many fewer programs serve three-year-olds
Family day care (FDC)	Provider's home	Usually one adult caregiver; an adult and one assistant for a group	Three to six children of different ages; average child-provider ratio is 3.5 to 1. 15 percent are larger FDC groups which serve seven to ten children (Hofferth et al. 1998)
Informal care	Provider's home	Generally one adult (not a professional provider)	Generally one child or a few children, some of whom may be the provider's

Hours (Time of Day)	Cost (Amount and Who Pays)	Care Characteristics
Part-day program (three- or six-hour), five days a week, 180 days a year; many programs blend funding and extend hours (Mitchell 2001)	Publicly funded care in schools for age-eligible children and where available; services are free	Early childhood education Supervised by state education department (Child Care, Inc. 2002) With HS and DCC, most likely to have a trained provider (Hofferth et al. 1998)
Generally full-day, providing longest hours of care	Parent pays an average of $52 per week (Casper 1995) or $1.84 per hour (Hofferth et al. 1998); subsidies available; 6 percent of families using FDC receive subsidized care (Hofferth et al. 1991)	Popular for infants and toddlers (Hofferth et al. 1998; Ehrle et al. 2001) More flexible than center care in terms of culture and language (Hofferth et al. 1998) More prevalent among low-income families
Generally flexible scheduling	Total cost ranges from $50 to $100 per week, depending on the care provider and the relationship between parent and provider, can be subsidized through welfare-to-work vouchers	Outside formal child care market and most publicly subsidized or licensed forms of care Often considered "babysitting" With kin care, oldest and most widespread form of child care (Brown-Lyons et al. 2001) Perceived as resembling parental care (Brown-Lyons et al. 2001) More prevalent among low-income families

(Table continues on p. 228.)

Table A.7   *Continued*

Type of Care	Setting	Care Provider(s)	Group Size and Composition
Nanny care (in-home provider)	Child's home	One adult	One child (possibility of siblings); average child-provider ratio is 2 to 1 (Hofferth et al. 1998)
Kin care	Home, child's or provider's	Kin (generally not a professional provider)	One child; possibility of other kin children (Ehrle et al. 2001); average child-provider ratio is 1.6 to 1 (Hofferth et al. 1998)
Father care	Home child's, kin's, or father's	Father	One child; possibility of siblings

Source: Author's compilation.

Hours (Time of Day)	Cost (Amount and Who Pays)	Care Characteristics
Full workday; some flexibility	High cost; parent pays an average of $65 per week (Casper 1995) or $3.02 per hour (Hofferth et al. 1998); can be subsidized	More parental control Generally unregulated (except some placement agencies) Rarest among low-income families (Ehrle et al. 2001)
Flexible	Low cost or free; parent pays average of $42 per week (Casper 1995) or $1.63 per hour (Hofferth et al. 1998); rarely but increasingly subsidized (Ehrle et al. 2001)	Care is usually given by female kin More prevalent among low-income families With informal care, oldest and most widespread form of child care (Brown-Lyons et al. 2001) Perceived as resembling parental care (Brown-Lyons et al. 2001) Children comfortable (Brown-Lyons et al. 2001) Least likelihood of having a trained provider (Hofferth et al. 1998)
Flexible, depending on relationship between mother and father	Generally free	Children comfortable (Brown-Lyons et al. 2001) More common in poor families, when fathers are unemployed or in nontraditional work, and when there is more than one preschooler in the family (Casper 1997)

survey responses indicate that families think center-based care offers more learning opportunities, greater safety, and more reliable care.

Constraints on Choices

Given the greater preference for center care than its use, it is important to account for what limits the use of center care versus other care types. Like all other markets, the child care market, from a consumption standpoint, is often viewed as a matter of preferences and choices. In practice, however, at least for low-income families, the child care that families use is determined as much by constraints as by choices, and the arrangements that parents arrive at often reflect quite limited sets of choices. These constraints include the relative availability of care, the information that parents have about care, the age of the child, the parents' work schedules, and the cost of care.

Supply Constraints   The supply of care for young children is severely constrained, especially for infant and toddler care (Fuller, Holloway, and Liang 1996; U.S. General Accounting Office 1997; Queralt and Witte 1998). Overall, there has been an enormous increase in the supply of child care in the last thirty years (Blau 2001). However, this supply growth has not fully kept up with the greater increase in demand for child care as many more mothers have joined the labor force in these years. The supply shortages are most acute for specific forms of care, such as institutional forms of care, care for infants and toddlers, and care for children in low-income neighborhoods, which have witnessed the greatest surge in increased maternal employment in the past decade. Center care arrangements, which some parents prefer, are generally the least available (Kisker et al. 1991), and their supply is particularly constrained in low-income communities (Queralt and Witte 1998).[9]

Information Constraints   The child care market is segmented by types, and there is little overall coordination within the market to offer information so that families can make informed choices about care arrangements. Families happen upon care choices through their circle of acquaintances as much as they seek care in an open market system. In the 1995 NHES, 59 percent of parents reported that friends, neighbors, relatives, and coworkers were their sources of information about primary, nonparental child care arrangements (Hofferth et al. 1998). This may be even more the case for low-income families in more isolated neighborhoods. In addition, there are often significant "asymmetries in information," or large differences in the information that parents have about the quality of specific care arrangements compared to the providers.

Age Constraints   Although the number of infants and toddlers in care has been rising rapidly, relatively few of them go to centers—partly because many families prefer a home setting for at least some part of their child's first three years, but also because many centers do not accept children younger than age three. Infant care is more expensive for centers since it requires more adults per infant. Those institutions that offer care to children younger than three often limit their numbers to a relatively small fraction of their total slots.[10] State and local administrative data indicate that the number of infants and toddlers on waiting lists for all forms of care far exceeds the number of children two years and older on waiting lists.[11] Data from the 1995 NHES indicate that mothers of younger children are the most likely to want to change care arrangements and that they prefer to change to center-based care (Hofferth et al. 1998).

Schedule Constraints   Some care arrangements are amenable to a mother's work schedule, and others are not. Mothers working full-time more often need to rely on formal care because the amount of time that care is available in relative or informal care arrangements is often significantly less than they need (Smith 2000). Many centers also operate on less than a full-time schedule—one-third of day care centers operate less than a full day (Kisker et al. 1991), and a majority of Head Start programs operate for only part of the day (Smith 2000; Schumacher and Irish 2003).[12] By contrast, nearly all family day care homes have full-day care, making this type potentially more appealing to those working full-time and longer hours (Hofferth et al. 1991; Kisker et al. 1991).

Single mothers and low-wage-earning mothers are more likely to work nontraditional hours and to have frequently shifting schedules (Heymann 2000; Hofferth 1995; Kisker et al. 1991; Presser 1995; 2000).[13] More than one-third of low-income mothers work nights and/or weekends. Almost no centers or family child care homes offer care during nights and on weekends, so mothers working these hours are most likely to rely completely on fathers, relatives, or informal home-based care providers or to use these in addition to center care (Emlen 1997; Hofferth 1999; Smith 2002). Many low-income mothers also have work schedules that may change often. Mothers from very low-income families are twice as likely to work seasonal jobs, to experience frequent job changes, and to work jobs with changing shifts (Presser 1995).

Cost Constraints   In a survey of average child care prices across urban areas in forty-seven states, Karen Schulman (2000) has found that full-time care for a twelve-month-old averages more than $6,000 per year for a child care center and more than $5,000 for a family child care home. This suggests that the high cost of child care may put these care choices out of the reach of most low- and moderate-income families unless the cost is significantly subsidized.

Most child care, however, is not subsidized. Data from the 1999 National Survey of American Families (NSAF) indicate that 38 percent of low-income single-parent families receive some type of financial assistance for child care from a government agency or other organization (Giannarelli, Adelman, and Schmidt 2003). Low-income families with children pay for child care somewhat less often than do all families, and when they pay they also pay somewhat less, but they still pay a substantially larger share of their income for child care expenses (Giannarelli and Barsimantov 2000; Smith 2002).[14] Smith (2002) reports that families with incomes up to 200 percent of the federal poverty line paid on average $61 in weekly child care expenses in 1997, or 20 percent of their income. At the same time, all those who earned more than that averaged $80 per week for child care, or 6 percent of their income.[15] Smith (2000, 2002) has found that child care expenses for all families have increased in recent years and that the large gap in the amount of income paid for child care has persisted since the census survey was conducted.[16]

The relatively high cost of child care even with subsidies puts many care choices out of reach for many families. This makes less expensive forms of care like informal and relative care more appealing, especially if the cost of care is discounted by the provider out of personal considerations (Heymann 2000; Singer et al. 1998). Because of cost concerns, parents may use this care even when it might not be a preferred care option or even as they worry about the care's quality and stability.

As a result of these constraints—supply, information, child's age, schedule, costs—low-income families face more limited care choices. These constraints interact and are multiplied for single mothers, those requiring care for children with special needs, and those working nontraditional hours, all of whom are disproportionately represented among low-income families. Constraints do often frame the child care choices made by single mothers. The care they use is the care that is available to them. Given this, they often face problems with the quality of the child care they do use.

Child Care Quality

There is a large, but diffuse, literature on child care "quality." Overall, child care professionals have developed some consensus on the main elements of what constitutes quality child care. Most definitions combine two aspects of quality: the *structural features* of the care that have been correlated with better child outcomes, such as group size, staff-child ratios, and training of staff, and the *care processes* that focus on the nature of caregiver-child interactions (Lamb 1998; National Institute of Child Health and Development 2002).[17] Many child care quality studies focus on the structural features of care, and some studies address care processes, using established rating scales to make quantifiable observational assessments (Cryer 1999).[18] Very few studies have looked at mothers' views of what constitutes good child care.

One child care assessment study, the Cost, Quality, and Outcomes Study (CQOS), used longitudinal developmental testing of more than eight hundred children from four hundred child care centers.[19] This concerted effort by an interdisciplinary team of researchers from four universities found that more than 70 percent of the children received care that was "poor to mediocre." Another 12 percent were in centers rated very low; these children received care that was considered unsafe or "developmentally harmful." Only 14 percent of the children were in centers rated "developmentally appropriate" (Helburn 1995).[20] Another study of home-based care by family child care providers and relatives, conducted by the Families and Work Institute, reported a similar breakdown for family child care homes, except that a higher percentage of the care was poor-quality and potentially developmentally harmful to children (Kontos et al. 1995).[21] The CQOS, Families and Work Institute, and other large-scale studies have found that overall quality is low in both centers and family child care homes and that quality varies with the structural features of the care.[22]

Deborah Phillips and her colleagues (1994) have found that care quality was significantly higher in centers serving children from high-income families than in centers serving low- and middle-income families. The study also found that care quality in centers that served predominantly low-income children was "barely adequate within a context of wide variation" (Phillips et al. 1994, 490).[23] Sandra Scarr and Marlene Eisenberg (1993) found that children from low-income families, families headed by lone mothers, and families whose mother had a complex employment pattern were all more likely to be found in lower-quality care, leading to less favorable child outcomes.

Several studies have further found that the quality of child care services may be particularly important in the lives of children from low-income families: low-quality care may place children at further risk, while high-quality care can compensate for a high-risk environment (National Institute of Child Health and Development 1999; Peisner-Feinberg et al. 2001; Phillips et al. 1994). Scarr and Eisenberg (1993) found that socially disadvantaged children were more likely to be influenced positively in their development by high-quality care and that children from low-income families were more vulnerable to the effects of poor-quality care. In contrast, children from families who had more advantages were not as affected (negatively or positively) by reasonable ranges in child care. The NICHD study found that infants from poor families enrolled in full-time, high-quality child care were more positively engaged with their mothers than were similar infants not in child care or infants in child care measured as low-quality (National Institute of Child Health and Development 1999). Scarr and Eisenberg (1993) suggest that the cognitive benefits of intellectually stimulating care are greatest for children from disadvantaged homes. The cognitive benefits are greater than they are for middle-class children; middle-class homes on average provide greater levels of intellectual stimulation, and the quality of child care has a more muted impact on these children.

Another dimension of child care related to quality that is very relevant for the present study is the stability of care arrangements. Instability in child care arrangements has been associated with increased child aggression, impaired relationships with adults and peers, and problems in peer interactions as children get older (Howes and Hamilton 1993; Howes, Matheson, and Hamilton 1994; Phillips, Howes, and Whitebook 1992; Scarr, Phillips, and Mc-Cartney 1990). The stability of children's caregiving relationships appears to be particularly important for younger children because of the strength and quality of the attachments that may be formed with stable providers and the greater emotional insecurity that can result from multiple, unstable caregivers. As developmental psychologists have discussed, the strength of early attachments is crucial to further emotional development and appropriate social behavior (Thompson 2001).

There has been relatively little study of child care stability and its variations by type, family income, or other relevant factors. In one of the only other longitudinal studies of child care arrangements, another NICHD (1997b) study found that children who started care in their first year experienced an average of 2.2 child care arrangements in just the first twelve months of life. Data from the 1990 National Child Care Study indicated that twelve months was the median length of children's current care arrangements at the time of the survey (Hofferth 1996). Kisker and her colleagues (1991) further reported from the same data that informal care arrangements were significantly shorter than center-based or family child care arrangements. Freya Sonenstein and Douglas Wolf (1991) tracked welfare recipients' child care arrangements in the 1980s and found that center care and care by a relative in a child's home were more durable than nonrelative care in the provider's home.

This study, through longitudinal interviews with mothers and detailed tracking of care arrangements from birth onward, focuses very much on the child care dynamics of low-income families and analyzes the duration of child care spells to understand the relative stability of child care.[24] To date, there has been little application of care spells analysis in child care research. Some research on turnover in care exists, and more is on the way. One major study has looked at spells of subsidy use for child care in five states using administrative data (Meyers et al. 2001). However, the reasons for turnover have never been explored for child care. Most of the analyses of poverty and welfare dynamics have used large-scale longitudinal datasets, but these do not exist in the same way for child care.[25]

Child Care Effects on Development

With more mothers working today than ever before, children's care arrangements serve as a primary context for their development because of the sheer quantity of time that they spend with child care providers in their earliest years. In the past decade there has been significant research on the developmental impacts of children's early care situations. In 1994 the Carnegie Corporation released *Starting Points*, a widely regarded report championing the cause of assisting children in their development from the cradle to kindergarten and highlighting the social implications of not doing so. New research in the past few years on early brain development in the fetus and the first years of life has also received significant scientific, policy, and popular attention. A White House Conference on Early Childhood in 1997 highlighted research suggesting that the first three years of life are "a critical period" for brain growth and learning (Blakeslee 1997). The findings by neuroscientists on the remarkable and rapid early brain growth complement the findings of developmental psychologists on the importance of early childhood relationships, experiences, and environments. The brain development research has not focused much on the relationship of particular contexts, like the home environment or the child care setting, to the brain's growth, except to suggest that early experiences matter a lot, and the earlier they occur the more they may matter.

Recent work by developmental psychologists is demonstrating that the earliest years of childhood are a period of extraordinary developmental importance (Bronfenbrenner and Morris 1998; Brooks-Gunn 1995; Ford and Lerner 1992; Lerner et al. 2002; Sameroff 1995).[26] Many of the recent findings about child care effects on children's cognitive, emotional, and social development have come out of data from a large multi-investigator longitudinal study begun in 1989 by the National Institute of Child Health and Development. NICHD's Study of Early Child Care (SECC) is a comprehensive longitudinal study of more than one thousand families from children's birth in the early 1990s through the year 2000 (Shonkoff and Phillips 2000). It is a large-scale effort to understand the relationship between children's care experiences and their development over time. The families were followed closely and assessed at regular intervals for changes in care arrangements, quality of care, and a wide range of developmental outcomes. In a compendium National Academy of Science report, *Neurons to Neighborhoods: The Science of Early Childhood Development*, the NICHD study researchers highlighted the importance of context for child development. The authors state:

> The scientific evidence on the significant developmental impacts of early experiences, caregiving relationships, and environmental threats is incontrovertible. Virtually every aspect of early human development, from the brain's evolving circuitry to the child's capacity for empathy, is affected by the environments and experiences that are encountered in a cumulative fashion, beginning early in the prenatal period and extending through the early childhood years. The science of early development is also clear about the specific importance of parenting and of regular caregiving relationships more generally. The question today is not whether early experience matters, but rather how early experiences shape

individual development and contribute to children's continued movement along positive pathways. (Shonkoff and Phillips 2000, 6)

Children's Social Contexts

The social contexts of poverty and neighborhood conditions provide a context for child development, which can be ameliorated or exacerbated by child care. Poverty serves as an important context for children's development. Greg Duncan and Jeanne Brooks-Gunn (2000) reviewed many studies and found strong evidence that poverty during childhood impairs children's well-being in a number of different areas. They found that poverty experienced in infancy and across early childhood is associated with adverse developmental outcomes in children's early cognitive abilities as well as in their later academic achievements. Poor children had higher rates of developmental delay and learning disabilities, including difficulty in learning to read between the ages of three and seven. Lawrence Aber and his colleagues (1997), when controlling for many of poverty's related factors, found that children in poor families had much higher risks of asthma, lower birthweight, and lower scores on several developmental tests at later ages. Children who experience long durations of poverty have also been found to show signs of depression and low self-esteem, to more frequently display antisocial behaviors during the course of childhood, and to have worse measures of early cognitive development (McLeod and Shanahan 1993; Miech et al. 1999; Patterson and Albers 2001). Among children in low-income families, those experiencing deeper levels of income poverty also had worse outcomes across several measures of cognitive and social development and among nonpoor families there was little difference in outcomes for families with greater incomes (Dearing, McCartney, and Taylor 2001).

Childhood poverty appears to have both short-term and long-term consequences for development. Growing up poor is associated with sizable cognitive deficits in early childhood (Smith, Brooks-Gunn, and Klebanov 1997) and with large earning deficits into adulthood (Corcoran 1995). Judith Smith, Jeanne Brooks-Gunn, and Pamela Klebanov (1997), using longitudinal data for children from the National Longitudinal Survey of Youth (NLSY), found large and significant differences in measured early education outcomes for poor and nonpoor children and concluded that the effects of poverty on children's cognitive development occur early in life. The research suggests that the long-run effects of childhood poverty on development are most severe when poverty occurs early in childhood and when poverty is long-term (Brooks-Gunn and Duncan 1997).

Neighborhood residence is also likely to affect children's development.[27] Brooks-Gunn (1996) has identified four broad categories of resources that researchers have found to be important to children in their development: income, human capital, time, and emotional and psychological resources. Almost all of these are lower for younger children in poor neighborhoods. Families in low-income neighborhoods have fewer personal and institutional resources for child development (Brooks-Gunn et al. 1998; Fuller et al. 1997; Klebanov, Brooks-Gunn, and Duncan 1997). Smith, Brooks-Gunn, and Klebanov (1997) found that neighborhoods with high concentrations of poverty provide fewer learning experiences in the homes of preschoolers, even controlling for the links seen between family income and learning experiences. Low-income neighborhoods also may affect children's development by providing poorer levels of social organization, fewer adult role models, and less collective supervision and monitoring of children (Sampson, Raudenbush, and Earls 1997).

The developmental research about the social contexts of poverty serves as a primary context for the children in this study. The effects of child care occur on top of these effects, and child care may mitigate or exacerbate some of the social contextual effects for children.

Children's Care Contexts

The earliest years of childhood are a period of enormous developmental importance, and children's attachment to their parents as primary caregivers holds great significance for their growth across all primary areas of early development (Thompson 2001). While parents have a greater impact on their children's development through the interaction, genes, environments, and resources they provide their children, children's relationships with their other caregivers are found to significantly influence development as well (Howes and Hamilton 1992; Scarr 1998). Among these relationships, Ross Thompson (2001) emphasizes that early care arrangements may most directly influence children's emotional security and early cognitive development.[28]

The developmental psychology literature generally reports that emotional development is affected by child care arrangements, that the effects are mediated by quality, and that they can be either positive or negative (Shonkoff and Phillips 2000). Secure, trusting, consistent relationships with caregivers often support emotional growth, especially when they are complemented with a strong, secure mother-child attachment (Howes, Matheson, and Hamilton 1994). Insecure caregiving or disruptions in care can inhibit emotional growth. Unstable care can compound the harm caused to emotional health by a chaotic family environment (Vaughn et al. 1979). Deborah Phillips, Kathleen McCartney, and Sandra Scarr (1987) found that both overall child care quality and caregiver-child verbal interactions were highly predictive of social development when controlling for family factors and child care experiences.

The effects of early maternal employment and early child care, particularly during infancy, has been studied extensively (for reviews of this literature, see Lamb 1998; Shonkoff and Phillips 2000). Jay Belsky (1986, 1995, 1997, 2001) has argued that early nonmaternal care is a possible cause for concern in the development of very young children.[29] Several studies have found evidence of negative effects of first-year maternal employment and nonmaternal care on the development of infants, including for cognitive and social developmental outcomes in later years (Belsky and Eggebeen 1991; Brooks-Gunn, Han, and Waldfogel 2002; Harvey 1999; Howes 1990; Waldfogel, Han, and Brooks-Gunn 2002). Brooks-Gunn and her colleagues (2002), using longitudinal data from the NICHD Study of Early Child Care, were also able to study the impact of variations in the type, quality, and other features of infant child care on later cognitive developmental outcomes and found that lower quality of child care and more hours of care led to more pronounced negative effects on developmental outcome measures at age three. These studies find that low-quality early care can negatively influence children's social and emotional development, particularly for disadvantaged children in families with other characteristics associated with more insecure mother-infant attachments.

Belsky's argument about the impact of early child care then may be qualified to say that early cognitive and social development may be further impaired by patterns of low-quality infant child care, particularly in the context of other family-related disadvantages.[30] Michael Lamb (1998) reviewed the literature on the effects of infant care and concluded similarly that infant care can be problematic "when it co-occurs with" poor-quality care at home as well as in unstable care arrangements. The findings from these studies and others (Clarke-Stewart 1989; Howes 1990; National Institute of Child Health and Development 1997a) suggest that we need at least to be concerned about the impact of infant child care and that future work should consider developmental effects in the context of the timing, quality, and intensity of the earliest child care arrangements, especially in families with working mothers.

Overall, there appears to be a consistent positive effect of higher-quality child care on children's social and emotional development across the range of child care types, and children from low-income families experience relatively more benefits from higher-quality child care (Helburn 1995; Howes and Hamilton 1992; Howes, Phillips, and Whitebook 1992; Phillips, McCartney, and Scarr 1987; Scarr 1998; Scarr and Eisenberg 1993).[31] Studies have found that higher-quality care is associated with modest increases in cognitive and language development. Scarr and Eisenberg (1993) found that children with involved and responsive caregivers display improved verbal and cognitive skills and more exploratory behaviors. An NICHD study (2000b) examined the relationship between care quality and cognitive development across a range of care types and among children from different family backgrounds. The study found that children experiencing higher-quality care scored higher on cognitive and language tests at several points in the first three years of life and that these differences occurred across a range of families varying by ethnicity, income, and home contexts. Other studies have similarly found that children with measured higher-quality care displayed improved cognitive and language development compared with those in lower-quality care, although the associations have tended to be modest in most studies (Burchinal 1999; Burchinal et al. 1996; National Institute of Child Health and Development 1998a, 2000a; Phillips et al. 1987; Whitebook, Howes, and Phillips 1990). Studies have further found that caregivers' relative influence appears to be greater for children in low-income families and for those facing other childhood disadvantages (National Institute of Child Health and Development 1999; Phillips et al. 1994; Scarr and Eisenberg 1993).

To summarize, for both social and cognitive areas of development, research studies find that children's interactions with parents and other caregivers influence early growth. Parents and the home environments they create remain the predominant influence on young children's growth, adjustment, and wellbeing even with the large amounts of time children spend away from their parents in care settings. The quality of child-caregiver relationships influences children's social development, including their emotional behavior, ability to form positive relationships with peers and other adults, and self-understanding. Similarly, caregiving relationships influence children's cognition positively or negatively, depending on quality. For both emotional and cognitive development, the research further suggests that the effects of care, whether positive or negative, are more sizable for children from disadvantaged homes. With the prevalence of child care in children's lives, the research has shown that it is a central context for early childhood development.

The Child Care Policy Context

In the United States child care and education for young children is primarily a family's personal responsibility. Stoney and Greenberg (1996) estimate that overall in the United States families pay 60 percent of child care costs, with the government paying 39 percent and the private sector contributing less than 1 percent. Not every family pays the full cost of child care because some families receive public child care assistance either directly through federal and state subsidy programs or indirectly through income tax credits that return some of the costs to families. (The major early care and education programs are presented in table A.8.) The amount of financial assistance that low-income families receive varies a lot, with many receiving no subsidy, some receiving assistance for part of their child care costs, and some participating in fully subsidized care programs (Giannarelli, Adelman, and Schmidt 2003).

The two common forms of public subsidies for child care are contracts and vouchers. Under contract systems, a public agency contracts with a provider for slots in a child care program. In a voucher system, parents are given vouchers to use to pay a certain amount for child care, which can be given to an eligible provider, who is either reimbursed directly from the agency or through the parent. In either case, contracts or voucher, the subsidy can cover all or some portion of the costs, often on a sliding scale based on income, with the parent making a copayment for the remainder. The relative use of each

(Text continues on p. 244.)

Table A.8 Summary of Major Federal and State Child Care and Early Education Programs

Program Name	Purpose	Eligibility Criteria	Funding Levels	Number Served
Child Care Development Fund (CCDF) (Gish 2001)	Child care subsidies for low-income families, including those who are receiving or have moved off of public assistance (TANF)	Children under thirteen whose parents are working, receiving TANF, or in training with incomes at or below a state-set income eligibility level; federal guidelines allow states to set income eligibility level up to 85 percent of state median income	$4.8 billion in federal funding and an additional $2.0 billion in state funding (FY 02)	1.81 million children (FY 01)
Social services block grant (SSBG) (Gish 2001) and Temporary Assistance to Needy Families (TANF) (Schumacher and Rakpraja 2002)	States can transfer up to 30 percent of SSBG or TANF block grant funds to CCDF to subsidize child care; states may also directly spend TANF funds on child care services	Needy children as determined by the states within broad guidelines set by the federal government	Forty-seven states either transferred or directly spent $3.5 billion of TANF funds on child care (FY 02); forty-three states spent $397 million of SSBG funds for child care (FY 99)	Not available

Program	Description	Who is served	Funding	Participation
Head Start (HS) (U.S. Department of Health and Human Services 2003) and Early Head Start (EHS)	Comprehensive early care and education program focused on social competence, learning, health, and nutrition	Head Start: children ages three to five from families with incomes at or below the poverty line; Early Head Start: children age birth to three from poor families	$6.3 billion (FY 02)	861,000 children (FY 02); 7 percent of these children are enrolled in Early Head Start
Dependent Care Tax Credit (DCTC) (National Women's Law Center 2003)	Federal tax credit for child care expenses up to $2,400 for one child, $4,800 for two children	Families that pay taxes and have children under thirteen	$2.5 billion in federal revenue loss (FY 02); some states made additional investments through state tax provisions	6.4 million taxpayers claimed the federal credit, with additional families accessing state provisions (FY 02)
Child and Adult Care Food Program (CACFP) (Food Research and Action Center 2002)	Subsidies for meals and snacks served in early care and education programs serving low-income children	Low-income children under six in public and nonprofit child care centers and family and group child care homes; funds are also provided for meals and snacks served in after-	$1.9 billion (FY 02) in federal funding	26 million children daily (FY 02)

(Table continues on p. 242.)

Table A.8 *Continued*

Program Name	Purpose	Eligibility Criteria	Funding Levels	Number Served
(CACFP)		school programs for school-age children and in adult day care centers		
Early intervention (EI) programs (part C of IDEA) and preschool special education program grants (Children's Defense Fund 2003)	Promotes development and remediates problems among children with identified disabilities	Children birth to six who have diagnosed developmental disabilities; states add other specific criteria	$807 million in federal funding (FY 02)	Not available
Title I preschool programs (Scrivner and Wolfe 2002)	Federal funding to school districts to improve the education of children in high-poverty schools; some school districts may elect to use some of the funds for preschool programs	Low-income, at-risk children; Title I program funding serves elementary and secondary school-age children, and some schools use some of their Title I funding for their preschool programs, which generally serve three-to five-year-olds	$204 million of Title I funding was spent on preschool-age children (FY 00)	Unknown
U.S. military child development program (Na-	Early care and education programs on	Primarily children who live on U.S. military bases in	$352 million (FY 00)	200,000 children worldwide (FY 00)

tional Women's Law Center 2000)	military bases that must meet the rigorous requirements that resulted from the Military Child Care Act of 1989 and be accredited by the National Association for the Education of Young Children	the United States or abroad		
State prekindergarten (pre-K) programs (*Education Week* 2002)	State-funded programs that provide preschool services in school-based or community settings	Varies by state; often programs are targeted toward low-income children or communities	$1.9 billion (FY 01)	765,000 children (FY 01)[a]

Source: Author's compilation.

[a]Calculated by dividing total funding by average cost per child served.

varies by states' administration of child care; more of the care in New York, for instance, is subsidized through contracted care.

The majority federal child care subsidy program is the Child Care and Development Fund (CCDF), which provides block grants to states for child care programs. Total federal child care spending grew tremendously over the decade, with the CCDF more than tripling between 1990 and 2002, reaching $4.8 billion in allocations to the states in 2002 (see table A.9). Added to this are states' required contributions to their CCDF budgets ($2.0 billion in FY 2002) and funds they can use from their federal welfare block grants for child care.[32]

In recent years states have extensively used the flexibility under the 1996 welfare reform law to use part of their welfare block grants—their Temporary Assistance to Needy Families (TANF) funds—to increase funding for their child care programs.[33] States have also directed some of their TANF surpluses that followed from large welfare caseload declines toward child care spending and transfers to their CCDF grants. In fact, TANF funds have been the largest source of the increases in states' child care funding since welfare reform, according to the Center for Law and Social Policy (CLASP), especially in 1999 and 2000, although state use of TANF funding for child care has leveled off since then (Schumacher, Greenberg, and Duffy 2001; Schumacher and Rakpraja 2002).[34] U.S. Department of Health and Human Services (2003) data for FY 2002 shows that states reported spending $3.5 billion in TANF block grant money.

Head Start is another federal program that funds child care and development programs. In FY 2002, $6.7 billion was appropriated for the Head Start program (U.S. Department of Health and Human Services 2003; see table A.2). Head Start was founded in 1965 as part of the federal government's War on Poverty, with the objective of breaking the intergenerational cycle of poverty by providing comprehensive services to low-income preschoolers (for a discussion of which children the Head Start program serves today, see Schumacher and Irish 2003). Head Start services are targeted at children whose family income falls below the poverty line or who receive public assistance and live in the catchment area of a local Head Start center. Most Head Start services go to preschool children ages three and four in centers that offer classroom-based care as part of a comprehensive child development and family services program.[35]

Most low-income families needing child care assistance are not served through publicly funded programs, even though child care spending in most states has increased significantly since the advent of welfare reform. A U.S. Department of Health and Human Services (2002b) analysis has estimated that 1.75 million low-income children received subsidies through the CCDF each month. This is a significant increase from the 1.0 million families it estimated to be funded in an average month in 1996 (U.S. Department of Health and Human Services 1998b). When we add in the children served

Table A.9   *Federal Expenditures for Child Care Development Fund and Head Start for Selected Years, 1990 to 2002*

Year	CCDF Spending	Head Start Spending
1990	$1.9 billion[a]	$1.6 billion
1992	2.0 billion[a]	2.2 billion
1994	2.7 billion[a]	3.3 billion
1996	3.1 billion[a]	3.6 billion
1998	5.3 billion[b]	4.4 billion
2000	7.2 billion[b]	5.3 billion
2002	8.3 billion[b]	6.7 billion

Sources: Adams and Sandfort (1992); Gish (2002); U.S. Department of Health and Human Services (2001a, 2003).
[a]Represents equivalent aggregate spending in programs that would be combined in 1996 consolidation of the federal child care funding stream into CCDF.
[b]Includes transfer funds from TANF.

through Head Start and other smaller federal funding sources (such as Title XX social services block grants),[36] the total number of children served and the recent increases look more encouraging.[37] Yet, despite large increases in child care spending and the number of children being served with government assistance, most families with children in need of care assistance are still not served with subsidies. Of the estimated 15.7 million children eligible for CCDF in 2000 using federal income guidelines, only 14 percent were served with CCDF and other federal funds combined (Mezey, Greenberg, and Schumacher 2002).[38]

In addition to less than full funding to meet their child care assistance needs, low-income families are also constrained by the complex and varying administration of subsidies in the states. Gina Adams, Kathleen Snyder, and Jodi Sandfort (2002) report that, owing to the complexity of the application and approval process, gaining access to child care subsidies is especially difficult for low-income families. They offer a qualitative analysis of families' experiences getting and retaining subsidies in twelve states. The process of applying for and securing child care subsidies entailed multiple visits, extensive documentation, and lengthy approval periods, greatly diminishing the accessibility to subsidies. According to their analysis, this has led to an underutilization of subsidies and high turnover rates for parents receiving subsidies.

Sometimes states make policy choices that screen out families and keep subsidy payments down since the system cannot meet a large portion of the potential need. Many states in recent years have prioritized the welfare-to-work population for child care services and moved their child care administration closer to their welfare system. This has added further complexity to child care administration and created problems for some applicants who are seeking only child care assistance. Pairing child care and welfare administration can make the process more confusing and discouraging to applicants and pushes child care administration to adopt some bureaucratic characteristics of the welfare system that families abhor: a focus on compliance, deterrence from use, cost control, and stigma.[39]

Adams and her colleagues (2002) report that some states have implemented innovative practices to make the process of applying for child care benefits simpler and the receipt of subsidies more continuous. These practices have included streamlining the application and recertification processes, using mail or fax rather than multiple in-person interviews, tighter coordination of the TANF and child care systems, and presumptive eligibility programs. Each of these steps can make program implementation easier and more efficient for states as well.

Another large source of financial support for child care comes through a federal income tax credit, the Dependent Care Tax Credit (DCTC), which can be used for reducing families' tax liabilities for a portion of their child care expenses if they qualify. The total tax credit amount generally works out to a maximum of $480 for one child and $960 for two or more children. This indirect subsidy for child care costs is unavailable to many low-income families, however, because they do not have significant tax liability and the credit is not refundable. As a nonrefundable credit, a family with no tax liability cannot receive a credit toward their care expenses, despite the fact that the lowest-income families often pay the highest proportion of their income for child care costs.[40] According to the most recent recorded year of IRS data, 6.4 million taxpayers claimed the credit and received approximately $2.8 billion in tax relief (National Women's Law Center 2003).

The Dependent Care Tax Credit is the most widely used form of child care subsidy: 6.4 million people received it compared to the 1.9 million who were assisted with CCDF funds and the 800,000 enrolled in Head Start programs.[41] The level of assistance is much lower, however, since more than twice as much tax revenue is spent for either the CCDF or Head Start programs as is forgone by families claiming the tax credit.

Conclusions

Millions of American children, including the majority of infants in their first year of life, spend a vast amount of their time in child care because their mothers are working. While a great deal has become known about care usage and its patterns through analyses of some relatively new larger national datasets, we still know much less about parents' preferences, how they choose among child care alternatives, and how these decisions interact with decisions about work, housing, and other family life decisions. We also know little about the care contexts of low-income families in particular, and of children living with a single mother in a disadvantaged neighborhood.

Several reviews of the research on the quality of child care confirm that child care is a very important developmental context, and that quality effects may be greater for children from low-income families—indeed, low-quality care may place children at higher risk, and good outside care arrangements can compensate for the risk factors associated with poverty. However, most of the research finds that overall child care quality varies within a relatively low range of quality and that the quality of care received by low-income families is generally worse. Deborah Love Vandell and Barbara Wolfe (2000) state that the overall quality of care is "fair" or "minimal," conclude that there is a lot of room for improvement, and note that this represents a lost developmental opportunity, especially for children from low-income families. Given that child care, if it is high-quality, can benefit children's development and support the great influx of working mothers, providing greater public support to low-income families would be consistent with both the social policy goals of welfare reform and the belief that developmental opportunities for children can address the adverse effects of poverty and help better set them on a path that avoids poverty in their future.

~ Appendix B ~

Discussion of Field Research Methods

In conducting this study of child care and work dynamics in low-income communities, I learned a great deal about how to do field research: how to develop, create, and refine methods to correspond to the research questions I was investigating. Since doing this field work, I have tried to teach students the research methods needed for community and family studies. I have felt at a serious loss when I could not find revealing methodological discussions accompanying some of the very good qualitative studies that have been produced. In that light, I wanted to supply some background about the methods I used when I published my own research, so that readers could interpret the findings accordingly and so that others doing similar work might have an example of one approach taken.

My approach in the research design was to use detailed ethnographies to understand children's care arrangements over time and across neighborhood-based samples of single-mother families with young children. These qualitative data were gained primarily from longitudinal interviews with forty-two low-income single mothers living in four diverse urban neighborhoods with high levels of poverty and complemented with participant observation of their young children in child care and other settings where they spent time.

The term "ethnography" is often used interchangeably with other research terms—"field-based research," "qualitative study," "naturalistic inquiry"—to refer to methods of social science inquiry that rely on talking to people and observing life in their natural setting (and writing about it). This research method generally seeks to understand the subject of inquiry from an insider's perspective, usually using narrative data rather than the numeric data used in quantitative studies. Qualitative research generally explores a line of inquiry in more depth with its subjects in a particular context, but most often with a relatively small study sample.

I used qualitative methods in this research for several reasons. Most of these reasons followed the general uses and purposes for which practitioners have applied field-based inquiry, many of which were reinforcing reasons in this case:[1]

- Qualitative methods are useful for *identifying patterns* in child care choices. There has not been much research to describe the patterns of care arrangements among low-income families who are relatively new entrants into the labor force and the ways in which mothers make their initial child care choices.

- The qualitative approach describes *what may be missing in existing data* on child care arrangements. More private arrangements like kin care, informal care, or even family day care are relatively less visible and short-lived. These forms of care may be systematically underestimated in the quantitative data. Some mothers may also give these types of care a different meaning—not truly considering some care they are using to be a "care arrangement" even though it may be the primary and necessary care used that allows them to work.

- A qualitative study helps to *provide meaning for concepts in their context*. In this case, low-skilled, inner-city residents rely more often on informal care arrangements and on kin and cultural networks for their family support needs, such as child care, and it was important to understand the meanings they gave to these forms of child care.

- Qualitative data allowed me to *uncover, describe, and interpret complexities* in child care choices, dynamics, and strategies and examine how these choices are seen by the mothers who live with them. Understanding which factors led to care choices required open-ended interviewing, follow-up with respondents, and interpretation of their responses.

- Studying child care dynamics and the ways in which strategies changed over time required detailed profiling of the sequencing or simultaneity of events. The qualitative collection of data helped to preserve the chronological flow of events, allowing me to *explore precisely which events led to which consequences*.

- Analyzing the detailed qualitative data across the sample helped me to *generate a conceptual framework* to understand and explain child care choices and dynamics and to revise it with the integration of more data.

- Finally, and possibly most important for my purposes, the rich descriptive data and the deeper understanding of contexts helped me to organize what I found to *tell stories* and offer a concrete, more powerful account of the findings.

Doing this kind of ethnography entails detailed descriptive research in the field of study (Cicourel 1964; Glaser and Strauss 1967; Jorgensen 1989;

Lofland 1971). When doing it for the first time, I found it helpful to follow the qualitative methodologies that have been effectively employed elsewhere (Edin and Lein 1997; Liebow 1967; Newman 1993, 1999; Stack 1974, 1996; Sullivan 1989). The steps in my research included: making contacts in the communities, establishing rapport with potential respondents, selecting informants, designing interview protocols, transcribing interview texts, observing and noting behavior in the field, developing diagrammatic schemes to analyze or explain relationships, mapping communities, and keeping diaries. As Clifford Geertz (1973, 7–14) has pointed out, this kind of research requires a lot of writing, and written description serves as one's data of "what is interpretive in the flow of social discourse."

The bulk of the data for this study came from a series of in-depth interviews with low-income mothers. I conducted taped, semistructured interviews with mothers at least four times and as many as nine times over twenty-four to thirty-six months. Through these interviews, I gained knowledge of the aspects of family life that are most relevant to children's care arrangements and then followed these families to observe changes in their situations and the care arrangements they made. I met and spoke with families on the phone many more times than this over the course of the field research and made notes on these regular ongoing conversations.

This analysis was structured as a relatively narrow and focused study.[2] Although the sampling method was specifically designed to focus on low-income single mothers in four neighborhoods in order to permit comparison across racial and ethnic groupings, almost all of the analysis in this study was for the forty-two families in the sample as a whole. The neighborhoods and families were selected to offer diversity in the sample. Given the small sample size and the initial focus of this analysis on the range of child care arrangements that working mothers used and their care dynamics, an analysis of all the families in the sample as a whole was most appropriate.

The Study Sample

The sampling for the study took place in three overlapping stages:

1.   Sampling of neighborhoods

2.   Sampling of child-serving community-based organizations in neighborhoods

3.   Sampling of families using multiple recruitment methods, including initial referrals from community organizations and direct recruitment from neighborhoods

I conducted the research in four neighborhoods with relatively high concentrations of child poverty. Two neighborhoods were primarily African

American in composition, and two were more demographically mixed, with high concentrations of Latino families and immigrants (see table 1.3). Relative to a one-neighborhood study, drawing the sample from four neighborhoods provided a potentially more heterogeneous sample and some possible variations in the types of strategies adapted. Within these neighborhoods, I made arrangements to gain access to and observe behavior in community-based locations that offered child care programs, as well as other locations where children spent time. I volunteered my time to these organizations, in part to participate in and observe activities there and to gain access to families. In the four neighborhoods, more specifically, I spent a significant amount of time during the week visiting child care locations, including most of the settings where children in the sample study received their primary care, as well as several other care settings that were not used by children in the study but that I came across in the research. I visited more than thirty centers in all and visited more than seventy home settings where children received care, more than half of which were family child care providers' homes.

I developed a small sample of families living in the four neighborhoods. The mothers were working, earning a low income, and single, and the children were between the ages of two and four at the time of initial contact. The criteria I used for selection were:

1. *Residence*: Living within neighborhood boundaries defined through a combination of: existing political boundaries, such as community boards, school districts, and social service catchment areas; continuous census tracts of similar demographic composition; and respondents' definitions of neighborhood boundaries

2. *Work status*: Employed at the time of the initial contact

3. *Low-skilled*: Measured as relatively low in educational attainment (less than fourteen years of formal schooling)

4. *Family structure*: Mother self-identified as not married at time of initial contact

A small sample was selected to be as heterogeneous as possible. The key methods used to generate a sample were:

- Developing contacts and getting initial referrals from child-serving organizations

- Reaching out directly to the families I met through voluntary neighborhood-based activities

- Writing and calling families on waiting lists for child care services

- Asking initial respondents to help me find other families

To select the sample, I began with referrals from family and child-serving organizations in the community; I did not begin with child care centers, because I did not want to select families with knowledge of what type of care they used, since this was what I was studying. I also met families through the community agencies serving low-income families where I volunteered. Both of these methods allowed me to gain initial access through trusted community contacts or to establish some personal connection. This step was important given that I was going to be asking respondents for detailed information on potentially sensitive topics and for significant amounts of their time. These are traditional means for developing a sample for an in-depth ethnographic study of this type (Edin and Lein 1997; Liebow 1967; Stack 1974; Sullivan 1989).[3] In three communities I developed at least my first few interview respondents through an organizational contact, and in the final sample twelve of the families were referrals from community-based organizations. Five came from personal contacts made through volunteer activities in community-based organizations.

I tried to build and diversify my sample pool to guard against getting information only from those who were most readily approachable in the community settings. I asked mothers to help me find other mothers they knew who met my selection criteria but might be "less connected," did not receive services from the organization that referred me to them, and did not use the same child care sources they did. This technique, which is called "snowball sampling" in qualitative research terminology, allowed me to get referrals from the earlier participants in the study and diversify my sample further. Snowballing from initial respondents led me to eleven of the families.

I tried to ensure that I was getting a diverse sample in several other ways as well. First, I started with a few community-based agency contacts but did not get more than one to three families from the same source (institution, agency, other respondent). Second, when I asked families to introduce me to other families, I generally asked them to introduce me to people who they knew used some other strategy or resource for child care and who have been more isolated than they were. Third, I sometimes used "skip-step sampling": if a respondent introduced me to other families, I would complete a shorter interview and ask them to introduce me to still other families before building my recruiting pool for a full interview and the longitudinal sample. I used this method when a respondent referred to me another potential respondent who seemed in some respects to be similar to the first respondent. Fourth, I continued over time to enlist the help of the families I had previously interviewed to introduce me to families who were relatively isolated and unattached to the social services organizations they used.

In two neighborhoods I obtained old waiting lists of families who had previously applied for child care services. These lists were about a year old and included the children's dates of birth and family contact information, but not information about whether or where they may have received care, and nothing regarding the other selection criteria. The fact that families had applied for child care subsidies did not necessarily mean that they were very likely to have moved into a subsidized care arrangement by the time I approached them for participation in the study, since New York City has such long waiting lists for child care that the majority of families applying do not receive subsidized care placements. In fact, when I analyzed the data, I found that the number of months of subsidized care received by the mothers I got from child care waiting lists was no greater than the amounts gained by mothers from other means.

From these lists, I randomly selected a smaller set of names and contacted families, first by letter and then with phone calls, to ask them whether they met the selection criteria and to seek their participation. Fourteen of the total respondents emerged from wait-list contacts. By these varied means, I was able to reach a relatively heterogeneous group of respondents. I wanted diversity in the sample to get a greater sense of the variability in experiences among mothers and possibly to develop more encompassing policy recommendations.

Sample Characteristics

Overall, half of the mothers in the sample were African American and half were Latina. The mothers ranged in age from twenty-one to thirty-nine, with an average age of twenty-nine at the start of the study. The average age of the mothers at the birth of their first child was about twenty-one, and thirteen had become mothers in their teens. The children were all between two and three years old at the time of their initial interview. Twenty-eight of the children had siblings at the time of the initial interview—twenty-one had older siblings, ten had younger ones, and three had both older and younger siblings. Two mothers also had a second child during the time of the field study.

The family composition varied across the sample, and within families it changed over time. Most of the mothers had never been married. Seven had been married and were divorced, and two married in the course of the longitudinal interview period. The mothers were for the most part lone parents, but in some cases the fathers of the children lived with them consistently or "stayed sometimes." Five of the fathers appeared to live with their children consistently for the length of the interview period, and in three other cases the father lived with the family for a portion of the time. In some cases, mothers were living with a man with whom they were involved in a durable relationship but who was not the father of the children. Even in cases where mothers were living with a partner, they often considered themselves single because they said the apartment lease was in their own name and the partner's tenure was uncertain. Thus, they often defined whether it was a fully shared household based on the formal status of the apartment.

The sample was selected to include only mothers who were working at the point of initial interview. Most worked full-time, and one-third had more than one job. The mothers worked from twenty-five to more than seventy-two hours per week, with an average of forty-two hours. Overall, the mothers earned between $4.35 and $15.20 per hour in their primary jobs and fairly evenly covered this range. The average per hour earnings for all hours mothers worked was $9.27.

Mothers ranged in their years of formal education from seven to fourteen years, with the average of 11.8 years, or just less than high school completion. Twelve mothers had dropped out of high school; eighteen had a high school degree (including five who received a general equivalency diploma); twelve had some postsecondary education, including six who had two years of college or had obtained an associate's degree.

Thirty-two of the forty-two mothers in the sample had received cash welfare assistance at some point. Most of the mothers were not receiving welfare payments during the time period of the interviews. Of the thirty-two women with any welfare history, eight received cash public assistance for some part of the interview period, but generally for short durations as they were working their way off of welfare. Three mothers received some cash public assistance throughout the interview period, though two had several administrative disruptions in their benefits, and one's benefits continued but declined steadily as her earnings increased.

During the interview period more mothers received other forms of social services assistance besides cash welfare payments, including housing assistance, food stamps, Medicaid, and child care subsidies. More than anything they relied on housing assistance. More than two-thirds of the sample lived in public housing or received rent subsidies. A notable surprise in the sample was the housing history of the mothers: many families in the sample had unstable housing dynamics that had led to frequent moves, including homelessness, and changes in neighborhoods that had caused them to move away from extended family, friends, and known resources. Nine of the forty-two mothers had been homeless with their families in the shelter system, and six more had been homeless for some time during the study child's first four years of life. More than two-thirds of the sample lived in public housing or received rent subsidies. In addition to the child care and work dynamics discussed in this book, mothers had to coordinate work and care choices with sometimes frequent changes in housing.

The mothers in this sample also relied on governmental help in the form of food stamps, Medicaid, and child care subsidies. Given their low incomes even when they worked full-time, many mothers still needed help, particularly child care assistance, so that they could work, and they needed health insurance for their children since only nine received medical benefits from their employers throughout the interview period. However, many who were eligible for this form of assistance did not receive it because the city's welfare administrators did not inform them of their eligibility or because they could not overcome, or did not wish to confront, bureaucratic intransigence.

Research Procedure

The research design consisted of these elements:

- Semistructured repeat interviews with a sample of mothers of young children, including regular follow-up (every three to four months) through more than two years to assess changes over time

- Observation of children in their care settings to provide the context of the child care arrangements

- Informal interviews with child care providers and other community-based social services staff with knowledge of these children's development and family situations

Most of the data for this analysis came from interviews with low-income single mothers. The quality of the research depended directly on how well I could get mothers to share their stories about child care and the related factors in their work and family life.

I took several steps to test whether I could gain access to hard-to-reach families, collect reliable interview data, and ensure its validity. Prior to beginning the field research for this project, I did a smaller, preliminary study in Boston on a related research topic. I also worked for two months as a field-based census enumerator in New York City in some of the neighborhoods in this study to gain access while also learning more about the neighborhoods and their residents. (None of the census work was used as a source of data for this project.) Next, when I made initial contacts with the respondents, I structured my interviews so that they occurred in the time, place, and manner most convenient to them. I ensured complete confidentiality to the respondents, used initial questioning to build rapport, and started the interviews with factual, focused questions. Over time I asked more probing questions, particularly in follow-up interviews.

Informed Consent and Confidentiality

At the initial point of contact with potential respondents, I made sure that I informed them of my interest in talking with them about a study I was doing on urban family life in their communities. I standardized the presentation and made it during a first home visit or initial neighborhood-based conversation. I further separated the introductions from the interview activities and followed up with a phone call after a few days about the research and to schedule another date for an interview if they preferred to wait. I found that discussing the research possibility openly in the context of an initial thirty-minute conversation helped to build rapport with potential respondents.

Given that I found many of my initial respondents through relationships with neighborhood institutions, I clarified my role and actively responded to any questions. I emphasized that participation was completely voluntary and confidential and that there was no relationship between my research and any referring agent if they had any concerns about possible service-related implications from their responses.

Most of the women I was able to contact were willing to participate, and I generally scheduled a time for a follow-up interview. I made every effort to get every mother I contacted to participate because I did not want to get just the most willing respondents, but also the most skeptical and hardest to recruit and retain as well. This made recruitment and retention a constant struggle, but it was successful in the end. Of the fifty-two mothers I initially contacted, forty-nine agreed to an initial meeting. Of the forty-nine, in seven cases during the first interviews I determined that the respondent was not eligible by some of the selection criteria. I conducted a shorter first interview with them, and those seven initial interviews were not included in the analysis.

In return for the interview time and confidence the respondents were giving me, I wanted to give the families something in exchange as a token of my appreciation. I wanted as much as possible not to make this a primarily monetary exchange, and so I decided to bring children's books with me to the initial meeting with families, which I also thought would serve the purpose of placing the immediate focus of the meeting on the child. The gift of books and reading in general served as a good opening to the conversation, helping to establish rapport. It also provided me with an opportunity in most cases to read to the child, if he or she was present, and get a sense of the child and to discuss with the mother how much she generally read with the child.

I gave the mothers the option of accepting either the books I brought or $20 for the initial interview, which was on average more than two hours long, and $10 for subsequent interviews. I made it clear that I was indifferent about which option they chose. Most mothers (forty-five of the forty-nine with whom I had initial meetings, and thirty-nine of the forty-two in the sample) elected to take the books. In later interviews, most mothers also took the books, though at a slightly lower rate. Thirty-six of the forty-two took the books at the second interviews, and thirty-eight of the forty-two took them on the third interview. The mothers who chose to take the money were in most cases those in the greatest need for cash.

Interviewing Mothers

The principal sources of qualitative data were the series of semistructured, repeated, and longitudinal interviews and many less formal conversations with the respondents wherever and whenever it was most convenient for the mothers—in their homes, workplaces, locations where their children received care, local community centers, or local eateries. A minimum of three (and in most cases four or more) semistructured interviews were conducted between May 2000 and April 2002, usually between three and six months apart. Of the forty-two mothers who were chosen for the research sample, I was able to arrange second and third interviews with all forty-two, though this required a great deal of persistence. Final interviews were conducted by telephone with two mothers who had relocated from New York. Thus, there was no attrition among the selected sample.

In the interviews I sought basic data on children's care arrangements, children's activities and development, child care and work dynamics, use of social services and other resources, the basics of family history, child health and development factors, and housing dynamics. Sometimes I probed these areas further for the mother's perceptions about what underlay her choices and outcomes (see the interview protocol in appendix C). During the initial and subsequent interviews, each mother was asked about how the children spent their time, current child care arrangements and history, how these came about and what caused them to change, and her work situation and history.

I sought a relatively complete profile of information for certain primary question areas, but I did not follow a particular script in raising interview topics. I made the discussion as informal as possible, allowing for the natural flow of conversation to shape the ordering and wording of questions related to the topics. Over time and with repetition, I improved how I asked the questions, using respondents' language and building on initial understandings of their contexts. Also, as the interviews proceeded, I arrived at a more natural balance in the emphasis and pace of the interviews, streamlining less relevant question areas and probing for more specificity in those that proved most relevant.

The first interview was often more structured and started with a concrete topic. Before beginning the first interview, I would make some introductions and discuss consent, confidentiality, and other preliminaries. Then I began asking questions about children's daily time use patterns, a relatively benign topic but one that prompted specificity. I asked the mothers to tell me in detail how their children spent their day, focusing on the day before, and also how they spent their own time in a day. With more follow-up questioning, I constructed a specified pattern of time use for each mother-child set that served as the initial primary data for my analysis. This provided a base of information from which I could develop a numeric analysis of the time spent working, parenting, and in other activities.

I used this initial questioning to build rapport with the respondents and to seek specificity. After establishing rapport, I moved on to a topical near-life history, often using this initial questioning as a direct basis for a more in-depth exploration of the respondents' strategies for work and child care. The primary areas for questioning beyond time use patterns were the children's care arrangements and care histories, children's health and development, mothers' work effort and status (current employment and earnings and recent work history), resources they used for the children's care, and their perceptions of their children's care and developmental needs.

Over the course of the interviews, mothers revealed much more to me as I became more familiar to them; they recalled additional detail and understood more clearly what I was asking. Repeat interviews provided valuable opportunities to further probe earlier responses, raise new topics for discussion, and interpret the responses over time. Repeat interviews also provided a richer and more complete set of longitudinal data. In the later interviews I was also able to discuss additional topic areas with mothers that provided a more complete picture of the family situation, including more details on family background and residential histories, views about their neighborhood and its effects on their family life, and specific strategies related to child care in the context of single-parenthood.

The total amount of interview time per mother varied depending on the level of interviewing needed to obtain information on a range of topics particular to the family's circumstances, the complexity of the family child care arrangements and other dynamics, and the length of time needed to develop a complete picture of the child's and mother's activities. The first baseline interviews were the longest, averaging more than two hours and ranging from about 100 to 225 minutes. For all the interviews the amount of recorded interview time with each mother averaged almost eight hours and ranged from seven to more than thirteen hours. In addition to the longer, recorded interviews, I spoke to the mothers more frequently by phone to maintain contact and track changes on a regular basis. For these conversations, I took interview notes that I summarized after the conversation.

Observing Children

Watching, listening, and interacting with children were important supplementary elements in the data collection. In all, I spent close to one-quarter of my time in the field. This was where I learned the most about context—how children spent their time in various care arrangements—and developed an understanding of the differences among the types of care arrangements and the effects of care arrangements on development. I volunteered time and participated for several months in care settings where two of the children in the sample received care—a center and a family day care home. I also observed and interacted with many of the children in the sample and sometimes followed children from one setting to the next when there were changes in arrangements. This part of the fieldwork provided the most valuable information about the children's activities. I recorded these written narratives of my observations in my field notes. As I made repeated observations of the same child or the same setting, I asked questions of the providers about particular children's needs and experiences, adding some more detail to the narratives.

Data Analysis

For the forty-two mothers, the total interview data amounted to more than 320 hours of taped interviews, a few more hours for which detailed interview notes were made, and more than 3,900 pages of transcriptions. A few of the interviews were not taped, generally at the respondent's request. The first two interviews with each mother were transcribed verbatim, and the subsequent interviews were more often targeted transcriptions, noting the information on a key topic of discussion. The field notes from observations in the families' homes and child care settings totaled more than 400 pages.

Once I completed the first interviews, I developed an interview summary memo, added field observations, diagrammed timelines of the relevant elements of family life (child care, work, living arrangements, social services), and made a note of any missing data. The summary memos also began to highlight emerging themes of mothers' strategies around work and child care. I developed a coding scheme around what I identified as twenty major themes in the data collected, including eighty-six specific codes for the narrative interview data as well as over sixty short-form data elements for family information and child care, work, and social service use and history. The coded data were then inputted into a database, designed specifically for this project, that allowed both quantitative analysis of child care dynamics over time and narrative analysis of the transcribed, coded, and inputted data.

I developed a timeline for each mother's work patterns and child care and living arrangements from the time of the child's birth, providing retrospective longitudinal data to compare with the longitudinal data that I collected over time. These led to the timelines presented at the end of the featured stories in each chapter, all of which were color-coded and more complex in the analytical stages of the research. I showed the respondents the timelines and reviewed all of this data with them in later interviews for accuracy so that they would have additional opportunities to add to their previous accounts or rectify discrepancies. Also, I took great care to make sure the data for the spells analysis were complete and accurate. The start and end of every child care spell and work spell were verified several times and related to the other information on the timeline to make sure they corresponded, especially when collecting retrospective data.

There was very clear consistency across the sample in the quality of the data on the use, intensity (number of hours in care), and duration of primary care spells both current and retrospective, as well as consistency in the quality of the data on the use of secondary care spells, though perhaps somewhat less consistency on the number of hours and duration of prior secondary care spells. The primary child care spells were the focus of the analysis, in any case, and the data on secondary care spells were mostly used to calculate the number of such spells being used and the hours in secondary care at the point in time of the interview.

Use of and Integration of Qualitative and Quantitative Data

I used the qualitative data in this study for descriptive purposes—to reveal how the participants in their own contexts viewed choices and made decisions and what they thought about those decisions. These are subjective perspectives for which qualitative data can help explicate what otherwise might not be known. I also pulled quantitative data (such as for the child care spells analyses) from the interviews to identify the distribution and prevalence of key patterns at one point in time and across time. Documenting each spell, including the dates of entry and exit and the cause for entries and exits, was an arduous process but the only way to provide a quantitative analysis of this qualitative data. As mentioned, it required repeatedly confirming dates and timelines with mothers and going over the circumstances for the care spells endings with them and in the analysis of the data several times to make sure a correct primary reason for exit was assigned, especially in cases where several closely timed factors contributed to changes.

This level of detailed data collection and analysis is important for research purposes because there are no data with which to do this analysis on a broader scale. These results can be used both in evaluating the data from this study and in designing larger longitudinal surveys that can collect such data in the future, though with somewhat less specificity and much less depth of understanding of the causal sequence of events. These results also demonstrate the importance of deeply integrated combinations of methods to truly understand difficult social policy questions.

Finally, once I identified the initial, most focused findings to emerge from the data, I used the codes to select key data elements for further analysis. I then generated separate data reports to review the evidence, analyze the data, and interpret findings related to child care arrangements, strategies and dynamics, and the interaction of child care and employment. This was a messy, iterative process, but it helped to reveal the most interesting patterns among the coding categories, as well as unexpected issues that emerged as a result of each round of interviewing and participant observation. I used a preliminary analysis of these to develop some follow-up areas for the third interviews, where the data might be incomplete. Further analysis led to the findings in this book.

Some aspects of the research process came naturally to me. I grew up in New York City during the 1970s in a mixed-income community, one that was bordered nearby by a very elite, intellectual society of whites and also by a mixed black and Hispanic, low-income, and culturally vibrant community.

I felt like I lived in the "no-man's land" between these extremes. Growing up, I drifted often and easily between the two areas, had friends in both, loved aspects of both, felt alienated by the separation, and hated that among my friends there were few who accompanied me in both worlds. Drifting into and out of different communities for this project came naturally since I had spent a lifetime blending my identity to fit into varying worlds in order to understand them and help bridge them. The communities in which I did this study felt very much like home to me. It was also easy enough for me to drift (so easy that I never thought about it until writing this self-description for the methodology appendix, per a reviewer's suggestion) between the relationships with the families in the study in these neighborhoods and my work at the New School for Social Research, where I was teaching, and my studies at Harvard, where I would return monthly to meet with my advisers on the project.

I developed an enormous sense of trust with the women in my study, far more than I had expected. They spoke to me of many aspects of their lives, and they seemed to know that I was very deeply interested. They revealed troubling aspects of their histories, of the pain of their pregnancies and even the times they terminated pregnancies, of the violence in some of their relationships. A few sought to know more about me, and I shared what I could. Many sought my opinion about the day-to-day events in their lives, and I lent my ear, and if I had something worthwhile to share from my experience, a little of my voice. My relationships with the children were most gratifying. I usually started each visit by initiating engagement with the child, not only because it seemed the natural thing to do but because I came bearing children's books on almost every visit and would talk to them about what they liked to read. Most visits I would read some to the children if they liked at varying points in the visit (some at the beginning, some at the end). The families invited me to their family gatherings, especially to children's birthday parties and Christmas and Easter activities but also Thanksgiving dinners, Fourth of July barbecues, and visits to community parks. Many invited me to attend church with them and shared their faith with me; some invited me to school events and to graduation ceremonies. I attended these activities whenever I could.

I had some interaction, but not a lot, with the men in these families. They were often very private, and some were skeptical of research. No one ever showed any hostility, but a few of the fathers and other men in the study, if they were present when I came to visit or to do an interview, would stay in another room or head outside. Others would also sit with us, sometimes listening and sometimes participating in the discussions, a couple of them very actively. In a handful of cases I had opportunities to interact some with the father outside of the home on his own, but these were more informal, general conversations. The men did not offer to talk about more private aspects of their lives, though most would have done so if asked.

I thought there would be topics that would be more difficult to discuss with the mothers because I was a man, so I planned to bring up those topics after I built a rapport with the families. I was amazed to find that I very often was able to establish a rapport quickly with the mothers and came to feel that there were few topics they would not discuss openly with me over time. And mothers very much wanted to share their stories given the chance. I do not think there was much that I could not explore with them because I was a man. In some ways they may have explained their thinking to me in more detail, or explained things they thought I might not know, because I was a man. This in some ways helped the research process and the gathering of more complete data. I do not think my presence and research affected their relationships with the men in their lives, and though many men were skeptical about what I was doing, the women seemed quite able to handle it.

I was also of a different ethnicity from every family I studied. My family originated from India, and all of the families in this study were African American or of Latin American origins. It helped me to have grown up and lived most of my life in very close proximity to the ethnic groups I studied, with many of my most significant early friendships with members of these groups. Since I had previously done work in many of these communities with small community-based organizations, many thought of me as potentially familiar with their circumstances. Families explained their cultural backgrounds and how these informed their experiences and choices. I speak some Spanish, but not with a lot of confidence, so when I spoke to them in Spanish, they found it endearing and were patient with me in speaking more slowly or clearly to help me.

I conducted this research while attending Harvard, a well-known university that they had all heard of, and I think that initially this may have increased their interest in participating in the study. Because they saw me as a student, I think they wanted to help me with my research if they could and maybe wanted less in return. In addition, they may have been more open and trusting because of my student status and my affiliation with a distant and respectable institution; I also spoke highly of my principal adviser on the project. The perceived class differences between a Harvard graduate student and teacher at a local university and women struggling in low-income jobs to meet their family needs did not seem to appear very much in the content of our conversations, especially as the fieldwork progressed. These aspects of my identity seemed to diminish in importance as they came to see me as a familiar person who came and asked them a lot of questions and brought books for their children. In general, they did not appear to "talk up" their stories to me, focusing more on higher aspirations, than I think they normally would have done. (Families focus a lot on their aspirations and goals as part of their survival strategies in general.) One area in which their discussion of their aspirations may have differed most from their actual behavior was reading. I think because I often arrived with children's books and they knew how important a "value" this seemed to me, which in part may be class-derived, a few may have talked up their reading behavior with their children.

Discussion of Methods

This research was not a purely inductive qualitative study like much ethnography, but rather included some areas in which I started with a priori frames or hypotheses to be tested. A primary aim of this research was to identify detailed qualitative information about care preferences and choices that could be categorized across respondents with qualitative analysis. The work seeks to identify from this level of detail strategic patterns being employed by different but similarly situated individuals. A second goal was purely interpretive: to understand and describe what people did for child care and to probe the explanations that mothers gave for how and why they chose their care arrangements over time and what they learned along the way. I tried to be very flexible in my approach to accomplishing these objectives.

Among the objectives for this research was to show how policy can be developed based on grounded, primary data from women's and children's lives. Policy approaches are more likely to be effective and realistic if they take into account the contexts of the real-life situations of families—the barriers, resources, and innate capacities of humans to respond resiliently and resourcefully to changing circumstances. This research illustrates some of the many creative ways in which mothers are responding to the constraints posed by child care options, work options, and policy changes as they seek to integrate their strategies for work and child care. It would be a mistake to infer that families' care choices necessarily reflect their highest preferences. It was my hope to show why the families in this study chose the care they did and what they might have chosen in a different policy or market context. In this study I referred to the care that many mothers used as their "second-best" care choice, because the care they preferred did not exist in their communities or they could not afford it. Observers who looked only at the behavioral frequency of a particular child care choice and not at the underlying motivations might erroneously infer that the patterns they saw were actually the care that mothers wanted.

Individual stories of urban families grounded in the real-life experiences of families and children can make significant contributions to social science research. I wanted to write about families in New York City, a place I know through personal experience, to offer some understanding about low-income families who were like the people I knew growing up. I wanted to tell these families' stories, and I believed that the telling of their stories would be, in many cases, a much better way of communicating the findings of my research than even the more systematic analysis across the sample that followed the stories in each of the chapters of the book.

A danger in qualitative research is that one can too broadly sketch the policy implications of the research without necessarily tying them strongly to the findings. In this study I tried to emphasize the most direct implications of the findings in the resultant recommendations.

This research adopted the grounded theory methods of Barney Glaser and Anselm Strauss (1967), who suggested that ethnographic study could be used to discover conceptual categories, models, and theories within a field of study. In this research, I studied individual cases and then used the findings to illustrate and define some meaningful characteristics of child care and how these interact to influence choices within a particular context. The findings in some cases are most relevant to the specific context—low-income families in New York City—but many can be used to hypothesize about conditions in other contexts based on their relative similarity to this context.

In a small-sample qualitative research study, one cannot make broad claims to representability. The book's conclusions are thus time-bound and context-bound: to a time of rapidly increasing work activity among low-income mothers, and to the context of a small sample of mothers who worked consistently and for many hours. Even though I varied the selection methods, there are likely to be portions of the low-income communities I studied that I did not reach because they may have been less connected to the types of organizational sources I used or to other working mothers in the neighborhood. Ultimately, although the sample is neither randomly derived nor very large, based on quantitative research standards, the patterns revealed in this study are not likely to be idiosyncratic. The sample, while small, is relatively heterogeneous and reflective of the communities for most key demographic variables. Further supporting the reliability of the data are the longitudinal interviews, which provided repeated opportunities to confirm the data and pursue the findings that emerged from the preliminary analysis across the sample. I made a concerted effort to select a diverse sample so that it could be at least adequate for starting scholarly inquiry into the nature of children's care dynamics and resulting policy implications. Providing detail for how the research was conducted may allow others who are interested in building on or testing the findings to add to the understanding of family life in low-income communities.

~ Appendix C ~

Interview Guide: Study of Child Care Arrangements in Low-Income New York City Neighborhoods

The goal is to get families to tell their stories regarding their child care arrangements, how their children spend their time, and the specific ways mothers' work, neighborhoods, and other contextual factors influence child care arrangements. The major method used to get this information is by conducting open-ended interviews. These interviews are as informal as possible. There is no fixed set of questions or strict protocol for the questioning, i.e., the questions are not read or asked in a precise manner or in the same order as they are arranged here. There is a series of topics that are important to explore in each interview and for which data are collected from each respondent and recorded.

In the first interview I begin with the same initial topic area, to be quite specific at the outset and to get respondents to focus on the topic being studied, as well as to build rapport and a flow to the interview. The actual interview flow depends on each respondent and varies accordingly, but the interviews touch on the same key themes. After coding the first interviews, I analyze the data for questions that had not been covered and ask these questions in subsequent interviews.

Through an open-ended approach and a series of longitudinal follow-up interviews, there is the opportunity to ask further questions on topics not covered in prior interviews, as well as new questions developed from studying and coding previous interviews and from findings from the participant observation component of the study. More directly, I track changes over time in the longitudinal interviews and ask some of the same key questions about child care arrangements and work patterns at different points in time.

Given that this is a grounded research method study, some interesting aspects of families' choices and influences surrounding child care are likely to emerge and to require further probing in specific topic areas for some respondents. Some of these topic areas might be anticipated, and for those there will be some questions I prepare in advance to ask, but most of the specific factors affecting choices cannot be so anticipated and will require spontaneous, direct follow-up questions or introduction of specific topic areas in subsequent interviews.

I. Interview One: Introduction and Explanation of Confidentiality of Interviews

(I begin by introducing myself . . .) My name is Ajay Chaudry, and I am studying the child care arrangements that working mothers make for their children in New York City neighborhoods. (. . . *and introducing why I am doing this study and what, if any, affiliations I have.*) I study and teach public policy, and the research is the basis for my thesis at Harvard. (*Skip if they know this.*)

We are studying the child care arrangements that working mothers make for their children. Some of the things we want to know more about are what kind of child care assistance mothers receive when they work, how children spend their time in different child care situations, the child care options available to families in their neighborhoods, and how mothers make choices about their children's care.

The goal for this project is to understand as much as possible about child care choices so that we can analyze policies related to child care and see how child care programs could be improved in communities. The best way to learn how to improve services is to talk with the people who use and work with these services and therefore know them the best.

You are a very important part of this research. We are planning to talk to about twenty families in this neighborhood and to meet with each of them a few times over the next year (if that is all right with them), so what we learn from each family is a very important part of the story we're trying to tell. Basically, we want to know and tell what it is really like for mothers to be working and at the same time to try to make sure their children are taken care of, and that's a story we can't tell without you and other mothers in this neighborhood and the city.

Once all the interviews are done, I will write a report on what has been learned from you and other families about life in your neighborhood and the strategies you use to work and provide for your children's care, so many people will read your story. I can tell you that while I will share what I learn, I will not share the identity of anyone we speak with; I will keep your identity completely confidential. I will not use your name or any other information that would allow someone else to figure out who you are or what you said. I will substitute names for everyone discussed in the report, including each mother, each child, and any other family member.

Let me tell you about my obligations to you. The most important thing, as I mentioned, is that we will keep your identity confidential. The second thing is that I want to do something in exchange for you agreeing to be part of this project and sharing your story and time with me. I have a book for *child's name* that I would like to give you, and I like to bring a book each time I come to see you. Another thing I would like to do is to offer my services and time in reading to your child and helping him or her with reading—I could do this at the times I come to interview the family or other more convenient times, or I could provide a few hours of child care for you in circumstances when you know you will need that.

If you'd prefer, I could pay you a small amount of money for the time you are giving to this work, in appreciation for your help. I can pay $20 for this interview, and $10 for each additional interview, which I expect will be shorter than this one. Which would you like? (*If she prefers a payment, pay the $20 now.*) Good, then here is your $20, and if next time you prefer I read instead, I can do that too.

Third, if it's okay with you, I would like to tape-record the interviews. I want to make sure that I get your story right, and I don't want to miss anything you're saying while I'm taking notes. I am also glad to do the interviews without tapes, though, if you would prefer that. I and one person helping me with this project are the only people who will listen to the tapes, and if you like, we can even use a made-up name during our conversation today so no real names will be on the tape.

Fourth, you have the right at any time to change your mind about participating in the study, and if there are some particular questions or topics that you do not want to discuss, you can tell me and we will skip over those questions. Just as well, if there is something you think is important that I am not asking about, I hope you will also tell me about that. If you decide after the interview that you do not want to be part of the study, I will give you the tape of the interview and tear up the notes.

Okay! Does all of this sound okay to you? (*If it does . . .*) I have two copies of a piece of paper that explains what I have just said. One copy is for you, and if you could please sign the other copy to say that you understand what I have explained to you and that you are willing to participate in the study.

Great. Now I would like to talk to you about your and your child's experience with child care. It should take about two hours. Do you have any questions before we begin?

(*Turn on tape recorder.*)

II. Initial Topic

A. Children's Time and Daily Life

1. Please describe for me how your child spent the day yesterday (*name day*) from the time *he or she* woke up in the morning until when *he or she* went to bed at night.

(*Help along by asking follow-up question. Seek answers in detail, including asking how much time the child spent in activities, who interacted with the child, where these activities took place, and how the child got from place to place. Ask whether this pattern is typical for that day of the week or the days when she is working; whether it is different on other days; and how it differs for weekends or days she is not working.*

*Ask this set of questions at each point of time in the longitudinal interview set.)

2.   Who does *your child* spend *his or her* time with regularly? Each day? Each week? How much time with you? Care providers? Siblings? Father? Relatives or friends?

3.   Where does *your child* spend *his or her* time? Each day? How much time?

III. Primary Interview Topic Areas

B. Child Care Arrangements

(*These questions should be covered in the first interview.*) Now I'd like to ask you more specifically about the child care arrangements *your child* is in right now and the ones *he or she* has been in in the past. (*For each example of an arrangement, which all together constitute a child care history, get all of the following information in as much depth as possible. For questions already fully or partially answered, confirm responses and follow-up as needed.*)

1.   What is *your child's* current primary care arrangement? What hours of the day does it cover? Where does *he or she* receive this care? How does he or she get there? Who provides the care? How long has *your child* been in this arrangement? What other (*secondary*) child care arrangements is your child in now? (*Get similar detailed data on all current arrangements.*)

2.   When did you first start using child care? How old was *your child* at the time you started this arrangement? How did this arrangement come about? How did you learn about this provider? What were the events surrounding the choice?

3.   Who was involved in making the child care arrangement? What were the child care options that were considered? How are child care decisions made for your child generally?

4.   How do you pay for this child care arrangement? What assistance do you receive, either in money or in help from the government, local agencies, or people you know?

5.   Can you tell me about all of the child care arrangements *your child* has been in? (*Get information on all of them and for each ask the same detailed*

questions.) What hours of the day does (did) it cover? Where did *he or she* receive care? Who provided the care? How old was *your child* at the time you started this arrangement? How long was *your child* in this arrangement? How did this arrangement start? How did you learn about this provider? What were the events surrounding the choice?

6.   What led to a change in your child care arrangements? What events or circumstances led to ending the old child care arrangement and making new arrangements?

     (*Make sure to cover beginnings and ends for all care arrangements mentioned.*)

7.   Who takes care of *your child* on weekends or other off-hours when you might need to work or go out or something comes up?

8.   What do you think are the good aspects of the child care arrangements *your child* has been in or is in right now? What do you think is most important to look for when you're trying to find good child care?

C. The Child

(*Some of these questions are likely to have been answered by now, but they serve as a checklist to make sure these child background topics are covered before moving on to questions that focus on the mother and work.*)

1.   How old is *your child?* When is *his or her* birthday? (*Record child's age.*)

2.   How many children do you have, and how old are they? Do they all live at home? Are they in school? In preschool? (*Record child's place in the family [oldest, youngest].*)

3.   Tell me about *your child.* What is *he or she* like? Can you tell me about any special gifts or needs in *your child's* development? Can you tell me about any events or situations that have affected *his or her* development?

4.   Where has *your child* lived? Has *he or she* always lived with you? If not, with whom else? When? For how long? How old was *your child* at the time of the move(s)? What were the reasons for the move(s)? Who made the decision? What options were available?

5.   What has raising *your child* been like? What are the best things about your relationship? What are the hardest things about your relationship? What would you like to change about this relationship? Why?

6.   What is *your child's* relationship to the (*biological*) father? To the father's family? How much time does *he or she* spend with the father? Does the father play any role in child care? Provide care? Provide financial assistance for child care or some other help?

7.   What other adults does *your child* spend significant amounts of time with and receive care from? What are *your child's* relationships with each of these other adults like? How much time does *he or she* spend with each of these people? Are they providing care? Do they provide any financial assistance for child care?

8.   Is there anyone else who provides financial assistance or some other help for child care?

9.   Which adults does *your child* consider to be *his or her* care providers? What does *your child* call *his or her* care providers?

(*Draw a care map from the child's point of view.*)

D. Mother's Work History: Dynamics and Patterns

I'd like to get a better idea about your work history and how it may or may not have influenced your child care decisions. (*At a minimum, get near-term work history [since birth of study child]. For questions for which context has been given in previous responses, do not ask again, but acknowledge and confirm information and possibly follow up.*)

1.   Do you have a job (or jobs) right now? What kind of work do you do? How long have you been doing this work?

2.   Where is your (*primary*) job located? What hours do you work? How many in a day? In a week? How do you get to your job?

3.   How much does your job pay? (*Ask this question for each job.*) What other income sources do you have (to supplement and/or replace work income)? Does your job have any benefits related to child care?

4.   How did you find your job? What other work options did you have?

5.   What has led to changes in your work situation? What events or circumstances led to a change?

6.   What impact did changes in your work situation have for *your child's* care arrangements?

7.   Can you tell me about your work history since *your child* was born? Were you working when (before) you had *your child*? (*Alternatively*) How soon after *your child* was born did you start to work? What kind of work did you do? What hours did you work? How much did this job pay? How long did you do this job? Why did you leave this work situation? Did changes in your work situation have any impact on your child care arrangements?

8. What other jobs have you had? Do you do any other work (or other activity) for pay? Second jobs? Next jobs?

   (*Repeat question 7 for each job.*)

9. Over the time you have been a single parent, have you ever received welfare?

   (*If yes . . .*)

   a. When did you receive welfare? Did you receive it steadily for some time? What was the time period? For each time you received welfare, what was the reason you went on welfare? What were the reasons you went off? How much did you receive in welfare support? (Grant? Emergency assistance? Food stamps?)

   b. Do you think you are better off working than on welfare?

   c. Do you receive any public (*governmental*) assistance now? With child care? What kind of assistance do you receive? How does it work?

   (*If no . . .*)

   a. Did you ever think about receiving welfare or some other form of public assistance?

   (*Other possible follow-up work questions, if they seem relevant and time permits:*)

10. Since having children, have you participated in any training and education programs to help you find a job or be able to get a better job? What was the situation? When was it? How long did it last? What child care arrangements did you make when you were doing this?

11. Are you generally satisfied with work, or would you want to change something about work or switch jobs?

12. What kind of job situation would you prefer to have? Do your jobs match your skills and experience? What other kind of jobs do you think you could get with your present education, skills, and experience?

13. How does your job situation compare with your friends' jobs?

E. Evaluation and Discussion of Different Types of Child Care Arrangements

(*Many of these questions are likely to have been discussed or answered in the context of section B, but follow up and get more detail on responses. If there is not much time, begin to probe and plan to return [noting this] as a whole topic in the second interview.)*

Of the child care arrangements your child has ever been in, what do you consider the good aspects of each (*starting with the current primary care arrangement*)?

(*List types of arrangements mentioned, both current care arrangements and previous care arrangements.*)

1. How does *your child* like *his or her* care arrangement(s)? What does *he or she* say about the provider? What does *your child* call the provider?

2. What activities does *your child* engage in when *he or she* is with the provider?

3. Do you know all of your providers? How often do you see them? What is *he or she* like?

4. What do you like about the type of child care (*name the type*) that *your child* is now in? What don't you like about it?

5. When you're looking for a child care arrangement, what factors are you most interested in? (*Start by being very open-ended with these questions rather than priming respondents for answers they might think you are seeking. Once some spontaneous responses are elicited, then probe for further responses.*)

Location

Flexibility

Setting

Reliability

Hours

Continuity

Age appropriateness

Type of provider (kin, professional)

Type of care (individualized, group, home-based)

Content of care

Other factors

6. If you could choose any type of child care arrangement for *your child,* what would it be?

7. Who would you consider to be an ideal child care provider? Yourself? A family member or friend? A professional child care provider?

8. What would you consider to be an ideal child care setting? A home? A community center?

9. Are there child care options you have considered but decided against using?

10. Has there ever been a time when you needed child care but could not arrange it? When did that happen to you (*last time*), and how did it affect your circumstances or *your child's*? What did you do?

11. Have you ever had to leave *your child or children* unattended because of difficulties in making child care arrangements? Tell me about the circumstances.

12. Have you ever had to rely on another older child, such as a sibling or a related child, to care for *your child or children*?

13. Does *your child* ever spend time at the homes of relatives when you are working?

14. Does *your child* ever spend time at the homes of friends (supervised or unsupervised?) when you are working? When you are not working? Do *your child's* friends spend time at your home when their mothers are working?

Conclusion of Initial Interview

1. How would you characterize the relationship between your work experiences and your child care arrangements? Do the two go together or does one hurt the other? How does that work?

   (*Probe to determine ways in which respondents see their work and their child care arrangements as conflictual or as convergent, and whether one precedes or determines the other.*)

2. What do you think your child care situation and work situation will be six months from now? A year from now?

This is the end of the (*initial*) interview. Thank you so much! This has been incredibly helpful, and I am very grateful for your time and your openness and honesty. I only got to some (*most, about half*) of the things I'd like to learn about from you, and I would like to ask you how things are going over time. Could I come back and talk to you again in three months? I can offer you . . . (*restate proposed compensations*).

Interview Cover Sheet

(The interview cover sheet is a one-page form that should be completed by the end of the first interview and include the following information:)

Mother's name

Mother's age

Mother's birthday

Child's name

Child's age

Child's birthday

Neighborhood (name and location)

Household or family size and number of children

Marital status or history

Educational attainment

Work status (principal job, weekly work hours, time in job)

Child care arrangements (primary care arrangements, hours, time in care arrangement, all other care arrangements)

Race-ethnicity and immigration-citizenship status

Initial interview date (place, time, duration)

Dates of follow-up interviews

Interview Two: Protocol

Interview Goal

The goal is to get families to continue to tell their stories regarding their child care arrangements and the specific ways in which mothers' work, their neighborhoods, and other contextual factors influence child care arrangements. Another goal is to track changes in these since the last interview through an open-ended interview. This interview is likely to be even more informal than the first. Again, there is no fixed set of questions, and the questions are not read or asked in a precise order in each interview; rather, they are arranged as appropriate given the analysis of the first interview and the relative context of the care, work, and family situations.

Asking about changes, tracking the longitudinal changes, and clarifying the data collected in the first interview are priorities in the second interview.

Beyond asking follow-up questions from findings in the first interview, it is appropriate to introduce some limited new topics as secondary concerns, such as child health, housing dynamics, and neighborhood context.

Thus, the topics in the second interview are:

- Child care (track changes and review data)

- Mother's work (track changes and review data)

- Other income supports, assistance, and expenses (track changes and review data)

- Father's assistance and involvement

- Social services assistance; welfare and food stamps history (track changes and review data)

- Child health

- Housing changes and questions

The second interview is also an opportunity to go over the dynamics worksheet and the timelines for child care, work, and living arrangements; the summary of care arrangements and work history developed in the first interview; and the data collected on child care costs, subsidies, durations, and exits.

Finally, if the questions on respondents' perceptions of child care (section E) were not asked in the first interview, they are asked in this follow-up interview.

F. Resources Used for Making Child Care Arrangements

1. Do you have any relatives or friends that you rely on for child care? Who are the people you rely on? What is their relation to you or to *your child*? Do you pay for this care arrangement? How did the payment arrangement come about?

2. *(If some kin are mentioned and others are not, probe to find out if there are other close kin and for views of kin care.)*

3. *(If respondent is receiving kin assistance)* do you give or receive child care assistance from these kin as well? Why or why not?

4. Are there any organizations in your community or elsewhere that you have turned to for assistance with child care? What are these places? Where are they? How did you learn about them or get involved in them?

5. Have you ever sought assistance from churches or religion-based organizations? From schools? From social service organizations? From organizations or resources connected to your job?

G. Housing Dynamics and the Neighborhood

(*If the interview is taking place in the home, make sure to fully describe the home* [*size, number of rooms, and qualitative details*] *and the location in the neighborhood, in the building, and on the block.*)

1. Where are you living right now? How long have you been living there (*months, years*)? How long have you lived in your present home? (*If less than five years, ask respondent where she moved from, when, and why.*)

2. Who else lives with you in your home? What are your current living arrangements? Who do you live with? (*Ask about changes in household composition.*)

3. Where did you live before that? For how long? And before that? For how long? Where were you living when *your child* was born? (*Get full near-term residential history.*)

4. Where has *your child* lived? Has *he or she* always lived with you? If not, who else has *he or she* lived with? When? For how long? How old was *your child* at the time of the move(s)? What were the reasons for the move(s)? Who made the decision? What options were available?

5. What were the circumstances each time you changed location or living arrangement?

6. What is your rent? Is your rent subsidized in any way, such as through the section 8 program? If so, what kind of section 8 do you have? Do you live in a public housing project? Have you ever received rental assistance or lived in public housing?

7. What does your rent include? What are your other living expenses? Utilities? Gas? Electric? Telephone? Cable? Others? How much were each of these last month?

8. What is your housing like? What are the good and bad parts about it?

9. How difficult would it be for you to move? Where would you and your family move if you ever did?

10. And my last question on housing is, have you ever been homeless or lived in a shelter? If so, when?

11. What do you call the neighborhood you live in? Describe what your neighborhood is like to me. How would you define its size (dimensions)?

12. What is it like living in this neighborhood? What do you like most about living here? What do you like the least?

13. What are your neighbors like? Do many of your friends and family members live in the same neighborhood as you?

14. Did you grow up in this neighborhood? How long have you lived in this neighborhood? If you have lived here less than five years, where did you move from and when?

15. Could you describe the places in the neighborhood to which you and the members of your family go regularly (*service organizations, schools, churches, health clinics or hospitals, work sites, shopping, friends, etc.; map these*). When do you go to these locations? How often?

16. What are the best and worst things about your neighborhood?

    (*Begin to probe some of these—for example, neighborliness, safety, crime, resources and services, cleanliness and trash, graffiti, loitering, drugs and alcohol, housing conditions, schools—and return to these neighborhood characteristics in the context of their impact on child care arrangements.*)

17. What are the neighborhood resources you use for your children's care? How did you learn about them?

18. What do your neighbors do for their child care arrangements? (*Probe types of care arrangements.*) Do your neighbors work? (*Probe what kind of jobs—formal or informal, legitimate and illegitimate.*)

19. How is your access to transportation? How do you go to and from child care arrangements, work sites, and other regular neighborhood locations? (*Also ask specific transportation questions while asking about child care arrangements and work.*)

20. How would you characterize the relationship between your living environment—your housing and neighborhood—and your work experiences? And your child care arrangements? Do these go together or does one affect (*hurt or help*) the others? How does that work? Of your living situation, your work, and your child care, which has been the most dynamic and subject to change? Which is most important in your experience? (*Probe to determine ways in which respondent sees these as conflictual or convergent and whether any one area or concern dominates the others.*)

Conclusion to Second Interview and Opinion Questions

1. What do you envision will be your child care situation and work situation six months from now? A year from now?

2. If you were advising a young woman like yourself, say, five years ago, what would you tell her? (*Ask open-endedly and wait for spontaneous*

response. If respondent needs more specification, ask about the advice one would give about balancing work and child care responsibilities, strategies for combining both, or child care specifically.)

3. If the mayor or governor were to ask what the government could do to assist working single mothers, what answer would you want to give him?

4. How would you sum up your experiences? (*If possible, ask comparative questions about the respondent's child care arrangement or work situation. For example, what is different about the current care situation compared to earlier ones? What is better or worse about these?*)

5. Is there anything else you can think of that I should have asked but didn't?

Interview Three: Protocol

Interview Goal

The goal is to get more updated information on family child care arrangements, review previous data, discuss care dynamics and the influence of factors relating to care dynamics, and the strategies that mothers employ for child care. This interview is likely to be shorter and very informal. The most important goal here is to track longitudinal changes since the last interview and discuss care strategies if time permits.

The topics in the third interview are:

• Child care changes (review data and discuss implications)

• Mother's work and income changes

• Other family changes

• Survival strategies

The third interview is also an opportunity to go into more aspects of the mother's life history and experiences and to ask some of the opinion and conclusion questions that there may not have been enough time for in the previous interviews. After asking all of the questions about changes since the last interview in care, work, and family living situations, move to section H—a general discussion of mothers' survival strategies.

H. Survival Strategies of Single Mothers

1. What is it like being a single mother? What are the advantages and disadvantages?

2. Do you receive any child care subsidy? Any child support that helps you cover the costs of child care? Financial or in-kind contributions from the father? From family or friends? From church or community organizations? Do you receive the Earned Income Tax Credit? (*Ask whether the respondent filed a tax return. Probe for all sources of income that might be used for child care costs.*)

3. For most people it is hard to earn enough to support a family and to meet the responsibility for raising and caring for children, and this is especially hard for single mothers. What do people you know do to meet both these demands, for work and child care? (*Probe for details about the relationship between the respondent's working and child care arrangements, and whether these are conflictual or convergent. Can probe further for other possible effects: Do people in the respondent's life live together? Share income? Share resources and responsibilities for caring for children?*)

4. Where do women turn for child care assistance when they start to work? To family and friends for support, money, and care? To organizations and groups in their community? To government agencies?

I. Mother's Life History

(*Get a better sketch of the mother's life history by asking about important life events.*)

1. What are some of the important events in your life? (*Follow-up questions*) Please think of four or five important things that have happened in your life that stand out in your memory. These can be anything for which you might remember the time it happened (*month and year*), such as leaving school, starting a job, meeting someone new, an event that happened to you or a family member, a death, a birth, a wedding, or anything that comes to mind. Can you tell me some of these and when they happened in your life (*month and year*)?

2. Have you ever been married or come close to getting married? When? How long were you married? What led you to decide to get married or not? Do you plan to get married (*again*)? What factors are important to you in deciding whether to marry?

3. What was the first job you ever worked in? When was it? How long did you have the job? What did you think of your first work experience?

4. Where did you go to school? Where did you go to high school? How did you like your school experiences? What kind of student were you? What skills did you learn when you were in school (or out of school) that have helped you in jobs you have had (or tried to get)? What skills did you not develop that you wish you had or could now?

Conclusion to Third Interview and Opinion Questions

1. How would you sum up your experiences? Your situation? (*If possible, ask comparative questions about the respondent's child care arrangement or work situation.*) What is different about your current care situation compared to earlier ones? What is better or worse about your care situation or your work situation?

2. How would you characterize the relationship between your work experiences and your child care arrangements? Do the two go together, or does one hurt the other? How does that work? (*Probe to determine the ways in which the respondent sees these as conflictual or convergent, and whether one precedes or determines the other.*)

3. What do you envision will be your child care situation and work situation six months from now? A year from now?

This has been most helpful, and I am very thankful for the information you have shared with me over the past year, and I feel indebted to you and your family for making your life and story open to me. I have learned and appreciated much from this experience and will always feel deep gratitude to you. Thank you again.

~ Notes ~

Chapter 1

1. The welfare reform law marked the most fundamental changes in thirty years in American social policy, which had existed for almost sixty years. It replaced child-centered federal entitlements to poor families with work mandates and block grants to states. Underlying the law were two ideas: that at the root of persistent poverty among a large portion of American families is a lack of personal responsibility, and that work is a necessary first step for any family or individual seeking assistance.
2. The names of most places and people have been changed.
3. The New York City Housing Authority charges 30 percent of income but deducts child care expenses.
4. The current poverty measure used in the United States is an updated version of a simple formula established in 1965 that was based on how much a family needed for a minimally adequate diet, scaled upward to reflect the proportion spent on food in a minimal family budget of basic needs. This poverty threshold established in 1965 used a 1955 survey that had shown that, on average, a family of three spent one-third of its income on food. This poverty standard then has been indexed for price changes using the consumer price index (CPI) and revised annually to maintain the standard set in 1965.

   Any poverty line by its nature is an arbitrary attempt to distinguish between the poor and the nonpoor in order to have some social indicator of want across a society. The current metric has become increasingly problematic over time as societal expectations of families' basic needs have changed, as have the relative prices of different components in a family's budget. The poverty line is an absolute measure, and as such it is less meaningful as a relative measure of economic well-being in a society where the overall average standard of living has grown faster than the poverty threshold. When the poverty standard was set in 1965, it was at almost 50 percent of median family income in the United States, but as a relative measure it had declined to 35 percent of median family income by 2000.

5. Kathryn Edin and Laura Lein (1997) studied the actual levels of expenditures needed by families to cover their basic minimal needs. Their analysis suggests that the poverty threshold underestimates poor families' needs by 40 to 60 percent. Patricia Ruggles (1990) also finds that since the poverty threshold was established the proportion of families' budgets used to buy food has declined from one-third to less than one-fifth as food prices remained relatively constant and the prices of basic nonfood items increased. Adjusting the poverty thresholds to reflect this change would mean increasing the thresholds by 40 percent. Edin and Lein report that when asked in public opinion polls what they consider the minimal amount of income a family requires for subsistence, Americans gave responses on average about 60 percent higher than the poverty thresholds at the time.

    The official poverty threshold is an absolute measure that estimates the minimal income needed by families. It can create gross simplifications when there are variations in how it is calculated, when geographic variations are missing, when some resources are counted, and when others are missed. A national panel has recommended significant changes to the poverty measure (Citro and Michael 1995), and others have suggested additional measures of want, such as material hardship measures (Edin and Lein 1997; Mayer and Jencks 1989) or income-to-needs ratios.

6. I use the term "low-income" more generally to describe the families in this book, who face many of the disadvantages associated with the socioeconomic conditions in poor neighborhoods that extend beyond just "income-poverty."

7. The poverty measure, though probably inadequate, takes on significance because of the portrait it paints of the number of poor; it also provides a social metric, and the measure itself is used extensively to establish eligibility for many programs and services, including food stamps, Medicaid, housing, Head Start programs, and child care subsidies in many states.

8. According to the March 2000 Current Population Survey (CPS), 43.7 percent of all children under six in single-mother families were officially poor. In Hispanic families 49.6 percent of children under age six in mother-only families were income-poor, and in African American families that level was 50.8 percent. In cases like Aaron's—two children in a single-mother family—the rates for children under six were even higher: 57.2 percent of all such children were poor, and more than 60 percent of Hispanic and African American children in single-mother families of that size were poor.

9. Many social scientists who study American political thought and pub-

lic opinion data have identified long-standing basic tenets and analyzed the interplay between American attitudes on matters of inequality and American social policy. Some of these underlying tenets include economic individualism, equal opportunity, limited government, communitarian values, and norms of reciprocity (Bowles and Gintis 1999; Heclo 1986, 1993; Kinder and Sanders 1996).

10. "Child care need" as discussed here refers to the need for supervision for children—that is, the child care services, broadly defined, that families may use for their children when the parents are working—not the need for greater early care and education services as a normative good in and of itself for children's development. This study finds both needs are significant. The developmental needs are discussed more in the literature review of child care in appendix A as well as in the findings in chapter 4 regarding how the mothers in the study viewed the child development and care needs of their children.

11. An analysis of the impact of welfare reform in New York City found that in the year before the new law was passed public assistance supported a total of 440,000 children (age twelve and younger) and 221,000 children between ages zero and five. At that time the budget for all forms of publicly subsidized child care (including Head Start) was $877 million, serving 110,000 children from poor and low-income families. For care overseen by the city's Agency for Child Development, the average cost per child was $6,300 for 63,000 children in 1994 (Chaudry 1997).

12. Prior to the 1996 welfare reform law, federal child care assistance included several separate child care programs, including two welfare-related child care entitlement programs: a guarantee of child care for families on welfare, and a guarantee of transitional child care assistance for families for one year after leaving welfare. The 1996 act included provisions that combined three former child care programs (some of which had been created as part of the previous welfare reform efforts and legislation, the Job Opportunities and Basic Skills [JOBS] Act of 1988)—AFDC/JOBS child care, Transitional Child Care, and At-Risk Child Care—into one entitlement funding stream and combined it with the Child Care Development Block Grant (CCDBG). The CCDF (which is also sometimes referred to as the CCDBG) became the principal source of federal funding for child care subsidies.

In addition to ending the AFDC entitlement, the law eliminated child care as an entitlement when it consolidated the program funding. Overall, the welfare reform law increased child care assistance over a five-year period by $4 billion, which was not nearly enough to serve low-wage working families in need of assistance and those moving from welfare to work. Faced with a fixed amount for child care, the loss of guaranteed child care assistance for each welfare-to-work client, and an immediate need to move families from welfare to work, many states approached child care assistance by targeting welfare families at the expense of working families. Furthermore, given the need to move people off welfare quickly, many states did not move to a simplified system, which the lump-sum block grant funding might have allowed, but either maintained multiple child care programs or created new ones or new layers on old ones, many of which had conflicting rules.

13.   Child care administration had always been mostly a state responsibility, and with the consolidation of federal funding streams, control over subsidized child care was further transferred to the states.

14.   The federal FY 1997 appropriations included $1 billion in CCDF discretionary funding that was not released to states until the start of FY 1998 (October 1, 1997). CCDF funding combines two federal funding streams: mandatory funds, which totaled almost $2.7 billion in FY 2002, and discretionary funds, which totaled $2.2 billion in FY 2002.

15.   The U.S. Department of Health and Human Services (2000b) estimated that only 12 percent of children potentially eligible under the federal government's maximum family income level received assistance through CCDF funds. The federal maximum is 85 percent of state median income (SMI). However, states may adopt any income eligibility level, and many have adopted a level below the federal maximum income level. Using states' adopted maximum income levels, the same study found that 15 percent of eligible children were assisted through CCDF funds.

Further analysis by the Center for Law and Social Policy estimated that 2.25 million families—or 14 percent of families eligible under federal maximum eligibility levels—were served through CCDF and other federal programs (including Title XX Social Service Block Grant funds). Using the state maximum eligibility levels, this translates into approximately 20 percent served through CCDF (Schumacher and Rakpraja 2002).

16.   Part of the formula for determining federal CCDF funding to the states is based on the prior level of funding they received before welfare reform. Since New York State had provided a greater level of child care assistance, it continued to receive slightly higher funding after welfare reform, though by 2002 this difference had declined and its funding amounted to 6.5 percent of the total federal CCDF funding, corresponding closely to it share of (and rank in) population. (It was receiving the third-highest CCDF allocation after California and Texas.)

17.   In 2002 New York City's budget for child care totaled $467 million, of which $285 million came from federal CCDF and TANF block grant funding, $180 million from city funds, and $2.5 million from the state. Prior to welfare reform, the state and city contributed equally to child care expenditures (more than $80 million each in FY 1997); combined

they contributed half of the total child care budget, and the federal child care funds accounted for the other half ($164 million in FY 1997). In subsequent years the state has steadily decreased its contribution, the city has increased its share, and the federal share has also increased from the additions of TANF transfers (Child Care, Inc. 2002; New York City Independent Budget Office 2002).

18. In 2002, 85 percent of the 92,000 children served by all forms of subsidized child care (vouchers and contracted care for welfare recipients and low-income nonwelfare families) were in families with annual earnings less than $18,000.

19. A follow-up study by Giannerelli, Adelman, and Schmidt (2003), using 1999 National Survey of American Families (NSAF) data, finds that the estimates of the percentage of families paying for child care, the average expenses, and the average percentage of earnings consumed by child care expenses are virtually unchanged from Giannerelli and Barsimontov's (2000) analysis of the 1997 NSAF. In a similar study of the 1997 Survey of Income and Program Participation (SIPP), Kristin Smith (2002) finds that in families that pay for child care and have a mother who is employed full-time, the cost of care averages $75 per week. Those with incomes up to 125 percent of the federal poverty line paid on average $52 in weekly child care expenses in 1997, or 22 percent of their income. At the same time those who earned above that level averaged $78 per week for child care, or less than 8 percent of their income.

20. Carol Stack (1974) was among the first scholars to identify "coping strategies"—how the poor respond to the conditions of their lives—when she looked deeply at the broad organization of life in one inner-city community that she called the Flats. In her field research, Stack relied on prolonged immersion, participant observation, and interpretation as much as on regular interviews. She identified the use of kin-based support networks as a broad coping strategy and documented how this strategy was used for sharing food and clothing as well as responsibility for children and financial resources and how these relationships reinforced a sense of mutual obligations.

Edin and Lein (1997) used focused, repeated interviews to determine the specific sources and uses of welfare recipients' budgets. They interviewed mothers to develop a detailed accounting of their family budgets, income sources, and expenses. Edin and Lein found that mothers met their families' most basic needs by combining welfare and work with any other economic resource they could gain access to, including those available through kin networks and social service agencies. They found that these strategies were generally irregular and unreliable sources of income and that mothers therefore had to constantly adapt and vary their strategies.

The research approach in this study is closer to that of Edin and

Lein, given the heavy emphasis on interviewing and the narrower focus on one area of women's strategic behavior, but it also includes some of Stack's focused, prolonged interactions in the community.

21. In their original welfare dynamics study, Bane and Ellwood (1983) found a highly dynamic welfare system: there was considerable movement on and off welfare and a great deal of heterogeneity among those who received welfare, with most people who ever received it staying only for a relatively short term (two years or less) and a smaller proportion being very long-term recipients (spells of eight years or more). In their follow-up work, having found a significant amount of recidivism in welfare use (many of those who exit welfare return for additional spells), they added "cyclers" as an important third category of recipients.

22. The differences between an analysis of the dynamics of care subsidies and an analysis of the dynamics of child care arrangements parallel in some way the study of welfare dynamics versus the study of poverty dynamics. In both cases there is an analysis of similar population dynamics, but with different dependent variables—one that says more about a program variable (welfare use or child care subsidies) and one that is more about a social condition (changes in poverty status or the use of child care arrangements). Both the program and the social condition are important and deserve study in their own right, as well as analysis that relates one to the other. There may be less overlap in these populations: a smaller subset of child care users receive subsidies (in the current time period) compared to the subset of poor families that use welfare programs (when many of the poverty and welfare dynamics studies were being conducted, though few poor families are now receiving public assistance since the implementation of welfare reform).

23. The dynamics studies have been employed to understand the basic nature of poverty and work; to measure levels of "dependency," "chronic poverty," and "cyclical unemployment"; and to shape understanding about the people within a policy area—the poor, "the welfare poor," and "the welfare-dependent." This research has also been used to guide public policy responses. For example, "two years and you are out" as a welfare policy was developed in part after research on welfare spells found that most people who ever received welfare payments received it briefly (for less than two years) and that those who received it for longer periods tended to leave the welfare rolls at much lower rates. A time limit or tough work requirement was seen as a way to decrease the dependency of these longer-term welfare recipients.

24. According to an analysis of CPS data by Mark Levitan and Robin Gluck (2002), the percentage of single mothers who were employed increased from 42 percent in 1996 to 61 percent in 2001, a five-year increase in the employment level of more than 40 percent. This was

higher than the increase in single mothers' labor force participation nationwide, which increased from 66 percent to 75 percent, though the national level of single mothers' employment was significantly higher at the start of the period. The median hourly wages for single mothers in New York City was $11.31, and the average for single mothers with a high school education or less was $9.04—very close to the average wage of mothers in this study, which was $9.27.

25. Home relief, also called general assistance, refers to cash assistance to income-poor single individuals, while the AFDC program provided cash assistance to income-poor families with children. Following welfare reform changes, AFDC was converted to TANF and the home relief/general assistance program became the State Safety Net Program. In addition to benefits for single individuals, it provides some benefits to immigrants and families that may have reached their time limits for TANF assistance.

26. Families losing welfare benefits, or at risk of losing them, often sought SSI disability benefits, if eligible, because it exempted them from work requirements and the time limits imposed on welfare benefits. Also, prior to the welfare reform changes, many localities, including New York City, often determined eligibility for welfare, Medicaid, and food stamps together, since welfare recipients were eligible for these. Some families received only Medicaid assistance. The data in table 1.2 show that while there was a sharp decline in the receipt of cash public assistance, there was a sharp rise in the number of families receiving only Medicaid. The increase in Medicaid-only cases was equal to 90 percent of the decline in cash benefits.

27. The two most common forms of public subsidies for child care are contracted care and vouchers. Under contract systems, a public agency contracts with a provider for slots in a child care program. In a voucher system, parents are given vouchers for child care, which can be given to an eligible provider, who is reimbursed either directly from the agency or through the parent. In either case the subsidy can cover all or some portion of the costs, often on a sliding scale based on income, with the parent making a copayment for the remainder. In New York most child care had traditionally been subsidized through contracted care, including most ACD-funded care. However, most of the recent increases in subsidized care have been channeled through vouchers, and all of HRA's assistance to families moving off welfare comes in this form.

Chapter 2

1. "Spells" in care for this analysis differ somewhat from "arrangements." A "care spell" is the number of consecutive months in which a child is in the same primary care arrangement. The aggregate number of spells

slightly exceeds the number of care arrangements by a few cases—there are 215 care spells in the sample and 209 arrangements. When a child continued in the same care arrangement after a break in care, this was counted as a single arrangement but as two (or more) spells.

2. Barney Glaser and Anselm Strauss (1967) developed the concept of "grounded" theory, whereby ethnographic inquiry is used to discover conceptual categories within a field of study and a theory or model is developed that bears a close relation and follows the logical form of the data. In this child care study, I analyze directly gained evidence and then use that analysis to illustrate and define some meaningful dimensions of child care and how these interact to form mothers' child care choices. The findings in some cases are most relevant to the specific context—low-income families in New York City—but they could be used to hypothesize about conditions in other contexts based on their relative similarity.

3. The early intervention programs in most states and localities were developed through a federally funded program created in 1986 for children with special needs and developmental delays. Under part H of Public Law 99-457, the early intervention program provides states with funding to address the developmental needs of children ages zero to three who need specific specialized services such as speech therapy or occupational therapy. Part H attempts to prevent long-term disabling conditions or delays in development by providing very young children and their families with a comprehensive array of educational, health, therapeutic, and family support services. The early intervention program seeks to increase the focus on preventive services and ensure that children with special needs get services in natural settings.

4. Smith (2000) found that for all children younger than five years old, including those whose parents were not working, the average was twenty-eight hours per week in care arrangements. As noted earlier, non-employed mothers also use child care regularly, and their usage levels have increased recently, though their use patterns differ some by age, types of care used, and hours spent in care. Kathryn Tout and her colleagues (2001) analyzed National Survey of American Families (NSAF) data and found that children with a non-employed parent who were in care arrangements spent an average of fifteen hours per week in care compared to almost twenty-nine hours for children in care with employed mothers.

5. Jennifer Ehrle, Gina Adams, and Kathryn Tout (2001) report that in the NSAF almost twice the proportion of infants and toddlers in employed single-mother families were in care full-time compared to two-parent families with both parents working (60 percent versus 34 percent). African American infants and toddlers were also in care more extensively than any other racial or ethnic group, with 58 percent in

care for more than thirty-five hours per week. The study also showed that infants and toddlers of working mothers spend more time in non-parental care as family income increases and that as children get older they spend more time in nonparental care. At age one and younger, 32 percent of children are in care full-time (thirty-five hours or more per week), and then at age two it increases to 43 percent.

In the NICHD (1997b, 2000a) studies, children spent on average thirty-three hours per week in child care. Black non-Hispanics in the study averaged the most hours of care, while white respondents averaged the fewest hours of care. The NICHD findings indicate a very high reliance on and very early entry into infant care, with low-wage earning families the most likely to place their infants in child care before three months of age. Most infants spent the first year of their lives in informal arrangements.

6. Every care spell was coded for whether it was paid (provider paid by parent, subsidy, or a combination) or nonpaid (caregiver provided care for free, in-kind), whether the care was publicly subsidized, and what the parents' payments were for care spells.

Chapter 3

1. As discussed in chapter 2, a primary care arrangement is the one in which a child spends the most hours of care when he or she is in multiple care arrangements. With the exception of a few spells during which two types of care were used simultaneously in nearly equal proportions (and these were taken to be blended arrangements), most of the time the primary care accounted for the bulk of the care time—an average of about 80 percent of the care hours.

2. I look at monthly care arrangements, yet child care arrangements can change weekly or even daily. Although it is possible to collect the data and do the analysis using continuous weeks in a care arrangement—at least for the time period in which prospective data were collected (retrospective data with that level of specificity would not be more reliable)—a preliminary analysis using the finer time measure of weeks found that there was little difference in the durations analysis. In this analysis, spells that lasted beyond an exact month were rounded off: six or seven weeks, for instance, would be counted as two months.

3. Nonmaternal care arrangements covered an average of thirty-eight months, and sample children had their mothers as care providers on average for ten months during their first four years.

4. Although the sample size in a qualitative study of child care dynamics is too small to lead to statistically significant conclusions about dynamics, it is very suggestive of how child care dynamics work in terms of the reasons for turnover. A qualitative longitudinal analysis of dy-

namics can help to define a child care dynamics framework that can then be better and more easily analyzed quantitatively with larger survey data once such data start to be collected longitudinally. A small-scale qualitative analysis can also map out some of the complicated interactions that lead to child care changes, providing some impetus for looking at the dynamics of care spells more systematically through in-depth ethnographies.

There are also some advantages to applying qualitative, in-depth research methods to the study of dynamics, as is done here. All of the arrangements are looked at over the same time span for each family in the sample, and because they start at the initial point (birth), all initial spells can be included. The collection method allows for compiling detailed longitudinal data that can be confirmed with respondents, who can provide the most accurate explanations for entries and exits. Also, given the possibility of following up with the small group of known respondents to determine the end of the last arrangement prior to the child turning four, there is no need to exclude the last observed care spells at age four.

5. Because many of the entries into new care spells are determined by the reasons for the exit from the prior spell, analysis of entries becomes somewhat secondary.

6. The care spells analyzed in tables 3.6 and 3.7 are for all 215 primary, nonmaternal child care exits. Note that the exit reasons for all care spells were determined based on data collected through completion of the last spell that was started before age four. Through follow-up interviewing, the end of all the last arrangements were determined, eliminating the need to exclude any observed care spells, or "right-censoring," the data.

7. Analyzing the data across the four-year care timelines, we can analyze all the breaks between care spells and identify the primary reasons associated with them. Given the complexity of many of the single mothers' lives—they were coping with dynamic changes that sometimes happened simultaneously—the reasons for care changes can be multiple. With the interview data and follow-up, it was possible in most cases to assign a primary exit reason and to confirm this with the families.

Chapter 4

1. In *The Truly Disadvantaged: The Inner City, the Underclass, and Public Policy* (1987, 62) and in subsequent works, Wilson shows how several simultaneous and interrelated problems, or "a complex web of . . . factors," as he puts it, have led to the social deterioration of family life in inner-city neighborhoods. The model he develops could be characterized as a relationship between several elements:

Social (exogenous) forces: Dramatic losses in urban labor markets; historic flows of migrants; the exodus of better-employed neighborhood residents who provided communities with a broader income spectrum; changes in the nature of family composition and gender relations; and declines in social institutions in the community that offer constructive forms of neighborhood social organization. These forces, in combination, lead to:

More constrained opportunity spaces (or) social isolation: A higher concentration of poverty in isolated urban communities; greater income segregation; greater racial segregation; joblessness; declines in community institutions and resources; and lower expectations and sense of control. These social factors, in turn, lead to:

A rise in urban social problems: Seen by some as negative cultural adaptations or behavioral pathologies, these include declining urban schools, crime, violence, drug use and trafficking, and gang formation. All of these factors contribute ultimately to:

Widespread social deterioration: Recently Wilson has emphasized joblessness as the central element in this social isolation model, and he has added an emphasis on the role of contemporary racial discrimination as a significant exogenous force.

2. Wilson discusses what he sees as three dimensions of neighborhood social organization: the prevalence, strength, and interdependence of social networks; the extent of collective supervision and personal responsibility in addressing neighborhood problems; and the rate of residential participation in (formal and informal) neighborhood institutions.

3. All of the mothers in this sample were employed at the time of the initial interview. The amounts that mothers worked in their primary jobs ranged from twenty-five to more than seventy-two hours per week, with the average about thirty-six hours; the total amount they worked averaged forty-two hours. Overall, these mothers earned between $4.35 and $15.20 per hour in their primary jobs, and they fairly evenly covered this range of pay.

4. When asked about their preference for starting nonmaternal care, mothers' responses ranged from three months to three years after the child's birth. The average of the response was a little over fourteen months, which was more than twice as late as the time when the mothers in the sample actually started initial care arrangements—an average of a little more than six months. Twenty-nine of the forty-two mothers stated a preference later than their actual start, eight stated a preference within a month of their actual start, and five would have preferred to go to work and make their first care placement earlier than they actually did.

5. Overall, ten mothers say age three is the appropriate time to start cen-

ter care as the primary care arrangement; fourteen think between ages two and three is the appropriate time; twelve think around age two is the right time; and six express a preference for center care at age one or earlier. Of the forty-two mothers, eleven feel that their child started in center care at about the time she preferred, and thirty-one feel that they started in center care later than they would have preferred.

6. As discussed in chapter 2, the factors leading to placement included the number of child care programs in the neighborhood, mothers' knowledge of service providers in the community, timing, persistence, and special circumstances leading to subsidies.

Chapter 5

1. Following Stack's (1974) pioneering research, Katrina Bell-McDonald (2003), Kathryn Edin and Laura Lein (1997), Elaine Bell Kaplan (1997), Katherine Brown Rosier (1997), and Ann Creighton Zollar (1984), among others, have made important additions to the scholarly understanding of women's strategies and the use of networks. In *Making Ends Meet*, Edin and Lein (1997) make a specific application to one dimension of family life that women manage—how they meet the basic material needs of their family by combining minimal amounts of money from several sources.

2. A surprising finding in the study was the number of kin who had spent the better part of their lives in New York City but then migrated to the southern United States, where they had extended family or historical ties. Many African American mothers in the sample also expressed a strong desire to move to the American South.

3. Interestingly, there was as much kin migration for families in the sample between New York City and the American South as there was transnational migration by relatives of immigrant families.

4. The sample in this study was targeted at single mothers who were working and not the other sets of women who were coping with poverty and might not have been working as much who were represented more in Stack's (1974) and Edin and Lein's (1997) studies. Notably, work is much less of a focus in Stack's portrayal of survival strategies. Stack conducted her field research in the late 1960s, when both welfare benefits and the minimum wage were comparably much higher in real terms, and she devoted relatively little attention to women's work or their needs for child care because the population in the community she studied had high levels of chronic unemployment and was largely welfare-reliant. Also, the lesser attention on work in Stack's study may also reflect differences in the times: in the 1960s poor mothers of young children, and mothers in general, were not expected to work, and concerns about child care had not reached the levels they would later. By

1990, when Edin and Lein's work began, employment was a clearer expectation. It is also important to note the differences in what Stack was looking at: her analysis of a community with chronic unemployment and welfare dependency focused on family and community, aspects of life in which work does not play a foremost role.

5.   Edin and Lein (1997) found much the same when it came to sharing money across personal networks. Their results were different from Stack's (1974) in part because in her examination of how networks serve as resources for many areas of family needs, Stack covered a much wider swath of sharing behavior, from passing along clothes to transporting kin, raising one another's children, and sharing food and living accommodations, while Edin and Lein looked primarily at money supports, for which there may be more redistribution among low-income families than reciprocal exchanges. Reciprocity, as Stack argues, takes on a more intense form of exchange of goods and services when families are more peripheral to the labor force. Also, Stack took a much deeper look at how personal networks operate as she spoke to many kin within networks, explored all branches of the exchanges, and followed kin relationships over time and from all angles of exchange in a community where she lived during the study. She was thus more likely to see more of the potential reciprocity of exchanges across networks and over time.

6.   Viviena Zelizer (1994, 2000) has differentiated between types of exchanges in personal relationships, such as the child care provided by kin that is discussed here. Within many forms of exchange she identifies three broad forms (all of which I found in this study): *compensation* or monetary exchanges (money in direct exchange for child care); *entitlement* (rightful claims or expectations of assistance); and *gifts* (one person's voluntary, not obligatory, assistance to another, but not to be expected at all times). To these I might add *reciprocal exchanges*—either direct care for care or care for other assistance. Mothers in this study regularly differentiate forms of assistance for child care in accordance with their definitions of the sort of relationship that existed between their kin and the structure of the exchange.

7.   For example, Stack (1996) has also found that over the life course older kin who were on the giving end of child care, financial, or other assistance for young kin may be on the receiving end of care for health, monetary, and other needs when they reach the stage of needing elderly care.

Chapter 6

1.   Jody Heymann (2000, 22–23), looking at combined federal and state funding in the states, finds that the amount of government funding per

child is paltry compared to the need and that "given the cost of pre-school, the lack of government funding means that many families simple cannot enroll their children."

2. Anne Mitchell, Louise Stoney, and Harriet Dichter (2001) estimate that families contribute approximately 60 percent of the financing for child care arrangements; all government funding combined accounts for 39 percent, and businesses and philanthropies account for 1 percent. This analysis was based on data originally reported by Louise Stoney and Mark Greenberg (1996) and is based on the assumption that while public expenditures have increased since the earlier study, it has been in relatively the same proportion as overall spending on child care.

3. It is at the state level that most child care and education policies are developed and administered in the United States. There are large differences in the extent to which states support and oversee child care and education services to very young children, and wide variations in how child care programs are organized and run in the states. Yet what most states have in common is that the child care and education systems serving young children are decentralized, incomplete, and fragmented across several programs with little coherence and coordination.

4. Many other advanced industrialized countries provide broader guarantees of support for children's care and education (Gornick and Meyers 2001; Neuman 2001; OECD 2001). In many European countries, the care and education of young children is guaranteed to families, beginning at the age of one in Denmark, Finland, and Sweden, at age two in France, at two and a half in Belgium, at three in Italy and Germany, and at four in Britain. The early care and education systems in these countries are financed primarily by the government, which covers on average 70 percent of the costs of the system in these countries; early care and education is thus a public good, and the government's support significantly reduces the high burden of financing care in these countries, as compared with the United States, where parents pay 60 to 80 percent of the cost of care. These government-financed systems are also designed, funded, and regulated to ensure a high level of quality. For example, in many Western European countries center-based and school-based staff with primary responsibility for young children are required to complete at least three years of training in universities or other higher education institutions. In the United States, there is no national set of qualifications for child care staff, and most states have either standards well below national European standards or no standards.

5. In New York and several other states (Michigan and Wisconsin, for example), the work requirement waivers for mothers of newborns applies only to mothers of infants up to twelve weeks of age. Massachusetts and New Hampshire choose to exempt mothers with newborn children

from TANF work requirements for the first two years of the child's life (State Policy Documentation Project 2000).

6. The U.S. Family and Medical Leave Act, administered by the Wage and Hour Division of the U.S. Department of Labor, took effect in 1993. The act requires employers with fifty or more employees to provide up to twelve weeks of unpaid, job-protected leave each year to eligible employees to care for a newborn, newly adopted child, or foster child or for a family medical emergency. Workers in the private sector are eligible to take leave if they have worked for a covered employer for at least one year and for at least 1,250 hours during that year. Workers in the public sector are covered by the FMLA without regard to the number of employees. Employers must continue health insurance coverage if they provided it before the leave, but they may require employees to repay the health insurance premiums paid by the employer during the leave if the employee does not return to work at the end of the leave. An employer may deny leave to an employee within the highest-paid 10 percent of its workforce (a "key employee") if letting the worker take leave would create substantial and grievous injury to the firm. About 11 percent of private-sector work sites in the United States are covered by the FMLA, and these employ about 60 percent of the country's private-sector workers. Most of those covered had been or would have been eligible for leave even without this legislation, if only on a voluntary basis (Kamerman 2000).

7. The FTDI program is fully funded by employees' contributions through a 0.08 percent payroll contribution, similar to the disability insurance program. The average California employee will pay $27 per year (a minimum-wage worker will pay $11.23 per year) and is eligible to receive six weeks of family leave per year. The size of the benefit will be 55 percent of earnings up to a maximum of $728 in 2004 (California Employment Development Department 2002).

8. The largest long-term study of a broad-based preschool program is a twenty-year longitudinal study of nearly one thousand mostly poor children enrolled in several inner-city Chicago preschool programs. A comprehensive analysis found that attending preschool at ages three or four positively affected child outcomes for low-income children compared to those who did not attend preschool. The program's participants also had differentially better outcomes as adolescents and young adults compared to those in a control group not enrolled in the program (Reynolds et al. 2001). Those attending the preschool program were 29 percent more likely to graduate from high school, 33 percent less likely to be arrested for a juvenile crime, and more than 40 percent less likely to be arrested for a violent crime. These are robust differences and notably better relative outcomes than for those who did not receive the interventions, yet in absolute terms the outcomes were only so

good. Forty-seven percent of those who were in the school-based pre-school Chicago program fifteen years ago have since dropped out of high school, 9 percent committed violent crimes, and 17 percent were arrested for juvenile crimes; these are still troubling rates compared to societal norms. Reynolds and his colleagues (2002) did a follow-up cost-benefit analysis of the program's positive long-term gains compared to the average program participation cost of $7,000: the program provided benefits averaging about $48,000 by the time participants were twenty-one years old; of that total, $26,000 represented benefits to the general public in saved taxpayer costs and crime.

Analyses of well-known, but smaller, individual preschool programs, such as the analysis of the High/Scope Perry Preschool program in Ypsilanti, Michigan, provide additional evidence of program benefits. Many of the noted early findings reported that children who participated in the program had higher levels of academic success: higher achievement test scores and grades; less need for special education; less grade retention; and higher high school completion rates. Follow-up studies have continued for more than twenty years, the most recent analysis being for the preschool children who are now young adults. The studies show that program participants have higher earnings at twenty-seven years of age and are engaged less in criminal activity or in receiving welfare supports (Schweinhart, Barnes, and Weikart 1993). A similar program and research study has been the North Carolina Abecederian Project, a more intensive program in which children were in full-time, year-round care from birth through age five in a high-quality university-based center, with a curriculum that emphasized language development. Those in the preschool intervention had higher scores on achievement tests, with the greatest differential in reading scores, less grade retention, and less special education placement; they were also twice as likely to attend a four-year college.

9. Of the $1.98 billion invested by states in pre-K programs in 1999, $1.76 billion was invested in eleven states: California, Connecticut, Georgia, Illinois, Massachusetts, New Jersey, New York, North Carolina, Ohio, Oklahoma, and Texas (Mitchell 2001).

10. According to more recent program data, the Georgia pre-K program was serving approximately 67,000 children at an annual cost per child of between $3,000 and $4,000 (Davis-Canteen 2002).

11. New York passed legislation establishing a UPK program in 1997. It was envisioned that all four-year-olds would eventually be served in UPK classes. The program was to be phased in over five years, with one-quarter of all four-year-olds served in the first year and full enrollment reached by the 2001–2002 school year. The pace of expansion has been slowed considerably in the state's budget process during each year of the planned expansion, and in the 2001–2002 school year, when the pro-

gram was originally scheduled to be fully funded, funding for the program was frozen at the prior year's levels owing to budgetary constraints. Governor George Pataki proposed in his executive budget covering the 2003–2004 school year that the program be eliminated altogether. Although the final budget preserved the program at current funding levels, any expectations of full universality have been all but abandoned.

12. The New York City Independent Budget Office has estimated that of the UPK population served in the city, 82 percent were in part-day programs, 16 percent in school-day programs, and 1 percent in full-working day programs (New York Independent Budget Office 1999).

13. A comprehensive meta-analysis of studies summarized by Ruth McKey and her colleagues (1985) found an association between participation in Head Start and short-term improvements in children's cognitive and socioemotional development, nutrition, and physical and mental health. While children are in Head Start, they show significant positive effects in cognitive and socioemotional development compared to poor children who are not in Head Start. It has been more difficult to draw conclusions about the long-term impact of Head Start. Some studies have shown that the cognitive gains from Head Start diminish over time, and others raise methodological concerns about those research studies showing gains and those showing fading effects (Barnett 1995). Eliana Garces, Duncan Thomas, and Janet Currie (2000), using national longitudinal data, find that participation in Head Start increases the probability of completing high school and attending college, elevates earnings in early adulthood, and leads to less likelihood of criminal involvement.

14. Head Start is almost entirely federally funded, although agencies are expected to make a 20 percent local match, a requirement that is generally met through in-kind, noncash contributions. Head Start is one of the few federal programs in which grants are made directly to local programs without going through state agencies. In New York City the local grantee for most Head Start programs is the city's Agency for Child Development, which then makes grants to individual Head Start programs. Such an arrangement is uncommon for Head Start.

15. Since Head Start generally allows for continued eligibility, most three-year-olds in Head Start would continue in the program as four-year-olds. The ideal mix would be to have equal proportions of three- and four-year-olds, with most children participating continuously until they are ready for school.

16. The income eligibility guidelines ranged from less than $18,000 in annual income for a family of three in South Carolina and Alabama to more than $38,000 in annual income for a family of three in Minnesota and Connecticut (U.S. Department of Health and Human Services 2001a).

17. In 2002 only five states extended eligibility to families with income at 85 percent of SMI, according to information they submitted in their CCDF plans to the Child Care Bureau (U.S. Department of Health and Human Services 2002a). Melinda Gish (2001), in a Congressional Research Services report, finds that eleven states were setting their maximum income limits at 85 percent of SMI, the maximum level of CCDF funds. The U.S. Department of Health and Human Services (2001a), in its annual report on submitted state plans, noted that nine states claimed to set income eligibility levels at the federal maximum of 85 percent. The Children's Defense Fund (CDF) (Schulman, Blank, and Ewen 2000) reports that forty-seven states set their guidelines at levels below 85 percent of SMI. States typically set their maximum income eligibility levels lower to target limited funds to lower-income families. In fact, according to the U.S. Department of Health and Human Services (2001a) annual report, twenty-one states lowered their eligibility ceilings between 1997 and 2001.

18. Though New York guarantees assistance to both of these groups, as we saw in this study, those who were transitioning off welfare rarely received the twelve months of transitional child care for which they were eligible. Contributing factors included the complicated nature of the bureaucracies involved, the two different child care systems, poor management systems in HRA's child care program, and a policy strategy of diversion, whereby eligible families were discouraged from receiving benefits. Some mothers were not even informed of their eligibility for transitional assistance.

19. Because Illinois has maintained eligibility at the 50 percent level of 1997 SMI, its income eligibility threshold has diminished some over time relative to the state's rising median income. However, it also established a 10 percent income disregard in 1998, meaning that up to 10 percent of the caseload can have incomes above the 50 percent 1997 SMI cutoff (Saterfield 2003).

20. According to state data, of the January 2003 caseload of 81,000 Illinois families receiving child care assistance, 62,000, or more than 75 percent, were not receiving TANF. The state gives no preference to families transitioning off TANF, but its data show that 5,000 of the 62,000 who were not receiving TANF had received TANF in the previous year and that another 19,000 had received TANF within the previous five years (Saterfield 2003). According to Linda Saterfield, Illinois is committed to treating all families similarly within a "uniform, universal system . . . to erase the lines between families." The state wants to "help anyone," she says, "who is low-income and trying to be self-sufficient."

21. Some of the complexities of administrative practices in the child care system grow out of the welfare bureaucracy's system and culture of dis-

trust. In New York City the focus of child care has shifted more strongly toward the welfare-to-work objectives and controlling costs. The development of the separate HRA subsidy system was created specifically as part of welfare reform, and its development and procedures followed from a welfare system's emphasis on compliance and self-sufficiency with less concern about the forms of child care that families use or the qualifications of providers. Most of the increased spending on child care in New York City in the past seven years has been through vouchers issued by the HRA child care system, resulting in greater usage of lower-cost forms of subsidized care such as informal care.

22. Marcia Meyers, Theresa Heintze, and Douglas Wolf (1999) find low levels of subsidy usage among welfare recipients. Studies by the Center on Law and Social Policy on "welfare leavers" have found low utilization rates among parents leaving welfare (Schumacher, Greenberg, and Duffy 2001). Rachel Schumacher and Mark Greenberg (1999) find that the proportion of parents using subsidies in their first year after leaving welfare ranged from 8 to 46 percent.

Meyers and her colleagues (2001) have conducted the only study to date on the duration of child care subsidies. They analyzed administrative data for care subsidies across five states over a two-year period and observed that the length of time families received subsidies ranged between three and seven months. The finding that families who received subsidies did not stay in the system for very long might be attributed in part to administrative problems within state systems. The study was limited to administrative data and looked only at completed spells within a short two-year time frame, and it did not account for recidivism. Nevertheless, this finding is consistent with the finding from this study that families experience frequent changes when negotiating care in an uncoordinated system.

23. Of the 47,000 children on the waiting list, 34,000 were from families seeking child care for work eligibility reasons, and an additional 4,000 were from families with a parent who was looking for work. The waiting list would have been longer except that the agency at times discourages further applications by freezing eligibility determinations. Of the 47,000 on the waiting list, about 28,000, or 59 percent, had already completed the eligibility application process and been found eligible, but were waiting for service. The others were placed on the waiting list after a preliminary intake with eligibility to be determined in the event of further vouchers becoming available.

24. After taking application information over the phone, Washington sends a request to employers to verify employment and income. Many families use the mail/phone/fax options, but others have made applications in person because they did not know they could apply by other means,

because they preferred to do so, or because they thought it improved their chances of getting services without errors in the processing of their applications (Adams, Snyder, and Sandfort 2002).

25. Illinois has considered using its existing wage-verification system for income verification, but these data are often six months out of date and provide no information for the newly employed (Saterfield 2003).

26. In South Dakota families can download applications or fill out the child care application form online. When they submit the form online, the form is sent to Child Care Services and a form for the parent to sign is printed out, to be sent in by mail or fax with income documentation. A day or two after Child Care Services receives the documentation, the agency sends a certificate of eligibility to the family and a letter to the child care provider. The state has seen steady increases in the number of families using the online option, especially during the second half of 2002. Families without computer access can access the online application in two ways: TANF families can enroll with their caseworker using the caseworker's computer during a meeting; or all families can also apply and recertify by using a computer in the home of some family child care providers (Schaefbauer 2003).

27. Florida appears to be the only state to have tried something like this. A 1999 state law provides that if a child enters a child care program anytime from birth until age five, the child can stay in the program for the entire period until age five. However, the income cutoff for continued subsidy eligibility remains at 150 percent of the federal poverty level; when a family's income exceeds that level, the family can stay in the child care arrangement but is no longer subsidized and has to bear the full cost of the care. A state official who oversees child care administration in Florida suggested that children are not staying in the subsidy system or in their care arrangements any longer as a result of the 1999 law and that there have been no significant changes in enrollment since 1999 (Perkins 2002).

28. According to ACS staff, nearly 35 to 40 percent of subsidy recipients miss their initial recertification interview appointment. (This may include people who know they are no longer income-eligible and do not seek to renew, as well as those who are asked to schedule at times that are inconvenient to their work schedules.) Parents are then given a fifteen-day grace period to come in for their face-to-face interview, which most do. Most who do their recertification interviews are found to remain eligible. Four to 6 percent are found ineligible because their incomes exceed eligibility thresholds (Finch 2003).

29. To promote continuity among children enrolled in blended Head Start/child care partnerships, Vermont allows families to have their eligibility redetermined annually rather than every six months. Similarly, Maryland allows families in its combined Head Start and day care pro-

grams to remain eligible for a subsidy until the end of the Head Start year, regardless of any change in the family's situation (U.S. Department of Health and Human Services 2002a).

30. When their eligibility for TANF child care subsidies expires, families in Minnesota are then expected to continue their care eligibility simply by contacting the child care administration and updating their income information just as they would for their child care redetermination: they submit their paperwork by mail and no face-to-face meeting is required.

31. There could also be variation across states within this narrower range of 60 to 85 percent of SMI for which care assistance to working families is guaranteed.

32. The number of families requiring child care assistance is potentially very high but hard to quantify because current estimates of the number of people in subsidized care do not effectively combine data about child care from different sources, break down unmet need estimates by age, or include uncertainties about potential levels of subsidy usage. Incorporating the first of these would involve the difficult but achievable step of getting a rough census of care for other forms of subsidized care that low-income families use, such as Head Start and pre-K programs, then adding those numbers to the number of families served by CCDF-funded programs and subtracting any families that were double-counted. The potential usage of different forms of care would probably vary by age as well; very young children would be somewhat less likely to use available care resources, for instance, and Head Start and pre-K programs serve only three- and four-year-old children.

There is very limited data on the number of families eligible for subsidized care that would take advantage of assistance if it were more universally offered. A few recent studies have begun to look at the question of potential take-up ratios for child care subsidy programs—the percentage of families that would use subsidized care under a variety of scenarios. Ann Witte (Witte and Queralt 2002) reports that in Rhode Island, which guarantees child care assistance to all eligible families up to 225 percent of the federal poverty level, the take-up proportion has consistently been close to 40 percent of all those eligible. Given that the percentage of all families served through subsidies is estimated at 15 to 20 percent, it is an educated guess that with a child care assistance guarantee the amount of subsidy funding required would be about twice what is currently spent.

Depending on how such a guarantee was structured and on whether such a guarantee was offered just to families with children younger than three, whose take-up ratios may be lower, my guess is that the increased spending required could be significantly less than that. Obviously, without more information the range of the increased costs would vary considerably. Ideally, we would prefer a model that includes as variables the type of care offered, the age of the children, the amount of the subsidy, the ease of arranging and maintaining subsidies, and the expected level of parent copayments for subsidized care.

Appendix A

1. "In the labor force" includes mothers who are working and those looking for work. The number of actually employed mothers is on average a few percentage points (three to six) below labor force participation rates, but labor force participation data for women by child age groupings are more generally available for longer time spans.

2. Analyzing the data from the 1997 Survey of Income and Program Participation, Smith (2002) found that in addition to the 10.1 million children under five with working mothers in child care, 29 percent of the 9.1 million children with mothers who were not employed were in regular child care arrangements in a typical week. In total, more than 12.4 million of all the 19.4 million children under five were in care. Earlier, Smith (2000) had found even higher rates of child care use when analyzing the data from the 1995 SIPP. She found that in addition to the 10.1 million children in care in 1995 who were under five and had a working mother, 846,000 were in care because their mother was attending school, and that in total more than 14.4 million (or three-quarters) of all the 19.2 million children under five were in care. Along with the times when care was used because mothers were working, families often used child care when mothers were in school or looking for a job and for developmental purposes even when mothers were home (Papillo et al. 2001; Smith 2000).

   The SIPP is a panel survey administered by the U.S. Census Bureau that follows a continuous series of national panels with representative sample sizes of 14,000 to 36,000 for durations of three to four years each. The first panel began in 1984, and the most recent panel for which child care data are available is the four-year panel that began in 1996; that panel collected child care data in the spring of 1997 and the spring of 1999.

3. Tables A.2, A.3, and A.4 present the usage patterns by age, income, and family structure, combining data from the two most recent waves of published SIPP child care data, 1997 and 1999 (waves 4 and 10 of the 1996 panel), which were combined to offer coherent data from a single source and minimize unexplained variations in individual waves of the annual data.

4. Data from the 1999 National Survey of American Families (NSAF) revealed patterns in child care use by income that are very similar to patterns in the SIPP data, but that survey found a somewhat greater dif-

ferential in the use of parental care between low-income families and higher-income families and a smaller differential in the use of relative care. In the 1999 NSAF, 33 percent of children under age five in families below 200 percent of the federal poverty level (FPL) were in parental care, compared to 24 percent in parental care in families above 200 percent of FPL; the use of relative care was 29 percent for low-income families (below 200 percent of FPL) and 26 percent for higher-income families (above 200 percent of FPL). Center care use was lower for families with income below 200 percent of FPL (23 percent) than it was for families with income above 200 percent of FPL (30 percent).

5. The 1999 NSAF also found that there was little overall variation in the use of center care and family child care by family structure, but it did find variation among single- and two-parent families at different income levels. For example, among two-parent families, the higher-income families were more likely to use center care (39 percent for two-parent families with incomes above 200 percent of FPL, compared to 29 percent for families below 200 percent of FPL), while the opposite was true among single-parent families, among whom 35 percent of low-income (less than 200 percent of FPL) families used center care, compared to 16 percent of families with incomes above 200 percent of FPL.

6. Becerra Rosina and Iris Chi (1992) examined low-income minority families' child care use and preferences compared to those of low-income non-Hispanic white families in Los Angeles. They found high differentials between Hispanics and whites in utilization of center care and care by relatives, even when they had the same amount of need. Rosina and Chi explain the sharply lower utilization of center care by Mexican Americans in their sample as a combination of cultural and institutional factors—limited knowledge of the available child care options; limited availability of centers in the Mexican American neighborhoods; differences in employment patterns; language barriers; cultural differences in child-rearing; and the greater availability of nearby extended family networks. Fuller, Holloway, and Liang (1996) have found that African American families were more likely than white or Latino families to use center-based care and that cultural differences in child-rearing practices contributed to these differences. Liang, Fuller, and Singer (2000), in an analysis of whether and at what ages a national sample of more than three thousand children first entered center-based care, found sharp disparities by ethnic group in center care and preschool participation, particularly for Latino children, whose enrollment was lower than for white and black preschoolers, controlling for maternal employment and family income.

7. Hofferth (1995) has found that for three- to five-year-olds there was a comparable increase in children of nonworking mothers using pre-

school center programs for developmental enrichment even when not needed primarily for care.

8. Analyzing the 1995 NHES data, Hofferth and her colleagues (1998) found that 68 percent of the low-income parents who wanted to change child care arrangements said they preferred to change to center-based programs, and that families using center arrangements were the least likely to want to change arrangements at all ages of use.

9. Ellen Kisker and her colleagues (1991) report that in a 1990 survey 12 percent of centers indicated having space available, significantly less than for other forms of care. Magaly Queralt and Ann Dryden Witte (1998), in a study of the neighborhood supply of child care in Massachusetts, have found that low-income communities had the lowest overall supply of available child care and the fewest slots available for young children. Lee Kreader, Jessica Piecyk, and Ann Collins (2000) similarly found a much more restricted child care supply in low-income areas of Illinois and Maryland.

10. Kisker and her colleagues (1991) found that only about half of all centers surveyed in the 1990 National Child Care Survey accepted very young children and that fewer than 10 percent of all vacancies in centers were for infants.

11. The scarcity of center care available for very young children creates a spillover effect into other forms of licensed care, particularly family child care. Most states specify that no more than two young children (under two years or under eighteen months) can be in a family child care provider's home at one time. Family child care arrangements also cannot accommodate much of the spillover, which may in part explain the much higher number of infants and young toddlers than preschoolers on waiting lists for child care.

12. In an analysis of 1995 SIPP data, Smith (2000) found that 55 percent of children in Head Start had parents who were not employed, and 17 percent had parents employed part-time. Among all children in care arrangements, 28 percent were in families in which a parent was not employed. Parents who used Head Start were more likely than those using other care types to use multiple care arrangements, doing so 69 percent of the time. For families using multiple arrangements, the Head Start arrangement accounted for only 56 percent of the total hours in care on average.

    In recent years the number of families in Head Start that are working and need full-day, full-year care has grown, and many local Head Start programs (with encouragement from Head Start at the federal level) have increased their capacity to provide longer hours of care, either by extending their program days or by blending Head Start and other child care and early education funding. Of those families that reported a need for full-day, full-year services, the proportion that received such services through a Head Start center (either through Head Start only or with blended funds) increased from 25 percent in 1997 to 45 percent in 2002, according to an analysis by the Center for Law and Social Policy (CLASP) (Schumacher and Irish 2003). Also, the percentage of parents with children in Head Start who were employed increased from the 45 percent that Smith (2000) found in 1995 to 68 percent that Schumacher and Irish (2003) found in 2002. Schumacher and Irish (2003) found that about one-fifth of families in Head Start in 2002 were receiving welfare.

13. Harriet Presser (2000), in her analysis of 1997 Current Population Survey (CPS) data, found that 43 percent of employed mothers with a high school education or less and with young children worked nontraditional work schedules, resulting in an incongruent fit between the hours of child care availability and the hours they worked.

14. An Urban Institute study, based on NSAF data, found that there was more than a 20 percent difference in the rate of low-income parents paying for care *and all those* earning more. The study found that 40 percent of low-income families (under 200 percent of the poverty line) pay for child care compared with 53 percent of families above 200 percent of poverty (Giannarelli and Barsimantov 2000). Smith's (2002) analysis of 1997 SIPP data indicates that low-income families (with incomes under 200 percent of the poverty line) pay for child care (in 33 percent of cases) about one-quarter less often than middle-income families (42 percent of the time), who pay for child care about one-quarter less often than families with incomes in the top third of all families with children (who pay 52 percent of the time). All working families average $71 in weekly child care payments, while those with earnings less than 200 percent of the poverty level average $64 per week for child care expenses. Thus, the actual amounts paid for child care vary less with family income than do payments as a share of income. In economic terms this means that the cost of child care is relatively inelastic, which creates disproportionate cost burdens for lower-income families. David Blau (2001) has demonstrated the inelasticity of child care and the effects of price on parents' child care choices, which provide further empirical support to the observations that many parents are priced out of some forms of care they might prefer and that cost serves as a significant constraint in child care choices.

15. An NICHD (2000a) analysis found that in 1993 child care expenses for a preschool-age child averaged $215 per month, or approximately 18 percent of the budget of a low-income family. For higher-income families, the average cost was $329 per month, approximately 7 percent of the household budget.

16. Smith (2000, 2002) reported that the average weekly family payment for child care increased from $57 in 1985 to $71 in 1997 (in constant

1997 dollars), an increase of 24 percent. Hofferth (1996) showed that there was very little increase in child care payments between 1985 and 1990, indicating that the period after 1990 saw very steep increases in child care costs. Hofferth concludes that the recent rate increases, particularly for subsectors of the care market (centers and family child care), suggest that the demand for child care has been growing more quickly relative to its supply (Hofferth 1996).

17.   Many reviewers of the child care quality research suggest that process quality studies are more useful than studies of structural features, but that the latter are more common because they cost less and the measurement is less intrusive (Hofferth 1995; Lamb 1998; Zaslow 1991). Even among process studies, standardized rating studies are far more common than direct, detailed, contextual study of the pertinent aspects of the developmental environment, since detailed contextual assessments are more difficult and time-intensive and more subjective.

A recent NICHD (2002) article seeks to relate the links in child care quality studies that focus on structural features to both processes and outcomes, arguing that, prior to this article, people have argued that structural quality leads to process quality, which leads to better outcomes for children (for example, smaller groups allow for better teacher-child interaction), without ever showing this empirically. Using NICHD data, the authors tested this and found that there is a mediated path from both caregiver training and child-staff ratios to care quality to cognitive competence, as well as to caregivers' ratings of social competence, that holds up even after controlling for family variables. In other words, the authors suggest, structural quality is associated with process quality and then associated with outcomes. They argue that this provides empirical support for policies that improve state regulations covering caregiver training and mandatory adult-to-child ratios.

18.   For observational studies, researchers mostly use established scales of quality measures to assess quality, the most prominent being the Early Childhood Environment Rating Scale (ECERS) and the Infant/Toddler Environment Rating Scale (ITERS). Both cover a wide range of care factors related to health and safety, facilities, staffing, use of materials and toys, developmentally appropriate activities, and interactions between staff and children. The ITERS excludes some areas more specific to preschoolers and includes others particular to infant and toddler development.

19.   In the CQOS, the researchers spent two to three hours observing rooms in each of the four hundred centers across four states and rated them using the ECERS (Helburn 1995).

20.   In the CQOS study, the distribution of quality ratings for infants and toddlers in centers was even worse, with only 8 percent of infants and toddlers in "developmentally appropriate" care and 40 percent in very

low-quality care that could endanger their health and safety (Helburn 1995).

21.   In this study of more than 800 children in the care of 225 home-based providers, overall quality was measured as "good" in only 9 percent of the care settings, while 56 percent were "adequate" (rated as neither growth-enhancing nor growth-harming), and 35 percent provided poor-quality care that was potentially developmentally harmful to children. Half of the children were not securely attached to providers. Positive and adequate care ratings were associated with care providers' motivations to be caregivers. Among family child care providers, those who sought out and received training and cared for relatively larger groups of children often provided relatively higher-quality, more sensitive, and more responsive care (Galinsky et al. 1994; Kontos et al. 1995).

22.   The NICHD has done an extensive longitudinal child care study across a range of settings. One NICHD (2000a) study assessed the overall quality of child care for toddlers in their longitudinal sample and the characteristics associated with positive caregiving in five types of care. With multiple longitudinal points of observation, they concluded that in terms of overall quality observed, positive caregiving was "highly characteristic" of the care received by just 12 percent of the children and "somewhat characteristic" for 32 percent. Compared to the combined 44 percent of children in the two highest categories, good care was "somewhat uncharacteristic" for 51 percent in the NICHD sample, and for 6 percent it was "very uncharacteristic."

23.   Both Phillips and her colleagues (1994) and Whitebook, Howes, and Phillips (1990) found that center-based programs attended by those who are not poor but low- to moderate-income—between the poverty line and median family income—were of lower quality than both the center-based programs attended by children from low-income families and those serving high-income families. Centers serving high-income children had the highest quality ratings. They referred to this as a "curvilinear relation between family income and quality" (Phillips et al. 1994, 473).

24.   The analysis of care spells dynamics is a major method that social scientists have used to examine changing social conditions and statuses of families over time and to study the dynamics and durations of particular elements of family life, most notably income, poverty, welfare, and work dynamics. An examination by spells to analyze the dynamics of family situations or program participation has been widely used in studies of family poverty, child poverty, family income, work, welfare receipt, and other issues (Bane and Ellwood 1986, 1994; Harris 1993; Pavetti 1993).

25.   In their study of poverty and welfare dynamics, Mary Jo Bane and David Ellwood (1994) used data from the Panel Study of Income Dy-

namics (PSID), which is a particularly good large dataset for studying dynamics because it tracks a large sample over many years (from 1968 to the present) and has relevant data for income, work, welfare receipt, marital status, and children in families. LaDonna Pavetti (1993) and others have used another longitudinal data source, the National Longitudinal Survey of Youth (NLSY), which as been collecting similar data monthly, starting in 1979. Neither the PSID nor the NLSY track child care arrangements.

26.   Scholarship in developmental psychology has built on Urie Bronfenbrenner's (1979) ecological framework and extended it in several ways. Bronfenbrenner (1979, 1986) was a pioneer in the contextual movement in studying child development. In his early work he sought to change the theoretical framework used to study children, and particularly disadvantaged children. He called his framework an ecological model (Bronfenbrenner 1979): it explicitly regards the multiple contexts that surround a child and influence development and explicitly stresses the importance of contextual variables, including changing family dynamics, parents' work situations, and children's care contexts. Bronfenbrenner and Pamela Morris (1998) more recently described and mapped the various contexts that influence children's development. Jeanne Brooks-Gunn (1995) proposed a family and community resources framework that draws from the disciplinary tradition of developmental psychology and focuses on environmental risk factors, community resources, family resources, and the intersection of intervention and family resources to better understand the development of and intervention with young children in families and communities. Others have applied general systems theory to identify principles for the functioning of complex developmental systems, such as the transition of children to kindergarten (Ford and Lerner 1992; Lerner et al. 2002; Sameroff 1995). In individual empirical studies and through concerted research efforts like the NICHD study, developmental psychologists have tried to understand and explain the importance of the first relationships between children and parents and between children and their early caregivers. This research generally emphasizes that early experiences and relationships matter for development and that the fundamental association between children's situational contexts—homes and other environments—and their early development affects later outcomes (Bronfenbrenner 1979). Recently, the importance of context (defined as environments and experiences) for child development was highlighted by the National Academy of Science report *Neurons to Neighborhoods: The Science of Early Childhood Development* (Shonkoff and Phillips 2000).

27.   Although there is still only limited empirical research available for understanding the impact of neighborhoods on child development, some

theoretical frameworks have recently been proposed for understanding these impacts (Furstenberg and Hughes 1994; Shonkoff and Phillips 2000). Jack Shonkoff and Deborah Phillips (2000) identify four major bodies of theory: stress theory, social organization theory, institutional explanation, and epidemic/peer theories. Felton Earls and Stephen Buka (2000) have proposed a stress theory, which emphasizes the importance of exposure to social and psychological conditions (for example, community violence) as well as physical toxins (such as lead paint). Robert Sampson (1992) and others focus on the extent of social organization and disorganization in a neighborhood and are interested in the processes in which parents frequently come into contact with one another and share values and therefore are more likely to monitor behavior and dangers to children (Sampson 1992; Sampson and Groves 1989; Sampson, Raudenbush, and Earls 1997). Institutional models stress the resources available to families in a neighborhood, such as parks, libraries, and health services (Leventhal and Brooks-Gunn 2000).

Several studies that focus on disadvantaged neighborhoods find that conditions exist in which children would not be expected to flourish developmentally. For example, Laura Taylor and her colleagues (1992) found that one in ten children witnessed a violent event prior to age six. This exposure to violence is known to be linked to psychiatric problems such as post-traumatic stress disorder (Singer et al. 1995). The difficulty in measuring the degree to which neighborhoods specifically matter is complicated by the methodological challenge of estimating the impact of neighborhoods when neighborhood conditions are so highly correlated with families' socioeconomic status.

28. Thompson's studies (1998, 2001) of early development show how young children's relationships with caregivers affect the security of their attachments, temperaments, self-awareness, confidence, and social understanding. Quality and stability in caregiving relationships can enhance these aspects of development, while adverse care experiences can lead to insecure attachments with caregivers. Insecure attachments with caregivers are associated with early anxiety, distrust and uncertainty that children may feel with a caregiver, their difficulties coping with stress, and negative self-perceptions.

The degrees of security and insecurity in attachments with caregivers are not strictly determinative of later psychosocial development, for a couple of reasons. First, the care that children receive from their parents remains the primary developmental influence on them. The care children receive at home interacts with that of the outside caregivers both positively and negatively. Second, attachment security is not static—early attachments are quite important psychologically, but the quality of attachment changes in response to other changes in a child's care situation and family dynamics. Responsive, nurturing care is needed from all of the contextually significant settings where children spend their time throughout early childhood as they move through care situations.

29.   Beginning in the mid-1980s in his periodic review of recent empirical research on the effects of infant day care, Belsky noted what he saw as an emerging link between the use of child care in the first twelve months and avoidant attachment of infants toward mothers: "There is an *emerging* pattern here in which we see supplementary [by which he means all nonmaternal care] child care, *especially that initiated in the first year*, whether in homes or in centers, sometimes associated with the tendency of the infant to avoid or maintain a distance from the mother following a series of brief separations" (Belsky 1986, 4, emphasis in the original).

Belsky's conclusions that the security of attachment in maternal-infant relationships was harmed by the use of infant child care and that the use of early care may constitute a developmental risk for children led to some controversy among developmental psychologists in early childhood research. Other child development researchers disputed his arguments and presented evidence to the contrary, arguing that Belsky had not accounted for the quality of care or the family characteristics influencing both attendance in early care and child outcomes and that he had not defined the negative developmental effects he was measuring (Clarke-Stewart 1989; Phillips, McCartney, and Scarr 1987; Scarr Phillips, and McCartney 1990).

Nevertheless, Belsky's point that secure maternal-infant attachments may be harmed by certain patterns of infant child care use spurred new directions in research that have led to improved understanding. The emphasis his supposition placed on the timing of child care spurred the child development research community to focus on timing and to define quality of care and measure developmental effects within a contextual perspective that includes relevant family and care characteristics.

30.   Belsky (1997) himself appeared to qualify the argument as well when he said that higher-quality child care can foster somewhat more positive outcomes, but that because the routine nonmaternal care children receive when beginning care in their first year is often not high-quality care, they are more likely to develop insecure attachments to their parents.

31.   Looking across studies that provide data on care quality, family background, and child outcomes, the research finds that overall quality affects children's attachment security, social competence, language, and cognitive development, controlling for differences in family characteristics. Carollee Howes, Deborah Phillips, and Marcy Whitebook (1992) found that children in higher-quality center care were more likely to be securely attached to their caregivers. Howes and others have also found that children who are more securely attached to their

providers have better interactions with adults and other children (Howes and Hamilton 1992; Howes, Matheson, and Hamilton 1994). Ellen Galinsky and her colleagues (1994) found the same to be true for family child care and other home-based care providers. Children with providers who measured higher along several individual ratings (including sensitivity and responsiveness) and global ratings were more likely to be securely attached to their caregiver.

32. CCDF funds are passed from the federal government to the states in the form of a block grant. Each state qualifies to receive its block grant amount of federal funds, which it combines with state contributions; the state administers this combined fund with broad discretion, within some general requirements set by federal law. Within the federal CCDF funding, the federal government differentiates between four sources of funding: "mandatory" funding, "discretionary" funding, "matching" funds, and TANF transfer funds. These funding streams have different sources of allocation and rules about state matching requirements and different time limits for obligating and spending the funds. Mandatory funds are based on states' historical spending on child care prior to the 1996 consolidation of child care funding streams under CCDF and is a "guaranteed" portion of funding. Discretionary funds are a share of the funds that states qualify for based on annual congressional appropriations. Some of the amount of the mandatory funding requires state matching funds, for which the state must spend at least an amount based on its historical level of spending to meet its "maintenance of effort" requirements and receive the equal amount in federal matching funds. The discretionary funds require no state match and are based on an allocation formula that factors in the number of children in the state and the level of need. Finally, states can elect to transfer up to 30 percent of their TANF block grant funds to their CCDF block grant. A state may also directly spend TANF funds on child care rather than fold these funds into its CCDF block grants. For a more complete discussion of the CCDF program and its component levels of funding, see Gish (2002).

33. States can both transfer some of their TANF funds to their CCDF grants and spend TANF funds directly on child care. In FY 2002, forty-two states transferred $2.0 billion of their TANF block grants to their CCDF programs. In addition, thirty-two states reported spending $1.6 billion directly from their TANF funding for child care (Schumacher and Rakpraja 2002).

34. TANF funding for child care has been particularly high since 1999 because of large TANF caseload declines in many states. Rachel Schumacher and Tanya Rakpraja (2002) report that from FY 2000 to FY 2001 there was a slight decline in TANF child care spending from $3.8 billion to $3.6 billion, and U.S. Department of Health and Human

Services data for FY 2002 show a further slight decline to $3.5 billion. State use of TANF funding for child care has largely leveled off, however, and with further worsening of fiscal conditions in many states, TANF spending on child care may be vulnerable to further reductions.

35. In addition, Head Start began the Early Head Start program to offer care to children younger than age three. These more recently offered infant and toddler services are still a small component of Head Start's services and spending (U.S. Department of Health and Human Services 2003).

36. The social service block grant is a flexible federal block grant that states may use to support their social service programs, including child care. States receive a specific allotment of SSBG funds based on population. No state match is required for the receipt of funds, and these funds can be used to help pay for social services to children and families with incomes below 200 percent of the federal poverty level. Federal funding appropriations for SSBGs has decreased from $2.5 billion in FY 1997 to $1.7 billion in FY 2002. Of the total SSBG funds, $400 million was expended by states for child care in FY 1999, the latest year for which there are expenditure estimates for child care spending with SSBG funds (Gish 2002).

37. Douglas Besharov and Nazanin Samari (2001) have estimated that the number of children served through federal and state child care resources increased by 1.2 million from 1994 to 1999.

38. Using data reported by the states and a model developed by the Urban Institute, the U.S. Department of Health and Human Services (2000b) estimated that only 12 percent of children potentially eligible under the federal government's maximum family income level (85 percent of SMI) and 15 percent of children eligible under the states' adopted maximum income levels (mostly less than the 85 percent of SMI federal maximum) received assistance through CCDF funds in FY 1999. Using the same model and applying it to revised U.S. Department of Health and Human Services data for FY 2000, Mezey, Greenberg, and Schumacher (2002) estimate that only 14 percent of children potentially eligible under the federal government's maximum family income level (85 percent of SMI) received child care assistance in FY 2000. Using the states' recent maximum income thresholds and other state eligibility requirements, the U.S. Department of Health and Human Services (2002b) estimated that 30 percent of eligible children would be served in FY 2003.

It is important to recognize that child care programs cannot be expected to have 100 percent utilization, since not everyone who is eligible may need or use subsidized child care. Absent data from programs or experiments that allow full access to child care subsidies, it is empirically difficult to determine the "take-up" levels for child care subsidies.

Based on an analysis of subsidy utilization in Rhode Island—the only state to have a child care guarantee (up to 225 percent of the federal poverty line) and in which families are broadly eligible—Witte and Queralt (2002) estimate that 40 percent of families used available child care subsidies in early 2000.

39. Studies of welfare administration have reported that clients are stigmatized, treated with suspicion, and humiliated within the cash welfare system (Golden 1992; Piven and Cloward 1971; Stack 1974).

40. The DCTC was first introduced in 1954 and has changed significantly in subsequent reauthorizations. In its current structure it provides a credit of between 20 and 35 percent for allowable dependent care, which can include child care for children up to age thirteen or care for an elderly or disabled person. The size of the DCTC depends on the number of children or dependents in care, the family's income, and the amount the family paid for child care during the year. Families can claim a limited amount of their child care expenses: in the 2003 tax year, families with one child or dependent could claim up to $3,000 and families with more than one dependent could claim up to $6,000. Eligible families receive credits worth between 20 and 35 percent of care expenses, depending on their income. Benefits are reduced by half a percentage point from 35 percent for families with adjusted gross incomes of $15,000 (or less) for every $1,000 increment above $15,000, until they reach 20 percent for all families with adjusted gross incomes above $43,000. Because at the lowest income level families have limited tax liability, the tax is nonrefundable to those at the applicable income levels for the start of the phaseout, and because the phaseout begins at such a low level of income, most who are eligible and receive the tax credit receive the minimum 20 percent credit. Although the full credit is worth up to $1,050 for families with one child or dependent in care and $2,100 for families with more than one dependent in care, in practice the credit maximums are $600 for families with one child and $1,200 for families with two or more children. The credit can be used to cover most child care expenses in a variety of settings or a variety of providers (National Women's Law Center 2003).

41. More than 29 percent reported taking the credit on their federal income taxes, in the 1990 National Child Care Survey, compared to 7 percent who received direct subsidies (Hofferth 1995).

Appendix B

1. Some of the primary purposes of applying qualitative research methods include: developing new lines of inquiry and identifying general patterns of behavior; finding information that is generally missing from less detailed, more detached forms of study, like surveys that may not

adequately uncover some underlying activities or may underestimate the prevalence of some other activities; providing meaning for social behavior as seen by those who experience the phenomenon being studied; understanding respondents' reasoning for their actions in order to explain possibly unexpected outcomes; describing the more complicated interactions between variables of study in order to help develop new or better-integrated explanations and concepts within the field of study; developing new theories, models, and analytic frameworks from a grounded analysis of data that can describe and help explain social processes or mechanisms; and telling stories so as to relate findings in compelling and illustrative ways.

2. The research design described here builds methodologically on several qualitative studies (Edin and Lein 1997; Liebow 1967; Newman 1993; Stack 1974; Sullivan 1989) but borrows most from elements used in research by Edin and Lein (1997) and Stack (1974). The research approach in this study lies closer to that of Edin and Lein, given the heavy emphasis on interviewing and the narrower focus on one area of women's strategic behavior. It adds to this some of Stack's elements of prolonged interactions in the community and added interpretations within this context.

3. Edin and Lein (1997, 12) say that in fieldwork like theirs—the researcher is asking for information on potentially sensitive topics like income, expenses, informal work, and living arrangements—"a stranger has almost no chance" to get enough access or accurate information without referral from a knowledgeable and trusted community source.

~ References ~

Aber, J. Lawrence, Neil G. Bennett, Dalton C. Conley, and Jiali Li. 1997. "The Effects of Poverty on Child Health and Development." *Annual Review of Public Health* 18: 463–83.

Adams, Gina, and Monica Rohacek. 2002. "More Than a Work Support? Issues Around Integrating Child Development Goals into the Child Care Subsidy System." *Early Childhood Research Quarterly* 17(4): 418–40.

Adams, Gina, and Jodi Sandfort. 1992. *State Investments in Child Care and Early Childhood Education*. Washington, D.C.: Children's Defense Fund.

Adams, Gina, Kathleen Snyder, and Jodi Sandfort. 2002. "Getting and Retaining Child Care Assistance: How Policy and Practice Influence Parents' Experiences." Assessing the New Federalism occasional paper 55. Washington, D.C.: Urban Institute.

Anderson, Mark. 2003. Child care program analyst, Child Care Services Division, Oregon Department of Employment, interview with Elizabeth Rigby, research assistant, April 16, 2003.

Bane, Mary Jo. 1997. "Welfare as We Might Know It." *The American Prospect* 30: 47–53.

Bane, Mary Jo, and David T. Ellwood. 1983. "The Dynamics of Dependence: The Routes to Self-sufficiency." Report prepared for the assistant secretary for planning and evaluation, U.S. Department of Health and Human Services. Cambridge, Mass.: Urban Systems Research and Engineering.

————. 1986. "Slipping into and out of Poverty: The Dynamics of Spells." *Journal of Human Resources* 21: 1–23.

————. 1994. *Welfare Realities: From Rhetoric to Reform*. Cambridge, Mass.: Harvard University Press.

Barnas, Mary V., and E. Mark Cummings. 1994. "Caregiver Stability and Toddlers' Attachment-Related Behavior Towards Caregivers in Day Care." *Infant Behavior and Development* 17(2): 141–47.

Barnett, Steven W. 1995. "Long-term Effects of Early Childhood Programs on Cognitive and School Outcomes." *The Future of Children* 5(3): 25–50.

Bell-McDonald, Katrina. 2001. "De-romanticizing Black Intergenerational Support: The Questionable Expectations of Welfare Reform." In *Race and the Politics of Welfare Reform*, edited by Sanford F. Schram, Joe Soss, and Richard C. Fording. Ann Arbor: University of Michigan Press.

Belsky, Jay. 1986. "Infant Day Care: A Cause for Concern?" *Zero to Three* (National Center for Infants, Toddlers and Families) 6(5): 1–7.

———. 1995. "Expanding the Ecology of Human Development: An Evolutionary Perspective." In *Examining Lives in Context: Perspectives on the Ecology of Human Development*, edited by Phyllis Moen, Glen H. Elder Jr., and Kurt Lüscher. Washington, D.C.: American Psychological Association.

———. 1997. "The Effects of Day Care: A Nation Still at Risk." In *Marriage and Family*, 23rd ed., edited by Kathleen R. Gilbert. Guilford, Conn.: Dushkin/McGraw-Hill.

———. 2001. "Developmental Risks (Still) Associated with Early Child Care." *Journal of Child Psychology and Psychiatry* 42(7): 845–59.

Belsky, Jay, and David Eggebeen. 1991. "Early and Extensive Maternal Employment and Young Children's Socioemotional Development: Children of the National Longitudinal Survey of Youth." *Journal of Marriage and the Family* 53(4): 1083–1110.

Besharov, Douglas, and Nazanin Samari. 2001. "Child Care After Welfare Reform." In *The New World of Welfare*, edited by Rebecca Blank and Ron Haskins. Washington, D.C.: Brookings Institution.

Blakeslee, Sandra. 1997. "Studies Show Talking with Infants Shapes Ability to Think." *The New York Times*, April 17, p. A17.

Blank, Helen, and Nicole Oxendine Poersch. 2000. *State Developments in Child Care and Early Childhood Education*. Washington, D.C.: Children's Defense Fund.

Blau, David M. 2001. *The Child Care Problem: An Economic Analysis*. New York: Russell Sage Foundation.

Boushey, Heather. 2003. "Who Cares? The Child Care of Working Mothers." Data Brief 1. Washington, D.C.: Center for Economic and Policy Research.

Bowles, Samuel, and Herbert Gintis. 1999. "Is Equality Passé? Homo Reciprocans and the Future of Egalitarian Politics." *Boston Review* 23(January): 4–35.

Bronfenbrenner, Urie. 1979. *The Ecology of Human Development: Experiments by Nature and Design*. Cambridge, Mass.: Harvard University Press.

———. 1986. "Ecology of the Family as Context for Human Development: Research Perspectives." *Developmental Psychology* 22: 723–42.

Bronfenbrenner, Urie, and Pamela A. Morris. 1998. "The Ecology of Developmental Processes." In *Handbook of Child Psychology: Theoretical Models of Human Development*, 5th ed., edited by William Damon and Richard M. Lerner. New York: Wiley.

Brooks-Gunn, Jeanne. 1995. "Strategies for Altering the Outcomes of Poor Children and Their Families." In *Escape from Poverty: What Makes a Difference for Children?*, edited by P. Lindsay Chase-Lansdale and Jeanne Brooks-Gunn. New York: Cambridge University Press.

———. 1996. "Children in Families in Communities: Risk and Intervention in the Bronfenbrenner Tradition." In *Examining Lives in Context: Perspectives on the Ecology of Human Development*, edited by Phyllis Moen, Glen H. Elder Jr., and Kurt Lüscher. Washington, D.C.: American Psychological Association.

Brooks-Gunn, Jeanne, and Greg Duncan. 1997. "The Effects of Poverty on Children." *The Future of Children* 7(2): 55–71.

Brooks-Gunn, Jeanne, Wen-Jui Han, and Jane Waldfogel. 2002. "Maternal Employment and Child Cognitive Outcomes in the First Three Years of Life: The NICHD Study of Early Child Care." *Child Development* 73(4, July–August): 1052–72.

Brooks-Gunn, Jeanne, Marie McCormick, Pamela K. Klebanov, and Cecilia McCarton. 1998. "Young Children's Health Care Use: Effects of Family and Neighborhood Poverty." *Journal of Pediatrics* 132: 971–75.

Brown-Lyons, Melanie, Anne Robertson, and Jean Layzer. 2001. *Kith and Kin—Informal Child Care: Highlights from Recent Research*. New York: National Center for Children in Poverty.

Burchinal, Margaret. 1999. "Child Care Experiences and Developmental Outcomes." *ANNALS of the American Academy of Political and Social Science* (special issue, "The Silent Crisis in U.S. Child Care," edited by Suzanne Helburn) 563(1): 73–97.

Burchinal, Margaret, Joanne Roberts, Laura Nabors, and Donna Bryant. 1996. "Quality of Center Child Care and Infant Cognitive and Language Development." *Child Development* 67(2): 606–20.

Burstein, Nancy, Jean Layzer, and Kevin Cahill. 2000. *National Study of Child Care for Low-Income Families: Patterns of Child Care Use Among Low-Income Families*. Cambridge, Mass.: Abt Associates.

California Employment Development Department. 2002. "Paid Family Leave Insurance." Sacramento, Calif.: California Employment Development Department.

Capizzano, Jeffery, Gina Adams, and Freya Sonenstein. 2000. "Child Care Arrangements for Children Under Five: Variation Across States." Assessing the New Federalism policy brief B-7. Washington, D.C.: Urban Institute.

Carnegie Task Force on Meeting the Needs of Young Children. 1994. *Starting Points: Meeting the Needs of Our Youngest Children*. New York: Carnegie Corporation of New York.

Casper, Lynne. 1995. "What Does It Cost to Mind Our Preschoolers?" *Cur-*

rent Population Reports, series P70–52. Washington: U.S. Department of Commerce, Economics and Statistics Administration.

———. 1997. "My Daddy Takes Care of Me! Fathers as Care Providers." *Current Population Reports*, series P-70-59. Washington: U.S. Department of Commerce, Economics and Statistics Administration.

Chaudry, Ajay. 1997. Unpublished analysis prepared for the New York State Task Force for Sensible Welfare Reform (June).

Child Care, Inc. 2002. *Child Care Primer Series, Update 2002*. New York: Child Care, Inc.

Children's Defense Fund. 2003. "2002 State Developments in Child Care, Early Education, and School Age Care." Washington, D.C.: Children's Defense Fund.

Cicourel, Aaron. 1964. *Methods and Measurements in Sociology*. New York: Free Press.

Citro, Constance, and Robert Michael, eds. 1995. *Measuring Poverty: A New Approach*. Washington, D.C.: National Academy Press.

Clarke-Stewart, K. Alison. 1989. "Infant Day Care: Maligned or Malignant?" *American Psychologist* 44(2): 266–73.

Coleman, James S. 1990. *Foundations in Social Theory*. Cambridge, Mass.: Belknap Press of Harvard University Press.

Collins, Ann, and Barbara Carlson. 1998. *Child Care by Kith and Kin: Supporting Family, Friends, and Neighbors Caring for Children*. New York: National Center for Children in Poverty.

Corcoran, Mary. 1995. "Rags to Rags: Poverty and Mobility in the United States." *Annual Review of Sociology* 21: 237–67.

Cryer, Debby. 1999. "Defining and Assessing Early Childhood Program Quality." *ANNALS of the American Academy of Political and Social Science* (special issue, "The Silent Crisis in U.S. Child Care," edited by Suzanne Helburn) 563: 39–55.

Currie, Janet. 2001. "Early Childhood Education Programs." *Journal of Economic Perspectives* 15(2): 213–38.

Currie, Janet, and Duncan Thomas. 1995. "Does Head Start Make a Difference?" *American Economic Review* 85(3): 341–64.

———. 1999. "Does Head Start Help Hispanic Children?" *Journal of Public Economics* 74(2): 235–62.

Davis-Canteen, Glenda. 2002. Office of School Readiness in the State of Georgia, interview and personal communication with the author, November 13, 2002.

Dearing, Eric, Kathleen McCartney, and Beck A. Taylor. 2001. "Change in Family Income-to-Needs Matters More for Children with Less." *Child Development* 72(6): 1779–93.

Duncan, Greg J., and Jeanne Brooks-Gunn. 2000. "Family Poverty, Welfare Reform, and Child Development." *Child Development* 71(1): 188–96.

Duncan, Greg, and Christina Gibson. 2000. "Selection and Attrition in the

NICHD Child Care Study's Analyses of the Impacts of Child Care Quality on Child Outcomes." Unpublished paper. Northwestern University, Evanston, Ill.

Earls, Felton, and Stephen Buka. 2000. "Measurement of Community Characteristics." In *Handbook of Early Childhood Intervention*, edited by Samuel J. Meisels and Jack P. Shonkoff. Cambridge, Mass.: Harvard University Press.

Edelman, Peter. 1997. "The Worst Thing Bill Clinton Has Done." *Atlantic Monthly* (March): 43–58.

———. 2001. *Searching for America's Heart: RFK and the Renewal of Hope.* Boston: Houghton Mifflin.

Edin, Kathryn, and Laura Lein. 1997. *Making Ends Meet: How Single Mothers Survive Welfare and Low-Wage Work.* New York: Russell Sage Foundation.

Education Week. 2002. "Building Blocks for Success: State Effort in Early Childhood Education." *Quality Counts* 17.

Ehrle, Jennifer, Gina Adams, and Kathryn Tout. 2001. "Who's Caring for Our Youngest Children?" Assessing the New Federalism. Policy brief. Washington, D.C.: Urban Institute.

Emlen, Arthur. 1997. "Quality of Care from a Parent's Point of View: A Place at the Table for Child Care Consumers." Washington: U.S. Department of Health and Human Services, Child Care Bureau.

Emlen, Arthur, Paul Koren, and Kathryn Schultze. 2000. *A Packet of Scales for Measuring Quality of Child Care from a Parent's Point of View.* Portland, Oreg.: Portland State University, Regional Research Institute for Human Services.

Fenichel, Emily, Erica Lurie-Hurvitz, and Abbey Griffin. 1999. "Seizing the Moment to Build Momentum for Quality Infant/Toddler Care." *Zero to Three* (National Center for Infants, Toddlers and Families) 19(6, June–July): 3–17.

Finch, Robert. 2003. New York City Administration for Children Services, interview with the author, March 2, 2003.

Food Research and Action Center. 2002. "Child and Adult Care Food Program." Washington, D.C.: Food Research and Action Center.

Ford, Donald H., and Richard M. Lerner. 1992. "Developmental Systems Theory: An Integrative Approach." Thousand Oaks, Calif.: Sage Publications.

Fuller, Bruce, Susan Holloway, and Xiaoyan Liang. 1996. "Family Selection of Child Care Centers: The Influence of Household Support, Ethnicity, and Parental Practices." *Child Development* 67(6): 3320–37.

Fuller, Bruce, Susan Holloway, Marylee F. Rambaud, and Constanza Eggers-Pierola. 1997. "How Do Mothers Choose Child Care? Alternative Cultural Models in Poor Neighborhoods." *Sociology of Education* 69(4): 105–25.

Furstenberg, Frank F., and Mary Elizabeth Hughes. 1994. "The Influence of Neighborhoods on Children's Development: A Theoretical Perspective and a Research Agenda." In *Neighborhood Poverty: Policy Implications in Study-ing Neighborhoods*, edited by Jeanne Brooks-Gunn, Greg Duncan, and J. Lawrence Aber. New York: Russell Sage Foundation.

Galinsky, Ellen, Carollee Howes, Susan Kontos, and Marybeth Shinn. 1994. "The Study of Children in Family Child Care and Relative Care: High-lights of Findings." New York: Families and Work Institute.

Garces, Eliana, Duncan Thomas, and Janet Currie. 2000. "Longer-term Ef-fects of Head Start." Working paper 8054. Cambridge, Mass.: National Bureau of Economic Research.

Geertz, Clifford. 1973. *An Interpretation of Cultures*. New York: Basic Books.

Giannarelli, Linda, Sarah Adelman, and Stephanie Schmidt. 2003. *Getting Help with Child Care Expenses*. Washington, D.C.: Urban Institute.

Giannarelli, Linda, and James Barsimantov. 2000. "Child Care Expenses of America's Families." Assessing the New Federalism occasional paper 40. Washington, D.C.: Urban Institute.

Gira, Carla. 2003. Policy unit lead, Division of Child Care and Early Learn-ing, Washington Department of Social and Human Services, personal communication with author, February 28, 2003.

Gish, Melinda. 2001. "Child Care: State Programs Under the Child Care and Development Fund." Washington, D.C.: Congressional Research Service.

———. 2002. "Child Care: Funding and Spending Under Federal Block Grants." Washington, D.C.: Congressional Research Service.

Glaser, Barney, and Anselm Strauss. 1967. *The Discovery of Grounded Theory: Strategies for Qualitative Research*. Chicago: Aldine.

Golden, Olivia Ann. 1992. *Poor Children and Welfare Reform*. Westport, Conn.: Greenwood.

Gomby, Deanna S., Mary B. Larner, Carol S. Stevenson, Eugene M. Lewit, and Richard E. Behrman. 1995. "Long-term Outcomes of Early Child-hood Programs: Analysis and Recommendations." *The Future of Children* 5(3): 6–24.

Gornick, Janet C., and Marcia K. Meyers. 2001. "Support for Working Fam-ilies: What the United States Can Learn from Europe." *The American Prospect* (special report on children and families) (January 1–15): 3–7.

Harris, Kathleen Mullan. 1993. "Work and Welfare Among Single Mothers in Poverty." *American Journal of Sociology* 99(2): 317–52.

Harvey, Elizabeth. 1999. "Short-term and Long-term Effects of Early Parental Employment on Children of the National Longitudinal Survey of Youth." *Developmental Psychology* 35(2): 445–59.

Heclo, Hugh. 1986. "The Political Foundations of Antipoverty Policy." In *Fighting Poverty: What Works and What Doesn't*, edited by Sheldon H. Danziger and Daniel H. Weinberg. Cambridge, Mass.: Harvard University Press.

———. 1993. "Poverty Politics." In *Confronting Poverty: Prescriptions for*

Change, edited by Sheldon H. Danziger and Daniel H. Weinberg. Cambridge, Mass.: Harvard University Press.

———. 1997. "Values Underpinning Poverty Programs for Children." *The Future of Children* 7(2): 141–48.

———. 2001. "The Politics of Welfare Reform." In *The New World of Welfare*, edited by Rebecca Blank and Ron Haskins. Washington, D.C.: Brookings Institution.

Helburn, Suzanne W., ed. 1995. "Cost, Quality, and Child Outcomes in Child Care Centers: Technical Report." Denver: University of Colorado, Department of Economics, Center for Research in Economic and Social Policy.

Henly, Julia, and Sandra Lyons. 2000. "The Negotiation of Child Care and Employment Demands Among Low-Income Parents." *Journal of Social Issues* 56(4): 683–706.

Heymann, Jody. 2000. *The Widening Gap: Why America's Working Families Are in Jeopardy and What Can Be Done About It*. New York: Basic Books.

———. 2002. "Low-Income Parents and the Time Famine." In *Tracking Parenting Public: The Case for a New Social Movement*, edited by Sylvia Ann Hewlett, Nancy Rankin, and Cornel West. Lanham, Md.: Rowan & Littlefield.

Hofferth, Sandra. 1995. "Caring for Children at the Poverty Line." *Children and Youth Services Review* 17(103): 61–90.

———. 1996. "Child Care in the United States Today." *The Future of Children* 6(2, Summer–Fall): 41–61.

———. 1999. "Child Care, Maternal Employment, and Public Policy." *ANNALS of the American Academy of Political and Social Science* (special issue, "The Silent Crisis in U.S. Child Care," edited by Suzanne Helburn) 563: 39–55.

Hofferth, Sandra, April Brayfield, Sharon Deich, and Pamela Holcomb. 1991. "Caring for Children in Low-Income Families: A Substudy of the National Child Care Survey, 1990." Washington, D.C.: Urban Institute.

Hofferth, Sandra, Kimberlee Shauman, Robin Henke, and Jerry West. 1998. "Characteristics of Children's Early Care and Education Programs: Data from the 1995 National Household Education Survey." NCES 98–128. Washington: U.S. Department of Education, National Center for Education Statistics.

Holloway, Susan, Bruce Fuller, Marylee F. Rambaud, and Constanza Eggers-Pierola. 1997. *Through My Own Eyes: Single Mothers and the Cultures of Poverty*. Cambridge, Mass.: Harvard University Press.

Holloway, Susan, Marylee F. Rambaud, Bruce Fuller, and Constanza Eggers-Pierola. 1995. "What Is 'Appropriate Practice' at Home and in Child Care? Low-Income Mothers' Views on Preparing Their Children for School." *Early Childhood Research Quarterly* 10(4): 451–73.

Holzer, Harry. 1996. *What Employers Want: Job Prospects for Less Educated Workers.* New York: Russell Sage Foundation.

Holzer, Harry, and Sheldon Danziger. 1998. "Are Jobs Available for Disadvantaged Workers in Urban Areas?" Discussion paper. Madison: University of Wisconsin, Institute for Research on Poverty.

Howes, Carollee. 1990. "Can the Age of Entry into Child Care and the Quality of Child Care Predict Adjustment into Kindergarten?" *Developmental Psychology* 26(2): 292–303.

Howes, Carollee, and Claire E. Hamilton. 1992. "Children's Relationships with Caregivers: Mothers and Child Care Teachers." *Child Development* 63(4): 859–66.

———. 1993. "The Changing Experience of Child Care: Changes in Teachers and in Teacher-Child Relationships and Children's Social Competence with Peers." *Early Childhood Research Quarterly* 8: 15–32.

Howes, Carollee, Catherine Matheson, and Claire E. Hamilton. 1994. "Maternal, Teacher, and Child Care History Correlates of Children's Relationships with Peers." *Child Development* 65(1): 449–60.

Howes, Carollee, Deborah Phillips, and Marcy Whitebook. 1992. "Thresholds of Quality: Implications for the Social Development of Children in Center-Based Child Care." *Annual Progress in Child Psychiatry and Child Development* 1993: 563.

Jorgensen, Danny. 1989. "Participant Observation: A Methodology for Human Studies." Newbury Park, Calif.: Sage Publications.

Kagan, Sharon L. 1993. *Integrating Services for Children and Families.* New Haven, Conn.: Yale University Press.

Kamerman, Sheila B. 2000. "Parental Leave Policies: An Essential Ingredient in Early Childhood Education and Care Policies." *Society for Research on Child Development Social Policy Report* 14(2): 1–15.

Kaplan, Elaine Bell. 1997. *Not Our Kind of Girl: Unraveling the Myths of Black Teenage Motherhood.* Berkeley: University of California Press.

Karoly, Lynn A., Peter W. Greenwood, Susan S. Everingham, Jill Houbé, M. Rebecca Kilburn, C. Peter Rydell, Matthew Sanders, and James Chiesa. 1998. "Summary: Early Childhood Interventions: Benefits, Costs, and Savings." In *Investing in Our Children: What We Know and Don't Know About the Costs and Benefits of Early Childhood Interventions.* Santa Monica, Calif.: Rand Corporation.

Katz, Michael. 1986. *In the Shadow of the Poorhouse: A Social History of Welfare in America.* New York: Basic Books.

Kinder, Donald R. and Lynn M. Sanders. 1996. *Divided by Color: Racial Politics and Democratic Ideals.* Chicago: University of Chicago Press.

Kisker, Ellen E., Sandra Hofferth, Deborah Phillips, and Elizabeth Farquhar. 1991. "A Profile of Child Care Settings: Early Education and Care in 1990." Washington: U.S. Government Printing Office.

Klebanov, Pamela K., Jeanne Brooks-Gunn, and Greg L. Duncan. 1997.

"The Intersection of the Neighborhood and Home Environments and Its Influence on Young Children." In *Neighborhood Poverty: Policy Implications in Studying Neighborhoods*, edited by Jeanne Brooks-Gunn, Greg Duncan, and J. Lawrence Aber. New York: Russell Sage Foundation.

Kontos, Susan, Carollee Howes, Marybeth Shinn, and Ellen Galinsky. 1995. *Quality in Family Child Care and Relative Care*. New York: Teachers College Press.

Kreader, J. Lee, Jessica B. Piecyk, and Ann Collins. 2000. "Scant Increases After Welfare Reform Regulated: Child Care Supply in Illinois and Maryland 1996–1998." New York: National Center for Children in Poverty.

Lamb, Michael E. 1998. "Nonparental Child Care: Context, Quality, Correlates." In *Handbook of Child Psychology: Theoretical Models of Human Development*, 5th ed., edited by William Damon and Richard M. Lerner. New York: Wiley.

Lerner, Richard M., F. Rothbaum, S. Boulous, and D. R. Castellino. 2002. "Developmental Systems Perspective on Parenting." In *Handbook of Parenting: Social Conditions and Applied Parenting*, 2nd ed., edited by Marc H. Bornstein. Mahwah, N.J.: Lawrence Erlbaum Associates.

Leventhal, Tama, and Jeanne Brooks-Gunn. 2000. "The Neighborhoods They Live In: The Effects of Neighborhood Residence upon Child and Adolescent Outcomes." *Psychological Bulletin* 126(2): 309–37.

Levitan, Mark, and Robin Gluck. 2002. "Mothers' Work: Single Mothers' Employment, Earnings, and Poverty in the Age of Welfare Reform." New York: Community Services Society of New York.

Liang, Xiaoyan, Bruce Fuller, and Judith Singer. 2000. "Ethnic Differences in Child Care Selection: The Influence of Family Structure, Parental Practices, and Home Language." *Early Childhood Research Quarterly* 15(3): 357–84.

Liebow, Elliot. 1967. *Tally's Corner: A Study of Negro Street Corner Men*. Boston: Little, Brown.

Lofland, John. 1971. *Analyzing Social Settings: A Guide to Qualitative Observation and Analysis*. Belmont, Calif.: Wadsworth.

Marcuse, Peter. 1997. "The Enclave, the Citadel, and the Ghetto: What Has Changed in the Post-Fordist U.S. City." *Urban Affairs Review* 33(2): 228–64.

Mayer, Susan E., and Christopher Jencks. 1989, "Poverty and the Distribution of Material Hardship." *Journal of Human Resources* 24: 88–113.

McKey, Ruth, Larry Condelli, Harriet Ganson, Barbara Barrett, Catherine McConkey, and Margaret Plantz. 1985. "The Impact of Head Start on Children, Families, and Communities: Final Report of the Head Start Evaluation, Synthesis, and Utilization Project." Washington, D.C.: CSR, Inc.

McLeod, Jane D., and Michael J. Shanahan. 1993. "Poverty and Children's Distress." *American Sociological Review* 58(3, June): 351–66.

Meyers, Marcia, Theresa Heintze, and Douglas A. Wolf. 1999. "Child Care Subsidies and the Employment of Welfare Recipients." Unpublished paper. University of California, Berkeley.

Meyers, Marcia, Laura R. Peck, Ann Collins, J. Lee Kreader, Annie Georges, Elizabeth E. Davis, Roberta Weber, Deanna Schexnayder, Daniel Schroeder, and Jerry A. Olson. 2001. "The Dynamics of Child Care Subsidy Use: A Collaborative Study of Five States." New York: National Center for Children in Poverty.

Mezey, Jennifer, Mark Greenberg, and Rachel Schumacher. 2002. "The Vast Majority of Federally Eligible Children Did Not Receive Child Care Assistance in FY 2000." Washington, D.C.: Center for Law and Social Policy.

Miech, Richard A., Aushalom Cuspi, Terrie E. Moffitt, Bradley E. Entner Wright, and Phil Silva. 1999. "Low Socioeconomic Status and Mental Illnesses." *American Journal of Sociology* 104(4, January): 112–47.

Mitchell, Anne. 2001. "Education for All Young Children: The Role of States and the Federal Government in Promoting Prekindergarten and Kindergarten." Working paper series. New York: Foundation for Child Development.

Mitchell, Anne, Louise Stoney, and Harriet Dichter. 2001. *Financing Child Care in the United States*. Kansas City, Mo.: Ewing Marion Kaufmann Foundation.

Montgomery, Deborah, Laura Kaye, Rob Geen, and Karin Martinson. 2002. "Recent Changes in California Welfare and Work, Child Care, and Child Welfare Systems." Washington, D.C.: Urban Institute.

Moore, Kristin, Sharon Vandivere, and Jennifer Ehrle. 2000. "Sociodemographic Risk and Child Well-being." Washington, D.C.: Urban Institute.

Murphy, Reeva Sullivan. 2003. Child care administrator, Rhode Island Department of Human Services, interview with Elizabeth Rigby, research assistant, March 3, 2003.

National Institute of Child Health and Development (NICHD). Early Child Care Research Network. 1996. "Characteristics of Infant Child Care: Factors Contributing to Positive Care Giving." *Early Childhood Research Quarterly* 11(3): 269–306.

———. 1997a. "The Effects of Infant Child Care on Infant-Mother Attachment Security: Results of the NICHD Study of Early Child Care." *Child Development* 68(5): 860–79.

———. 1997b. "Child Care in the First Year of Life." *Merrill-Palmer Quarterly* 43(3): 340–60.

———. 1998a. "Relations Between Family Predictors and Child Outcomes: Are They Weaker for Children in Child Care?" *Developmental Psychology* 34(5): 1119–28.

———. 1998b. "Early Child Care and Self-control, Compliance, and Problem Behavior at Twenty-four and Thirty-six Months." *Child Development* 69(3): 1145–70.

———. 1999. "Child Care and Mother-Child Interaction on the First Three Years of Life." *Developmental Psychology* 35(6): 1399–1413.

———. 2000a. "Characteristics and Quality of Child Care for Toddlers and Preschoolers." *Journal of Applied Developmental Science* 4(3): 116–35.

———. 2000b. "The Relation of Child Care to Cognitive and Language Development." *Child Development* 71(4): 960–80.

———. 2002. "Child Care Structure to Process to Outcome: Direct and Indirect Effects of Child Care Quality on Young Children's Development." *Psychological Science* 13: 199–206.

———. 2003. "Does Amount of Time Spent in Child Care Predict Socioeconomic Adjustment During the Transition to Kindergarten?" *Child Development* 74(4): 976–1005.

National Women's Law Center. 2000. "Be All That We Can Be: Lessons from the Military for Improving Our Nation's Child Care System." Washington, D.C.: National Women's Law Center. Available at: www.nwlc.org.

———. 2003. "Making Care Less Taxing: Improving State Child and Dependent Care Tax Provisions." Washington, D.C.: National Women's Law Center. Available at: www.nwlc.org.

Neuman, Michelle. 2001. "Hand in Hand: Improving the Links Between ECEC and Schools." In *Early Childhood Education and Care: International Perspectives*, edited by Sheila Kamerman. New York: Columbia University, Institute for Child and Family Policy.

Newman, Katherine S. 1993. *Declining Fortunes: The Withering of the American Dream*. New York: Basic Books.

———. 1999. *No Shame in My Game: The Working Poor in the Inner City*. New York: Alfred A. Knopf and Russell Sage Foundation.

New York City Human Resources Administration. 1994. *Monthly Case Load Management Report* (December). New York: Human Resources Administration.

———. 2001. *Monthly Case Load Management Report* (December). New York: Human Resources Administration.

New York City Independent Budget Office. 1999. "Implementing Universal Prekindergarten in New York City." Policy report. New York: New York City Independent Budget Office.

———. 2002. "City's Reliance on State and Federal Funds for Child Care Grows." Occasional paper. New York: New York City Independent Budget Office.

Nightingale, Demetra, and Robert Haveman, eds. 1995. *The Work Alternative: Welfare Reform and the Realities of the Job Market*. Washington, D.C.: Urban Institute.

Organization for Economic Co-operation and Development (OECD). 2001. *Starting Strong: Early Childhood Education and Care*. Paris: OECD.

Osterman, Paul. 1980. *Getting Started: The Youth Labor Market*. Cambridge, Mass.: MIT Press.

Papillo, Angela, Kathryn Tout, Sharon Vandivere, and Martha Zaslow. 2001. "Early Care and Education: Work Support for Families and Developmental Opportunity for Young Children." Washington, D.C.: Urban Institute.

Patterson, Stephen M., and Alison B. Albers. 2001. "Effects of Poverty and Maternal Depression on Early Child Development." *Child Development* 72(6): 1794–1813.

Pavetti, LaDonna. 1993. "The Dynamics of Welfare and Work: Exploring the Process by Which Women Work Their Way Off Welfare." Ph.D. diss., Harvard University.

Pavetti, LaDonna, and Gregory Acs. 2001. "Moving Up, Moving Out, or Going Nowhere? A Study of the Employment Patterns of Young Women and the Implications for Welfare Mothers." *Journal of Policy Analysis and Management* 20(4): 721–36.

Peisner-Feinberg, Ellen S., and Margaret R. Burchinal. 1997. "Relationships Between Preschool Children's Child Care Experiences and Concurrent Development: The Cost, Quality, and Outcome Study." *Merrill-Palmer Quarterly* 43(3): 451–77.

Peisner-Feinberg, Ellen S., Margaret R. Burchinal, Richard M. Clifford, Mary L. Culkin, Carollee Howes, Sharon L. Kagan, and Noreen Yazejian. 2001. "The Relation of Preschool Child-Care Quality to Children's Cognitive and Social Developmental Trajectories Through Second Grade." *Child Development* 72(5): 1534–53.

Perkins, Evelyn. 2002. Deputy director of fiscal administration and responsibility, Child Care Division, Florida Department of Children and Families, interview with the author, November 13, 2002.

Phillips, Deborah, Carollee Howes, and Marcy Whitebook. 1992. "The Social Policy Context of Child Care: Effects on Quality." *American Journal of Community Psychology* 20(1): 25–51.

Phillips, Deborah, Kathleen McCartney, and Sandra Scarr. 1987. "Child Care Quality and Children's Social Development." *Annual Progress in Child Psychiatry and Development: Developmental Psychology* 23(4): 537–43.

Phillips, Deborah, Miriam Varan, Ellen Kisker, Carollee Howes, and Marcy Whitebook. 1994. "Child Care for Children in Poverty: Opportunity or Inequity?" *Child Development* 65(2): 472–92.

Piven, Francis Fox, and Richard A. Cloward. 1971. *Regulating the Poor: The Functions of Public Welfare*. New York: Random House.

Polakow, Valerie. 1993. *Lives on the Edge: Single Mothers and Their Children in the Other America*. Chicago: University of Chicago Press.

Presser, Harriet. 1995. "Job, Family, and Gender: Determinants of Nonstandard Work Schedules Among Employed Americans in 1991." *Demography* 32(4): 577–98.

————. 2000. "Nonstandard Work Schedules and Marital Instability." *Journal of Marriage and the Family* 62: 93–110.

Queralt, Magaly, and Ann Dryden Witte. 1998. "Influences on Neighborhood Supply of Child Care in Massachusetts." *Social Service Review* 72(1): 17–46.

Ravitch, Diane. 1988: *The Great School Wars: A History of the New York City Public Schools*. New York: Basic Books.

Reynolds, Arthur J., Judy A. Temple, Dylan L. Robertson, and Emily A. Mann. 2001. "Long-term Effects of an Early Childhood Intervention on Educational Achievement and Juvenile Arrest: A Fifteen-year Follow-up of Low-Income Children in Public Schools." *Journal of the American Medical Association* 285(1): 2378–80.

————. 2002. "Age Twenty-one Cost-Benefit Analysis of the Title I Chicago Child-Parent Centers." *Educational Evaluation and Policy Analysis* 24(4): 267–303.

Romaner, Irwin, and Robert Finch. 2003. New York City Administration for Children Services, letter to the author, January 16, 2003.

Rosier, Katherine Brown. 1997. *Mothering Inner-City Children: The Early School Years*. New Brunswick, N.J.: Rutgers University Press.

Rosina, Becerra, and Iris Chi. 1992. "Child Care Preferences Among Low-income Minority Families." *International Social Work* 35(1): 35–47.

Ruggles, Patricia. 1990. *Drawing the Line: Alternative Poverty Measures and Their Applications*. Washington, D.C.: Urban Institute.

Sameroff, Arnold. 1995. "General Systems Theories and Developmental Psychopathology." In *Developmental Psychopathology*, vol. 1, *Theories and Methods*, edited by Dante Cicchetti and Daniel J. Cohen. New York: Wiley.

Sampson, Robert J. 1992. "Family Management and Child Development: Insights from Social Disorganization Theory." In *Facts, Frameworks, and Forecasts: Advances in Criminological Theory*, vol. 3, edited by Joan McCord. New Brunswick, N.J.: Transactions Publishers.

Sampson Robert J., and W. Byron Groves. 1989. "Community Structure and Crime: Testing Social Disorganization Theory." *American Journal of Sociology* 94: 774–802.

Sampson, Robert J., Jeffrey D. Morenoff, and Felton Earls. 1999. "Beyond Social Capital: Spatial Dynamics of Collective Efficacy for Children." *American Sociological Review* 64(5, October): 633–60.

Sampson, Robert J., Stephen W. Raudenbush, and Felton Earls. 1997. "Neighborhoods and Violent Crime: A Multilevel Study of Collective Efficacy." *Science* 277: 918–24.

Saterfield, Linda. 2003. Bureau chief, Office of Child Care and Family Services, Illinois Department of Human Services, interview with Elizabeth Rigby, research assistant, February 21, 2003.

Scarr, Sandra. 1998. "American Child Care Today." *American Psychologist* 53(2): 95–108.

Scarr, Sandra, and Marlene Eisenberg. 1993. "Child Care Research: Issues, Perspectives, and Results." *Annual Review of Psychology* 44: 613–44.

Scarr, Sandra, Deborah Phillips, and Kathleen McCartney. 1990. "Facts, Fantasies, and the Future of Child Care in the United States." *Psychological Science* 1(1): 26–35.

Schaefbauer, Wayne. 2003. Program specialist, Subsidy System, Child Care Services, South Dakota Department of Social Services, interview with Elizabeth Rigby, research assistant, February 21, 2003.

Schulman, Karen. 2000. "The High Cost of Child Care Puts Quality Care Out of Reach for Many Families." Washington, D.C.: Children's Defense Fund.

Schulman, Karen, Helen Blank, and Danielle Ewen. 2000. "Seeds of Success: State Prekindergarten Initiatives, 1998–1999." Washington, D.C.: Children's Defense Fund.

———. 2001. "A Fragile Foundation: Child Care Assistance Policies." Washington, D.C.: Children's Defense Fund.

Schumacher, Rachel, and Mark Greenberg. 1999. "Child Care After Leaving Welfare: Early Evidence from State Studies." Washington, D.C.: Center for Law and Social Policy.

Schumacher, Rachel, Mark Greenberg, and Janellen Duffy. 2001. "The Impact of TANF Funding on State Child Care Subsidy Programs." Washington, D.C.: Center for Law and Social Policy.

Schumacher, Rachel, and Kate Irish. 2003. "What's New in 2002? A Snapshot of Head Start Children, Families, Teachers, and Programs." Policy brief, Head Start series, no. 2. Washington, D.C.: Center for Law and Social Policy. Available at: www.clasp.org.

Schumacher, Rachel, and Tanya Rakpraja. 2002. "States Have Slowed Their Use of TANF Funds for Child Care in the Last Year." Washington, D.C.: Center for Law and Social Policy.

Schwarz, John, and Thomas Volgy. 1992. "Social Support for Self-reliance: The Politics of Making Work Pay." *The American Prospect* (9, Spring): 67–73.

Schweinhart Lawrence J., Helen Barnes, and David Weikart. 1993. "Significant Benefits: The High/Scope Perry Preschool Study Through Age Twenty-seven." Ypsilanti, Mich.: High/Scope Educational Research Foundation.

Scrivner, Scott, and Barbara Wolfe. 2002. "Universal Preschool: Much to Gain but Who Will Pay?" Working paper series. New York: Foundation for Child Development.

Shonkoff, Jack, and Deborah Phillips, eds. 2000. *From Neurons to Neighborhoods: The Science of Early Childhood Development*. Washington, D.C.: National Academy Press.

Singer, Judith D., Bruce Fuller, Margaret K. Keiley, and Anne Wolf. 1998. "Early Child-Care Selection: Variation by Geographic Locations, Maternal Characteristics, and Family Structure." *Developmental Psychology* 34(5): 1129–44.

Singer, Mark I., Trina M. Anglin, Li Yu Song, and Lisa Lunghofer. 1995. "Adolescents' Exposure to Violence and Associated Symptoms of Psychological Trauma." *Journal of the American Medical Association* 273(6): 477–82.

Smith, Judith R., Jeanne Brooks-Gunn, and Pamela K. Klebanov. 1997. "Consequences of Living in Poverty for Young Children's Cognitive and Verbal Ability and Early School Achievement." In *Consequences of Growing Up Poor*, edited by Greg J. Duncan and Jeanne Brooks-Gunn. New York: Russell Sage Foundation.

Smith, Kristin. 2000. "Who's Minding the Kids? Child Care Arrangements: Fall 1995." *Current Population Reports*, series P70–70. Washington: U.S. Department of Commerce, Economics and Statistics Administration.

———. 2002. "Who's Minding the Kids? Child Care Arrangements: Spring 1997." *Current Population Reports*, series P70–86. Washington: U.S. Department of Commerce, Economics and Statistics Administration.

Sonenstein, Freya. 1991. "The Child Care Preferences of Parents with Young Children: How Little Is Known." In *Parental Leave and Child Care: Setting a Policy and Research Agenda*, edited by Janet S. Hyde and Marilyn J. Essex. Philadelphia: Temple University Press.

Sonenstein, Freya, and Douglas Wolf. 1991. "Satisfaction with Child Care: Perspectives of Welfare Mothers." *Journal of Social Issues* 47(2): 15–31.

Spock, Benjamin, 1957. *Baby and Child Care*. New York: Pocket Books.

Stack, Carol B. 1974. *All Our Kin: Strategies for Survival in a Black Community*. New York: Harper & Row.

———. 1996. *Call to Home: African Americans Reclaim the Rural South*. New York: Basic Books.

State Policy Documentation Project. 2000. "Child Care Assistance: 50 State Policy Comparisons." Washington, D.C.: State Policy Documentation Project. Available at: www.spdp.org.

Stoney, Louise, and Mark Greenberg. 1996. "The Financing of Child Care: Current and Emerging Trends." *The Future of Children* 6(2): 83–102.

Sullivan, Mercer L. 1989. *Getting Paid: Youth Crime and Work in the Inner City*. Ithaca, N.Y.: Cornell University Press.

Taylor, Laura, Barry Zuckerman, Vami Harik, and Betsy McAlister-Groves. 1992. "Exposure to Violence Among Inner-City Parents and Young Children." *American Journal of the Diseases of Children* 146: 487–94.

Thompson, Ross A. 1998. "Early Sociopersonality Development." In *Handbook of Child Psychology*, edited by William Damon and Richard M. Lerner. New York: Wiley.

————. 2001. "Development in the First Years of Life." *The Future of Children* 11(1): 21–34.

Tout, Kathryn, Martha Zaslow, Angela Romano Papillo, and Sharon Vandivere. 2001. "Early Care and Education: Work Support for Families and Development Opportunity for Young Children." Assessing the New Federalism occasional paper. Washington, D.C.: Urban Institute.

Tyack, David B. 1974. *The One Best System: A History of American Urban Education.* Cambridge, Mass.: Harvard University Press.

Tyack, David, and Larry Cuban. 1995. *Tinkering Toward Utopia.* Cambridge, Mass.: Harvard University Press.

Urzedowski, Pat, and Sandra Scott. 2002. Former state child care administrator (Urzedowski) and current child care administrator (Scott) in Nebraska's Economic Assistance Division, interviews with Wendy Trull, research assistant, November 12 and 14, 2002.

U.S. Department of Agriculture. 2003. "Food and Nutrition Service: Child and Adult Care Annual Summary." Washington: U.S. Department of Agriculture. Available at: http://www.fns.usda.gov/pd/ccsummar.htm.

U.S. Department of Commerce. U.S. Census Bureau. 1990. *1990 Decennial Census Summary Tape Files.* Washington: U.S. Census Bureau.

————. 2000a. *Poverty in the United States. Current Population Reports Series P60–210.* Washington: U.S. Government Printing Office.

————. 2000b. *2000 Decennial Census Summary Tape Files.* Washington: U.S. Census Bureau.

————. 2001. *Statistical Abstract of the United States.* 121st ed. Washington: U.S. Government Printing Office.

U.S. Department of Health, Education, and Human Services. 1998a. "Child Care: Use of Standards to Ensure High Quality Care." Publication HEHS-98-223R. Washington: U.S. Government Printing Office.

————. 1998b. "Fact Sheet: State Spending Under the Child Care Block Grant." Washington: U.S. Department of Health and Human Services, Administration for Children and Families.

————. 1999. "Access to Child Care for Low-Income Families." Washington: U.S. Department of Health and Human Services, Administration for Children and Families.

————. 2000a. "Temporary Assistance to Needy Families (TANF): Third Annual Report to Congress." Washington: U.S. Department of Health and Human Services.

————. 2000b. "New Statistics Show Only Small Percentage of Eligible Families Receive Child Care Help." Washington: U.S. Department of Health and Human Services.

————. 2001a. "Fiscal Year 2000 State Spending Under the Child Care and Development Fund as of September 30, 2000." Washington: U.S. Department of Health and Human Services, Administration for Children and Families.

———. 2001b. "U.S. Welfare Caseload Information, Temporary Assistance to Needy Families Total Number of Families, September 2000 to March 2001." Washington: U.S. Department of Health and Human Services.

———. 2002a. "FY 2001 CCDF Data Tables and Charts." Washington: U.S. Department of Health and Human Services, Child Care Bureau.

———. 2002b. "State Spending Under the Fiscal Year 2001 Appropriations for Child Care and Development Fund (CCDF) as of September 30, 2001." Washington: U.S. Department of Health and Human Services, Administration for Children and Families, Child Care Bureau (August 2002).

———. 2003. "Head Start Program Fact Sheet." Washington: U.S. Department of Health and Human Services, Head Start Bureau. Available at: http://www2.acf.dhhs.gov/programs/hsb/research/2003.htm.

U.S. Department of Labor. Bureau of Labor Statistics. 2001. "Employment Characteristics of Families in 2000." Washington: U.S. Department of Labor.

U.S. General Accounting Office. 1997. "Welfare Reform: Implications of Increased Work Participation for Child Care." GAO/HEHS-97-75. Washington: U.S. Government Printing Office.

———. 2000. "Early Education and Care: Overlap Indicates Need to Assess Crosscutting Programs." GAO/HEHS-00-78. Washington: U.S. Government Printing Office.

Vandell, Deborah Love, and Barbara Wolfe. 2000. "Child Care Quality: Does It Matter and Does It Need to Be Improved?" Madison: University of Wisconsin, Institute for Research on Poverty.

Vaughn, Brian E., Byron Egeland, L. Alan Srooufe, and Everett Waters. 1979. "Individual Differences in Infant-Mother Attachment at Twelve and Eighteen Months: Stability and Change in Families Under Stress." *Child Development* 50: 971–75.

Wacquant, Loic. 1993. "Urban Outcast: Stigma and Division in the Black American Ghetto and the French Urban Periphery." *International Journal of Urban and Regional Planning* 17(3): 366–83.

Waldfogel, Jane. 1999a. "Family Leave Coverage in the 1990s." *Monthly Labor Review* 122: 13–21.

———. 1999b. "The Impact of the Family and Medical Leave Act." *Journal of Policy Analysis and Management* 18: 281–308.

Waldfogel, Jane, Wen-Jui Han, and Jeanne Brooks-Gunn. 2002. "The Effects of Early Maternal Employment on Child Cognitive Development." *Demography* 39(2): 369–92.

Whitebook, Marcy, Carollee Howes, and Deborah Phillips. 1990. "Who Cares? Child Care Teachers and the Quality of Care in America." Final report of the National Child Care Staffing Study. Oakland, Calif.: Child Care Employee Project.

Wilson, William Julius. 1987. *The Truly Disadvantaged: The Inner City, the Underclass, and Public Policy.* Chicago: University of Chicago Press.

———. 1993. "The New Urban Poverty and the Problem of Race." Tanner Lecture. Ann Arbor: University of Michigan.

———. 1996. *When Work Disappears: The World of the New Urban Poor.* New York: Alfred A. Knopf.

Witte, Ann, and Magaly Queralt. 2002. "Take-up Rates and Trade Offs After the Age of Entitlement: Some Thoughts and Empirical Evidence for Child Care Subsidies." Working paper 8886. Cambridge, Mass.: National Bureau of Economic Research.

Zaslow, Martha. 1991. "Variation in Child Care Quality and Its Implications for Children." *Journal of Social Issues* 47(2): 125–38.

Zelizer, Viviena A. 1985. *Pricing the Priceless Child: The Changing Social Value of Children.* New York: Basic Books.

———. 1994. *The Social Meaning of Money.* New York: Basic Books.

———. 2000. "The Purchase of Intimacy." *Law and Social Inquiry* 25(3): 817–48.

Zollar, Ann Creighton. 1984. *A Member of the Family: Strategies for Black Family Continuity.* New York: Burnham.

~ Index ~

stability of care arrangements: care
  choices, 45–48, 169–70, 222; care
  coping strategy, 182–83; duration,
  105–6; impact of, xviii, 13, 154,
  233–34; number of concurrent
  arrangements, 39–40, 73–75, **74,**
  101–2; policy issues, 188–89,
  202–9; poverty, 130; primary care
  timeline, 94–101, **96–97, 98**;
  quality, 233–34
Stack, Carol, 19, 164, 184
state and local programs: care assistance
  and eligibility, 202–13; developmental issues, 201–2; federal block
  grants, 13, 17–18; Head Start, 199–
  201; policy issues, 190–91; preschool
  and prekindergarten, xix–xx, 196–
  99; state median income (SMI), 18,
  203, 204, 208, 211–12. *See also*
  policy issues
strategies, developing care, 156–86;
  agency-based care strategies, 174–79;
  culturally based, 164; initial care,
  134, 139–40, 165–68; post-welfare
  reform adaptive strategies, 179–83;
  Sara and Christina's story, 156–63,
  162; second-best care path, 168–74;
  stable care as stabilizing force, 182–
  83, 210; subsidized care, 181–82;
  summary and conclusions, 183–86;
  work paths and care paths as interrelated, 180–81
Strauss, Anselm, 264
structural issues: family structure, 112,
  115–17, 195–96, 219–20, 223;
  quality care features, 232–34
subsidies and agency-based care: application process, 79–81, 206–7, 246;
  care choices, 63, 76–83, **77**; as care
  spell exit, 109, **110, 112**; "churning," 176–77, 205; community-
  based care, 174–79, 185–86; contracted care, xxi, 239, 244; defined,
  xxiii; duration and dynamics, 234;

frustrations with, 202; improve access and continuity of, 202–9; initial
  care, 165; vs. kin and informal care,
  49, 50; as maternal concern, 135,
  146–49; New York City, 20–21, 79–
  83, 135, 146–49, 204–9; obtaining,
  181–82; policy issues, 189–95, 202–
  13, 245–46; program summary,
  240–46, **241–43**; scarcity and complexity, 12, 135, 146–49; second-
  best care path and strategy, 165,
  170–79, 186. *See also* Agency for
  Child Development (ACD), NY;
  Human Resources Administration
  (HRA), NY
Supplemental Security Income (SSI),
  20, **22,** 24
supply of care, 63, 193–94, 230

TANF (Temporary Assistance to Needy
  Families), 14, 204, 209, 244
tax issues, xix, 195, 246, 313*n*40
Thompson, Ross, 237
time. *See* scheduling
Title 1 preschool programs, **242**
transitions (exits), care spells, xxi, 36,
  103–17, **110**
trust, and kin care, 43, 49

universal preschool, xviii–xx, 197–99
unlicensed care, defined, xxiii
unstable care. *See* stability of care
  arrangements

Vandell, Deborah Love, 247
voluntary care-related exits, 109, **110,**
  111
voucher care, xxiii, 193, 239, 244. *See
  also* Human Resources Administration (HRA), NY; subsidies and
  agency-based care

Wacquant, Loic, 129
welfare and welfare reform, 1–26;